MONKEYING AROUND AT SEA

MONKEYING AROUND AT SEA

ANGELA COE

The Book Guild Ltd

First published in Great Britain in 2019 by
The Book Guild Ltd
9 Priory Business Park
Wistow Road, Kibworth
Leicestershire, LE8 0RX
Freephone: 0800 999 2982
www.bookguild.co.uk
Email: info@bookguild.co.uk
Twitter: @bookguild

Typeset in 12pt Minion Pro

Printed and bound in the UK by TJ International, Padstow, Cornwall

ISBN 978 1912881 147

British Library Cataloguing in Publication Data.
A catalogue record for this book is available from the British Library.

Flick & Ann Fletcher
and
Lori Williams

Three friends,
true friends,
who gave us so much help.
All we said was "thank you",
poor words for what we felt.

Also of course Bobby
our captain, who it must be said
had many trials to bear.
A lesser man with such a crew,
would give up in despair.

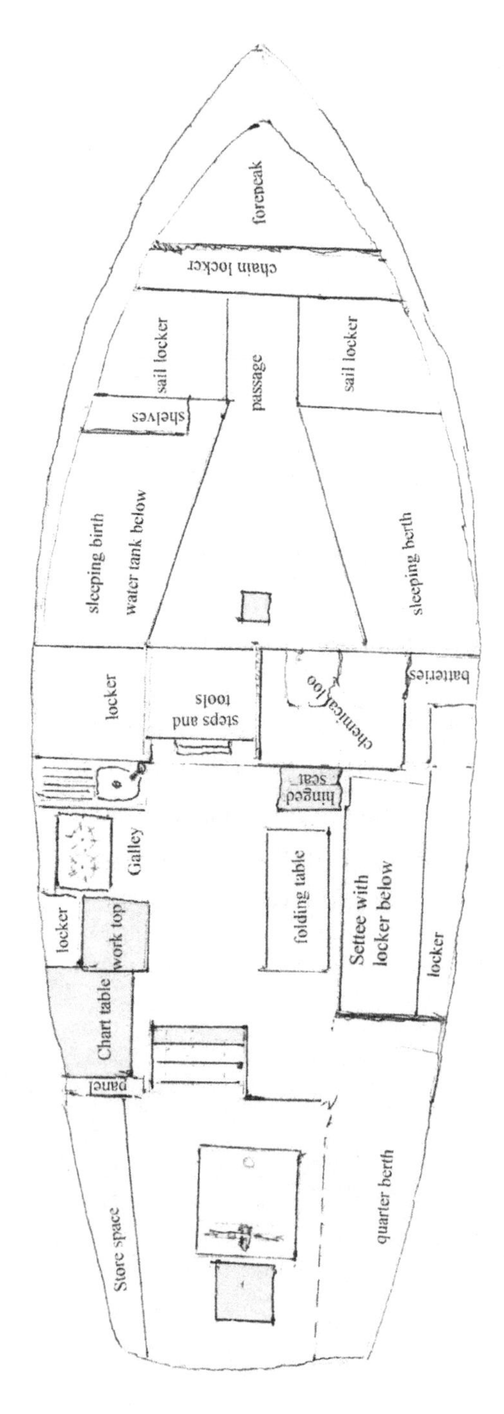

Original layout of 'Sandpiper'

CONTENTS

PREFACE

The manuscript for this book was written forty years ago during our forced stay in Spain, using diaries in which I had kept a daily account, and tapping them out on an old portable typewriter. At the time it was written as a memoir for family and friends, allowing me to ditch the diaries. Since then the manuscript has lain along with prints and slides in a trunk, the type fading on the yellowing pages and the photos often sticking together or changing colour and the slides growing mildew. Much has changed in the past forty years and other cruising friends that kept in touch have either passed on or left the cruising scene.

I fear many other yacht-sailing people will be aghast at our rather slapdash way at sea. I agree, we could not be called serious sailors, even though Bobby was a master mariner. Our belief was that life should be an adventure. Sailing then was fun. I do wonder, if now, cruising sailors will get the same enjoyment out of sailing as we and our contemporaries at that time did. The world now relies more and more on electronics: radio, navigational airs, etc. These in themselves probably cause more upset when they go wrong than anyone would experience without them.

I must stress from the outset that I sincerely hope that no one after reading about Pixie our monkey will ever consider obtaining a pet monkey. The place for all wild animals is in the wild. Sadly as humans we feel we own everything but a life is a life, be it human or any other animal, that life should be treated with respect. Pixie and other animals I have had were rescued. I can say with a certainty that had we not taken her, her life would have been both short and a misery. Pixie gave us an enormous amount of pleasure, a pleasure tinged with sadness that she could never live as a wild animal should. We did our best for her and she was happy, never knowing the life she should have been able to enjoy as her right in this world.

Pixie the monkey went to sea
in a second-hand cement boat with
Bob-tail her cat, Bobby and me
and this is the book I wrote

CHAPTER ONE
BRAINWAVE

"All my best ideas come to me in the bath."

This statement was made by a friend, in a tone of voice that implied that any idea not borne in the bath was not worthy to be considered. If his statement was fact we would have had little chance of ever having an idea of any kind. Our bath times were communal affairs with Bobby, my husband, and I under one shower, Pixie the monkey swimming in the full tub, up and down and round our legs, while Bob-tail her cat was perched on the edge of the tub, into which he would occasionally take a dive, much to the concern of Pixie who helped him return to dry land; she had had him as a kitten and obviously felt he was still far too young to take to the water.

It was all very jolly and we were far too busy trying to stop Pixie from eating the soap to have any time for profound thoughts. Most of our actions resulted from unplanned, impulse ideas that might pop into our heads unbidden, which for the most part made for a more interesting life.

On the night of August 28th, 1977, it was a full moon. Bobby and I were drinking our coffee on the patio of our house in Singapore. Our two dogs, Brownie and Goblin, lay contentedly at our feet. Pixie sat picking over the remains of her dinner, while Bob-tail lay curled up on his favourite chair. Life had been fun. We had travelled, worked and lived in several countries and now our time in Singapore was drawing to a close. We had recently visited England and bought an old Mill House in Devon situated not far from my parents, as was their wish. Bobby was to retire the following year and according to my parents it was high time we settled down. While wishing to comply I felt a sick feeling in the pit of my stomach that our roaming days would be over. Beautiful as the Devon countryside was, were we ready to settle down where our only worries would be if the snails ate all our intended homegrown produce before we did, or that the pipes froze in the winter?

Having resigned ourselves to this new mode of living there was one big snag: British law at that time demanded that all animals entering England from another country had to be quarantined for six months. Monkeys were also classed as wild animals and would not be quarantined along with the dogs and cat. We had visited the two wild animal quarantine places. We knew we could not subject Pixie to solitary confinement, they were worse than any prison. Concrete cells bare of anything resembling the real world with just wire mesh at human eye level. Many of the poor inhabitants were only able to hear who lived next to them and, as often as not, it might be a predator who would in natural surroundings be their enemy.

*

While neither Bobby nor I believed in keeping monkeys or any wild animal as a pet, there are times when it is the only thing to do. One day while living in Malaysia we had gone down to the dock area to buy tobacco. Outside the shop was this poor baby, pig-tailed macaque monkey. A thick wire tightly circled her neck with six inches of chain attached and nailed to the plank of wood she was sitting on. She was wet and shivering and a Chinese man tossed a lighted cigarette butt at her. I sat next to her and she clung to me. Bobby went into the shop and told the man to release her; he naturally wanted money, more than we had with us. Promising he would pay next day, the chain was prised off the wood. We walked the short distance home, the little wet creature, with ears too big for her, clung to me. This was not our first monkey. I love all primates and had read a lot about them so knew that none of them could be house trained!! The first thing we did on getting home was to cut the thick wire from her neck. It was tight and not easy getting the wire cutters between her neck and the wire. Had she remained with it and grown it would have dug into her neck as vets had so often found out. Then I needed to go to the loo, I took her off me and sat her on a towel rail. By chance, beneath the rail, was a floor drain. Monkey see, monkey do. She had a wee in the perfect spot. She did not need to be trained. She acted naturally, went either outside or in the bathroom.

*

As we sat sipping our coffee the thought of what we could do about the animals was uppermost in our minds. Buying a house in England had been one big bad idea. We tossed back and forth how we could get our pets to England without subjecting them to imprisonment. Suddenly Bobby turned to me, "I have just thought of a way we could take all the pets to England and not put them in quarantine."

"How?" I asked, not really expecting a sane answer; had we not debated the fact a million times? "If we had a boat, we could sail to England and then the pets would be on the boat well over the required six months and not need to go in quarantine."

Would it work? I wondered. It was certainly the only idea we had come up with after months of thought. I hardly liked to mention that we did not have a boat. "Perhaps," he said dreamily, "we could find a cheap boat for sale."

I was not sure how one went about finding a cheap boat for sale or, having found one, how we would learn to sail her. But it was an exciting thought and would be another adventure. Bobby was a master mariner so he at least knew about navigating the high seas. I stopped thinking of pottering around an English garden and pouring tea for the local vicar, the smell of which I can't stand: tea, not vicars. I now had visions of a boat with us all aboard and sailing off into the sunset in calm seas – overlooking the fact if it was a sailing boat we would need a bit of wind. My mental picture of the boat was a bit hazy. A cross between a fishing boat and Noah's Ark. I had been on a sailing boat before, for a few hours one Sunday with a friend, two years ago. My role had been purely as a passenger, having fortunately not been asked to help with the sails and had declined the suggestion I could have a go at steering, not wishing to endanger someone else's property, besides which I cannot swim. I did recall thinking what a network of ropes there appeared to be and that it was quite beyond me to fathom out how anyone knew what was what. I pushed that to the back of my mind. After all it was just an idea, we did not have a boat.

Three days after Bobby's brainwave he returned home saying he had been to the yacht club and thought he had seen a boat. I looked at him, even I knew you could not help but see boats if you went to the club. He now smiled. "Two of them are for sale, one is cheap, I think we could afford it."

Bobby had taken a look at this boat on the Monday while it was out of the water but, husband-like, had refrained from mentioning it until he had taken another look and talked it over with the owner, Charlie Green. As I tried to look as if I understood, he explained that it was an Endurance 35 Cutter Rigged Sloop. So far none of this meant anything to me. He continued, "It's made of ferro cement." Forget the ferro bit, I knew what cement was; had I not read somewhere that if you wanted to get rid of someone at sea you gave them cement shoes? He must be joking, any boat worthy of its name was surely made of stuff like wood that would float. I kept quiet and learned she had been built in Bangkok, just over three years ago. Her name was '*Sandpiper*'. I liked the name and as for the rest I would have to wait until the following Sunday when it had been arranged we would go for a trial run.

No lying in bed that Sunday, we arrived at the yacht club to find Charlie still eating his breakfast. The boat was pointed out. *'Sandpiper'* was there, floating just like any other boat, with the sunlight playing on her blue hull. She looked far better than I had anticipated, not the nasty cement grey bulk prone to sinking I had been picturing.

As we stood on the jetty, waiting for the club ferryboat to take us out to *'Sandpiper'* I felt a little apprehensive. The jetty was bobbing about a little too much for my liking. I tried to ignore the feeling, thinking what a fool I would look if I got seasick before we even got on the boat. Once on board, the first impression was the lack of room for us and our furry family, though she was in fact quite spacious. Steps from the cockpit led down to the cabin. Seating with locker space above, behind and under on the starboard side. Also, a quarter berth that went under the cockpit. This I felt no right-minded person would wish to crawl into but might make a suitable bed for the dogs. On the port side was a chart table, lockers and draws, a two-burner stove and a very large sink. A step down and there was a tool locker with the head opposite. Two bunks either side, right forward a sail locker. A strip of new carpet did not really hide the sparseness of the place. Charlie obviously had a thing against doors, nearly all had been removed, leaving only the hinge marks to show they had once existed. Even the lockers behind the seats were open, good for posture but I did wonder how anything put in them would remain in place once at sea. After our tour of inspection, if you could call it that, just about all could be taken in without moving. Bobby dropped down on his knees, not to pray for a safe run but to view the Volvo engine that lived like a monster under the floorboards, which were not for some reason referred to as floorboards but as soul boards, or was it sole? A term I never found natural to say. Imagine, saying 'We lifted up our soul to look at the engine'. I went along with the list of fancy nautical term, but floorboards remained floorboards on *'Sandpiper'* and in this book.

We both enjoyed our trial run. Walter and Carla, a couple from another boat with two kids and a lot of sailing experience, came to crew. The weather was perfect. We left most of the actual handling to the others, Bobby taking a go at steering. With a stiff north east monsoon wind we sailed for about four hours before returning. I was now happy to agree with Bobby that we should buy *'Sandpiper'*. Driving back to the house I felt on fire, not just with excitement but with a very bad sunburn and completely worn out, but happy that we were going to have one more adventure before retirement. We had never taken out a bank account. All money we had accumulated was tossed in a desk draw, it was more than enough to buy *'Sandpiper'*: Singapore dollars 35,000.00 – a thousand per foot.

September 8th was the big day. Bobby and Charlie went to the lawyer, forms were duly signed. Bobby handed over a large paper bag of money and in return was handed the key. *'Sandpiper'* was ours.

We have now read all the books and heard how our cruising friends landed up with their boats. As serious sailors we should have spent months thinking about what kind of boat would suit us, what material it should be made of, etc., then spent a few years either building a boat or looking for one to buy that fitted our requirements. Had we done that, of course, we would all be dead and buried, never having left Singapore. Ignorance is bliss and we have no regrets. For us buying a boat was buying transport to get us, we hoped, to England with our pets. If she could do that we would have no complaints.

O how we cried when we opened our boat
Fumes up our nose and into our throat
The loo was a new one and yet it did leak
The Aqua Kem liquid was what made us weep.

CHAPTER TWO

LEARNING THE ROPES

The following Sunday, a young newlywed couple, Ken Humphrey, the son of an old friend of mine, and his wife Ruth were in Singapore for a few days on their way to a new life in Australia. We were happy to be able to show off our new mode of transport to them and our American friend Chuck Russell joined us.

With pride we opened the hatch and bade our first visitors to enter. Before any of us could move, we became transfixed as fumes hit us and our eyes streamed with tears. Bobby cried his way into the cabin and discovered the cause. The blue liquid from the head had leaked out and down into the bilges. Charlie had fitted a new *handi magic* chemical loo just before we bought *'Sandpiper'*. It looked very grand but gave us trouble until it was discovered a pipe had been broken in fitting, causing the Aqua Kem liquid to leak out. Rather a shame it had waited until we had visitors to shame us. Meanwhile, we opened all the hatches and cried our way around the boat. Not sure how impressed our visitors were.

A few days later it was Hari Raya, a public holiday in Singapore. Normally we would have been visiting our Moslem friends, eating cookies and drinking soft drinks at each house. This year we excused ourselves. This was the day we would have our first go at sailing alone. The day was perfect, a little but not too much wind. The first hours or so were spent sorting out the sails and deciding which to use, and which way up they might look best. Getting off the mooring buoy was easier than it might have been, we moved off without mishap. Our sail was not such a speedy or as impressive a run as our trial run had been but then hardly to be expected as we ventured no further than having the main and staysail up. We enjoyed ourselves and gained confidence, realising that having put the sails up and that the boat actually moved as we steered her, it was relatively simple to know what was connected to what.

The hardest part by far was the effort it took of first getting the sails up and then taking them down and stuffing them back in their bags. I thought we'd die of tiredness as our shore-bound bodies were not used to that sort of thing. Still as Bobby pointed out we would not have to do that every day once at sea.

Charlie had left all cooking utensils, plates etc. and some canned goods on board. Bobby solved the mystery of lighting the kerosene stove – later I was to wish I had taken an interest and learned. I found a can of beans and some coffee; not exactly a meal but like a couple of kids we wanted to eat aboard, feeling we had earned it after our accident-free run.

"Do boats have curtains?" I asked. "Of course if you want to make some," Bobby replied. There were a surprisingly lot of small windows. I got going with the tape measure, thinking they would be the shortest curtains ever made and would have curtain wires top and bottom.

The following day we took our second sail and did a little better, having both jib and staysail up. On our return we investigated what all the lockers contained and found a pressure cooker. "That," I said firmly, "is going out."

Once in America, a friend and myself had been invited to a bachelor's apartment for a meal of chilli beans. A memorable experience. The poor man had left his beans cooking in a pressure cooker while he drove over to pick myself and my friend up. On arrival he opened his kitchen door and we stood speechless at the extraordinary sight before us. A blackened pan on the stove and beans in every direction: ceiling, walls and counters. That experience had naturally put me off pressure cookers I thought for life. As I trudged through the club, a friend saw me heading for the bin with my pan and extolled its virtues until I was convinced it was quite the most indispensable thing one could have at sea. Having now long since got over my fear of it, I fully agree. We cook the rice in it, turn it out and cook the curry. Used just as a heavy pan it makes a good bread oven and at Christmas we cook a good fruit cake. In fact, just about anything can be cooked in it. Its life was saved and instead of the garbage bin it was taken home, cleaned and I learned to use it.

Our third sail on the following Sunday was not quite as good. Perhaps we had got overconfident; the sails did not look quite right, we both agreed they looked the wrong size. Things looked better when we took them down and put the jib where the staysail had been and vice versa – well we all have to learn.

Although we had plenty of headroom on board, Bobby, who is all of 5'3", managed to bang his head three times while on board, then for good measure gave it another crack when taking a shower at home. He wondered if perhaps he had damaged a brain cell when he put his hand in his pocket and found he had brought back a shackle and left his watch on board.

It was a month before we sailed again. We had all the proper ideas of learning to sail before leaving Singapore and getting properly prepared but there was plenty of time we thought. As always it was Pixie and her Bob-tail, and the two dogs we had to think about, after all we had bought the boat to sail to UK because of them. We had decided that when we really knew what we were about we would start taking each of them, one by one, on trial runs to get them familiar with the new way of living and see how they reacted. If we took all four to begin with and they all started to dash around the deck, run up the rigging or dive overboard, we would be in trouble.

A lot of time was spent working on patterns for life jackets. The yachting magazines all advertised several brands of life jackets for all sized humans but nothing suitable for a family such as ours. Odd-shaped life jackets were drawn up and discarded, corks were collected with the idea they might be woven into a life jacket of some kind. What we never figured out was how we would get Pixie to keep one on for more than a second, before ripping it off and chewing it to show what she thought of it. Not only would she take hers off but divest the others of theirs. In the end the corks were chewed up by the lives they were meant to save and the whole idea of life jackets for them was given up as hopeless. In the event of bad weather we decided Pixie and the dogs would have to be chained. Bob-tail would, we thought, stick close to Pixie but we bought a net on a long pole so we could scoop him out of the water should he fall in.

As we only went for two more sails before finally leaving, the pets had not even seen the boat until we all left the house for good. It was not lack of interest, just that there did not seem the time. Bobby was still working and often, even on Sundays, he had work or meetings to attend. I was taken up with my pottery along with buying old furniture to refurbish the Mill House we thought we were headed for in Devon. There were also the tanks of marine fish which kept dying, and the freshwater fish in tanks that kept multiplying. We started to buy yachting magazines and bought each other life jackets for Christmas, but we still had not broken the ties of our usual way of life.

Bobby spent time working on the boat. The main thing being the leaking loo. Each time we went on board and opened the hatches our eyes ran and burned with the fumes from the bilge. Along with the loo problem we had an evil spirit that did not wish it repaired. Every time Bobby went on board to fix the leak, something happened. The first time he found he'd forgotten the instruction book so contented himself with pumping the chemical out of the bilge. He then found he had some oil down there by accidentally dropping his hat down the bilge. As his arms are not five feet long and he is considerably more than five inches round, he found he could neither reach it or get down to it, and so grabbed the boat hook to hook it out. Before perfecting his hooking technique he only managed to push it farther down into the oil. Finally, having hooked it, he sat up and banged his head on the table. He then had the job of washing his nasty looking hat in sea water and Vim. Recording what he had done on board, he put '*washed my hat and got a headache*'.

Another day he found the club had moved the boat to a different mooring. Busy below having finally found the cracked pipe, he heard a loud report like a rifle shot. Dashing on deck he realised he was drifting in a strong wind and tide. The mooring chain had broken. Almost falling down the steps in his hurry he attempted to start the engine, pulling the throttle to get more power the throttle lever came off in his hand. With the engine just ticking over there was not sufficient power to steer the boat in such weather conditions. By this time '*Sandpiper*' was bent on joining up with the small racing dinghies moored nearer to the shore. Quickly hoisting the red flag that was used to bring the club ferryboat out, he grabbed the boat hook and the fog horn and drifted amongst the small boats, blowing the horn for attention with one hand and fending off the other boats with the hook in the other. Snap! The hook broke off the end of the pole. Visions of half a dozen smashed up fibreglass boats floated through his head and the resulting bills, not to mention the anger of the owners who would probably lynch him. With a Superman act brought about by terrified desperation he managed to get a line on the mooring line of one of the small boats. Finally, after what had probably taken only a minute but seemed like hours, they saw or heard him from the club and help arrived.

We narrowly missed a collision when we went on our fourth sail. We had started the engine to motor away from our buoy but she would not answer to the helm, while I looked on in horrified fascination as we made a beeline for the next boat, Bobby having the presence of mind to fend us off. When we returned to our buoy after a pleasant sail we found the engine still useless and believed something had managed to wrap itself around the propeller. We tried sailing up to our buoy, almost, but not quite near enough, I could not reach the line, as we passed we went on and turned to make a second attempt. The club by this time had seen us and decided it would be prudent to come out and tow us to our mooring in view of the strong flood tide. Later we found that the propeller was covered with a solid mass of barnacles.

A new kind of life we thought we would have
so sold all our goods to the hoard
For we had a boat to sail round Good Hope
so with four furry pets climbed aboard

CHAPTER THREE
THE DAY DAWNS

Our original plan had been to leave Singapore in May. A contract for towing had come to an end for Bobby and business was low so we decided to sail at the end of January.

In December we beached *'Sandpiper'* and with the help of a good friend, Bill Benson, we got to work on the bottom, scraping and painting on anti-fouling. All rather fun, the anti-fouling we used that time was red and at the end of it we all looked like we had been attacked by sharks. We had cause to celebrate after having managed to get it all finished before the tide came in.

Friends on learning of our decision to leave so soon said we were crazy to leave when we had only been out in *'Sandpiper'* four times, for a few hours each time. To keep them happy we had one more run but figured that learning en route was just as good as going out and returning after a few hours to our home port. Navigation was not going to be a problem, Bobby was a master mariner, for him it was only a matter of getting used to the sails. For myself, I had just about everything to learn which made it more exciting. My only real worry was how the pets were going to behave, a worry as it turned out, to be fully justified.

Provisioning the boat was my responsibility. I bought several cases of dog food, that was easy as I knew what they liked and how much they ate. The only snag was that I did not know for how long I was stocking up. I tried Bob-tail on every kind of canned cat food. He turned his nose up at it all, quite happy to let the dogs eat it. He had been spoilt by the Amah who would cook him fish and rice and meat. It looked as if once at sea he would have to share the dog food and eat eggs. I still kept a few cans of cat food to put aboard just in case he changed his mind.

Stocking food for ourselves was more of a problem. We had a grocer and a greengrocer deliver every day except Sunday and I still ran out of things. Now I was having to think weeks, months, ahead. Lists grew and grew. I started on the spices, bought them in large quantities, sorted and sealed them. Then large amounts of dried beans and peas of every sort I could find. These my Amah sorted, removing all sticks and stones and spread them out in the sun to get rid of any unwanted passengers such as weevils etc. Cans of butter, ghee, oil.

Advice from sailing friends was sought and given. Eggs had to be greased with Vaseline to make them keep for months. The animals got tired of eating raw eggs off the floor as the slippery things fell from my hands. Cheese would keep if wrapped in paper sprinkled with vinegar. For this I ordered rolls of greaseproof paper and then found it was paper towel I needed for the cheese. Canned goods were my horror. For a start I was not good at opening the darn things. We only used tomato sauce and processed peas in cans, the latter being perfect for currying. We were advised to take cases of canned vegetables as they did not need water to cook unlike our dried goods. Bobby and I visited a supermarket picking up a can of this and a can of that, one of each kind, which we intended to try out to see if we liked them before leaving. As it turned out it was months later at sea before we opened the first can. We found meatless vegetarian food and of these we did buy a case of.

January was a month of bedlam. Everything in the house had to be put in piles and sorted out. Piles of things to go on the boat, another pile of things to be sold. Everything else for the packers to come and pack up for shipment to England. I kept shifting things from one pile to another, wondering if I was making the right choice.

By this time I had given up on my coral fish. I never had more than five at a time but large as the tank was they were not happy. The tank and all the equipment was sold. Next all the freshwater tanks complete with fish went to buyers. I hated the thought of leaving my beloved garden. I dug up a small curry leaf tree and planted it in a pot for the boat. Leaving was made easier when we heard the rumours that the house was marked for demolition, or to be fenced in and turned into a rehabilitation unit for drug addicts. Years later I returned and could not see the house, a high wall hid it from view and the other side, once jungle, was Changi Airport. Enough to make anyone turn to drugs.

Reluctantly I sold all my pot plants, which to my pleasure were mostly bought by friends where I knew they would flourish and get the attention they were used to. I first advertised the household effects in a small private paper and then waited expecting the telephone to ring. It remained silent and not a soul turned up. I later discovered the paper was not published until the following week. Meanwhile, I placed adverts in the local newspaper and then a flood of people were calling at the house and on the phone. In a short time all had been sold, things that had been part of our home for so long were now dispersed among many others.

The most harrowing day of all was getting the pets all injected and inspected for their exit permits. Both the vet for the anti-rabies shot and the place for the exit permits were a long way from where we lived in Changi. Fortunately, we discovered there was such a thing as an animal ambulance and they were also familiar with all the procedure and with a driver that obviously loved animals. The driver was quite prepared to take all four animals on his own, which was nice and surprising. As Pixie is a nicely brought up little girl and will not go off with strange men, I went along too.

Pixie is normally clean and house-trained but in cases of stress in new surroundings wets continually, or gets diarrhoea. With this in mind I intended to have a couple of towels ready. Then a friend, Lori, came up with a better idea, she still had some throwaway nappies that her young son no longer needed.

I sat next to the driver with Pixie's large bottom nicely clad in a perfectly fitting nappy and wrapped in a towel, sitting on my lap. Bob-tail had been brought up from a tiny kitten by Pixie; she allowed us and our Amah to touch him but no one else. He took this to mean he must also shun anyone else; I deemed it best to put a harness on him, made for the occasion. I think I may have made it too small, but I never got the chance to find out; he went quite mad, nearly escaping through the kitchen window. We had to haul him back by his legs, Pixie would have had a fit if she had seen. We got scratched in the process, which I felt we deserved, then popped him in a basket with a lid, wondering if the driver and the vet knew what they were in for. The dogs, much to their surprise, had leads put on their collars and were then shut in a room so they would not disappear before the ambulance arrived at 7.45am, at which time we first put the basket of howling cat in the back and the dogs were quite happy to jump in and join him. Pixie appeared to be unaware that Bob-tail was in the back in a less than happy mood. She sat nicely on my lap, clinging to me, ignoring the nice driver but taking a bit of interest in the passing scenery.

First stop vet. Pixie and I went in first. She was quite happy until the vet came at her with his needle then she screamed and clung to me. He had difficulty getting a leg stretched out for the injection. In the scramble, both nappy and towel fell off just at the moment when they were needed the most. Still she had had her shot and we dashed out into the vet's garden, leaving him a rather unpleasant mess to clear up but with a still clean nappy and towel. We had managed round one.

The job of getting Bob-tail, Brownie and Goblin done I left to the driver, while I followed Pixie around the garden, now quite happy and picking the head off some choice flowers. I saw the driver go in with Bob-tail still in the basket and crossed my fingers, I felt I should say a little prayer for him. He came out still with a smile and unscratched. The dogs were no trouble.

Next step was the exit permits. This was slightly more difficult and for a while it looked as if they were not going to issue them. The fact that they were going on a small private boat and not flying or going by a regular passenger ship put the authorities in a bad position, not knowing what to do. The problem was worse when they were told we would not be going to just one destination; though bound for England, we would not of course be there in one week's time. The problem was handed from one person to another. Pixie got bored and started to take things from the desk, I was politely told they had seen her, and she and I could leave. The driver was allowed to stay marching up and down with the dogs on leads and a basket of now silent cat. It was a long wait but a decision was taken and we got the permits. Singapore $20 for three of them but for some reason only S$3 for Pixie. It was all just a load of red tape as subsequently we were never asked to show any of their papers.

The packers were in for two days packing up our household effects and taking away everything for shipment. The house now was empty except for a pile of stuff for the boat. Bobby made trip after trip from house to clubhouse, each time saying, "I don't know where we are going to put all this on the boat." Neither of us had any suggestion as to what we could do without. To make sure the pets did not all disappear by the time we were ready for our final departure, I shut Bob-tail in one of the empty rooms, chained Pixie and Goblin up on the patio, then called and hunted for Brownie who always was near us but had suddenly vanished. When she did turn up she joined the others. Just in time. Bobby rushed in, the club was about to close. We all tumbled into the car. Full load, no room for remaining jerry cans or Mala the Amah and her daughter who were seeing us off. Ever helpful Lori was there with her car to take them and the rest of the stuff.

We reached the club just in time for the club boat to run us out to '*Sandpiper*' before finishing for the day. Hurriedly we chained the dogs outside the club and rushed aboard; with Pixie and Bob-tail safely on board we left our mooring buoy and motored alongside the jetty to collect the pile of stuff left in the club, the dogs, and bid our friends farewell.

Our first difficulty was getting Brownie and Goblin down the steps of the jetty. It was many years since Brownie had seen steps in Guyana. Since Goblin had joined our family he also had not seen steps. They both crouched down and went almost on their bellies.

Our good friends Flick and Ann were there waiting to see the boat and say goodbye; Lori and her son Mathew, and Mala, our lovely Amah, and her family.

It had just got dark and naturally we wanted everyone to see our new home. We had run the engine so the battery was charged up and we could, so we thought, turn on the light. Nothing happened. As Pixie was on deck chewing a bit of wire we put the blame on her, Bobby dashed off to buy large flashlights. Pixie had been blamed in error as later we found out we had forgotten to put one of the switches up. In an assortment of glasses, coffee cups and monkey mugs, everyone drank to our trip in Champagne, thoughtfully provided by Flick and Ann. I, in true form, forgot to take a photo of this momentous occasion and also to get anyone to sign the visitors' book which I had hastily bought and recovered for the purpose.

Soon we were alone. Bobby had to carry the dogs down into the cabin, Pixie and Bob-tail sat next to us. The cabin was full and we were content and excited as we ate our curry from a set of fitting stainless steel pans. Pans, the rice and curry was a very sweet and thoughtful gift from Mala. Our new life had begun. Soon we would be on the high seas – so we then thought.

Before we left harbour, we had a disaster,
Yet another still anchored offshore.
Then death added its toll to a sad week of woe
and the boat was a pleasure no more.

CHAPTER FOUR

HEARTBREAK AND DISASTERS

The following morning we moved back to our buoy, first making sure we still had Bob-tail aboard, he having been thought lost three times the previous evening when he did not answer to our frantic calls. He had obviously made a much closer inspection of the boat than we had and found his way into lockers and the bilge.

Bobby went ashore to clear up various matters and I set about finding places for all our goods, it being our intention to leave in two days' time. Pixie found plenty to do, chewing on things we did not want chewed and trying to let go the mooring lines, while Bob-tail continued his inspection of the cabin, not yet venturing on deck, both appeared happy. Brownie and Goblin on the other hand took a more than dim view of their surroundings. We had expected wild dashes round the deck accompanied by lots of barking. They had apparently lost the use of their legs and lay next to each other with the most miserable expression on their faces I have ever seen. Food and water had to be put under their noses as they were not going to move an inch for anything. Unfamiliar with steps, to get them from cabin to deck was a major operation of lifting, heaving and hauling, whereupon they sunk down on deck and lay down as before. Bob-tail used his kitty litter tray and was highly praised for being such a clever cat within the hearing of Brownie and Goblin. The contents of the tray were deposited on newspaper on the deck in the hope that the dogs would follow his good example. They turned their heads in disgust with a look that said quite plainly 'we will wait until we are ashore'. I had not expected this and was worried.

Towards evening a strong breeze blew up, very pleasant after the heat of the day. Bob-tail still refused to come on deck, despite the fact that Pixie was there whom, he considers, through some freak of nature, to be his mother.

I moved Pixie forward on a long chain attached to the jib boom. She liked this as it enabled her to swing down on her chain and touch the water. I sat on deck with the dogs and watched, happy that one crew member was enjoying herself.

At the time there was quite a fresh north east wind and a choppy sea. Then as the boat once more rolled, I caught sight of the end of the chain, still with the padlock attached but no Pixie! At first I could not take it in, I was paralysed for a moment with fear, before being galvanized into action. I went for the net which was attached to a long pole we had kept handy in case Bob-tail dived over board. I knew where it was but now it was buried under a pile of items temporarily stored on the cabin roof. Succeeding in freeing the net I looked down, stupidly expecting her to be where she had fallen in. All I could see were large waves and a strong current going out to sea. Yelling her name, I scanned the sea, I spotted her trying desperately to swim back against the current. I knew she was a strong swimmer but she had never swam in the sea or in such conditions. The waves now looked bigger than I ever remembered seeing, poor Pixie so small and too far away to throw anything to help her. As a non-swimmer it would have been pointless to dive in after her. Hoisting the flag to call the club boat out, at the same time not daring to take my eyes off Pixie who was being dragged farther and farther away and all I could see was her pink bottom. The foghorn was at hand but after two blasts it depleted to a mere inaudible grunt. Yelling did little to help, we were the farthest mooring buoy from the club and not within hearing distance. The other boats in the vicinity had no one on board.

Pixie was still in sight as the boat started coming but just before it reached *'Sandpiper'* Pixie, who I had not taken my eyes off, disappeared. I stared, willing her to reappear, nothing met my eyes. I was beside myself with the horror of it all, to see Pixie who I loved so, drowned, and I could do nothing to help her. As in a nightmare I took a life ring and had the boat take me much farther than I had last seen her and then back along the shore in a desperate, hopeless search. Pixie was gone. It was just getting dark when the boat returned me to *'Sandpiper'*. Bobby returned shortly after; to say we were heartbroken was putting it mildly. The whole idea of purchasing the boat was mainly to keep Pixie with us. Now even before hoisting sail, Pixie was gone and it was quite obvious that the dogs hated being on the boat. We no longer cared what we did but decided we could not risk the lives of the others. Pixie was the best swimmer of the lot and the most agile and if we could lose her while still at anchor there seemed little hope of a safe passage for the rest of them.

The next morning Bobby went ashore, searching the beaches and asking people if they had seen Pixie; good friends joined in the search but no one could report anything to relieve our anxiety. Our beloved little Pixie had gone; we became almost useless in our misery. Ann, Flick and Lori spent the next few days sorting out our problems and looking for homes for the dogs. Mala said she would take Bob-tail, she was the only one he trusted and we thought he would miss Pixie more than he would miss us.

Ann found Brownie a home at the Red Cross for crippled children. We felt this would be perfect. Brownie, who we had taken in as a stray with puppies many years ago in Guyana, was very old and apart from sudden spurts of energy about once a week, did not move about much but loved to be petted. We felt that these crippled children, who mostly could only move in wheelchairs, would be ideal for her. She was to be one boy's special pet and sleep next to his bed. The boy, David, took to her and she to him at first sight and we thought that we could not have found a better place for her; she seemed content and not worried when we left. We still felt we had betrayed her and the others who we said we would never give up.

Goblin had not been ours for very long. He had once belonged to a couple who worked for us but when they split up we landed up with Goblin, their dog. We did not even know his name so re-christened him and he seemed happy to stay with us, though often straying and knocking Chinese people off their bikes if they passed our house. Lori said she would take him, she lived just a little farther up from our old home and Goblin was always visiting her, and Ann's house opposite, so she would be almost home.

When we took the dogs ashore they had been on the boat three days and during that time had not moved about or been to the bathroom once. They were certainly happy to get ashore and relieve themselves. There was no doubt terra firma was their choice.

We still had Bob-tail, he had settled down very well in spite of not having Pixie. He never went on deck and we wondered if perhaps we dare keep him. Too much of our world was falling apart.

The following day, still with heavy hearts, we went ashore with the cases of dog food, their brushes, mats etc. While taking these from the wharf to the club one of the boatmen came to me and said his son had found Pixie. Miracles don't often happen. I had prayed and prayed for Pixie to be alive, Mala and all her family had gone to the Hindu temple and prayed. Ann said she felt sure Pixie would be returned. I could not forget that I had seen her disappear in the middle of a very rough sea and strong tide and that could only mean that the sea had taken her. I felt weak with joy as the boatman explained that Pixie was not only alive but in perfect health.

We shall never know for sure how Pixie reached land, looking back I believe she must have decided to swim underwater when she disappeared from sight. We knew she could do this and hold her breath far longer than expected. She frightened us the first time when we were in Malaysia by diving in a pond and not reappearing until reaching the other side. Perhaps she found it easier underwater than fighting the waves. Still it was a long way to swim for a little monkey in such sea conditions. Apparently, she did reach the shore that evening and was seen by the boatman's son sitting in a tree on the beach. Pixie went to the boy and, as she still had her belt on, he tied a length of string to it and took her in his little boat across to the large island opposite. No doubt Pixie was happy to get in his boat thinking she would be returned to us. Why it took so many days before we were told, we were not sure. Either the father, who was one of the boatmen for the club, was not on duty for those days and so did not know we had lost Pixie, or else he had not returned to the island and did not know his son had her. It mattered little, that she was alive and well was enough.

Naturally as soon as we knew Pixie was safe we wanted to go and get her at once. This was not to be. It was made very clear that they did not wish us to go to the island ourselves. Nor were they willing to take us. They claimed the house was far from where the boat could land and we would not be able to find it and, in fact, did everything possible to discourage us from going. Reminding them we had offered a good reward for her return did nothing to change their minds. However, as they had promised Pixie would be returned to the club that afternoon we waited, and waited, we waited impatiently all day. Afternoon came and went, still no Pixie; we began to get worried. It was getting dark and the boatman came off duty. We asked him if it was not possible for us to go and collect her together with him. Reluctantly he agreed if we use our fibre glass dinghy. So far we had only used the dinghy once and found it was too heavy for us to drag ashore so had left it at the club. The Seagull outboard engine we had for it had, that day, been returned from the repair shop and fitted on. We got in the dinghy letting the boatman steer. He took us to *'Sandpiper'*. He did not wish to take us both as the dinghy was a bit unsafe. I got on board *'Sandpiper'* so Bobby could go and get Pixie. Another delay, they found there was little gas left in the tank so had to return to the club for fuel. This turned out to be fortunate because as they arrived at the club so did the boat bringing Pixie. Bobby got out of the boat to see Pixie running up the shore on a long string to greet him. With the boatman now rowing and Bobby holding Pixie they returned to *'Sandpiper'* where she was handed up to me. How wonderful it was to have her in my arms again and none the worse for her adventure. Hugging Pixie and crying with pure joy, I took her down into the cabin and Bobby rowed the boatman back. Bob-tail came out of hiding and we sat on the seat in a happy reunion.

Time went on, I peeled an assortment of vegetables for dinner, letting Pixie take what she liked. Still Bobby had not returned. It got late, eventually Pixie, with Bob-tail in her arms, fell asleep. I could not imagine what was keeping Bobby so long as he had only been going to give the boy the reward and get gas for the outboard. Finally, I heard a boat coming alongside and went on deck with the flashlight to greet Bobby. I shone my light down, it was not Bobby who looked up at me but a complete stranger, without a word he handed me a note. As I read the note I was stunned: Bobby was in hospital with a dislocated shoulder and would have to stay the night. Just as I had been thinking that our troubles were over. Was *'Sandpiper's'* crew ever going to be complete?

Bobby had taken the boatman back and got gas for the engine. Just as he was starting the engine, a large wave caught the boat, which in turn went under the wharf and promptly sank with Bobby in it. He surfaced complete with rope and, with the help of a Malay that was just passing, they managed to pull the dinghy up. In doing so Bobby dislocated his shoulder very badly and found he was unable to use his arm. The man kindly offered to look after the boat for him as he was in such pain. Fortunately, the hospital is next door to the Changi Sailing Club.

He suffered more on arriving at the hospital. They seemed not to notice he was dripping wet and in pain, all they wanted was his passport or some kind of identification. He explained that as he had not anticipated an accident of falling into the sea and all it had entailed, he had not carried his passport which was just as well or that would have been soaked. Tired and in agony, he demanded that they cease their nonsense and take him to the doctor on duty. After further arguments a female doctor appeared on the scene. She tried to pull his shoulder back into place, failed; it was so painful Bobby was near fainting. Another doctor was called and the two then tried but all they did was to torture poor Bobby until he had to beg them to stop. The resident surgeon was called, who examined him and realised that it was impossible anyway as it had not come out front ways as they thought, but gone to the back. They would have to operate.

He was stripped of his wet shorts and shirt to be left naked. They then rolled them in a tight bundle so they would be just as wet for him the following morning. Kindly they covered his body with a sheet and stuck him in a room with an air conditioner on so low that he almost froze to death and had him wondering if they had given up on him and put him in the morgue.

While still alive two nurses came and put him on a trolley to take him to the operating room. One nurse supporting his injured arm. They kept up a two-way conversation much to the discomfort of Bobby, whose injured arm was forgotten and dropped. On arrival at the operating room they found they had forgotten the key and the door was locked. One nurse went back for the key only to find it must be the wrong one as it did not work. The other nurse, who had kindly resumed supporting his arm, dropped it abruptly to go and get the key herself.

Finally, they were able to get in the room. Two doctors arrived and started an argument as to whether they were in the correct room or not. By now Bobby was in great pain and everyone seemed to have forgotten all about him in their heated argument. Mercifully, the surgeon arrived and ordered an anaesthetic be administered.

The next morning Bobby woke to find his arm strapped to his body in a sling and feeling very much better. Getting off the bed he requested to have his clothes back. His request was refused, telling him he could not leave until the doctor discharged him. After that he was told someone would have to come and claim him and pay the bill. He said he did not wish to be claimed and there was no one to do so. He was perfectly capable of paying for himself if they would just give him back his shorts, in the pocket of which he had a large roll of money.

It was not only a painful night out for him but an expensive one also, at a cost of S$750. By noon I had Bobby back. Now that the two strong swimmers on board had had a ducking, I just hoped neither Bob-tail nor I would fall in. The chances of us coming up again, while still alive, were not very good.

We had thought that having Pixie back we would be able to leave but now Bobby's arm, his right one, was useless and we would have to wait for that to heal, then I thought our troubles would be at an end. I had forgotten the old adage that mishaps run in threes.

"Hi Lori, what are you doing here?" I said as I got off the club ferryboat the morning after Bobby had returned from his mishap. I was more than surprised to find Lori sitting on the bank. "Heard you had not left yet and thought you might like a lift to the shops," she volunteered. "Oh thanks," I replied. I could not help feeling it was a little odd. Lori seemed a bit preoccupied and I knew she was due by then to drive to her work at the airport. The shops were all an easy walking distance for me and she had no way of knowing if and when I would come ashore that morning. I told her about Bobby and his experience.

"Why don't you forget the boat and fly to Spain or somewhere and relax? It seems everything is going wrong for you." This did not sound like Lori, who had been keen about our proposed trip before. There was no time for further conversation as we had arrived at the post office, the farthest I had to go, and Lori now had to drive to work.

Something was wrong, I felt. No mention had been made of the dogs. I could not rid myself of a cold fear gripping me that something had happened to Goblin and that Lori could not bring herself to tell me. Had something so bad happened that she was afraid I would break down or get hysterical? Had she in fact been hoping Bobby would be the one to come ashore so she could tell him? Why had I let Lori go without asking her about Goblin? I hastened through with my shopping. I intended, as before, stopping on the way back to see Brownie but I was rather laden down and wanted to get back to the club where I could use the phone. I rang Ann, perhaps she could tell me about Goblin. Flick answered and was surprised I was not with Ann who, he said, had gone to Changi to meet me. I put the phone down. Why were both Lori and Ann wanting to accompany me shopping? As I gathered up my bags the phone rang and the barman handed it to me. It was Ann, who had just returned home. Gathering up my courage I asked her about Goblin, she would know if anything was wrong as she and Flick lived opposite, and Goblin was a playmate to their dog, Henry.

Ann was more than willing to talk about Goblin, I got a blow-by-blow account of almost every minute of his day. Goblin was fine that was clear. Perhaps with all the upset I was getting paranoid. Just because my friends show a desire to see me I suspect them of some secret motive. Feeling much relieved I now asked Ann, who did voluntary work for the Red Cross home, if she thought they would mind my visiting Brownie, who we had said goodbye to while we remained in Singapore waiting for Bobby's shoulder to heal. Surprisingly, she hesitated and said she did not think it was a good idea. She now sounded in a hurry and said to go back to the boat as she and Flick were about to leave to visit us.

As I replaced the receiver the cold fear was back. Something I was sure had happened and it could only be Brownie. Returning to the boat I told Bobby of my conversations with Lori and Ann, he agreed something definitely must be wrong. I refused to let my mind dwell on the worst scenario. Brownie had been happy on our last visit to say goodbye and had gone on one of her mad dashes round the field. Yes, we were worried, but thought that perhaps Brownie had run away and gone back to our old home, a distance which she could have made slowly, despite her old age. Flick and Ann arrived on board, it was lovely to see them, though I felt it a shame the cabin was in such a mess. With all that had happened since we moved on board I had done little in the way of cleaning. We talked of everything but dogs. Bobby and Flick went on deck. It was then Flick told Bobby that Brownie had been found dead under David's bed that morning, having passed away in her sleep. Brownie was old and we knew that she did not have much time left in life but the last time I had visited her she had seemed happy in her new environment and was running in the field on one of her occasional spurts of energy. That we had put her through three days on the boat, which she hated, and then abandoned her for her last few days after all the years together seemed unforgivable.

It was also very sad for the children who had been so happy to have her, in particular David who was so proud to have a dog to love.

Had buying a boat been a good idea? So far it had resulted in a lot of heartbreak and trouble for us all, for our pets and other people whom we had involved. We now longed to leave before anything else could go wrong.

In the end came the day, though cloudy and grey
when we started this journey so mad
the weather grew rougher and sailing got tougher
then a sandbank got right in the way.

Our route up the Malacca Straits

CHAPTER FIVE
ALL AT SEA

Bobby's arm slowly improved and he was able to lift it a little higher each day. Pixie and Bob-tail had settled down nicely and we all began to enjoy living on a boat, a boat that bobbed about but did not actually move. Until a friend asked me which way we were going I realised I had not given it a thought. I had travelled extensively but for the most part with no fixed destination. I asked Bobby. "I thought we would go to Malaysia first, see what charts we needed, and then head for Africa and go round the Cape of Good Hope," he replied. That sounded really exciting, I had not been to Africa. Later Flick tried to talk him out of going that way and for a time our route was not settled.

The weather remained good with not a drop of rain. Having decided to leave on the 18th February we once again said goodbye to our friends which seemed to have become a habit with us. That night rain poured down and we woke to find we had a depression on the way, the barometer had dropped considerably. Not a good day to start off. I did not even go ashore for my usual shower that day as I was beginning to feel foolish saying goodbye one day and hello the next. I had not known then that small boats rarely sail when planned. The next day the weather was not much better but we decided to take off anyway which, as it turned out, was not a very clever move.

The mainsail got jammed on the last foot of the traveller and the bobstay needed tightening which caused the jib to flap around. We soon found ourselves caught up in the depression and were foundering around in the water like a demented whale. Then not only the jib, but all the sails decided they had had enough, flapping like mad and making an awful noise and looking most *unsail-like*. I was completely petrified, feeling that this was just about the most crazy way to travel invented. Bob-tail did not think much of it either and sat in the cabin howling his head off. Pixie was very good though, when I had to take the wheel so Bobby could see to the sails, she sat with me as if to say she would help and hung on to the wheel, no doubt thinking she could do better and certainly no worse than I. Rain poured down and we got soaking wet and so cold I thought if we did not drown then we would probably be the first people to freeze to death in the tropics.

Giving up on the jib and then the stay-sail we got the engine started, the noise of which I usually hate but now sounded like music after the racket the sails had been making. Anyone watching would have thought we had gone mad, everything was happening at once. The plastic garbage bag I had attached on one of the winches got mixed up with a sheet (rope I would have called it) when we were trying to pull it in. Bobby was yelling at me to pull on the sheet and the more I pulled the more the bag twisted round the sheet; I grabbed a knife and cut the offending bag free. I object to dumping anything but vegetable matter in the sea, but at that point I was so mad with the sea and the garbage so over it went. Later I felt guilty but I suppose compared with all the good things we have left to the sea such as sun hats, mugs, buckets, plates, shorts etc., most of which Pixie tosses overboard with glee, the garbage bag was just a drop in the ocean, no pun intended. On our next tack Pixie's chain got caught in the cleat with the sheet, more struggles with Pixie taking an active part but getting more in the way than helping; the whole of our little world was going mad.

At one point I realised that padlocking Pixie's chain to the rails was fine as long as we stayed on top of the sea but if it looked that we were going to turn over and sink she would have no chance to swim free and the key hung in the cabin. Still doing my best to steer but on the whole making a hash of it I said, rather dumbly, "Do you think we will turn over and sink?"

"Not if you keep your head and steer properly," was his reply. *Golly*, I thought, *if it depends on that we have had it*. By this time we had got into the shipping lanes of the Malacca Straits and it was then that we decided to give up on all the sails and use the engine alone which apart from other things would give us a more dignified appearance.

For some reason we had on board a very old chart of the area. Bobby had bought a new up to date one and then forgot all about it and was using the old. He was now wondering why all the buoys were in different positions from that shown on the chart and all quite different from how he remembered it when captain of a cargo boat some twenty years before. It was the next day that he remembered the new chart lay still untouched.

We were just feeling that we now had command of the situation when the engine decided it was its turn to play tricks, stopping dead. No time to do whatever one does to an erring engine, instead we rushed to hoist the sails. Before we could even start hauling we felt a bump; we were aground! I have no idea why, as there were big ships all around us so presumably, unless they too had gone aground, which I thought unlikely, they had water under them. We must have hit the only mole hill, or whatever they have down there, in the area. At least we were now still, so I figured therefore safe. Bobby did not look too happy about it and felt an urgent desire to get off into deep water. He was more than pleased when a local cargo barge came along and pulled us off.

Deciding we had had enough adventures for the day, we anchored. We stayed anchored in the same spot during the next day, spending time putting things right. The bob-stay was tightened and there seemed no reason why the mainsail did not go right up as it did from then onwards, perhaps we just had not grown enough muscle at that point.

Most of the day Bobby sat talking to the engine and then attacking it with spanners etc. One spanner got away and fell into the bilge where we could see it nicely but not reach it. Pixie was the only one small enough to get it but she proved most unwilling to even try. Dropping things in such places was more in her line, not retrieving them. In the end we made a neat little hook and line and managed to get it up after considerable effort.

Next day, after a lot of tries, we finally managed to get the anchor up and we were off again. From then on we did much better. At least we acted more seaman-like and the sails, even though they did not carry us very fast, looked like sails should look. We planned to anchor for the night off Pulau Pisang (Banana Island) and arrived in the area well before dark, all we had to do was to go behind the island to anchor. Sounds easy but what a game it proved to be. The wind completely died and we had to start the engine but with such a strong southerly current we remained almost at a standstill.

We got sick and tired of the sight of that island. It got dark but the full moon still showed that island laughing at us; slowly we got round the island and then the engine decided enough was enough and it was tired. It stopped dead leaving us still in very deep water. We were tired too and tried to get the engine to take us just a little farther; it refused. Bobby now saw we were drifting down on one of the islands, when we were near enough we dropped the anchor in 17 fathoms and only about two hundred feet from the island. The rope caught on a hook in the chain locker and I dashed down to free it, catching Pixie playing with the echo sounder. It was 2300hrs by the time we anchored; we tied down the mainsail and lit the anchor light and fell into bed exhausted. That night, tired as we were, we got little rest. Pixie kept standing on my sunburn to look out of the port hole and Bob-tail at one point went on deck so he could jump down from the hatch on to my face. Bobby woke me again at three in the morning saying he felt sure the anchor was dragging. Upon investigating, we found we were surrounded by drift net fishing boats who had set their nets between each other and moved right across our anchor rope. They had caught one big fish, us. There was tremendous tension on our anchor rope and we were being dragged along. Bobby decided the only way to deal with the situation was to cut every fishing net rope in sight with our cutlass. More used to hacking paths through dense undergrowth, he hacked away until we were free. Who knows, perhaps we saved the lives of a few fish as well. It was hard to understand why the fishermen had done such a stupid thing as they could hardly fail to have seen us, it was a clear bright night and our anchor light had not blown out.

Two nights later we anchored off Muar in a heavy swell. That night a real gale blew up, we tossed and rolled and things kept rattling around in the lockers. Bobby appeared to be up all the time checking on the anchor. We got little sleep and in the morning felt sick with tiredness. For some reason whenever we have rough weather I get ravenously hungry, which is inconvenient as it's always the most difficult time to cook. I crawled out of the bunk and got some cereal and made up some milk. Returning to the bunk with it, Pixie ate all mine and Bobtail stuck his nose in Bobby's and drank all the milk. Later I found on the floor a pan, still with its lid on, of the leftover curry from the night before. Pixie and I finished that off like a couple of starving refugees. The next find was not so nice. Someone had vomited at the end of the bunk, I think it must have been Pixie though she did not appear to be troubled by the motion.

The sea was a nasty army green colour and it looked awful outside. At 1300hrs we made an attempt to get the anchor up. No way could we move it, it was quite happy where it was, so we stayed until the following day by which time the sea was calm and back to the colour the sea is supposed to be. We felt fit after our rest and the anchor came up without trouble.

The weather on the whole was not what we would have liked. Sometimes it was dead calm with hardly a breath of wind and loads of sun. The latter turned Bobby a lovely brown colour and made me look like a cross between a lobster and a snake shedding its skin. Other times we would be caught in a Sumatra, a local squall which would have us tearing around madly, dripping wet, changing or lowering sails. Still it all got to be more fun as the days went by. It was only the first day that I really hated.

As a rule we would find an anchorage before dark that was fine, but getting the anchor up again the next day was another matter, even with the winch. We would wait until the current was not against us, then using the engine to ride over the chain so the anchor hung down and using every bit of strength we both had we pulled like mad; rest, pull again; rest, and so on until it was finally up and we were exhausted. I hated that darn anchor, all the time my bones pained right through to my back and chest, even my hands hurt. I was beginning to think we had started this sailing business a little late in life. When I voiced this thought Bobby said, "What do you mean? When I was your age I could have pulled the anchor up single-handed." True he was 16 years my senior and how did he know what he could have done then?

Usually when we anchored before dark it was a lovely time of day when we would sit on deck watching the sun do down with a rum and water, in which Pixie shared, unfortunately her idea of sharing is two for me and one for you. One such evening we heard a funny noise. Pixie was standing up and looking across the water, her eyes far better than ours, then we saw what had attracted her: four beautiful dolphins jumping up and playing. We watched spellbound. That sighting was well worth all the hardships of sailing.

The engine we now found to be a very temperamental monster, we had had little to do with it before setting out, just running it now and then to charge the batteries. Perhaps it felt lonely stuck down in the bilge and so played up to get more attention in return for moving the boat.

We had to lift the boards up each time to start the engine and one day Bobby saw it had no oil, it was now all down in the bilge, having leaked out through the main seal. What a mess, pumping it all out and putting it into containers. Before entering Port Kelang, the port where he had once worked, he filtered all the oil so it could be used again. We had no more oil aboard and we would need the engine to make our way against the strong tides in Port Kelang.

We had seen no other yacht until the afternoon, just before entering Port Kelang. We sighted a small yacht going in the opposite direction, showing the Canadian flag, the distance was too far to see if anyone was on deck but we waved anyway feeling they deserved some form of recognition if they had come all the way from Canada. We then realised the flag did not mean that they had sailed from Canada. We were flying the Union Jack and had only come from Singapore.

Later we learned the boat was *'Seraffyn'* which had left Port Kelang just before we arrived. At the time the name meant nothing to us but later we read Lyn & Larry Pardey's book *'Cruising in Seraffyn'* and wished we had arrived sooner and met them.

"We have made it," I shouted happily as we anchored and dashed below just before the rain fell down. "Bit different from our day sails from Changi," said Bobby grinning. It certainly had been, no more after a few hours of sailing could we put the sails away and drive home to a nice freshwater shower, doctor my sunburn and relax over a meal Mala had prepared for us. This was real sailing and exciting, even if I did now and then think longingly of a shower with fresh water while Bobby dumped a bucket of sea water over me. We were right too, we had learned a lot on the way, far more than we could ever had learned just going on Sunday sails, however many we had done.

"You are doing all right, you know," Bobby said. "Am I?" I replied, grinning all over my face. I did think I was getting the hang of it all and glad Bobby thought so too. Bob-tail had settled down well and not fallen overboard, though he spent most of his time on deck. Before leaving Singapore we had bought a roll of fishing net and wrapped it all round the rails. It looked a mess but it would prevent Bob-tail falling off, though it would not help much if he fell off the cabin top which is where he preferred to be, if not with Pixie. Pixie had turned into a good sailor and did her best to help, pulling at any rope she could get her hands on, she got in the way more than she helped but still she was trying. However, she did have her bad points. One day I heard Bobby taking to her. "You are the worst second mate I have ever sailed with, Never, in all my seafaring career, have I had s second mate who chewed ropes." Oh well, we can't all be perfect.

It was nice to be back in Port Kelang. We had lived there for three years and had in fact rescued Pixie from a little shop down by the docks. Now we were back and very near our old home.

Freedom for Pixie is what we now sought
and we searched high and low but in vain
A husband to share it, just could not be bought
so Pixie did not change her name.

CHAPTER SIX

MONKEY BUSINESS IN PORT KELANG

Our arrival in Port Kelang was celebrated with a bottle of wine, in which Pixie had her hand full from my glass, though at home she had never been keen on wine. Bob-tail too had changed his eating habits once on board; he was quite happy to eat canned cat food that he would not look at at home. He was also happy to tuck into grated coconut and other odd things.

The first birds we saw after our arrival were the famous Kelang crows; we were glad to see that the Sultan had not succeeded in eliminating them all with his organised crow shooting. We also saw a pilot boat go out, this was of interest as it was one that Bobby had designed for the port authority before leaving Malaysia. Now it was built and in action but the uniforms he had also designed were no longer being worn, the crew wearing ordinary clothes.

Our mail arrived and with it more problems. My parents had offered to take delivery of our shipment of household goods sent from Singapore, but were having trouble as the customs' forms had been mislaid. Far worse than that was the news from the Agriculture and Fisheries in England. While in Singapore I had written to them telling them of our intention of coming to England with the animals, asking what rules we had to comply with in order not to put them in quarantine for the required six months. We had expected that for the six months prior to us reaching England we would not be able to take them ashore and wanted to know if we had to get special certificates to prove we had not done so. They had written back a long and detailed and kindly letter explaining the law. What it all boiled down to was the fact that no matter how long Pixie and Bob-tail stayed on the boat without going ashore, they would still be required to do the six months. We were back to square one. I wrote again asking if we could not come to England and anchor in UK waters and then stay on board with the pets for the six months allowing only quarantine inspectors on board. That too was in time turned down. I wrote more letters to everyone I thought could help, bar the Queen. There was no way out: if they were to go to England they would have to be put in quarantine and separate ones at that.

We loved Pixie dearly and the shock of what had happened in Singapore was still with us. We had to think what would be best for her. She would, we knew, not willingly be parted from us, we were her family. Surely she would be happier if we could return her to the wild to live the life she was meant to have. We had gone down this route before when we had her in Malaysia. We had sought advice from the zoo. They told us they often were given pig-tailed monkeys when they outlived their usefulness as coconut pickers. We saw none in the zoo, where were they? We were told they were too common to display so they just tossed them over the wall to fend for themselves. Did they monitor them to see how they managed? No, they were common and no one cared.

We had introduced Pixie several times to other monkeys, one lived in a large cage in a junk/antique yard we often visited. He was happy to see her but she ignored his advances and was more interested in the junk. She would never be able to join a troop and her ways would not be theirs. She had always shown fear of the bush. Whenever she went off in Malaysia or Singapore she always headed for people, never the frightening jungle. What we needed was an uninhabited island with water and vegetation. We learned of the Sembilan Islands farther north on the west coast of Malaysia which we thought sounded ideal. Rumbia, the larger one, we were told had water. So far so good but she would need a mate and preferably one who had also spent some time in captivity. We pondered on this idea, wanting to give Pixie the chance of freedom but also wondering how we could ever give her up. If it did not work we would have to give up the idea of going to England, which would upset my parents, but perhaps be nearer in Spain or some place with no quarantine rules. That was all in the future and we would see what happened meanwhile.

It was fun being in Port Kelang again, it was a nice calm anchorage and we met old friends and made new ones at the friendly little yacht club. The deck was a bit exposed to the heat for Pixie but she kept cool by sitting in a plastic tub of water and developed a passion for throwing everything into the sea. We were forever running out of mugs as she drank endless mugs of orange juice and when finished, unless we were quick off the mark, toss the empty mug into the sea. The shop in town where I bought suitable mugs must have thought I was making a collection of them. I would go in and buy three mugs at a time and the odd plate or two.

It was a luxury to wash in fresh water again after days of sea water bucket baths on deck. We were able to bathe in the club using their mandi bathroom. Big tubs of water with a dipper to pour the water over you. The typical and delightful Malay way of bathing.

Unwisely perhaps, in going ashore I would take the short cut across the rail tracks so I could walk past our former home. When we had left it to live in Singapore, the garden had been a blaze of colour from flowering shrubs and trees to a pond by the house with fish and the most beautiful ficus tree that spread its aerial roots and branches over a huge area. This was Pixie's tree. Now it was hardly recognisable as a ficus. It had been so badly mutilated I could not understand how anyone could have done it. No longer a spreading shade, all the aerial roots and branches had been hacked off making a shape more like a poplar than a ficus. The hedge too was gone and nearly everything in the garden cut down, that is except the grass which was about two feet high, completely hiding from view the pond, if it still existed, by the patio and the graves of our beloved Pablo (the dog that had arrived on the top of a basket of vegetables as a puppy when we first lived in Guyana, then British Guiana) and of Pixie's little rabbit, Arab. I had been warned not to visit it and told that Chinese owners had taken it over and cut everything down, but I had not visualised just how bad it would be. It looked far worse than when we had first moved in, the house had been empty for eighteen months then and the garden had been unattended, but the fantastic ficus tree had stood tall, spreading and proud.

Shopping expeditions often resulted in my buying more than I could carry so I would have to hire a tri-shaw, a three-wheel cycle with a seat for two at the back. The shop that once delivered to our house no longer had a van. Once when I bought too much to stock up the boat they sent a small boy back with me; to see this small thing struggling with half my bags was too much so I got a tri-shaw anyway. The burden of it all was now taken on by a poor old Chinese driver who looked as if he might not last the short trip. I said I would walk but he insisted I get in and we made it to the club whereupon the plastic bag of goods hanging on the handlebars came off and smashed to the ground. I was minus one bottle of monkey orange juice.

We had a surprise visit from Rashid, a man that had once worked with Bobby at the Port Authority, bringing with him a bag of fruit for us. He told us they had all been hearing rumours that we were back in Port Kelang and he was pleased that he was the first to track us down at the yacht club. Mr Lim, now working at the club, was also an old acquaintance; he had been in charge of the rest house when we first arrived in Malaysia some six-and-a-half years before. We had stayed for a few days prior to finding a house with our cats, birds and dogs who had just been reunited with us after about seven months in quarantine in UK and Hong Kong. Sadly, all had now passed away, Brownie being the last.

We had intended staying about two weeks in Port Kelang mainly for the reason of having to wait for the delivery of an Aries self-steering vane being sent out from England, then we would continue on to Sri Lanka before the monsoon set in. Now having decided to try and return Pixie to the wild it seemed inevitable that we would have to remain around Malaysia for the monsoon period since we would not leave her on an island unless we were satisfied and certain that she could fend for herself, and was safe and happy.

There was plenty to keep us busy. Having now lived on the boat for some time we started realising all there was to be done on her and every day, starting even before breakfast, we were scraping and re-varnishing, painting the inside of the cabin and making doors etc.. I, who had been worried that I might not have enough to keep me occupied, found that there was an endless amount of things and work to be done. The engineers of the Port Authority kindly came and worked on our engine for us which entailed moving Pixie from her favoured spot in the cockpit to the foredeck, whereupon she decided to work as well and ripped off all the canvas round the foot of the mast – she was right, it did need renewing!

The steering vane did not arrive for two weeks even though it was sent by air. When it did eventually arrive the customs charges etc. came to twice what we expected. It was several days more before we could actually get it delivered on board. We unpacked it in the cockpit, then sat down and read the directions for assembly. A good idea except we left the sheets of directions on deck and a gust of wind blew them away. Frantically we tried to see where they had gone and if we could undertake a saving expedition. They were gone, never to be recovered. We were now on our own and had to puzzle out how it should be put together without help. We thought we remembered the instructions had said it could be fixed in a matter of hours. It took days. For a start we had to drill holes for the bolts in the cement stern. This involved borrowing a drill and generator for the purpose.

I was terrified Bobby was going to fall in the water with it and get electrocuted as I stood by at the plug to turn it off if necessary.

The Aries vane proved itself in the future to be our most prized possession, saving us endless hours at the wheel, that is, once we had worked out how to operate it. Like most things, making it do its job was simplicity itself once we had understood how. Without the vane we doubt we could have even got as far as Sri Lanka. It made our whole trip so much more enjoyable.

The club had a dog, I don't believe it actually belonged to anyone but it was a friendly dog and had taken up residence at the club and been give the name Nicky. Perhaps Nicky sensed I was missing Brownie and Goblin and attached himself to me when I went shopping. At first I was suitably flattered at having his company. Then his loving nature changed, as we walked down the road he dashed off after chickens and goats, scattering them squawking and bleating off the road and into people's gardens. Very embarrassing, I walked ahead pretending I did not know him.

Life aboard was never dull, even cooking was fraught with dangers. One evening I was about to make dinner, having in my hand a bag of grated coconut. Taking a step backward to my horror and astonishment I dropped down into the bilge; Bobby had just lifted the floorboards up to look at the engine for some odd reason. Fortunately, I came up almost as fast as I had gone down and suffered no injury. Bobby was furious that I had been so silly, which I thought was a bit unfair as it was quite unintentional on my part. He pointed out I could have broken my leg. I saw his point; who wants a mate with a broken leg? Worse was the fact that half my grated coconut had shot out all over the engine and the bilge, and was sure to block the bilge pump, or if not it would go bad and we would have a rotten coconut smell on the boat for the rest of the trip. As it happened Bobby swept it all off the engine with such exaggerated care that neither thing happened. A few days later I did not have to cook as the pump for the kerosene stove gave its last sigh and would no longer pump air into the tank. Nothing could be cooked until we got a new one.

With all our work, the boat was beginning to look more homely. Living and working on the boat did have its problems, like keeping clear of wet paint and varnish. Then there was Pixie, always willing to join in and help, like the day she managed to get the varnish brush I'd left soaking in in turpentine. Before we discovered what she was up to, the floor, table and cushions had been painted with a nasty sticky mess. We had leatherette covered cushions made for the back of the seating, which hid the lockers and made sitting at the table more relaxing and comfortable. They looked very smart for a few of days but Pixie could not resist the temptation to keep having a little chew. Leatherette is very chewable, so we soon had cushions full of holes.

When not working on the boat our time was spent finding out things that would help in our plan to put Pixie back in the wild. We enquired about the island and wrote to the Malaysian Nature Society of which we had once been keen members, asking for any advice they could give us. We also wrote to the game department. Everyone was very helpful but we learned that troops of pig-tailed macaques needed a lot of room and that they are migratory. They will be seen in one area and then disappear for months. This being the case it was thought that an island might not have enough natural food on it. They also thought that it would be hard for Pixie to return to the wild. We thought so too, but felt we had to find out by giving her a chance. We did of course not intend to put her alone on an island. First we had to find at least two more monkeys, a male and female, so they would still be happy if Pixie decided to remain with us. If we could get hold of more that were unhappy in captivity, so much the better. One problem was going to be that she was used to cooked food. During the day we gave her uncooked fresh fruit and vegetables, she never ate a lot and much preferred rice and curry, spaghetti etc. at night. We planned to phase out the cooked meal and give her more natural things. That night it was raining which meant dinner was in the cabin. I made just enough roti and curry for Bobby, thinking Pixie would take hers better if I ate the same as I gave her. I could hardly give her a plate of wild fruits and seeds with a grasshopper on top. I made up our plates with pineapple, which she loves, tomato, lettuce etc. which I felt was a start in the right direction. Pixie sits between us at the table. When she sees me preparing the food she jumps about and takes her place expectantly. I put her plate of salad in front of her, she ignored it. I gave Bobby his roti and curry and sat down with my salad. Pixie looked at mine, hers and then at Bobby's then slapped her hand on the table, a new trick she had started on the boat to let us know she wanted something; swivelling round to face Bobby she stretched out a hand to take some of his dinner. I moved her plate in front of her, she poked at it, ascertained it really was just salad and returned her eyes to Bobby's plate. He gave her a bit of roti and told her to eat her salad whereupon she calmly picked up her plate and deliberately dropped it upside down in my lap. She was very decisive about it and not really cross, probably thought we were acting rather stupidly. I returned my lap of salad to her plate but gave in and added a little curry and roti, which she then ate, satisfied she had got her share and only then did she eat her salad. As usual she had outsmarted us.

Much as Pixie loved Bob-tail she objected to him eating the food we gave him, pulling him away from it when she got the chance. She appeared to think he should be vegetarian and not have stuff she considered not fit to eat. The same night we had tried changing her diet, we watched with amazement as Pixie stood up and managed to reach the plate of cat food I had left on the counter, lifting it down very carefully and putting it on the floor for Bob-tail, then sat watching him eat. Perhaps she thought we were going to deprive him of food too.

Still searching for any more scraps of information or pig-tailed macaques that might like to swap captivity for the wild, I went to Kuala Lumpur and to the zoo, heading straight for the monkeys and apes. They had a number of different kinds of primates, even ones from South America, but no pig-tails. Like Singapore they considered them too common to put on show. Looking at my former friends from South America I passed a small crowd of people among the trees and saw that the attraction was a black-handed gibbon perched on the shoulder of an Indian man who had a little boy in his arms. The mother got nervous and took the boy away, whereupon the gibbon got off the man. I was on the edge of the gathering but while on the man's shoulder the gibbon must have caught sight of my adoring look. Without hesitation he made his way to me. It was love at first sight. He was crazy about me and did not care who knew it; he climbed on my shoulder and admired my sun shades and kept nibbling at my ears. All a bit embarrassing in front of such a large crowd which was growing bigger. A European woman wanted her big son to hold the gibbon so she could take a photo. I tried to surrender my new boyfriend but was hugged tighter. The boy who wanted to hold my new friend was wearing spectacles and took them off, seeing how my shades interested the gibbon. Still having no luck in enticing him away from me he put them back on as an encouragement as mum impatiently waited to take his photo. Nothing worked. It was as if gibbon and I were to be part of a star attraction at the zoo for the day. I squatted down and tried to remove his clinging hands and feet but four to my two were more than a match for me. In the end, disappointed that I was giving him the brush off, he gave up, jumped off me and made for the nearest tree and disappeared from view. I hoped I had not hurt his feelings.

After a number of enquires I was told they had pig-tailed monkeys in the quarantine part of the zoo, not open to visitors. I was allowed in, however, and here I found three very skinny looking monkeys, the females with flat bottoms even though they were mature. The keepers could tell me little about them but as I persisted they showed me their history cards at the office. I was amazed, a pair had been sent from Sarawak and from their almost blank card I managed to gather they had been sent by a European. I was told again that that type of monkey is of no interest to the public but as they had been sent to them they would release them in the bush at the back of the zoo, where they assume they will be all right, having done it before with other monkeys. No check was kept of them after their release. I asked if I could have them so that they could be released with Pixie. They were not ready to be released and they preferred to do it themselves, why, when they took no further notice of their welfare, I did not understand. They could see no reason when I told them about Pixie and our plans why I needed more, and why I did not just send her off in the bush. I asked about their life span and mating habits. To the first they said they only live ten years but had no further knowledge. I was not impressed with their knowledge or lack of it and felt sure they should live longer than ten years or certainly hoped so.

A month had gone by since our arrival in Port Kelang and we were still busy doing things to the boat. No sooner was one thing fixed than we found something else needed our attention. The foot pump to pump the fresh water from the tank to the sink failed and there was not one to be had in the whole of Malaysia. Fortunately, a friend of a friend was going to Singapore and managed to track down, then bring us back, the one and only one there. All we really needed was a new diaphragm for the pump but they are not imported so we had to buy a whole new pump.

I painted the floor in the cabin, doing a very small section a day so we could walk over the painted parts. Bob-tail did not see the point of the operation and each time walked on the wet paint. I did not mind a few artistic paw marks on the floor but he would then walk over other places with brown feet and I would have to follow him with a rag and turpentine.

The outside of the cabin was blue like the hull, we preferred white. I started painting it. Twice Bobby forgot and brushed against it and then Pixie tossed her bath water over it and Bob-tail, not to be outdone, curled up against the wet paint and left a mass of hairs. By the time I had finished it looked as if it needed repainting. I managed to mess the last bit up myself, having run out of the paint I was using I found another can in the locker but failed to look at the label properly. I used it before I realised I was using plastic paint that had to be mixed in equal quantities with hardener. It looked very nice but never dried so that dust and everything else that touched it stuck. Turpentine failed to remove it and yet it still would not dry. Many unhappy days were spent scraping it all off.

Bobby and I asked ourselves and each other the same thing most nights. Was what we were planning for Pixie the right thing to do? She seemed so very happy with us on the boat, having us both in sight and Bob-tail was ideal. We never went ashore together so at no time was she left alone. If she did return to the wild would she really be happy and what of us and Bob-tail? It was hard to imagine life without our Pixie. We kept telling ourselves that as we loved her so much we should be happy knowing she would be leading a natural life and perhaps bringing up a family, so it was our duty to give her the opportunity. The more we thought about it the more we hoped she would not accept freedom and would return to us.

The boatman came and delivered us a note. Lori in Singapore had phoned and would we please phone her back, it was urgent. I felt sick. It had to be about Goblin. I was beside myself with worry. Bobby went ashore and managed to get through to Singapore, no mean feat in Malaysia. It turned out that Goblin was OK but was being naughty, back to her old tricks of chasing bicycles and mostly, if she did not knock them off, the riders fell and ran in fear. No one had ever complained about it before but apparently now someone had. A man from the Ministry had called on Lori and told her that Goblin must be controlled or they would take her away and destroy her. Poor Lori, as we well knew there was little we could do to control Goblin, the garden was not fenced in and Goblin had always run free and chased bicycles, which we were unable to stop her doing. Lori, who had lost her husband some years before in an accident, was working and had her own dog, cat and little boy to care for. She herself was due to leave Singapore in June and she could find no one who would take Goblin and give her a good home. All Bobby could suggest was that she send Goblin to England.

Before we left, we had discussed what should be done if Lori left Singapore. It was agreed Lori would either find Goblin a good home, or failing that send her at our expense to England. At first I was hoping she would send her to the UK so we would have her again. Now this did not seem a good idea. She would of course go into quarantine for six months. Now it was plain we would not be in England in six months, probably still in Malaysia. Goblin was not a one-family dog, she had arrived as a stray that our servants took on. When they split up and both left, Goblin stayed, so becoming ours. She was as much in the homes of our friends as she was with us. For her part I doubt she missed us unduly, so it would be selfish to leave her in kennels for our pleasure. The best for her was to stay in Singapore, if only we could find a good home. We thought of just two likely people who might know of a good home, people Lori did not know.

Armed with phone numbers, I went ashore the following morning to try my luck on the phone. My lucky day, not only did I get a Singapore operator first try – which must be a record – but I was put through to the person I sought. When we lived in Port Kelang many hours, and sometimes days, were spent trying to get an overseas call – even to Singapore which is more or less next door. Jan Mason, who I phoned, was in and I had hardly told her of our problems when she said she thought she knew of a good home with a family who had just lost their dog. Giving her Lori's phone number I felt at last things were working out. Wishing to leave nothing to chance I tried my other friend's number and got through again but found I had been given a wrong number. My luck had run out with the phone so I settled for writing notes to my other friend and to Lori to let her know what had happened.

A few days later we learned that Jan had found Goblin a good home in the same street where Jan lived. The houses had a fenced garden so Goblin could not chase bicycles and she had settled in happily.

We were still having trouble with the engine and had had the Volvo Penta people out time and time again. Bobby wasted one whole afternoon trying to get through on the phone to them when we discovered they had not put all the parts back in the engine after having *finished* one day. When he did get through on the phone it was too late and they were closed. Rather than just return to the boat he decided to go shopping, then found he had forgotten to take his footwear ashore. He returned very fed up.

"Gosh, snow." I had just woken up and the bunk was covered in white stuff. "What are you talking about?" said Bobby wearily, then found a bit of the 'snow' tickling his nostril. Pixie had performed an operation on her Teddy Bear and removed all its stuffing. What a mess, the stuff kept flying up as we tried to gather it in a sheet. Pixie took the limp body on deck and later it had disappeared so we took it she had buried it at sea.

Yee Awa, Yee Awa. A monotonous sound like the creaking of an old pump. It was a familiar sound, we had first heard it when we lived in Malaysia after every fall of rain – frogs! Did we had a stowaway? We shone the flashlight down the bilge, nothing. Put our ear to the freshwater tank, the noise rang loud and clear. "They are definitely in the water tank," I said. "Don't be silly, how could they be, its sealed," Bobby said as he crawled under the cockpit with his flashlight. "Perhaps we got some spawn in our water before putting it in," I suggested. We tried pumping a little water out of the tank to see if they changed their tune. It made no difference, the frog concerto went on. I unscrewed the top of the tank and no frog tried to make its bid for freedom. It went on at intervals for days and we stopped worrying about it; evidently our frog or frogs were quite happy wherever they were. I just hoped if they were in our tank we would not find we had boiled tadpoles in our coffee. We mentioned our stowaways to Bunny, who was a great English character and could mostly be found at the club. He lived on the other side of the river with his boat in his backyard. An ideal place to have one to work on. Bunny solved our mystery. "Cement hulls conduct sound very nicely," he said. Our frogs were safely ashore sending us sound signals through the water.

We thought we had finally got our engine in working order but when we ran it to charge the batteries something else was wrong with it. That was not all. In the evening I prepared the vegetables and for some reason the stove would not light. Bobby pumped it for ages but still nothing happened so we went to bed hungry; we were both in a bad mood next morning when we could not make coffee. All was not lost, we would not starve to death. Bobby found the tank was leaking air and fixed it. We could eat again.

Volvo Penta mechanics came and fixed the engine. I spent a jolly day picking out weevils in the atta flour. I appeared to have more weevils than flour. That done it was the turn of the rice. That too had some unwelcome guests, I believe they came from the garlic I put in to deter the weevils. Amongst our mail one day we received a very welcome gift from David and Annette Evans in Singapore. *'Cruising Under Sail'* by Eric Hiscock. Just what we needed and it was read from cover to cover. Half of what I read I did not understand but felt one day it would all click in place. It did strike me that they were in full command of their boat and did not undergo all the little emergencies we managed to have so far. I found a lot of new sailing words but by far the best was *baggywrinkle*. Even my seagoing husband did not know that word. What was more there were even directions on how to make the delightful things. When I informed Bobby what that delightful sounding object was, the fluffy things we had seen on the stays of other boats to stop the sails chaffing, he said it was just what we needed and I could go ahead and make some. He was rather more than reluctant to part with any old rope for the job but eventually did. I set to work. With baggywrinkles on our stays, Bunny commented that we now looked like a real cruising boat.

April the 19th was going to be the big day, we were all set to leave. We had not got the monkeys we wanted as yet, thinking we would explore the chosen island first. If suitable we could come back to Kuala Lumpur and get them at a pet shop. However, we had to wait for the Volvo Penta boys to come first so we could pay their bill. They came but while on board looked at the engine again, tried it, deciding that something else needed doing. Guess they thought they had found a couple who knew nothing about engines and would keep them in work for ever.

April 23rd dawned. A perfect day and we were all set once again to leave. Just before eight we moved away with the engine running nicely, fifteen minutes later it stopped of its own accord. We restarted it and clouds of black smoke bellowed out of the exhaust. Again it only kept going for fifteen minutes. Bobby restarted it yet again saying lots of nasty things about all the money we had paid out to have the engine fixed and it was worse than it had ever been. We turned around to head back to our anchorage but the engine stopped again and the wind died completely. We gave up and anchored. The engine was boiling hot, it was plain now to see it had not been getting cooling water. We had been out just half an hour.

Pixie was also keeping us busy. Since fixing the steering vane we could no longer put her in the corner of the cockpit where she liked to be as she then could reach the vane. We liked to keep her near us so we chained her on a short chain nearer the cabin. She soon found she could still just reach the wheel and when we were not looking, but seeing to the erring engine, she unscrewed the bolt of the vane. She could also now reach inside the cabin and cleared the shelf of things which I quickly grabbed back before they were tossed in the sea. Nothing then I thought was in her reach, but I had forgotten the fire extinguisher, until I saw her with it and chewing at the top. Fortunately, she had not found out how it worked before I caught her. She then settled for chewing off all the trim on one side of the hatch. All in half an hour.

We moved her forward again and waited for the engine to cool or for some wind to come our way. At 1220hrs we got a little wind. Up came the anchor and off we went again. Hardly any wind but the sails were up and the engine on slow and no black smoke. This time we kept going for forty minutes before the engine stopped and the wind died away. The Port Authority boat came along and gave us a tow back to our buoy and by 1330hrs we were back at our anchorage with sails put away as though we had never left.

"You know," said Bobby, "I think the intake valve might be blocked and stopping water from cooling the engine."

"Well," I said, "can't you unblock it?"

"Yes, but it will mean coming out of the water, but that might be cheaper in the long run than keep having the mechanics out."

We booked to go on the slip. We waited six days before they could take us on the slip, meanwhile the Volvo boys passed and seeing us still there came on board and found something else wrong and worked at the engine all day, after which we went on a short trial run with them on board. The engine kept going OK but black smoke still bellowed out. As we had booked the slip we felt it just as well to still come out of the water and do the bottom.

It felt strange to be perched up above dry land. Pixie thought it was fun when we took her down the ladder and chained her on a long chain under the boat. This gave her plenty of shade and plenty of things to play with on the tracks. She had her bathtub filled with water to sit in if she got hot. Bob-tail would not join her; he, seeing people around, kept hidden in the cabin all the time we were there. Pixie soon had another playmate in my friend Nicky, the club dog who had joined us and played with her. She got a few titbits from passing people, bits of sandwiches and once we found someone had unwisely given her a bottle of beer.

While on the slip we decided we might as well make a good job of the boat. I painted the deck and then we changed the colour of the hull from brilliant blue to white. A workman helped us with the painting; he always wore a sad-looking face and was so skinny we called him Mr Skin and Bones, only between ourselves of course.

Pixie, meanwhile, was happy under the boat and Bob-tail miserable under the bunk. Bobby had a bad cold, which he unkindly passed on to me. By the following Friday the boat was gleaming in her new paintwork and we got off the slip with the help of two Indian men who volunteered to help because they liked Pixie. As we came up to the mooring buoy one of the Indians suddenly jumped into the water and swam to get the mooring line. This was rather an unexpected move and the reaction from Pixie more so. She chattered loudly, got hold of the rigging, shaking it, and seemed very upset at her friend jumping into the water. *Good*, we thought, *if one of us falls in the water she will alert the other.*

Once again we were ready to leave, it would be nice to get to sea again but I was afraid. Would the Sembilan Islands turn out to be the future home for Pixie, if so how could we bear to part from her? Our thoughts were agonising and we talked it over again and again and came to the conclusion that it would be best to get the monkeys while still in Port Kelang and take them with us, rather than find the islands first and return for them. This too would give Pixie longer to get accustomed to them. They would not be as tame as Pixie and surely would enjoy the island even if Pixie decided not to stay. I tried not to think of what the boat would be like with two or more extra monkeys aboard, monkeys that would probably obey us less than Pixie. Would they mind sleeping on deck or in the quarter berth, or would they see Pixie and Bob-tail sleeping with us and demand equal rights?

To obtain the monkeys Bobby went off to the dreadful pet shop we had discovered soon after our first arrival some years back. A tiny shop packed full of animals, dozens of birds in cages only large enough for one. A few bedraggled monkeys chained outside, playing in the filthy drains and, most heartbreaking of all, several monkeys in a small cage without room to move. It was such a sickening sight, we vowed never to go near that area again. However, we now wanted monkeys and to buy such poor things and release them back in the wild would give us and them pleasure.

We needed at least one female and one male but would take all he had to save them from such a dreadful life. Bobby returned partly disappointed and partly relieved. He had found the shop with the same old Chinese man but now he only kept chickens. Perhaps the authorities had stepped in. This was good news but we still needed monkeys.

Bobby now went to Kuala Lumpur, touring the pet shops there that were not as horrific as the one had been in Port Kelang. He found several pig-tails but they were all babies, not what we wanted; we needed mature ones that were ready for mating, nearing three years old. Babies would not be able to fend for themselves. If Pixie took to them she would expect us to provide for them, and she the love. The shops said they could not obtain any adults for us. Without them we could not proceed with our plan and in the end we gave up our quest as hopeless.

We had planned and tried so hard it would have been understandable if we had sat down and wept with frustration. Instead it was as if a burden had been lifted from us and we felt more light-hearted and happy than we had since we had formed the plan to release Pixie. We had tried and failed. Pixie would continue her life with us.

Dinghy loaded rather late
With food and grog to celebrate.
Rip tide takes us in its grip
whirling down with tide we slip

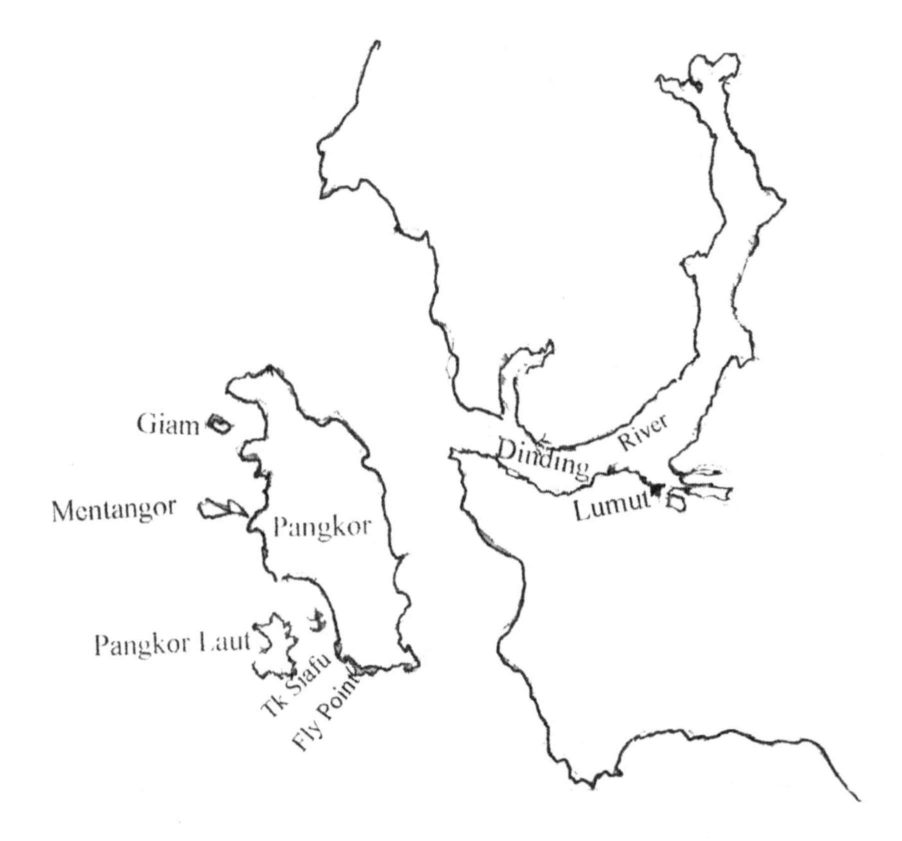

Pankhor Island and Lumut

CHAPTER SEVEN
A PLACE TO LINGER

May 13th, up anchor and away after double checking that it was Saturday and not Friday 13th. These were familiar waters for Bobby who had chartered the area and positioned the navigation buoys only a few years before, in pairs and numbered, now they were badly out of position, some missing and the beacons completely wrecked.

We started the engine while we put up the sails. The oil pressure was low and it was still not working as it should in spite of all the work done on it and the money we had spent. There was a nice breeze so we cut off the engine and decided we would forget it existed.

Drawing opposite Kuala Selangor, the tide was against us and the wind dropped a bit so the lighthouse stayed with us on the starboard side for some time, bringing back memories of the car trips we took in that area looking for monkeys that never turned up when we were around, watching the mud skippers hop along the wet sand and into their holes. Perhaps these fish were evolving into land creatures. Here we also found many interesting abandoned houses. The sort we would have loved. The rest house had told us that no one would live in them as they were near a burial ground and were haunted.

As I reminisced a small gull floated past us going in the opposite direction, standing on a small plank of wood. As it passed it flew off and joined another gull who had a similar plank. Perhaps the first advised a change of course was necessary. After a brief exchange the gull returned to its own plank, having no trouble locating it, even though it had travelled some way.

Not much distance was made that day and just as it got dark we dropped anchor, north of Pasir Panjang, opposite the lighthouse. A very choppy sea lulled us to sleep that night. By daybreak the sea was calm. We downed breakfast before moving on, a plan we always adopted in order to get our strength up to battle with the anchor.

Suddenly the wind sounded as if we might be in the northern hemisphere, the sea rose up to meet it and a raging battle of the elements took place, while the rain poured down. Pixie joined us to huddle with Bob-tail in the cabin. "That," said Bobby, "must have been a Sumatra," the name given to short violent squalls that frequent the Malacca Straits. Within an hour it had all died away as suddenly as it had arrived, taking with it all the wind. We used the erring engine again to get the anchor up and it managed to keep us going for the next hour, there still being no wind. After that we relied on the sails and made little headway. We anchored before dark in a good anchorage just before Tg Sauli. Apart from the fact Bob-tail over ate after fasting for three days and then threw up all over the strip of carpet; it had been an uneventful day.

The next day brought very little wind but our engine was in a good mood and helped us out a little. I was by then suffering very badly with swollen, blistered lips, brought on by sun and wind. I was not troubled with it on land or at anchor, once it had healed, but one day sailing would start it up again. I had several makes of lip salve, none of which did any good. I tried zinc ointment in which I put lots of faith in healing skin rashes. That proved so painful that I spent ages dabbing it all off again with baby oil.

Islands were now in sight and a large number of fishing trawlers. One indicated they had fish to sell, we waved them away and thought of a friend in Singapore who ate fish head curry. There were more birds on rafts, one slightly larger bit of wood held three birds. Several times fish would leap out of the water in a straight line. Jellyfish were very prolific and of a red-brown colour, some huge, others only babies.

We anchored at six in the mouth of Sungai Perak and were surrounded by transparent jellyfish. The swell increased that night making it quite rough. Bobby got up several times I learned, while I slept on. The morning was overcast, I came on deck to find the jellyfish still surrounded us which made it impossible to catch a bucket of water to bathe without getting jellyfish as well. Mostly they were the transparent type but some were almost salmon pink, others clear but with red around the edge of their mantles. Interesting to watch but not to bathe in. We wanted to get into a bay on Pulau Rumbia, the largest island in the Sembilan group. This was the island we had picked to see if we could release Pixie. That day the conditions were not right. Undecided what to do we tidied up the boat and then, finding the jellyfish had got tired of investigating us, we were able to get buckets of water and wash some clothes.

Although we had given up the idea of releasing Pixie on this island we still wanted to go and explore it. The swell and wind was heading in the direction which would give us an uncomfortable lee shore and it was not a good time to visit the Sembilan Islands. Pondering over the chart, we both rather liked the look of Lumut. We had time on our hands now and it would make a good base from which we could visit the islands after getting more local knowledge. The islands certainly looked inviting, high and densely wooded. To get to Lumut we had to sail up the Dinding River which would entail using the engine, we would have to keep our fingers crossed it would not let us down, once in the river with no wind. Lumut looked nice and undisturbed, the hill was wooded but at the start of the village near the sea they were cutting into the bush, leaving nothing but red soil. It is always a sickening sight to see wonderful wooded areas being destroyed by man. Later we found it was a new naval base being built. A poor exchange for nature, we thought. We dropped anchor near the little wooden clubhouse which was closed and looked deserted, no one around though several boats were at anchor, their owners' residents ashore. Pixie's reaction to Lumut was most strange, she got very excited as we came to anchor and started calling. Until then we had only ever heard her use this call for one of us if we were returning from shore, or at home if we had been out and she saw us returning. It was very useful as we always knew on the boat if anchored far from land, that whichever of us had gone ashore was returning. Pixie's eyes were very much better than ours, seeing who was returning long before either of us could see anything. Now she was calling continually and we were both with her and Bob-tail. There was not a person or animal in sight as far as we could see. Did the trees hide other monkeys? Could it be that it was here she was first caught before we rescued her from the shop in Port Kelang? We never found out what it was that made her call. After we got in that afternoon she never called again whilst there, except to one of us. Subsequently when we left to visit other islands, later returning to Lumut, she called again. This in all her sailing years was the only place she would act this way. What it was in that area that attracted her was a mystery. We were told someone had kept two pig-tailed monkeys as pets there, which they eventually freed while still young. At first we wondered if Pixie was one of these monkeys that were caught. That could not be when we found out that had happened only about a year previously and we had, by that time, had Pixie almost five years. No one had seen them since and felt sure they were not around. Did Pixie know better? We did hope Pixie would lead us to the source of her interest but as before she refused to go into the bush or take much interest in the natural surrounds, preferring to keep in sight of boat and club.

Bobby dug out our Avon dinghy and pumped it up to row ashore to see if the clubhouse was as deserted as it looked. After his ducking in the fibreglass dinghy that we had purchased with *'Sandpiper'* we never used it again and sold it back to the Changi Club where Charlie had bought it. We then bought ourselves a new Avon inflatable dinghy.

Bobby disappeared round the back of the clubhouse and a little later all the boards in the front of the club were removed. He had found an old Chinese couple at the back who opened it up for him and had insisted on seeing he had Malay money before handing over a beer. Having satisfied them that he could pay be was allowed to purchase a box of cold beers and two blocks of ice. This was the first time we had used the Avon. In both Singapore and Kelang, the clubs had a boat to ferry you to and from shore. Bobby looked competent handling the dinghy but said it felt strange. We sat on deck talking until midnight in subdued voices. The silence was so penetrating you could hear it. We had found the perfect spot to stay awhile.

Next morning, we both got in the dinghy and just went round the boat looking at the green slime and weed we were already growing on our water line. Pixie objected strongly to us both getting in the dinghy and jumped around on deck, upsetting her tub of bath water. We quickly got back on board to pacify her. Leaving Bob-tail on board to guard the boat we all went ashore. Pixie was not sure about the dinghy at first but consented to come, fearing I suppose that we might go off and leave her. As we tried to pull away she clung onto the boat but soon moved and cuddled down in the dinghy with me. Once she decided it was not as bad as expected she walked along the side and sat on the edge, pretending she did this sort of thing every day. The moment we touched land out she jumped and started grabbing handfuls of sand. We had a long chain clipped to her belt and wanted to walk to the trees in the hope of discovering what had made her call when we came in. The fascination of the fine white sand was too much and she kept sitting down and digging holes. After that she was all for going into the club but we walked her along the shore and mangroves where she found the odd berry to eat and picking around the mangrove roots picked very small sea snails off, trying to suck out the occupants from the shell. We all enjoyed the walk and on our return she wanted to go into the club again, the more so when she saw a cat who also saw her and stared in an amazed way back at her. We chained her to one of the trees near the club. Every now and then she would call, sometimes very loudly. We felt sure it was not us or Bob-tail she was calling but we heard no answering call.

We took advantage of the beautiful clean showers at the back of the club and felt the better for it. On the way back to *'Sandpiper'* Pixie got in the dinghy without hesitation and sat herself down at the back wearing her superior look. As we reached the boat she at once climbed on board and went to the hatch, calling down to Bob-tail who came up and was greeted with much monkey talk, perhaps telling him all her adventures. Worn out she soon fell asleep on deck, waking later to eat a large plate of spaghetti.

From then on Pixie was quite at home in the dinghy, and the tree by the club we tied her to she considered her property, making straight for it as soon as we stepped ashore. One day there was a few goats tethered near the tree which I thought she would like, she had not seen a goat before. Unlike cats and dogs, which she loves, she ignored them.

Rubbish from the boat I found was a difficult thing to get rid of in Malaysia. I had been laughed at in Port Kelang for bringing all my garbage ashore. I placed it in the bin but was told it would be dumped in the sea in the end. Here in Lumut it appeared they had no garbage collection at the club and it was plain they thought I was a little queer in the head for not just tossing it overboard, something I felt I just could not do. We did find a pit in the grounds where other rubbish had been burnt so we put our garbage there and set light to it every day.

May 25th was our wedding anniversary. We had celebrated quite a few and not sure how many years this one was but it was an excuse to celebrate. We had wanted to go to Pankor but first we had to wait for a mechanic to see about something we needed making. We found a very good and inexpensive workshop just along the shore from the club. Next we needed to get oil for the engine by which time it was too late to start off. We settled instead to just have a special dinner on board with wine. We gave up on the wine after going to every shop in Lumut, none of which stocked such luxury. We bought a lot of other groceries on the way. We left the club a little later than usual that evening and feeling that the groceries, ice and beer, together with ourselves, were a bit heavy for one trip, Bobby rowed back to the boat with the ice and beer. A strong current was now running so he quickly dumped the ice and beer on deck and came back for Pixie and me. There was an urgent ring to his voice when he said, "Quickly get in the dinghy." Pixie and I obeyed without hesitation. It was now getting dark and Bobby was rowing as if his life depended on it. We were halfway to '*Sandpiper*' when the rip tide caught us, carrying us off down to the few locally owned boats. We made a grab for one as we passed but could not get a tight enough hold.

"One more boat to pass and if we don't get that we will be washed out into the Malacca Straits," Bobby yelled. With that prospect before us we made an extra effort and grabbed at the side of the last boat we might ever see. Pixie sprang on board at once while we hung on like castaways and secured the dinghy. Sitting for hours in the dinghy in the dark in our wet shorts seemed a little crazy. We decided that the owner, under the circumstances, would not mind us going aboard and joining Pixie on deck. We huddled in the centre cockpit, glad we had not been washed out into the Straits but wishing we had the beer that was sitting on our own deck. We had to hope that Bob-tail had not seen us heading away from him and thought we had abandoned him without food.

By 2230hrs the tide had slackened; cold and weary we got back in the dinghy and managed without mishap to get back to '*Sandpiper*'. Bob-tail did not seem unduly upset as he tucked into canned cat food. We felt too tired to cook let alone celebrate so warmed up some refried beans with a fried egg each on top and tumbled into our bunks. We had done something a bit out of the ordinary for our anniversary after all.

The following day we sailed over to Pankor Island, dropping anchor between it and the smaller island of Giam. Giam was surrounded by large boulders, sandy beaches and trees. No sign of habitation though many fishing boats passed us by. The bay being accessible only by boat we could count on privacy, but unlike Lumut the anchorage was not very comfy, with a heavy swell all the time. Bobby spent all of the nights there with little sleep, getting up every time a squall passed to check the anchor, while I slept the sleep of the dead, blissfully unaware of what was going on.

We explored Giam first, making for the beach in the dinghy. We got swamped in the surf as we landed and Pixie fell overboard but climbed back straight away. We found sand covered in beautiful shells and broken coral. We surprised a small squirrel running up a tree. An abundance of orchid plants growing on the trees with large clusters of pods that almost looked like small bananas, evidently they tasted just as good as Pixie ate a lot. Strange footprints in the sand divided down the middle with a line; we guessed it must be a monitor lizard but saw none. Looking out at sea Bobby suddenly shouted, “Look.” There in the distance we saw what looked like half a dozen seals. Unfortunately we did not have the binoculars with us. Later we thought it more likely that we had seen dugongs, that fascinating sea mammal related to the manatee. When leaving to get back over the surf we tied Pixie’s chain to the dinghy to make sure she did not get left behind or turn back at the wrong moment. This proved unnecessary as she timed it perfectly and sprang at the same time we did.

We enjoyed Giam so much that we spent the next four days exploring the rest of the island. Although we found a lot of dead, broken coral on the beach there was no coral reef. The water was so clear that we could see small fish and other sea life in the depths. Pixie enjoyed climbing the rocks on which she appeared more at home than in the trees, which for the most part she avoided unless they contained something edible. The beach was a treasure trove of shells and though it did not seem a good idea to fill our locker space with bags of shells they were too beautiful not to collect a few special ones.

Pixie was, as had been proved, a good swimmer but she refused to swim in the sea. The waves frightened her and no doubt her long and unpleasant swim in Singapore was still fresh in her memory. She would wade around some of the rocks and even swim a little in sheltered pools of water between the rocks but refused to go into the sea, no matter how much we tried to entice her. The last two days we spent on Pankor where Pixie got a lot of exercise climbing up and down the rocks. The beach was pure sand, not a single shell to be found.

By then we had used up all our fresh fruit and vegetables, also eggs. I had a desperate longing for an egg. It was time to return to Lumut where on our return Pixie did her call as the first time. Again she received no answering call back.

We were no longer the only visiting yacht. *'Arauna II'* a French boat was now anchored not far from us with Max Herman and his crew, Michel and Shoo Shoo. Max we found in the club. We listened in fascination of his trip from France; he was now on his way to Singapore in the hope of getting work as a diver. Bobby having a number of contacts in Singapore, both in the diving and oil exploration business, was able to advise Max on his prospects and give him the addresses of people to contact. We both hoped he made out all right. Still longing for an egg, I dashed off to do my shopping. The first Chinese grocery I visited had no eggs. At the next I was so relieved to see a tray of eggs on the counter I said I would take the lot, not even bothering to count exactly how many there were. Before leaving the shop I found myself, along with some fresh fruit and vegetables, with 30 eggs wrapped in newspaper. I had never tried carrying thirty eggs wrapped in newspaper before and will certainly not try it again.

Back at the club Bobby was still talking to Max so I placed my purchases in the dinghy. The eggs carefully placed between the blow-up seat and our wash kit. While I went to get Pixie from her tree, Bobby got a block of ice. Pixie now wished to make friends with Max and so I stood with her, not noticing where Bobby put his ice, nor thinking to tell what the newspaper parcel contained.

Arriving back on *'Sandpiper'* I chained Pixie to the rails and Bobby started unloading the dinghy. I went to help and asked for the eggs – too late. "Eggs," said Bobby, lifting the ice then slightly losing his balance, moving his foot to where the eggs lay. No need to tell him where the eggs were. He handed up a now very soggy mass of newspaper which I carried below, dripping raw egg as I went. Was I even now fated not to satisfy my longing for an egg? Carefully unwrapping the wet mess

I extracted ten unbroken eggs, washed them and put on a tray on the counter in the galley. I managed to save a lot of egg from the broken shells. Pixie and Bob-tail helped clean up. Things did not look too bad, dinner was definitely going to be omelettes of some sort. I then set about cleaning up the spilled egg in the cabin. Bobby washed down the deck and all was back to normal if it could be said life was ever normal with us. Suddenly, for no apparent reason, Bob-tail jumped up on the small counter space. I believe it was the first and last time he ever got up there. Even so he was not very big and there was just room for him next to the eggs. Before I could move the eggs, with a flip of his paw he sent the whole lot crashing down. I stood transfixed with disbelief. Bobby appeared at the companionway and looked down speechless. I suddenly burst out laughing, it all seemed too funny for words. Bobby shook his head, deciding my craving for eggs had addled my brain.

"First you go and buy a large quantity of eggs when you could easily get fresh eggs each day and then roar with laughter when the last one is smashed," he said. Still laughing like an idiot I started scooping the remains off the galley, thinking it was fortunate I had only just washed it down. All ten eggs had broken this time but some were still almost intact in their shells, others floated around with unbroken yokes. All these I added to my large bowl of beaten eggs. We enjoyed dinner that night. Bob-tail had a very generous helping of raw egg on his rice and fish, while Bobby, Pixie and I had a delightful eggy meal which satisfied my craving. For any reader who might also suffer the misfortune of smashing thirty eggs in one go, here is what you do:

Cook half your usual amount of rice.
Fry onions, garlic curry powder and cumin.
Add the rice and then slowly all the eggs.
(Large skillet or wok required).
Prod around until all the egg is cooked and then
add a small can of processed peas.

Delicious!

The following two evenings Pixie acted very strangely. Our days had followed the usual pattern of taking her ashore and then returning to have dinner on deck. After we had eaten I would go below to do the washing-up bringing Pixie down with me. Bobby would follow a little later. This time she started screaming at him as soon as he appeared, making rushes to bite him without actually doing so. Bobby just stood there and she calmed down, then cuddled up to me and started crying. Both nights were just the same but what brought it on we could not think and never found out.

We had another occasion to celebrate on June 5th, the date we first got Pixie, five years before. She was just a baby but probably about one year old. We thought we would take another visit to Pankor but it was not to be. We were, during this time, working on the boat as well as having fun. Bobby had discovered that a lot of the ribs or frames that give strength to the hull had been sawn off behind the lockers. So, we required strong wood cut to shape to replace them. Also beam-knees (beautiful word) which tie the cabin top beams to the frames. The workshop said they would come aboard to take measurements for them so we had to wait. The carpenter did not turn up, instead the mechanic did and took our Seagull outboard for repair. Our battery, which they had taken the day before for charging, was not returned. We settled to go ashore at noon and have a picnic under Pixie's tree. She ignored the special fruit salad I had carefully prepared but grabbed the platter of cookies with a look that said plainly 'These are mine so hands off'.

The weather turned very windy so we returned to the boat earlier than usual and took the awning down. Pixie got in her old sack we had tied to shade her from the sun. She did not like strong winds. Her birthday dinner had to be celebrated down in the cabin where we had set out the toys we had bought for her. She was not very impressed with the toys, clearly she was growing up and wanted more sophisticated things that she could take apart. She approved of her tiny glass of sherry before dinner but could not manage the last drop so carefully poured it down a hole over the engine. We hoped it would help make the engine work better. She ate a good dinner but was too tired to eat the cake I had made for her and soon fell asleep. I looked at her sleeping peacefully, she was so much a part of ourselves. Was she as contented as she appeared to be? Were we giving her the best life possible under the circumstances? I hoped so.

The next day the weather continued very windy and Pixie did not feel very well. Her bottom, as is usual with females of mature pigtails, was very large. Their bottoms swell at the time of the month when they are ready to mate and decrease in size when they have their periods. Now her bottom was irritating her as is often the case when large. Pixie and I stayed on board and Bobby went off shopping. He returned with fruit and veg and a new pair of sandals. From the dinghy he handed up some newspaper parcels. One I saw contained bananas, in the next a poor dead fish stared up at me and I dropped the parcel which fortunately landed back on deck and another fish dropped out. Much as I love seeing fish swimming in the sea I get upset at the sight of any dead animal. I left the parcel on deck. I do, however, know that an animal like a cat is naturally carnivorous, so apart from canned cat food Bobby often buys and cooks fish for Bob-tail.

"How did you get that, it's dirty, give it to me," I heard Bobby saying. Obviously he was talking to Pixie who was chained on the foredeck. I could not think what Pixie had got so popped my head up through the hatch. Pixie had a dead fish in her hands which Bobby took away from her and then washed her hands. There was no way she could have got the fish herself being chained on the opposite side of the boat from where I had dropped the parcel. Bob-tail must have taken it and either given it to her or gone to eat it with her and she took it away. Bobby then collected the fish and started preparing and cleaning it ready for cooking. The next thing I hear is Bob-tail making odd noises. On investigation I found him eating a raw fish in between the bunks. Dead fish were appearing everywhere making me quite nervous.

Some days later we had company, *'Hai Lung'*, which had left Singapore some months before we had. Later another boat who we had also seen in Singapore, *'Syzygy'* arrived. At the club we talked to Eric Russell owner of *'Hai Lung'*. He had his son with him and another man, Terry, as crew. Eric was now on his way back to Singapore having been in Penang which he declared was a filthy place where the people were all thieves and you could guarantee having your dinghy or outboard stolen. "There was one good thing about it," put in his son. "We had an underwater garden growing on the bottom of the dinghy but the water was so foul that all the growth died and dropped off."

When living in Malaysia we had once spent a very enjoyable holiday in Penang. The beaches were clean and the water clear. We said nothing and decided we were having our leg pulled. Later, to our cost, we endorsed their sentiments.The captain of '*Syzygy*' now joined us,with his daughter and two crew members. The talk turned to other boats we had known. *'Tamorenos'* and another boat that had been wrecked and sunk three weeks before off Phuket, Thailand, when a typhoon hit. For us the saddest news was that Keith's boat *'Princess'* had also been there at the same time but he had managed to beach his boat and though it was badly damaged was not beyond salvaging and repair. However, the local inhabitants claimed it as a wreck from the sea and completely stripped it. Our hearts went out to Keith. We knew he had put all his savings into the boat and had so many plans. He had been one of Bobby's Australian friends and had asked Bobby's advice on if he should take out insurance or not. Regrettably Bobby had told him he never took insurance for anything and doubted if anyone would insure a boat that went much farther than its home port. We sincerely hoped he did not take that advice.

The captain of *'Syzygy'* had a radio, which appeared for the most part to give out bad news. "You heard about *'Ocean'* the Danish boat I suppose?" No, we had not heard about it. "Well," he said, "that is now wrecked on a reef in the Red Sea."

"Bad place the Red Sea," put in Bobby. "I don't think I would like to take a boat up there, it's not just the reefs and all the shipping you have to contend with, to say nothing of the bad weather, but these day with so many hostile countries you need a gun on board." I felt glad we were not planning to take that route.

"Yes," agreed the captain, "I was on my way to Europe via the Red Sea but changed my mind. Going back to Australia now."

"How far did you get?" we asked. "Just to Sri Lanka and that was enough, awful place."

"Why?" I asked. "You must have liked Sri Lanka itself, surely?" Sri Lanka was a country we were both looking forward to visiting again having many happy associations for us. It was the place Bobby and I first met and where I was given a baby monkey in Anuradhapura. Added to that we loved the food, the country and the people. Not everyone likes the same places; fortunately the very things we liked about Sri Lanka they did not, except for one member of the crew, Peter, who was English, who put in that he had enjoyed it.

"Did you see *'Whistler'* with Doug and Machteld?" we asked. They had left Singapore before we and we had met them again in Port Kelang, just before they left for Sri Lanka. "Oh Doug," someone laughed. "You know Doug, he lost his way and landed up in Sumatra. His engine broke down, he is now on the way back here."

Oh dear, I thought, *here we are with next to no sailing experience happily thinking it's no big thing to sail off round the Cape and over to the Caribbean, then crossing the Atlantic to England.* Now all these boats which we considered crewed by experience yachtsmen were getting lost, turning back or getting wrecked. "Has anyone we know got to where they were heading?" I asked.

"Oh yes, Walter and Carla and their two young children are now in Israel, having safely gone through the Red Sea." This was good news. Walter and Carla being the couple who crewed on *'Sandpiper'* on our trial run. We were amazed how quickly they had made it to Israel.

A few days later we were again the only visiting yacht left in Lumut. We too got up our anchor and went over to Pankor Island again. Passing the beach by Fly Point I could just make out shapes moving along the beach. "Quick," I called to Bobby, "hand me the glasses, I think I can see monkeys." Monkeys they clearly were, relations of

Pixie though not of the same species. These monkeys had long tails and were crab-eating macaques. They were all heading in the same direction, along the beach to the next set of rocks. It looked as if they would go over the rocks to Tg Siapu. We sailed ahead of them to drop anchor off that beach to await their arrival. While I had been excited at the sight of the monkeys, Pixie just sat on deck looking in their direction but with no particular interest. I felt I had been rather tactless, showing such interest over a troop of uncivilised monkeys with long tails. We thought it would be nice for her to meet up with them. To be honest it was ourselves who would have wished to see the reaction of Pixie if she had met a large group of these macaques. She had met one of their kind before, a pet of our gardener's brother; she showed no particular interest in him. Then she had never shown interest in one of her own type.

Having anchored and seen no sign of the monkeys we quickly jumped into the dinghy and rowed over to the beach, perhaps we thought they were still on the rocks between the two beaches, but no sign of the monkeys could we find, and Pixie refused to help by giving her monkey call.

The beach was beautiful; in the fine white sand we looked for monkey tracks. All we found were footprints of birds, lines drawn by hermit crabs and some large paw marks which we would have liked to believe were made by some kind of large cat but had to agree they looked more like dog paws. Pankor is populated to a small degree. The next beach to the one we had anchored off had a guest house and hotel which was barely visible from our anchorage and cut off from its neighbouring beach by the rocks.

A logging boat was on our beach the next morning not far from a sign signifying the land was a forest reserve. Perhaps they saw the sign and us watching, as later it left with no damage done. The logging boats were quaint with a house on stilts on the deck.

As usual we were surrounded by a number of large fishing boats. For the most part Malaysian fishing boats pose no threat to other boats, though there is always the exception to the rule. It is the boats that come in Malaysian waters from Thailand that find piracy more lucrative than fishing. Newspaper reports of Malaysian fishing boats being boarded and the crew being unceremoniously tossed overboard were common. We now had a marketing boat, that is the mother boat of a fleet of fishing boats to which the catch is transferred. To our surprise it came alongside. No word of greeting, it kept its engine slowly ticking over as it circled us. We waved and took a photo. No response.

"I think we will stay on board a bit and wait until they move off," said Bobby. "They are probably just curious but it is best to be on the safe side."

"What can be so curious about us?" I asked. "You, for one thing." he said. "You mean they have never seen a European woman before?" I enquired.

"Probably, but not one with purple lips and bright red skin."

It is easy to forget how one looks aboard a boat with no mirror. I had to agree when I thought about it, I probably did present a curious sight. Skin red and peeling, hair bleached in the sun nearly white and blistered lips covered in Gentian violet I had got from the hospital for my lips in Lumut. It so happened the sarong I was wearing had a lot of purple in the design. Perhaps they thought I was an odd creature trying to look trendy. The boat hung around until 1300hrs and then moved away. Off we went ashore. No sooner had we landed than the boat returned to circle '*Sandpiper*', again with only Bob-tail on board. It was not my pretty lips that was the attraction now. Bobby immediately returned and remained until the whole fleet moved out of sight.

For the first time we got Pixie to walk in the bush, up the steep slope behind the rocks. Ever since she had lived with us she had hated to be surrounded by trees or tall vegetation. Not unusual in tame monkeys, and macaques spend most of their time on the ground. Even in our own garden she would not go willingly into the parts with a lot of trees but would climb on me and cling tightly with her arms around my neck. Now she was walking, actually leading the way, not just sticking to the more or less clear slope but going short ways in the bush, picking things that took her fancy. A nice but prickly walk for me, the bush was not intended to be explored in bikini and bare feet. Once up the slope we found a very beautiful trail which was easy to walk along. On our return Pixie and I went down the last bit of slope twice as fast as Bobby, by sitting on a pile of leaves and going down on our bottoms. Bobby thought that was cheating and declared the race null and void. I was then given a swimming lesson and thought I did rather well by managing several strokes before sinking in the shallow water. I found floating easier and far less tiring. Pixie watched, no doubt wondering why I found it so difficult, and seemed a little concerned for my safety. We had had a good and enjoyable day and were now ready to leave. We unchained Pixie but to our surprise instead of walking along the sand to where we had the dinghy, she waded into the water and had a little swim. She then pulled at me, I was not sure if she was still nervous of the sea and wanted to make sure I was keeping near her or if she was giving me a swimming lesson, having observed my feeble efforts. I think the latter.

Pankor has a large variety of bird inhabitants but we were not lucky enough to see many or even hear their calls until one morning I went on deck and there was a deafening sound of different bird cries. *Bird Sunday*, I thought, but it was the most unmusical Alleluia chorus. Six large birds were at that moment flying overhead, looking white while still in flight but on landing in the trees appeared to have light and dark brown areas on their feathers. Unable to see clearly, I thought they were sea eagles. Whatever they were they were certainly considered to be unwelcome visitors to the island by the other birds. It had been no Alleluia chorus I had heard but a bird protest rally. The intruders sat haughtily in a tree for a few minutes, then pretended they had a business appointment on some other island and flew off. The birds were now silent.

Still with hope that we might find the crab-eating monkeys we fixed the Seagull engine on the dinghy and motored along to the beach we had seen them on the day we came in; they were not around.

A few feet inland we found a brackish pond full of small pipe fish that looked like sea horses that had been straightened and smoothed out a bit. Pixie tried to catch them with her hands without success. It did not seem prudent to stay too long on that beach from where we could not keep our eye on *'Sandpiper'*. Bobby went back in the dinghy, leaving Pixie and I to make our way back along the beach and over the rocks to our usual beach opposite *'Sandpiper'*. As soon as we were over the rocks I noticed a lot of tracks on the sand which were unmistakably made by monkeys. You have to give them credit. Uncivilised Pixie might think, but they were certainly outsmarting us.

Perhaps even then they were in the trees keeping an eye on us. If Pixie saw or sensed they were around she was not letting on, and I could see nothing. When Bobby returned with the dinghy to collect us we went halfway out to *'Sandpiper'* and then waited, hoping as the sun went down the monkeys might appear on the beach again. Their tracks had not gone the whole length of the beach but disappeared at the edge of the bush. They were not fooled and were probably by then back on the beach we had left, laughing at the stupid humans.

The weather deteriorated the next day, first a Sumatra that lasted an hour then a heavy swell set in with rain. We returned to Lumut.

In Lumut we lingered
for longer than planned.
Pixie found a wee boyfriend
but alas bit his hand

CHAPTER EIGHT
DOUBLE BUNK

"We have company," Bobby called from the cockpit. I watched as a small boat *'Kathena Faa'* came in and dropped anchor not far from us. The dinghy was soon put over the side and a mother and small son got in to row ashore. Not too unusual but the little boy was doing the rowing. After depositing his mother ashore he came back alone and over to *'Sandpiper'*, attracted by Pixie. I was shattered, my rowing attempts were nothing to boast about, rather a hit and miss affair. My arms were not strong enough. That excuse would no longer do. The little boy was professional and he was not much bigger than Pixie. As he drew near us we made our acquaintance with Kym. We asked him if he would like to come aboard. Very politely he asked if we were inviting him aboard. When we confirmed that was just what we were doing he looked very pleased and said, "I must first go and get permission from my father." Permission evidently received he returned. Our deck was high over his inflatable dinghy and having no ladder, Bobby had to haul him aboard. Looking at our compass he told us it was not the same type as his. "Your cockpit is very small," he observed. We had to agree it was. Seeing the outboard on the cockpit rails produced the query, "Is that a Seagull?"

"Yes," we replied. "Do you have one?"

"No, we don't have an outboard." When he asked Bobby how much anchor rope we had out I was convinced that this tiny boy knew more about boats than I ever would. In return we extracted from him the information that he was five years old, was not English, as we had thought, but was in fact from Germany and had sailed with his parents from New Zealand where they had gone to buy the boat. They were now on their way back to Europe. Kym would have liked to have made friends with Pixie but she had been upset when Bobby hauled Kym aboard. It upsets her if she thinks people are manhandling each other. Also, now older, she was not so tolerant with children as she had been when young. Fearing she might bite we prevented children from getting too near or playing with her. Before leaving Kym was able to pat Bob-tail, who was in one of the bunks. We were looking forward to meeting the parents of Kym, this fascinating bilingual little five-year-old.

Subsequently we met and became friends with Kym's parents, Astrid and Wilfried Erdmann. Here we thought were real sailing people. Wilfried was the first German to sail round the world single-handed. He went round a second time, taking Astrid with him, who became pregnant with Kym before arriving back in Germany. They then flew out to New Zealand, having decided just what kind of boat they now needed. They bought it and with Kym were sailing back to Germany via the Red Sea. We were sure this little family would reach their goal safely and arrive as planned before Kym was six and had to attend school. Within a week Wilfried and wee Kym had made firm friends with Pixie, sitting under her tree with her. With Wilfried I was not surprised, she takes to most men as long as they are not afraid of her, but inclined to be jealous with women and children. It was nice that Pixie had a small friend to play with but we worried lest she ever turn on him and had to keep out of sight when they were together, knowing she was quite likely to get cross with him if she saw us watching. Unfortunately, what we feared happened. Just before they were due to leave Kym was found crying in the long grass with a bitten hand. A nasty bite, but I was relieved to see it was not as bad as it could have been. If Pixie had really attacked him in anger he would not have got away.

Kym was a smart little fellow and he must not have screamed when she bit him which would have resulted in him angering her. Pixie knew she had done wrong. When I went up to her she made noises and ran round her tree then stood with her head on the ground and bottom in the air to be smacked, after which she held me and had a little cry.

Kym was taken to the hospital and given a tetanus shot and returned with a bandage on his hand. He was a very honest little boy and told us what had happened. Playing with Pixie with a long mangrove pod, he had passed it to Pixie, who took it and then in play he had tried to take it back. He had broken the basic rule we warn everyone about. Never to try and take back anything once offered and accepted.

It is always very upsetting when a child gets bitten by an animal it loves when just playing with it. The bite heals but so often the memory of it stays and the child loses all trust in the animal that bit him or her. We hoped it did not destroy Kym's faith. He himself said he had done what we told him not to do. He was a very sensible little chap, so we trusted it was a lesson learned and not confidence destroyed.

Pixie's bottom was bothering her again. It was large and should have gone down weeks before, but showed no sign of doing so. Also Bob-tail developed a lump on the side of his face and in a couple of days it got very large. We were now bathing his lump and Pixie's bottom with Dettol and hot water twice a day. The lump on Bob-tail's face when squeezed released a lot of puss and then went down but Pixie's bottom remained large and worried us. Her monthly cycle had got out of order in Singapore and the zoo vet Dr Lee had given her an injection which made her bottom go down. I now wrote to him and asked if there were any pills or medicine I might be able to purchase and administer to her. Dr Lee kindly replied on zoo headed paper, giving a list of different preparations that would work. Having no luck obtaining any of the listed drugs in the medicine shops, I tried the

Government hospital where I had attended as an out-patient with my blistering lips. The problem was I could not expect free medicine for Pixie and doubted that they would be allowed to sell it. The normal procedure at the hospital was to go along and pay 50 cents at the reception desk where you are then given a slip of paper with a number on. You then wait for your number to be called, when you can go in a see a doctor. Any medicine he prescribes for you is then collected at the dispensary in the next room. Fine for humans.

Being averse to wasting either the doctor's or my own time I went to the desk and asked if I could purchase one of the drugs on the list. One of the assistants took it and read Dr Lee's letter and then said I could get the drugs at the dispensary, no need to pay, first though I had better see the doctor. Thinking he meant to see the doctor to get permission to get the drugs I agreed and waited for him to give me a number and write my name in the book. The hospitals there keep all records. Though I had gone just for stuff for my lip they had kept a card for me. I now realised he was getting my medical card out, which was rather irrelevant to the case. I pointed out that the doctor hardly needed my card to issue medicine for my monkey. He had read the letter written on zoo veterinary headed paper but was still under the impression that it was medicine for myself I required. I had repeated monkey, and *kera monyet* in Malay several times without it penetrating. Finally, everyone really understood and there were grins on all the faces and they all kept repeating monkey in English and Malay, and we all nodded our heads at each other like puppets and grinning like a Chinese Buddha, until we were all quite convinced it really was a monkey we were talking about. Someone suggested a vet. I explained I doubted they would have the required drugs which were the same commonly prescribed for women, that is human ones. Two orderlies were called, given the story and told to take me straight into the doctor, ahead of all the other waiting patients and without paying the usual fifty cents. At least they had their priorities right, monkeys before people. On our way to the doctor's office other staff were passed and let in on the joke. I could not really see what was so funny but it was nice to be spreading so much joy around the place, and it was easy for me to keep on grinning too.

One of the nurses had met Pixie when she was around the club so it was proven that she really did exist and not a figment of my imagination. The doctor was the same one I had previously seen and asked me about my lip, which was getting better with less sailing. I told him what I had come about and he understood at once. After looking at the list he said he thought they must have one of the things on the list or some substitute. He then came with me and searched for the drugs himself, found suitable pills and also decided, while we were at it, I should have some more Vitamin C pills even though I had not mentioned the fact that Pixie had managed to get the bottle of pills and I had only got them back after she had discarded them from her mouth in a rather damp condition, and all sticking together. Some people criticised the government hospitals in Malaysia but I always found the staff quite delightful.

To get Pixie to take a pill is difficult. It is impossible to force it down her throat like one can – if you are clever – with a dog or cat; Pixie would just hold it in the pouches and then take it out and toss it away the moment you turned your back. The only way was to pretend you did not want her to have them, leave one within her reach and go out of sight, whereupon she would steal it. The drawback to this was that if whatever it was did not taste good she would spit it out. To crush it in food was risky; if she had any suspicion it had been doctored she would not eat. I settled on the idea of crushing it up in honey and spreading it on a small piece of bread, then making two more similar bits minus the pill. Chewing one piece I went on deck with my plate of honey bread and sat near her with the plate just out of reach. Taking the other undoctored piece I started to eat, naturally Pixie wanted it but I refused to give it to her, then I suddenly jumped up as if I'd forgotten something, giving the plate a knock so she could reach it. She immediately grabbed the remaining one with the pill and ate it in such a hurry she never knew the difference. By using much the same method the next two days the prescribed amount had gone down and so had her bottom.

The club was rarely patronised on weekdays by anyone other than ourselves and the owners of other visiting boats. Every third Sunday of the month the club members would gather, go sailing or fishing, and had a big lunch at the club. At these times we kept out of the way, staying on the boat, not wanting to intrude or have Pixie ashore with so many people and children around.

We did strike up a friendship with two members who came to the club more frequently. Stewart McCulloch we found was the owner of the boat we had sought shelter on when caught in the rip tide. Stewart had been a planter in India and Burma, he was now retired and living in a lovely old Malay-type bungalow that had once been part of the Sitiawan Estate. He invited us to his house, such invitations usually have to be turned down as we will not leave Pixie on the boat on her own. Stewart had thoughtfully invited her too, they having already become friends. Stewart collected us in his car, Bobby sitting in the front and I at the back with Pixie sitting nicely on a towel in case of accidents which fortunately did not happen. Looking out of the window she took a big interest in all we passed, now and then standing up and looking over Stewart's shoulder. He told us that Sitiawan got its name from a story of two elephants. These two elephants were friends. One day one got sick and fell down into the mud from which he was unable to get out. The other elephant stayed by his side showing true friendship, hence the name Sitiawan which comes from the two Malay words Setia and Kwan; meaning steady and faithful friend.

Before taking us to his house Stewart showed us some of the surrounding countryside and the beaches with holiday chalets built there. We admired his house and two-acre garden. A garden was something we missed on the boat and he had planted a number of citrus trees and coconut palms. Pixie looked quite at home under a velvet flower tree and was brought fruit by some local boys. Little outings like that were quite an event to us now that our life was spent on the boat.

Our social life grew when Gerald and Terry Hinxman with their two charming young sons, Quintin and Tristan, joined the club. Gerald was working in Lumut in connection with the new naval base that was being constructed. They had just bought a weekend sailer, *'Overdraft'*, that we had previously noticed was for sale in Singapore. Gerald had gone to Singapore and bought it and with the help of a friend brought it down to Lumut to join the small group of moored boats there. Gerald and Bobby soon found they had a number of things in common, while Terry became an invaluable friend knowing the shops where things we wanted to buy could be found, and taking us on many shopping trips.

The method of coming out of the water in Lumut we thought rather quaint. Outside the workshop, a little farther along the beach from the club, stakes were positioned so that at high tide you could position your boat between them and tie up so that at low tide you'd be high and dry on the mud. Our bottom once again was covered in an interesting assortment of sea life. We motored along to the stakes. While the tide was going out we went to the club. For the first time Pixie refused to come with us, preferring to stay aboard and look at the new view. The bottom was scrubbed and painted and we were back in the water at high tide the following afternoon.

Towards the end of June we spotted *'Whistler'*, with our friends Doug and Machteld aboard, coming up the river. No sails and moving along at a snail's pace. "They must have repaired their engine," Bobby said. As they passed us and swung round to anchor we saw their method of propulsion: their dinghy was tied to the side of their yacht and a Seagull engine was supplying the power. They, like us, decided to wait out the monsoon season in Lumut.

Pixie got little exercise ashore, spending most of her time on a long chain fixed to her tree where she would mostly just sit. So we would walk her in the long grass where she caught grasshoppers. We liked then to go along the mangroves. Not keen on the mangroves, she spent as much time as I'd let her sitting down playing with the sand. This gave me more time to take in small happening of this world which otherwise I might have missed.

There were tiny crabs that made holes surrounded by wee balls of sand. They dived down their holes as I approached but if I sat still long enough they decided the monster was harmless and I could see now they had little paths from their holes. The balls of sand were not as first suggested, taken from the holes, the crabs make and widen their paths by taking sand and rolling it under their bodies and out come perfect little balls. As the ball-making was in progress along came a small black ant ignored by the working crabs. I dismissed him from my observations as a wandering tourist in crab land. He caught my eye though and I saw he was carrying off a tiny crab, perhaps a baby, about half the size of the little workers, Were the crabs going to allow this blatant kidnapping to go unchallenged? It appeared so, as the working crabs just carried on making balls of sand without turning their heads. Minute as the victim was, the ant was having trouble, the baby crab being on the heavy side. With a twig I flipped the crab away, only to find it was dead. I let the ant have it back and off he went. The ant was no kidnapper but the crab's undertaker, they themselves being too busy manufacturing balls of sand to take time off to bury their dead. As road building and ball-making appeared to be so time consuming I thought a little help was needed. I added a few extra roads from one of the holes and added a few link roads which might be an advantage to them if chased by the enemy. Then, getting really into this crab road building, I added a linking road to a neighbour. All workers fled into their hole when I took a hand but two stayed at the entrance, watching these miraculously fast roads appearing. I bet they could hardly believe their eyes and were probably thinking of an early retirement.

When I finished giving them a comprehensive road system they came out of their holes but were singularly unimpressed by my work. Some of the crabs were detailed to go on my road and make balls of sand out of the wee heaps I'd left at the sides of the roads. They were very sulky over the extra work I had given them. I noticed that they took longer now to make each ball, not only that but the balls were not as good. I had evidently left out some vital ingredient, perhaps they dampen the sand first. One crab went up the road I'd made, linking it to another, thinking he might like to visit his neighbour and boast about their new road system. Poor guy never got a chance. Out jumped the guard of the hole and they were clasped in battle for a while. They parted, the resident went back down his hole leaving the intruder to dash back the way he had come. I blocked off the road as it was obviously not going to add anything to friendly relations. I felt a bit mean about the whole thing really, but there was nothing much I could do about it so left things as they were and Pixie and I resumed our walk.

Apart from birds, the sea and insect life, there was little wildlife around Lumut. It was a delightful surprise one day when Machteld and I were sitting in *'Sandpiper's'* cockpit while I taught her to do macramé, to see a head pop up in the water and take a look at us. It did not stay for lessons and we never saw him again but decided it was a baby otter.

We thought our cabin looked quite nice after all our painting and varnishing. It certainly looked better than when we had first got the boat but after being invited on board the boats of our friends we realised how very spartan still our cabin was in comparison. *'Whistler'* in particular we admired, a wooden Choy Lee boat built in Hong Kong. We came back from that visit and started drawing up plans to make changes in the interior of the cabin. We wanted to move the galley, just where, we were not sure. I was all for doing without one, cooking not being my favourite occupation, but Bobby thought that was going a bit too far. We both agreed what we really wanted was another long seat where the galley was, it would not only look much nicer and give us more room if friends came aboard but it would also give us a lot more locker space under and behind the seat. The galley at present with such a small locker and counter space was just taking up room.

The other thing we badly wanted to change was our two single bunks. As the mast was in-between and in the way, we could not make a wider double bunk and we would not be able to get past. Our forepeak was a sail locker with anchor chain locker situated behind. We had seen boats with a double bunk positioned where our sail locker was. It would have to be an odd shape, wide at the bottom end and tapering to a blunt point at the top. We could keep the sails under the bunk and have the added advantage that we could then stand on the bunk and push the sails through the hatch above. Originally *'Sandpiper'* was just transport, now we were beginning to consider it home.

We set to work to make a nice big bunk that all four of us could sleep in with ease. Removing the two existing bunks was a small matter, they were just canvas stretched out on metal frames with foam mattresses. The frames we took to the workshop where we knew they would make use of them in some way. The canvas we used to make awnings for Pixie to sit under on deck and the foam much later would be turned into long cushions for the seat we planned to make one day. Half our bunk would be the sail locker extending out a couple of feet to where our existing bunks had been. That would leave us with space each side at the end. One space we thought one day could be the galley. What to do with the other bit of space we were not sure but felt by the time we got to that point we would have thought of something. With the bunks out of the way, Bobby set about dismantling the bulkhead of the sail locker. Easier said than done. Soon the cabin was snowed under with sail bags, tools and all the shelves and doors we had removed. The deck was piled high with the frames of our bunk beds and all the junk that went under them. Old wood we would keep for reuse. Fortunately, for me, there was not enough space for two to work. I left the honour to Bobby and Pixie and I went ashore, leaving him to prise away at the plywood bulkheads. Thus I was chatting to Terry, who had become a daily visitor to the club, with Quintin and Tristin, on holiday from school. They had not then bought a dinghy to get out to their boat so had borrowed Doug's. Suddenly Terry jumped up in a panic having just noticed the dinghy was no longer pulled up on the beach. The boys were called, they could shed no light on the disappearance. The last they had seen of it, like us it was sitting on the beach, now it was nowhere in sight. Bobby having rowed Pixie and I ashore had returned to *'Sandpiper'* in our dinghy. All together we yelled his name. Amazingly he heard above the banging he was making and came on deck expecting to hear that Pixie had done something terrible. Now we all had to shout, "Doug's dinghy." Understanding he looked all around and spotted it farther upriver stuck in the mangroves which was out of our view. Had we not resorted to panic but used our brains we might have guessed it would have landed up there and just walked along and got it. As it was Bobby rowed over and towed it back. Crisis over.

After a couple of days' work everything in the fore-end of our cabin was stripped out, leaving just the cement sides of the boat. It was getting rather difficult to move around and we now had to sleep on deck. No doubt Pixie thought we were behaving in rather an odd manner destroying everything in a far grander scale than she could even contemplate. Bobby went in the dinghy and started chipping away at any rust marks he saw on the hull resulting from the wires in the hull getting near the surface, then filling in the resulting holes. Now the sides were a patchwork of unpainted cement, blue and green showing through. In the evening while Bobby concocted one of his famous vegetable stews in the muddle of the cabin, I gave the hull a coat of undercoat, finishing it next day with gloss.

It was more satisfactory after that to see the bunk taking shape rather than the destruction of our boat. Deciding how high we could have the bunk and still get in with ease and plenty of headroom, he now made a nice frame for the base of the bunk using two by two lengths of wood he had salvaged from the bulkhead. We were getting up extra early now, finding sleeping on deck not very inducive to lying in. This gave us a good start to the day. However, there were days when little or nothing could be done owing to one setback or another.

One such morning we had both done a considerable amount of daily chores before breakfast, after which we pumped out the loo. We still had hate relations with the loo even after Bobby had fixed the leaking pipe. In Singapore we had no more trouble in that direction but we did not like the idea of the holding tank, feeling it would be much better to just pump it out each time it was used. Natural waste we felt sure could not be as harmful as the chemical we had to put in, but it was necessary to pump the tank out every few days, if we did not then it smelled foul. Even so it always had a bad odour. We then found it was not possible to purchase any more of the chemical and wondered what to do when it was all finished. As Charlie had fitted it in new, before selling the boat to us, we still had all the literature aboard. I wrote to the manufactures, Thelford in Australia, asking if they could send us out the chemical. The reply came back that they could not send us any and appeared as bewildered as we were as to what we could use instead. The cost of airmailing Aqua Kem to us, they said, would be enormous (they did not say how much), to comply with the air regulations the one-gallon kegs would have to be packed in sawdust and the in a strong wooden box. Guess they did not want to chance making all their passengers and crew cry. We loved their fourth paragraph that went as follows: *Perhaps a mild detergent such as pine-o-clean would at least deodorise the waste to some extent, although we are not sure whether pine-o-clean would damage Slide Ez Valve seals.*

Well that was all very jolly except that no detergent in all the many shops we went to was called pine-o-clean. That apparently, along with Aqua Kem, was an Australian brand name. Anyway, we were not sure we wanted to risk damaging our Slide Ez Valve seals, whatever they were.

I now tried to pump it out but the pump refused to work. Bobby tried with no better luck. It must be blocked, this meant he had to take it apart. By now I was getting used to things going wrong and having to be taken apart. Feeling no concern I got on with some painting – not the artistic kind. Suddenly a glugging noise, a bad word from Bobby and the most awful stench filled the cabin. If the smell was bad the sight was worse, gagging I rushed up on deck. Having cleared up the most awful mess, Bobby now found there was nothing wrong with the pump. The outlet over the side was blocked. All it needed was a few pokes with the broom handle from the dinghy to clear it. I suggested that in future he might try doing that first and got a withering look.

Our new sleeping quarters were beginning to take shape. I thought then we might use it to sleep on, finding sleeping on deck getting a little wearisome, wondering if we were to be hit by a rain squall any time. However, we decided that to have to keep removing all the tools and bits of wood from the bunk each time would only delay things as small items would get lost in the muddle of the rest of the cabin.

The completion of the bunk took about a month in all. It was well worth waiting for. Once the base of the bunk was put in place filling the width of the boat from one side to the other, we had a huge bed, even for the four of us, one end being well over eight feet wide, tapering down to just over one foot at the end that had been the chain locker. Down the middle it was almost seven feet in length. The largest area of clear space we had on the whole boat. Stretching ourselves out at various angles on the plywood we found we had more than enough room whichever way we arranged ourselves. We ruled out sleeping across the bottom, this left the narrow end superfluous unless Pixie and Bob-tail made it their end rather than cuddling up to us. At sea we would have our heads or feet pushing against the side of the boat, depending on which tack we were on. If we slept as Doug and Machteld did, with our heads up at the wide end, we would be sleeping in the centre to get the length of the bed. Our head and pillows would have no backing, as we now had a new bulkhead that Bobby had made of wooden planks with an opening in the middle to enable us to get on the bunk. The best way was the one that we planned at first, with heads up at the small end. The wide end was then a bit useless and no sheet would cover it.

Clearly our bunk needed a little reshaping. It took time but we finally hit at the obvious plan of making the widest part only four-and-a-half feet wide and it could remain that wide for the first three feet. After that it would taper off. The extra space each side would become lockers for what clothes we possessed. These did not entail much work and looked very professional with teak louvred doors. We had cheated with the doors, taking the door that had been the sail locker and cutting it in half. The original door had been perfect for this having a solid piece of wood in the middle between the louvred parts. We also used the frame of the door. We had worked together on the last part and now started getting more ambitious. We had a number of attractive bits of wood to use up. The cement sides were not attractive, even when painted, so the more locker and shelves we could put up the less the cement would show. Shelves for books would go along above the bunk at the sides. Shelves we agreed were easy. I left it to Bobby who had done very well and I was full of praise for his work. I spoke too soon. When I saw the result of the shelves I thought he had gone crazy.

First, he had to make a frame for them as of course he could not nail or screw anything to the cement side. He solved this problem by using an assortment of glues and fibreglass along with an odd assortment of bits of wood which ranged from varnished or painted to bare wood with nail holes in. When something did not hold the rest firm he added another bit of any odd-sized wood in desperation. All thought of what the finished thing would look like fell out of his head and he worked away like a mad man for several days just to get something to support a couple of planks of wood. I said nothing but looked on as this outlandish work of art took place and thought we would have done better to leave it to Pixie to build. I got brave and pointed out that I thought we were trying to make the boat look nice not just practical, and that I would rather have no shelves at all than the monstrosity we now had. Tempers got frayed, I cried and Bobby glowered. Next day Bobby went off ashore for something and I went and took another look at the thing that was going to be shelves. I sat willing it to fall down or just wither up and disappear. As it unobliging did neither I gave it a helping hand and got two bits dislodged.

Suddenly I knew I had the solution as to just how two nicely made shelves could be fixed and that if I could rip it all down I could start again and put something up myself. Fortunately for me Bobby then returned. It is often easy to see what could be done and not so easy to actually do it. I moved from the bunk hoping he would not yet notice a couple of bits of wood were now missing from his work, or if he did would take it that it had fallen down. Bobby never looked at it, I think by that time he too could not bear the sight of it. No mention was made of the shelves that day but next morning he went back to work on it. Taking my courage in both hands I went to tell him in the nicest manner possible that it could be done another way. He said nothing. I peeped in and to my joy saw he was no longer building a monument to agony but attacking it with a hammer to demolish it for ever.

The second set of shelves looked like shelves should look. With the minimum of frame work. All once more was going well. Another locker was added with room at the top to add three pigeonholes with flap doors. Our bunk at last was complete. With all the woodwork sanded down and given a few coats of satin varnish the result looked quite professional and cosy.

At first we put straw mats over the plywood base to sleep on, which also gave us a good place to sit crossed-legged and work over small jobs. I added brightly coloured pillow cases and made some long bolster-shaped pillows with a draw string at the top which, during the day, contained our sheets and blankets. It looked nice but would be more comfortable at sea with a mattress; we measured our odd-shaped bunk for a two-section mattress. Being in two parts it would be easier for us to remove and get at the lockers under the bunk. We decided on a kapok or cotton-filled canvas mattress, such as we had been used to sleeping on at home. We gave the measurement to Stewart who kindly said he would take them to the mattress maker for us. Later Stewart said he thought it would have been better filled with coconut fibre. On reflection we felt he was right but it was too late to change our minds.

While Bobby was making the new bunk, the whole boat, deck and cabin looked as if it had been struck by an earthquake. Working and living in such a confined space at the same time was not easy. '*Whistler*', who we had admired and who had looked so well cared for when we went on on board, was now in much the same state, Machteld informed me. Tools everywhere. Doug, who rivalled Pixie in his desire to take everything apart, was happily dismantling his engine, taking it piece by piece to the workshop where he would work on it himself. It looked an unfathomable heap of parts to us but Doug was enjoying playing with it all.

One of our Sunday pastimes when we were in Port Kelang had been watching a very attractive middle-aged couple sailing their Snapdragon: a long narrow fast sailing boat. They looked very picturesque and serene as they sailed past our anchorage, the lady dressed in a large hat and wearing white gloves. We heard they were leaving Malaysia and putting the boat *'Umtagati'* up for sale. To our surprise we now saw *'Umtagati'* had joined the moored boats in Lumut and we made the acquaintance of Aynsley and David Bell. The new owners, David and Aynsley, were living in Kuala Lumpur and would spend their weekends sailing from Lumut. Kindly they would also bring any items we had asked for. With all the help we were getting from our shore-based friends we were doing well.

Feeling it would be showing a bit of good sense and seamanship to have a few spare parts on board, we agreed to buy a lot of spare parts for our engine from Doug. He also had a Volvo Penta and wished to sell parts he did not need to pay for others he now wanted. We also bought an oil warning gadget that would set off a siren if the oil in the engine got too low. I fervently hoped we would never need it as neither Pixie nor I could stand the noise but agreed it was a good precaution. Doug's engine had been ruined through lack of oil.

We had been given a book *'Survive the Savage Sea'* by Dougal Robertson. This got us wondering what we would do in the same situation. We turned down the dreadful idea of slaughtering turtles and fish. Well I felt we could do neither. Bobby agreed about the turtles but said catching a few fish to save ourselves would not be wrong. OK if he and Bob-tail wanted to eat them but I, and I expected Pixie, would have no part of it. Bobby disagreed and said if we were starving we might change our minds. Before we got in to a deeper discussion over this issue we recalled that as things stood we did not stand a chance of finding ourselves adrift in a life raft. We did not have one.

That was until Bobby asked Doug if he wanted to sell his. He agreed and said he would open it up for us to take a look at it. Personally, I thought it would be fun to see just what one day we might have to fit ourselves into. However, Bobby preferred not to have it opened. We knew Doug was expert at taking things apart but did not know if he was just as good at putting things together. It was just not worth taking the chance; if we had to use it, something we had not thought about until reading the book, and if it did not open because it had not been packed properly it would be a sad state of affairs.

We had not fully understood. Doug had to open it having done so before and putting personal things in it, which he now was removing, and added a new flashlight and knife for us before selling it. We had missed our opportunity of seeing it and we still wondered if it would open if needed.

The little wooden clubhouse that had looked so deserted on our arrival was now the meeting place where we could all get together and chat over cold beers. The old Chinese couple would open it up as soon as they saw one of us coming ashore. They could, if asked, produce a simple meal or a sandwich. First this usually entailed the old man getting on his bike and peddling off to buy the makings. He and his wife lived at the back of the club and gave the impression that we were all rather a bother they could do without. We were lucky and got on reasonably well with them. I remembered just enough Malay to ask for anything we required. The fact that they did not have a word of English coupled with their grim faces upset a lot of people. As visitors we paid ten Malay dollars for the privilege of using the facilities which included showers and where we could also do our laundry. On an earlier visit one couple had fallen foul of the management and decided not to pay the fee or use the club. That would have been fine except one day the couple in charge caught them using the showers. From then on they were particularly vigilant.

One day I got up at dawn, Bobby still slept. Rather than banging around making breakfast and waking him I decided to row ashore for an early shower. All was fine until I came out of the shower to find I was trapped. The large gate that was always open and had been when

I went in, was now closed with a huge padlock. I was left to yell for a while before the old boy came out and released me. I think he was rather put out that he had not captured the victim he had hoped for. He had heard the shower and thought it was the non-paying couple sneaking a free shower. I wondered if he had caught the non-paying guest what he proposed to do about it.

The old lady was obviously the boss. One day she was not around and for the first time the husband was, for him, looking very cheerful. We all responded to his happier mood by smiling. Then speculated amongst ourselves as to whether he had chopped her up with his meat chopper. Naughtily we asked him if that was what he had done. He gave us a rare smile, not understanding a word, the question having been put in English. Next day his wife reappeared stepping out of a car. She had been on a trip to Ipho.

One really could not blame them for wanting a bit of peace and quiet in their declining years, instead of having to put up with us chattering away in what to them probably sounded as bad as Chinese did to us. They got their own back now and then by closing the club to us when they had their family and friends visit. We hoped on these occasions they relaxed and were both able to smile.

At the club one afternoon Machteld and I watched as another boat came in to anchor. Machteld got quite excited feeling sure she knew the boat and the couple on board. Strangely only one person could be seen on deck. Just a girl we thought, easily identified by her long ponytail. We watched in admiration as alone this young girl managed everything herself and anchored nicely. "Something must have happened to her husband," voiced Machteld. We did not have to wait long. The girl rowed over to the club. Machteld and I grinned at each other realising our mistake. The *girl* turned out to be a Chinese male.

Lin Wah-ye was single-handed for the time being, having come from Hong Kong on his boat *'Sylvero'*. His American girlfriend Ruth having gone home for a visit. They were not the couple Machteld thought they were. It was the first and last time I ever met a Chinese man with a cruising yacht. Ruth returned and she and Wah-ye were part of our little community. They too were headed for Sri Lanka where we hoped to meet up again. They were a very unusual and enterprising pair as they decided to leave their boat for a while and flew to Nepal to go trekking.

The mattress we had ordered arrived and now our bunk when made up looked, we thought, grand. It was covered over during the day with a batik sheet in blue and white, pillows of contrasting colours, upon which I placed Andre Baby, a small teddy bear with long dangling legs. I had that toy, now called a mascot lest I be thought rather childish, since being given it by my favourite aunt on my first birthday. Every night I took off the sheet before bedtime, placing Andre Baby on top of the locker. By chance Bobby removed the sheet one evening. A lot of sand used to come down the hatch when a Sumatra blew and so invariably the sheet had to be shaken over the side. This Bobby also did and we went to bed.

Later that night I woke to find Pixie was being very restless and had been standing up. I got the impression she might have taken something off the top of the locker. I was mistaken, Pixie had nothing but where was Andre Baby? I searched around the bunk thinking Pixie must have moved him, no sign, then I remembered Bobby had uncovered the bed. I looked places he might have put him, still nothing. Bobby now woke and asked what I was doing. "Where is Andre Baby?" I asked. "I don't know, I never touched him," he replied sleepily. "But you removed the top sheet and he was on it." As I uttered these words the awful truth dawned, Bobby must have tossed my lifelong toy/mascot overboard. "That's the end of me then," I said. "I have always had Andre Baby so if he has gone I must be going to drown or something." Very unreasonably I felt sure this to be the case. "Don't be silly, he'll get washed ashore, I'll find him tomorrow," Bobby said and went back to sleep.

The chances of being able to find him again were remote. So there was I, as a middle-aged woman, crying myself to sleep over a lost toy received forty years before. I was certainly very careless with him, I had lost him once before at the age of four. I had him tied to my tricycle and he must have fallen off. I had been so upset my father had put a notice in a shop window, fortunately he was returned minus his glass eyes. I vowed then I would always keep him. I like to keep my vows, even if only to a toy.

Bobby was up early next morning and went off in the dinghy. I stayed in bed, waiting to be struck down now I had lost my mascot. He returned after a two-hour search of the mangrove beach where he figured Andre Baby should have been washed up with the tide, provided he floated.

"I am sorry," he said when he returned. "I could not find him." Rather surprisingly I could still function without my mascot, so I got up and had the breakfast Bobby had prepared. When tide went out again that afternoon, we both went ashore to search before I had despaired of ever seeing him again, but now I was determined to find him – it seemed very important. Bobby cautioned me there was little hope. We searched again among the mangroves' roots, going over the whole ground and turning over any pile of flotsam. No sign, we turned back still searching where we had already looked. Suddenly Bobby gave a shout. He had found Andre in a heap of leaves with just his sandy feet showing. We sat hugging each other, I holding my little bear, and had a good cry from joy. What a crazy picture we must have presented but there was only the crabs to see us.

Later, having taken Andre Baby in the shower with me and putting him in the sun to dry, I found I was now minus my sun shades. Back we went to the mangroves and sure enough there they were where we had sat down and had our jolly little weep.

Back on board Bobby found he must have left his shades in the shower. "Don't worry," I said. "They will turn up, everything does." They did.

I go to town to get a jab
the run around fair drove me mad.
Return to boat to tell my tale
and find poor Bobby looking pale

Pulau Buluh

Some of the Sembilan Islands

CHAPTER NINE
LOOSE ENDS

When we first started out from Singapore we had anticipated spending most of our time at sea. Our idea was to stay a couple of weeks in Port Kelang after which to sail directly to Sri Lanka. We visualised another stop of a few weeks, then on down the Indian Ocean to Mauritius and around the Cape of Good Hope in January 1979. Next, we would continue on to the Caribbean, stopping in Guyana which was once our home, exploring a few of the islands, before crossing the Atlantic to arrive in England in the summer months. Yes, we had it all worked out.

Oh, how naïve we were. It would perhaps have been a reasonable plan for someone in a hurry with plenty of sailing experience behind them and a boat that had all that was needed for the long voyage. This description hardly fitted us. It had not taken us long to find out there was much that needed doing to the boat first, and that any repairs always took at least twice as long as expected to complete. Having been inadvertently delayed in starting from Singapore and then spending much more time in Port Kelang with our erring engine and trying to find playmates for Pixie, and getting the steering vane delivered and fixed, the months had rolled by. On arrival in Lumut we again had work done on our engine and spent time putting things that were essential to rights by which time the cyclone season was well advanced and we decided to wait that out. We felt in no particular hurry now, as we were enjoying our life aboard and working on the boat and meeting interesting people. This trip might well be our last adventure. We were now not sure just where we were heading as it appeared England would not let us in under our terms. So, we would have to think of some other European country. At the moment we wanted to make the most of our present lives.

We got our charts out and studied the weather conditions at different times of the year in different places trying to work out when it would be best to arrive where. We fancied spending Christmas in Sri Lanka and it was also a good time to go there, but then we could not expect to get round the Cape of Good Hope in January. This would then give us a whole year to enjoy ourselves between Sri Lanka and the Cape, to arrive in Europe a year later in the summer of 1980. We were both in favour of taking things easy and seeing as much as possible on the way. Also giving us plenty of time to fix the many things that would undoubtedly go wrong on the way.

I knew my parents were eagerly awaiting to know just when they might expect to see us in England. We had been very vague in our replies and did not mention the fact we would not put Pixie in quarantine which would change things. Having no experience of boats or weather conditions outside England, they did not understand why we did not just sail directly, non-stop, and arrive in a few months, warning us to arrive in the summer months as the coasts of England are dangerous in the winter. I could quite understand how they felt as only a year before I too thought it all might be just plain sailing to England. I now wrote to them explaining our new plan telling them that we intended to pick the best time of year which was also the safest, and that as we were now too late to go round the Cape that summer it would have to be the next.

With the bunk finished we planned to embark on moving the galley at some time in the future. We had, however, made up our minds on what to put in the space on the starboard side: a water tank. We had one tank that held thirty-five gallons but on some of the longer trips we planned it would be more comforting to have a lot more water. The workshop in Lumut was very versatile and they said they could make a tank to fit the space. Bobby got out his tape measure and drew out a tank with a V-shaped bottom. While this was being made we could go off and visit the Sembilan Islands. However, the weather conditions were not very good and Terry had invited me to spend a few days with her in her house in Ipho, something I was looking forward to. Bobby thought he would come out of the water again so we would have a clean bottom to start with.

On the morning of the day we were to come out of the water and I would later go to Ipoh, we woke early intending to catch the morning tide. We had had a bad night with heavy rain and our pillows were very wet. The rain had come down the hole in the deck that had once been for the anchor chain. In hindsight it had been rather foolish in co-operating the chain locker as a part of our new bunk. We were now left with no real chain locker but had made a hole in the empty forepeak bulkhead and the chain went through there, but it still had to come through the hole in the deck, which of course was a fixture and the end of our bunk. We realised too late that we did not really need the extra foot of bunk that the chain locker gave us. It was too narrow anyway for our heads, so served no real purpose.

Our wet pillows were not all we found on waking. Pixie had woken first and found the best way to open the small lockers was to completely remove the turn screws which kept them closed. The engine must have also had a bad night as it took us ages to start it. By the time we got it going it was 0630hrs and by this time the tide was on the ebb. It was still raining so we left Pixie in the cabin and went to get the anchor up, having thoughtfully put the coffee on. All our efforts could not move the anchor which seemed to be glued fast to the bottom, even though we had the engine now running it did not appear to be helping one bit. Deciding that the propeller must be fouled, we gave up.

Returning to the cabin we found Pixie had amused herself while we were out of the way by pulling shells from a shell picture I had given to me in Singapore. The coffee had boiled over the burners and doused the flame so we were met by a conglomeration of coffee and kerosene, to say nothing of sea shells all over the place. Not the best way to start the day.

That afternoon Ah Sue from the workshop came and dived down and cleared the propeller of barnacles and then he and Bobby were able to move '*Sandpiper*' over, ready to come out of the water, while I was already ashore and gaily waved goodbye to such problems and was driven off to Ipoh.

I had three very enjoyable and relaxing days with Terry and her family. A bedroom all to myself with a huge bed and no fear of squashing a monkey or cat if I rolled over. Even more amazing was to see a real bathroom again, with a loo that flushed and a tub with hot and cold running water where I could lie and soak and try to work out how many weeks of drinking water I was relaxing in. I became very lazy and would get up after Gerald had gone to work and Terry had taken Quintin and Tristan to school. I would then roam around their lovely garden picking off dead flowers and pretending, for a while, it was mine. I would not have changed our boat for a house and garden at that time but it made a wonderful change. While I was there, their long-awaited Avon dinghy was delivered to the house, much to the boys' delight. The big box was opened and the dinghy blown up on the living room floor. On our return journey packing the car took some doing and we only just managed to get the last item stowed. All the shopping I had done had to be taken out of the bags and distributed in any space between the boys at the back with the outboards, or in the trunk with the dinghy.

'*Sandpiper*' was back in the water with her clean bottom. Bobby had apparently had quite a time after I left. It was dark by low tide so Bobby had to work all night with the help of two men from the workshop, by the light of gas lamps. It was the last day of the very high tide and if he did not get off the following morning he'd be stuck there for a month. He had chained Pixie on deck but she objected violently to the men helping to do the bottom and kept swinging down on her chain and making noises at them. This frightened the men so much they were unable to work. Bobby then took her in the cabin, attached her lead to the table and was happy to see she fell asleep almost at once. So Bobby went back to work. Next time he looked in at her she had decided to clear out the locker behind the seat and everything was strewn all over the cabin. Her biggest find was a roll of tissue with which she obviously had a lovely time unrolling and spreading it all over the cabin. Perhaps she was trying to cover up the fact she had also made a few more holes in the cushion covers.

The tank had not yet been finished and we still had not received the bill for our mattress. While waiting for these we went off to the Sembilan Islands after borrowing a coral anchor from the workshop. We needed a day with little wind to be able to anchor off the island so first went back to our now familiar Pankor Island where Bobby and Pixie could swim and I tried to. I preferred hunting for beautiful shells. A Sumatra hit us the third night and we were rolling around so much that all the things in our lockers sounded desperate to get out. At sunrise we got our anchor up and went over to Pankor village; little houses among the coconut palms and a calm anchorage. We got pushed around a bit in the wash of fishing boats going in and out; the fishermen were all friendly and would wave and call to Pixie who sat making faces at them.

We finally set foot on Pulau Rumbia on the 4th October, the Sembilan island that we had originally picked for Pixie. We had given up that idea but still wished to see it. Originally we thought if we tried to let Pixie go we would hang around for six months. All things considered it was fortunate we had not got the other monkeys we had been looking for in Port Kelang. In Lumut we had learned it was far too dangerous to go to those islands at that time of year, and even now we must wait for a calm day and keep our eye on *'Sandpiper'* to enable us to get out at the least sign of wind.

We now arrived on a clear calm day with so little wind that we had to use the engine. The island looked beautiful as we edged our way slowly in. The water was deep and now we could see why it was so dangerous, the rocks were too near for comfort when we anchored in 13 fathoms. The tide was low when we went ashore to explore, a nice coral sand beach with a few shells. Thick vegetation which would have made keeping track of monkeys rather difficult and we were only able to explore one side of the island, wanting to keep an eye on '*Sandpiper*' in case the wind returned. There was no sign of water but Pixie was finding plenty to eat: grass tips and a small vine, related to the passion fruit, with lots of small fruit on it, a brown-headed grass, the seeds of which tasted good and plenty of grasshoppers. Surprisingly we found a young pawpaw growing and a clump of lemon grass. The island was uninhabited and difficult to get to but certainly it was visited by humans. One hill had only secondary forest on it and parts were burnt. A pit containing old cans, modern man's visiting card. Also, a Chinese shrine with joss sticks in pots on the rocks. It certainly appeared it was visited more often than we had been led to believe. Pixie enjoyed exploring and we let her lead us round and up the hill behind the shrine. We did not go far, planning to come again the following day with our jungle boots and long pants. Before we left we shampooed ourselves in the sea where we came face to face with a large boxfish who appeared more surprised to see us than we it. We returned to '*Sandpiper*' before sunset, not wishing to stay the night so close to the island, the anchor came up easier than expected making us realise it would not have been any good with much of a wind. At first we tried anchoring between Rumba and Lalang where the chart showed shallow water but, finding nothing less than 30 fathoms, we went back to the mouth of Sung Perak. By then there was a strong and steady wind so with all sails up we raced along in the dark, the best sail we had had for a long time; a good end to a perfect day.

The next morning there were squalls and we waited for the weather to clear, leaving just after ten. Good sailing weather again but not what we wanted for another visit to Rumbia, but decided to give it a try anyway. We now had some exciting sailing between the kelongs: Malay fishing stakes which extended for about two miles. The fishermen live on their stakes by building platforms on top and small houses perched over the water. We thought it was rather amazing that we had managed to avoid them in the dark. Some men were adding new poles, standing in a small boat holding onto a very long pole; they chanted as they worked the pole down into the sea bed. Sailing up to Rumbia we saw the beach was no longer deserted, a fisherman had beached his boat and was busy cleaning it. Lowering the sails we started the engine before dropping the anchor. We had made a wise move for once as we found the wind was far too strong for safety and the rocks too near. Quickly but sadly we pulled our anchor up again and moved out. Within minutes a storm was on us, no rain but the wind blew its hardest and the huge waves threatened to engulf us. Our dinghy, tied behind, was being pulled out of the water like a huge fish on the end of a line. The noise of the engine coupled with the racket the wind was making was nerve-racking.

"Can't we stop the engine and put the sails up?" I shouted. "What? In this weather, they would be torn to ribbons," he yelled back. *Dumb me*, I had not thought of that. Poor Bob-tail did not like it one bit and sat in the cabin howling his head off. "Can't you stop him making that noise?" Bobby now shouted. "It will bring us bad luck." Strange what being at sea does. Bobby ridiculed people who believed in such things as bad luck. Superstitions were all rubbish. But that was on land.

This was a far cry from our lovely sail from Rumbia the evening before and I was not enjoying it one bit. Only Pixie was taking it all calmly. She was on the foredeck and looking quite unconcerned, just sitting on deck trying to take the shackle off the spare anchor, happy that we were otherwise occupied and not around to stop her. Because of the violent motion we appeared to be racing along. In fact, we were making very little headway, our engine not being strong enough. Once I got used to it all I went on deck and made my way to join Pixie, wrapping my arms and legs round the mast to stay put.

The strong winds continued for hours allowing us to make no headway. When finally the wind lost a little of its strength, we got the sails up and stopped the engine. It then started to be more fun and we again raced along. Seven hours after leaving Rumbia we thankfully dropped anchor in the shelter of Pangkor. A distance of just ten miles from our starting point that morning.

Pixie had gone down in the cabin before we anchored. Perhaps with the idea of making dinner she got out a packet of soup powder, finding it rather strong to eat she smeared it over the cushions and bulkheads. Before anchoring I switched on the depth sounder which fascinates her, she sat staring at it which I thought would keep her out of mischief for a bit. Unwisely I switched it off after we anchored but was still busy on deck. Naturally she thought something had gone wrong with it and she had better take it apart. We soon discovered what she was up to but not before she had time to unscrew the electric cable leading to the transducer.

Bob-tail was a very unhappy little cat the next day. He kept crying and following me around. I tried to understand what it was he was trying to tell me. In the end he gave up and did a big puddle on the carpet. Too late, Bobby grabbed him and put him in the cockpit. This made Pixie furious with Bobby for treating him in such a manner and she started screaming at Bobby and then she too wet the carpet. As usual it was our fault. We had covered Bob-tail's sand tray with a sail bag the evening before.

The weather returned to normal so we moved our anchorage and went ashore on Tk Siapu. Passing the rocks with the lighthouse on we saw a fishing boat wedged between the rocks. The men were bailing her out. A victim of the storm perhaps. We hoped they would manage to repair her between tides and re-float at high tide.

Our favourite beach looked different from before as it was now very low tide, still Pixie acted as if she remembered it. This time she was more interested in the trees than the rocks and she did not mind so much if we wandered farther away and looked for shells while she searched for food in the trees.

Returning to Lumut after nine days away was a little disappointing. Usually it was nice to get back to our familiar surroundings but now '*Whistler*' was anchored where we had always been, no reason why he should not of course, and we found out later that it was hardly his fault as he had dragged anchor. At the time we felt put out about it and anchored near him, then feeling we were too close had to move and anchored again. We went ashore only to find we could not go in the club, the old couple having taken it over and filled it with all their relations and children round Pixie's tree. We returned to '*Sandpiper*'. We felt things were really falling apart when Machteld arrived and told us she was leaving and flying back to Holland. We cheered up a little when she produced a nice pile of mail for us that she had collected from the post office. We were not happy for long. One letter was from our maid in Guyana giving us the sad news that Sixpence, a monkey we had taken from a small summer zoo in Wales and later to Guyana, had died in the zoo in Georgetown where we had left her feeling happy that she now had company, even if not of her own species. We had so hoped we might see her again when we got to Guyana.

Eagerly I had opened a letter from my parents only to find that they were very upset to learn how long it would take us to get to England. The old Mill House we had bought they said was deteriorating and needed living in. The garden was getting overgrown and they pointed out they were getting older and wanted to see us again soon. We felt shattered, they wanted us to either sell the boat or the house. We now realised that, unintentionally, we had put the burden of the house on them, we had not asked them to take responsibility of the house but they had done so. We had been under the impression that as the house had stood for hundreds of years it was good for a few more. We never realised it needed to be lived in. Apparently it had been spoilt and now needed to have a fire in the winter to stop its old bones getting damp and dry rot; how it could be both damp and dry we had no idea. We had bought the house as they so wanted us to settle down near them. At the time we had thought we would finally live in Spain as that would be near, but that too they did not like, and had stipulated to the house agents it must be within 20 miles of where they lived in Somerset. This was not near the sea which Bobby thought impossible but we went ahead and bought the house.

If we now went ahead and sold the house that would not make them happy as then they would know we certainly would not be coming to England. We still wanted to come to England if only we could find a way around the problem of quarantine for Pixie. It was the question of quarantine that loomed over us like a dark cloud. We tried to put it out of our minds in the hope something would change, like the laws in England. I had written dozens of letters while in Lumut to different people and organisations who might help. Everyone replied and were sympathetic but so far our problem remained unsolved but we were determined to keep trying.

Bobby had salt in his veins and the sea had been his life until we married. Even then, though we lived on land, we were always near water and he had work connected with it in some way or another. Now he had his own boat but so far we had not sailed it very far. We did not want to give it up almost before we had started and how could we with Pixie and Bob-tail? Why oh why did we always get ourselves in such muddles? Pondering on what to do for the best we came to the resolution that there was only one thing to do to keep us all reasonably happy. We would return to England that coming summer. I could go from Spain, or wherever, to visit if we still had not found a way to get the pets in. To be able to do this we would have to go through the Red Sea. I remembered the stories we had been told. All the shipping in the narrow sea, the reefs on which many a boat had been lost. The weather and the hostile shores frightened us but it was the only way. Sadly, we had to forget our dreams of sailing round the Cape and of seeing Guyana again but we could look forward to still more happy months living on and sailing '*Sandpiper*'. I just hoped in the coming months I would gain enough experience and knowledge to pull my weight when it came to it.

My cholera shot we found was out of date so I took myself off to Sitiawan to get my shot and my card stamped up to date. I left Bobby to fix the new water tank in place which was now finished and on board. How he was going to do it I could not imagine. The measurements were correct and it would fit nicely in the space allotted for it but we had failed to take into account that the mast was in the way. Another bit of brilliant planning on our part.

Arriving in Sitiawan I went straight to the market as I had been told the clinic there was the best place to get my cholera injection and health card stamped. I hunted round the market and could find nothing resembling a clinic. It started to rain, I gave up and went to the Indian provision shop where we usually purchased things not available in Lumut. I asked the shopkeeper about the clinic. His suggestion was that I go to one on the Ipho road. He thought it was the only one that would chop my card. "It is rather far to walk, would you like to borrow a bike?" he asked. *Well yes*, I thought, *that would be a bit of fun*. Hoping I did not sound too fussy, I requested it to be a bike without a crossbar. I like falling off without hunting myself. The shopkeeper disappeared and returned with a near new sturdy little blue bike which was just the thing. Off I went feeling very happy and the shopkeeper followed on his motorbike delivering newspapers and things on the way.

Each time he passed me on a stretch of road he pointed that it was farther along. This clinic was big enough not to miss and I had high hopes of getting what I had come for. Entering and explaining what I had come for, they told me to go to the one by the market I had first tried. I told them that one had completely disappeared. Patiently they explained exactly where it was in relation to the market and then added that it would not be open until that afternoon at two. Then they told me, when I had obtained the jab and chop on my card, I should return to them and the doctor would put his signature to the chop. I had never heard of the doctor and had no desire for his signature. I asked if I could do without that privilege as I had only borrowed the bike and could not keep it all day. No, they insisted, that was the way things had to be done. Back I went and returned the bike. I thanked him and told him what had happened and that I might need it again if still available.

Having done my shopping, I was now at a loose end, wandering round an emporium until that closed. I located a nice little Indian eating place and stuffed myself with rice and curry eaten with my fingers off a banana leaf. The food cost just one Malay dollar however much you eat, this the owner kept impressing on me as he tried to get me to take a third helping of everything. Not being used to eating a large meal in the middle of the day I now felt as if I could hardly move, but if I stayed he would start trying to fatten me up again. Leaving my bag of shopping with them I went off in search of the clinic. When the doors opened I was right there on the doorstep waiting to bound in and get my jab. Being first I was shown straight into the doctor's room who looked up expectantly at me, no doubt in hope I had some interesting complaint that he had read up on. When I told him what I wanted he told me he was not qualified to give injections. *What about one of the nurses?* I proffered. No. They could not either. By then other patients had drifted in and I just hoped they had nothing more serious than a cut finger or headache to be attended to. I tried to encourage him to widen his knowledge and just try and give me a jab. If he could not bring himself to do that I told him I would not really mind just as long as he pretended and just chopped my card. No, that too was out of the question, but being helpful suggested I go to the clinic on the Ipoh road, the one I had been to. I told him what they had said and he had a little think. He now said he would chop my card for me if I got a jab somewhere else first. "Where," I asked, "can I get a jab?"

"Well," he said, "there are plenty of private clinics." An orderly standing by then took a hand and said he would give me a lift to a private clinic if I had no transport. I agreed to this, expecting something on four wheels. We went out to the yard and there was his motorcycle, an unusually small one. I was not very keen but got on the back only to find my legs were too long. Hanging down they just touched the ground and there did not appear to be anything to rest my feet on. It was either designed not to take passengers or for a midget. The driver failed to give me any instructions as to what I might do with my legs so I just bent them backwards and clenched my toes to prevent my flip flops from falling off. With a roar from the engine we started off. I felt terrified as not having even been introduced to the driver I hardly liked to hug him too hard and thought I might be thrown off at any moment. Thankfully we arrived at the first place within a minute, it being little farther than across the road. I had noticed the building before, it appeared to be in the process of being demolished, with piles of wood and a lot of workmen. Closer inspection revealed a new stairway that looked safe. Up I went.

The place looked more stable on the second floor with a girl sitting at a desk. "Yes," she said, "the doctor will be able to give you a cholera shot but he is not in yet." I did not know if I wanted to laugh, scream or cry. Instead I calmly asked what time he was expected. She shrugged her shoulders. Back down I go to tell my driver and he suggested we find another clinic. Easy, we soon found one, it was closed. Off again, this time right out of the main town. I now had the feel of the thing we were riding on and was beginning to enjoy it, but my poor legs were longing to unbend and it was only a matter of time before they, or I, dropped off. Thankfully I saw what looked like another clinic and pointed it out, he thought it was a dentist. I did not really care but had to stretch my legs so insisted it was a clinic, which by good luck it turned out to be. I was the only patient but was given a card with the number three on it, indicating two were ahead of me so asked how long I might have to wait. She did not know, the doctor had not come in yet. My little motorbike driver was supposed to be on duty at the first clinic so of course I could not keep him out all afternoon. If he left me where we were I would have miles to walk back. We agreed to return to the first clinic which was only a short walk from his. Back up the stairs again where I was greeted happily with the information that the doctor had come in, and gone out again. I sat on the top of the stairs, the place only ran to one chair for the receptionist. Eventually a doctor arrived, gave me a cholera shot and signed my card, a bit of good luck as I would not have to return to the morning one just for a signature. At last I was getting somewhere, but not fast. I now had to return to the first to get the chop on my card. First they had to find a chop suitable for stamping my card. This took ten minutes and two men turning out every drawer they could open. Deciding one was just the job, my card was chopped and they charged one dollar for the pleasure. Same as my lunch. I told them I thought it was free. "Oh no, only the shot is free."

"But I just paid five dollars for the shot," I replied.

"Yes, but you went to a private clinic."

"I went," I said, "because you could not give me one here."

"No, I am not qualified." Mission completed and adventures over I collected my shopping from the eating house and returned to Lumut.

I was greeted with such a sight of devastation on board *'Sandpiper'* I just stood speechless. The cabin was a mess, tools all over the place, a large jagged hole had been cut in the bulkhead and the new tank lay at an angle the other side. All this I took in while my eyes were riveted on the pools of blood that liberally decorated the place. In the midst of all this stood Bobby, ashen-faced, with one foot wrapped in a large towel which had once been light pink and was now stained bright red with blood. "I cut my foot," he said weakly, and rather unnecessarily. "It does not hurt but the blood will not stop running out."

Averting my eyes from the blood-soaked towel lest I add to our troubles by fainting, I searched through the lockers for the safety harness we had bought in Singapore and not yet used. With this attached to the grab rail it made a good sling to told his foot up as he lay on the seat, so letting his blood, or what little of it that remained in his body, stop leaking all over the place. I then learned what had happened. As there was obviously no way to get the tank in position as things stood, he cut into the bulkhead so the tank could be got in round the mast. After that he figured it could be pushed back into position and the hole in the bulkhead repaired. Having cut the hole he then tried to lever the tank in position but dropped the sharp V-shaped edge of the tank on his foot, making a gash between his big toe and the next. At first he did not think it was too bad. After binding it up he went on working until he found he was stepping in pools of blood.

The bill for our mattress had now arrived. I went back ashore to pay the money and told Stewart what had happened. I was grateful when he said he would come the following morning and take Bobby to the hospital. Bobby, however, said he'd had enough of hospitals and refused to go. He was back working on the tank the next day which took another nine days to get in place, bedded down then panelled in front with wood planks and a valve fitted.

Meanwhile, he doctored his foot himself and looked very dashing hopping around in swim trunks and a sock on one foot to hold the bandage in place.

Penang was just as we had heard
our Seagull engine disappeared
with its loss we sailed away
to islands where the otters play

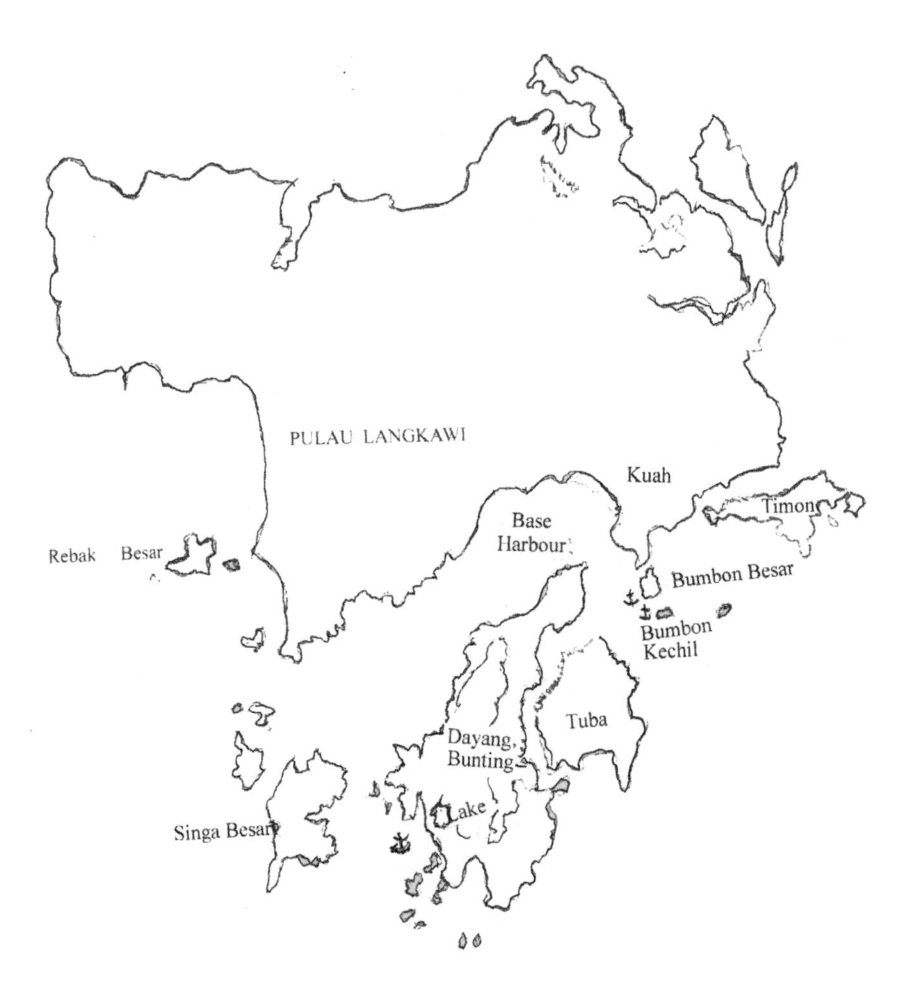

Some of the Langkawi Islands

CHAPTER TEN

LANGKAWI ISLANDS

We were off. Next stop Penang. Not only were we actually leaving Lumut but we were having a race, as arranged the evening before. Gerald, Terry and their boys thought they would go about halfway to Penang with us in *'Overdraft'*. *'TontineII'*, a trimaran which had arrived a few days previously, was also leaving for Penang and Ruth and Wah Ye were going along as extra crew.

Cruising rules were agreed – everyone leaving when they were ready to do so. I saw my chance at last of getting a photo of *'Sandpiper'* with sails up and actually sailing. Ruth agreed she would take a photo of us as they passed and in return I would take one of *'TontineII'*. This having been settled we set off in fine spirits. Doug, now alone, was the only one now remaining in Lumut.

Feeling sure the others would out-sail us, we got off to an early start. Passing *'Overdraft'* we waved to all the family on deck. We were not to see them again until many, many years had passed. We learned later that they had not sailed that day after all. The *'TontineII'* crew said they had to go shopping first but would soon catch us up. A good westerly wind sped us on our way, squalls built up around us but never hit us directly. We kept a sharp look out for '*TontineII*' in the hope she would pass us in good light for our photo session but, lo and behold, there was no sign of her. It was a good sail and Bobby was grinning and looking rather smug. "I don't think anyone is going to catch up with us now, and if this weather holds we should arrive in Penang about midnight," he said happily. I felt rather less jubilant, to win a race through virtue of having set off first I considered less important than having a nice photo of '*Sandpiper*' racing along as we were doing at that time. Ten minutes after Bobby's joyful words the wind dropped and we found ourselves becalmed. After that we had little or no wind until about four the following morning when a moderate wind sprung up for two hours, before it dropped again. There was still no sign of '*TontineII*' and we felt sure they must have used their engine and passed us in the night. Slowly we made our way towards Penang. The wind returned as we reached the coast but was dead ahead. At 2030hrs we gave up and anchored off Telok Temaayak for the night. After anchoring and tidying the sails Bobby suddenly got a dizzy spell when he bent down. I then felt I was about to faint. Had we got sunstroke we wondered. Then we remembered we had not eaten that day. A good meal put that right and we fell into our bunk. "I wish," I said drowsily, "we had not left Lumut so early. I so wanted a photo of '*Sandpiper*'."

"Never mind," Bobby consoled me. "We will get someone to take a photo before the end of this trip."

Next morning who should we see coming round the point but '*TontineII*'. We quickly got the anchor up and the sails all set and went out to meet her in a good light for our planned photo taking. We were not exactly bowling along but the wind filled all the sails nicely, As I stood on deck taking photos of them I could see Ruth doing the same for us. We had not only managed to win the race handsomely but had our photo taken as well.

We continued up to Chaucht Pier to anchor, quite near immigration. '*TontineII*' decided to anchor the other end. They certainly had picked a better anchorage but we did not fancy the long row to immigration they would have. We were near the ferry route, the water was just as dirty and oily as we had been warned. We were also anxious about our dinghy and outboard engine as we had heard more reports about the prevalent thieves there. *'Edna Marie'* from Australia was the only other boat to share our anchorage. Immigration were on the ball coming alongside as we anchored and taking our passports. Bobby was told to report to the office as soon as possible, making it sound very urgent.

After bandaging his foot which was still not completely healed and blowing up the dinghy, Bobby went ashore armed with a length of chain with which to secure the dinghy to the dock. We were taking no chances here. After seeing immigration the customs office was closed so that was put off until the next day.

Bobby had a lot of fun the following morning. On going ashore he was pleased to find customs had now opened its doors. He was rather less pleased to find they were only open to tell him he would have to go over to the mainland on the ferry. From there he was told it was just a mile to walk to customs. This was fine but he found it was more like three miles than one, and on arrival told he needed to have forms. That was OK until he was told to get them he had to take the ferry over to Penang where he could buy them at any stationary shop. She said it in such a happy manner he thought she must be joking, until she returned to her desk and he realised she was not kidding. The long walk to the ferry and then on arrival back in Penang he managed to locate the needed forms. Back again to the ferry, his injured foot now throbbing, he limped along to the customs which he felt they must have moved even farther away than it was on his first visit. Here he saw the same girl as before who was evidently new to the job. She now requested the name of his agent. Bobby carefully explained he just had a yacht and had no agent, nor did he have any intention of engaging one. She looked thoughtful, she had not handled such a case before, in spite of all the other yachts that go to Penang. She sought advice from a co-worker. The forms that Bobby had taken so much time and trouble to obtain were not necessary! Tired and fed up with it all Bobby got his clearance at the same time. On his way back to *'Sandpiper'* he met the crew from *'TontineII'* also looking a little glum. They were in trouble with the immigration authorities for not anchoring in the correct place.

Just before Bobby returned from his ordeal, I started to have my own little bit of excitement when a squall blew up and we started dragging anchor and heading fast to plough into *'Edna Marie'*. Just my luck with only one boat any place near us and it has to be right in our way. No point in trying to get the anchor up so I started letting more rope out without the slightest hope it would help matters, but the only thing I could think of that I could try. Fortunately, Bobby returned to take over. We then spent a miserable hour on deck in pouring rain trying to get the anchor up and re-anchor, and finding the engine just would not work. Bobby then got out another anchor and rowed off with it in the dinghy to drop it.

In spite of having our clearance and not liking our anchorage we had to stay a few more days in Penang. Bobby had taken my watch to a repair shop as it had played dead after I dropped it. We now fully agreed with Eric who had told us in Lumut about Penang being dirty and full of thieves. We moved our Seagull engine on the cockpit rail so that it was opposite the companionway and in sight from our bunk and all the cabin. Just for good measure it was then secured with a chain and padlock. At night we took the dinghy on deck.

A few days later with our shopping complete and having picked up my now working watch, we made plans to leave the following afternoon with the tide. A squall hit in the night and at three Bobby got up to check the anchor. All was well and the dinghy and Seagull were still on board. We then all woke again at five, why, we were not quite sure; Pixie was sitting up and looking forward and we thought she had woken us. To make sure nothing was amiss Bobby again went on deck. I, only partially awake to start with, was just dropping off to sleep. A shout from Bobby made me almost wake up. "The Seagull engine has gone," I heard his shout. Half-asleep I answered, "I know," as if it was a thing of little importance. Realising I was not dreaming and just what it was Bobby had said I sat up, I could see right through the cabin to the cockpit and there in the moonlight was the rail that should have had the Seagull chained to it but was now empty. Now wide awake and very mad we scanned the water in hope of seeing the boat that contained the thieves and our outboard motor.

Nothing moved, the sea was flat, not a ripple in sight. No boats in the water near us and all quiet ashore. "Well that's that," said Bobby, "we will not see our engine again." I thought he should report our loss to the police, we had time, not wishing to leave until the tide changed at one in the afternoon. Bobby thought it would be a waste of time but reluctantly agreed. After an early breakfast, he rowed ashore to the police station. It was two in the afternoon before he returned. To start with there was no English-speaking policeman to take his report. When one did arrive he wanted the story repeated several times. We had found out how it had been taken, two half links of chain we had round the engine were on the deck, having been cut with large wire cutters. These together with the Seagull manual, which gave the engine number, Bobby showed the police, suggesting that they keep the number and check it out with all such engines they see. The police then decided they should come in force and take a look at the scene of the crime. They were led to our dinghy which was met with great disapproval, they wanted something a little more solid looking. They voted to wait for the launch to bring them out to us. They arrived, stood and stared at the now empty rail and we pointed out the exact spot on deck where we had picked up the cut links. Satisfied they had now seen all there was to see they departed, much to Pixie's relief. She had been jumping up and down on deck making rude noises at them. Bobby had been right, it was a waste of time and we had then missed the tide. Though they took our next address and later, while in Sri Lanka, Bobby wrote to them asking if they had found our Seagull, we never heard another word from them.

Before leaving the following day, Bobby had to use the cutlass to chop away what looked like a whole banana plantation, complete with bananas, that had entwined itself around our anchor rope. As we worked on freeing the anchor a dead rat floated past and a ton or so of garbage. We now had to wait for the tide as we found that our engine would only go in reverse gear, something having happened to the gear box and forward gear. Penang was one place we were not sorry to leave. The Langkawi Islands now beckoned, a beautiful, mostly uninhabited group of islands.

Langkawi Island itself has a small town, a rest house and hotel, both of which we had visited in former years but then had only been able to admire the other islands from a distance. To be able to sail among them would be much more satisfactory. We experienced a heavy sea and swell, though the wind was moderate, so did two-hour watches. During the daylight hours the sun would burn me; I would have to cover up with a short kaftan-type dress I called my angel dress that I had made out of white sheeting. At night we both would add a lot more clothes as the temperature dropped considerably. At dawn the islands lay ahead; magical islands that changed shapes as our position in relation to them changed as we tacked back and forth. For the most part the islands took on the appearance of prehistoric monsters stretched out on the water.

We headed for Pulau Dayang Bunting. We saw from the chart it had a freshwater lake and longed to bathe our salt-encrusted bodies in the fresh water. Dropping our anchor off Dayang Bunting in perfectly calm and crystal-clear water. Having had very little sleep the night before we postponed going ashore. After tidying up the peanut shells Pixie had covered the cabin with we sat on deck, Pixie and Bob-tail between us, wrapping ourselves in contentment. Nobody we thought could be enjoying a better view than we had and to add to it, for a little while, we had the company of a school of dolphins playing in the water.

The next nine days were idyllic. The first day the wind blew strong over the tops of the hills but there was no swell in the bay. Even the fact that we had emptied the coffee grounds from our coffee pot, and then left the pot on the cabin top where it had blown overboard could not dampen our spirits. The setting was just too beautiful to be sad in.

Most of the islands were uninhabited and unexplored by virtue of the fact that it's not possible to land on them. They rise up from the sea like miniature mountains and have no beach. Dayang Bunting differs in so much that it boasted a couple of small beaches on which one could land a dinghy at low tide. We explored the larger of the two beaches first and to our delight found a cave. I crawled in after Pixie. I was very surprised that she wanted to enter but enter she did as though this was an everyday occurrence. The cave opened out and we found ourselves amongst stalactites, with one large stalagmite in the centre. Pixie was as fascinated as we were and we all explored in awed silence. When we did speak we never raised our voices above a whisper. We felt we had entered a holy place. After exploring Pixie sat herself atop of the stalagmite meditating. Higher up was another opening and the sunlight poured down into the cave. Looking out we could see the sky and trees and *'Sandpiper'* at anchor.

On leaving our cave we found the tide was now lower and that the smaller beach would be uncovered so rowed over to investigate. The moment the dinghy touch the beach Pixie jumped out and headed straight for the rocks and started to climb. Had she read our thoughts or had she sensed or smelt the fresh water? She was going up the way we had decided on to get to the freshwater lake. I had put my running shoes in the dinghy to wear for climbing but Pixie dragged me off before I had time to put them on. She led the way at first but the rocks were easier for us to climb than for her as the spaces between suitable hand holes were a bit far apart for her. In such places we had to go ahead and then hold her chain. Giving it a couple of tugs to make sure we held it firmly, she would then, like a mountain climber, climb up hand over hand on the chain, her feet finding toe holes on the rock face. Once at the top we had our first view of the lake. It lay there large and clear, surrounded by tree-covered hills. A perfect spot and we had it all to ourselves. Making our way down to the lake we fancied we heard some movement in the bush. We turned in the direction we thought we heard the noise and sure enough we saw a face. A small face. A male monkey was looking at us. Pixie saw him too, stopped and pulled faces at him but made no noise. She then continued on her way and the lone monkey disappeared. At the lake we stripped off and had a good bath and shampoo. Pixie liked washing but we could not get her to swim in the lake. The lone monkey came back to stare at us several times and we had hopes that he would join us. Was he the answer to our prayers. Was this the spot that could become Pixie's home with a ready mate? He did not join us and Pixie showed no interesting in trying to follow him. She was polite and pulled friendly faces at him but left it to him to join us only if he wanted to.

The next day we had to wait until later in the afternoon for our beach to be uncovered for another excursion ashore. This time we took piles of washing to do in the lake and a bag of peanuts with which we hoped to entice the monkey we had seen to make friends with us, or rather Pixie. We neither saw nor heard the monkey on our way to the lake.

I was sitting in the water doing my washing, Bobby was sitting nearby on the bank and Pixie was on look-out up a tree. Suddenly there was a big splash in the water near me. I thought either Bobby had thrown a stone in the water or that Pixie had taken a dive. Pixie was still in her tree and Bobby said he thought I had made the splash. We then heard another splash just the other side of a rock then a chattering noise. We looked but saw nothing, wondering if it was the monkey trying to make friends. The chattering stopped. The next time we heard it we also saw a head sticking up, looking at us from the middle of the lake. Then satisfied that we had seen him he dived down and was seen no more. Was it our monkey friend? I rather doubted it, its language and behaviour did not quite fit, but we had certainly seen a monkey and only a monkey on our first visit. We talked it over, still undecided. We had seen the head but it was too far away to see just what it was. We knew Pixie could swim underwater so it could have been the monkey. When we left we spread the peanuts on a rock and returned to the beach.

How lucky we were to find such a beautiful place, unspoilt by any signs of garbage. Pixie, however, managed to find a plastic comb.

Surrounded by all these beautiful things of nature, to her the comb was the most interesting and she refused to be parted from it. We thought when we left the lake to climb down the rocks she would discard it. No way, she just transferred it from her hands to her mouth. Back on the beach we looked in some more caves. They were not as deep as the ones we found on the first day but had multicoloured rocks which put me in mind of the raku pottery I had been experimenting with just before leaving Singapore.

The next day we took the water containers ashore to fill at the lake. We had a long length of rope so Bobby could haul them when full, up the rocks and down the other side. Our offerings of peanuts lay as we had left them and no sign of Mr Monkey. While bathing in the lake several herons flew over. This time Pixie enjoyed a long swim after her shampoo, staying in the water long after we came out. Leaving us by the lake Bobby started carrying back the water containers. He returned very excited, telling us to hurry. He had seen seals on the beach. "Seals," I said, "surely not."

"No," he agreed. "Not seals, the other things: otters."

Pixie not being excited by this news refused to hurry, so leaving her to follow with Bobby I climbed quickly back to the beach and was rewarded by the sight of eight otters. They soon saw me and all went back into the sea. Otters are very inquisitive little people and all popped their heads up to take another look at me. They were delightful and of course I then realised that it had not been the monkey we had seen in the lake but an otter. They were as fascinated by me as I was by them and kept popping up in the water to take another look at me before swimming off to the other beach. I hurried along trying to keep up with them as they swam. Bobby and Pixie were now on the beach and Pixie saw the otters but did not like me going off after them and started to call. Before I got to the other beach they had been and gone. I followed their tracks which were rather dog-like. They had been playing round a large pile of mixed shells. We had investigated these shells the first day wondering why there were so few shells on the beach yet with this pile just in one spot. Had the otters left them in this neat pile after making a meal of the occupants? Or had they, like us, just been looking at them?

We never tired of going ashore and never had a dull moment on Dayang Bunting. One late afternoon we had a little more excitement than we had bargained for. I often took my camera ashore but this time it was luckily left behind. It was the first time we had surf on the beach, the sea just tossed us ashore. We took our usual bath in the lake and Bobby filled the containers. Back on the beach we saw the breakers were now very big. Pixie was none too keen to get in the dinghy. The sun was going down so we put everything in the dinghy pushed it out and made Pixie jump in. Too late, a breaker caught us and the next thing I knew I was rolling around under water in the sand, still clinging to Pixie's chain, terrified she would get it caught underwater. A very long second passed before I heard Bobby calling, "Are you OK?" then I was on the beach, Pixie ahead of me. I let go of her chain and she rushed up and sat on top of a rock as if afraid the sea was on her tail. It was some time before we could persuade her to come down. Meanwhile, we searched the beach for our wash kit etc. Bobby had made a dash for the oars and had them and the water container but the length of rope was gone as was most of our wash kit. We tried again but Pixie hesitated and the dinghy filled with water. Third time lucky. Pixie now realised the importance of jumping in at the correct time and we made it. Our freshwater bath had been a waste of time. Our hair and Pixie's fur was full of sand and salt. We had to take a wash down in sea water on deck.

Next morning, after sitting on deck watching about a dozen dolphins playing in the water, we went ashore to hunt for our lost things. Bobby particularly hoped to retrieve the lost rope. We found nothing.

There was another beach farther along, out of sight of our anchorage. From this beach we found another way to the lake where boats could take tourists. Here there was a well-defined path so no climbing was necessary. In what might have been difficult parts, wooden steps had been built. We were glad there were no tourists about the whole time we were in Langkawi and we had it all to ourselves. It was an interesting walk with squirrels and some really lovely butterflies. Pixie found a number of tasty insects. She did not eat just anything, many she did not even try, instinct perhaps telling her they were not for eating. Her biggest find was a fungus that took her fancy, perhaps owing to its odd shape. She never tried to eat it but continued her walk holding it in her mouth. It certainly looked more attractive that the plastic comb she had done the same with some days before. The walk to the lake was enjoyable but it ended at a part of the lake we had not been able to see before and turned out to be a big disappointment. At one time a floating pontoon or pier had been placed there. Now it was all broken and sunk and all the oil drums that had kept it afloat were rusting away. The water lay still and stagnant, not even good enough to paddle in, let alone wash or drink. We stayed for a while watching the birdlife and giving the insect life a good supply of our blood and then left for the beach. Here we found some fishing boats and Malay men and women having a meal, cooking their rice on a fire on the beach. Pixie sat down on a rock at a little distance and watched them and they her. The meal over, they dug holes in the sand which filled with water and then they started to wash themselves. Pixie watched all this for a while and then went to the edge of the sea and sat in shallow water. The men were now washing their heads and Pixie scratched hers making it wet in the process. Everyone laughed, thinking she was copying them. Continuing to return each day, sometimes twice a day depending on the tide, to our part of the lake over the rocks, we soon regarded it as our own private place, so were rather startled one day while bathing to hear voices. Quickly we came out of the water and got some clothes on. Just in time as a guide appeared at the top of the cliff. We asked him to give us a few minutes while we attached Pixie to her chain and moved a bit farther along the bank. We were not disturbed for long as only the guide and one Chinese man made it to the lake and took a quick dip in the water. Bobby going down with the water container met two other members of the party, two women: one American the other English. Both had travelled from Hong Kong. Unfortunately, they had hired the boat to take them to the lake, not realising they would have to do any climbing, so had no footwear which they felt they needed to make the climb. We felt sorry that they had missed seeing such a lovely area just because they had not been told what to expect. They said they were finding it very difficult to find out about anything. They had become a little cautious after having heard of an English doctor who had joined a tour at one place where there were slopes they had to slide down. Sadly no one thought to tell the doctor the last slope ended in a sheer drop. He slid down, went over the edge and was killed on the rocks below.

After nine wonderful days we reluctantly decided we must now go over to the main island to the village at Kuah to replenish our now depleted stock of fresh food. That morning we made our last trip ashore. Bobby had always done all the rowing on previous trips, this time I said I would row back. I felt that I was rowing reasonably fast but *'Sandpiper'* did not appear to be getting any nearer. I made a silly remark that *'Sandpiper'* was farther out and that Bob-tail must have moved her. Finally back on board we got the sails ready and then started the engine to charge the batteries and went down into the cabin. We had been on board less than an hour when Bobby happened to stand up in the companionway and look out. "Quick," he yelled, "we are almost ashore."

I jumped up hearing the urgency in his voice though his words did not make sense. Horrors, he was making sense, we were only about thirty feet from what remained of our little beach we had left so recently. No time to ponder how this could have happened, we quickly hoisted the sails we had so very fortunately got ready earlier. The engine was still running but that would only help if we wished to go in reverse. It would not stay in gear either as you had to have a stick to hold the gear lever in place. That of course had disappeared. There was just enough breeze and we swung around just in the nick of time, we were almost in touching distance of the rocks.

We must have pleased the spirits of the island as according to the chart we should have run aground.

At least we were not delayed by having to pull the anchor up. It had not dragged as we at first thought. It was gone! Up came the rope with nothing on the end of it. Our best anchor – 38lb CQR – lost with ten fathoms of chain. I had been right in thinking *'Sandpiper'* had moved farther out when I was rowing. Then the tide turned and she came back in. We did wonder if, while ashore, a fishing boat had come along and taken our anchor but on second thoughts we decided that was highly unlikely, knowing we were ashore and that the tide was on the turn, they would hardly have risked our boat going on the rocks just for the sake of an anchor. The only logical answer was that the shackle pin had worked its way out. Our fault again, we should have wired the pin and buoyed the anchor. We now only had a thirty pound anchor and a small fifteen pound one. Still all told we were lucky to still have a boat to need them.

That afternoon we anchored off Kuah. A pleasure boat came round us from the *'Dari Laut'*, a new floating hotel farther along from us. They were taking a lot of photos of Pixie. We also saw *'TontineII'* anchored near them but without her crew who had returned to Singapore to bring out another boat. A charming Indian girl, Chandra, came alongside later and invited us to a meal on *'Dari Laut'*. We declined at first as we felt they might not wish to include Pixie and also the menu might be all fish or something we could not eat. She left and later returned saying she had been told an offer of a freshwater shower before the meal would change our minds. Having ascertained that Pixie was also welcome and that they had plenty of vegetarian dishes, we gladly accepted. First though we would do our shopping, and then move our boat nearer to them as they felt it might be too far for us to row.

Pixie we now found had a small tick on her eyelid, right on the edge. She is usually very good at letting us attend any cut or injury she has, but the eye is a sensitive spot, and the tick was very small. Try as we might we could not remove it. After a couple of days it grew to pea size and fell off. It was quite a time for creepy crawlies. Unwrapping a piece of cheese we found a family of maggots had taken residence on the cloth. We soaked the cheese in sea water, remove the maggots and boiled the cloth. When the cloth was dry wrapped it all up again after soaking the cloth in vinegar. We also started noticing the odd cockroach, very unwelcome visitors. Useless to try and catch them and ferry them ashore, we just had to hope they would not multiply too fast.

Going ashore at Kuah could not compare with the island we had just left but Pixie enjoyed it with lots of children to watch playing, water buffaloes and goats, and soft mud which even she sank in. Shopping left a lot to be desired. We were unable to replace the coffee pot that had gone overboard or the dust pan that had gone the same way. In the end we had to buy a tea kettle to serve as a coffee pot which was maddening as there had been a kettle on board which, having no use for, we had given away to the old Chinese couple in Lumut. I never grew to love that kettle. All the coffee grounds would block up the bendy spout so we would have to prod around with a bit of wire to get our coffee. Later I joyfully gave it away in Sri Lanka and felt I never deserved the delighted thanks I got. We found no eggs, and vegetables were few and rather less than fresh but quite expensive. On the plus side we were able to get bottles of wild honey. We stayed a week anchored off the village. All my fault as, for some reason, I fell sick, got pains and fainted. We could only conclude there was something on that island that affected me. Some years before, while living in Malaysia, we had gone to that island for a short holiday. I had been fine but on arrival was taken ill and even had to spend a day in hospital. I only recovered fully when we left.

That first day, after getting what stores we could, we anchored near *'Dari Laut'*, which at that time was not quite completed. The plan they had was to bring out German tourists that wished to go fishing. The charming Indian girl Chandra visited and we arranged to visit them that evening. Here we thoroughly enjoyed ourselves. First we luxuriated in the beautiful bathroom with all mod cons and a whole shelf of shampoos etc. until we looked quite civilised enough to grace their dining table. Pixie did not join us in the bathroom or dining room. We chained her to the pontoon where she could get up the steps on to the deck where we thought she could do no damage. We enjoyed good company and food. On returning to Pixie, we found she had busied herself by scraping off the freshly painted white paint that was not quite dry, getting it all over her mouth.

Another week was spent anchored off Bumbon Besar; Pixie liked the island as we did but we did not always have the beach to ourselves. Kevin and Berte, who were working on the *'Dari Laut'*, became welcome and regular visitors to *'Sandpiper'*. Kevin gave us a lot of help by working on our engine. He confirmed that the forward gear had gone but he straightened the lever so it no longer needed a bit of wood to hold it in position, a bit of luck as we were running out of bits of wood as, given half a chance, Pixie would take them to toss overboard. Kevin also dived down and cleared our propeller of barnacles which we hoped might make it whizz round a bit more proficiently.

Apart from enjoying ourselves we were still doing a number of hours of work on *'Sandpiper'* each day, as we had continued to do since leaving Lumut, apart from when we were at sea. Varnishing and painting became a daily routine. Keeping the boat generally clean and tidy took up more time than I expected in such a small place. Sand from Bob-tail's tray and food tossed around by Pixie did not help. I often added some way or another to the confusion. One morning I opened a can of molasses, in levering the top, it came off with a bang, splattering all over Bobby, the deckhead and table. It was a nasty mess to clear up but I had a laugh as it had missed me completely.

Kevin suggested we go to Paya Island where the best snorkelling was to be had. Not at that time possessing any snorkel or masks he kindly lent us two sets and flippers. Paya Island is not part of the Langkawi group but a little farther south on the way back to Penang. We set off with a light breeze which died away to nothing after about one hour. From then on we had to be content with short bursts of light wind. An army helicopter came and flew round us. We waved to show we were alive and well. It was after dark before we made the island. A group of three islands, Paya being the largest, but still only a narrow strip of an island looking singularly uninteresting but OK as it was the snorkelling we had come for. We first anchored almost at touching distance of the island, but then feeling we were too near, anchored in seventeen fathoms having no wind to go farther round. As soon as we anchored the wind blew up but it came from the island so posed no threat.

Bobby got up in the night as we were rolling badly and found we had dragged anchor so far the island was now out of sight. He was able to re-anchor but we felt a bit put out that after all our trouble to get to the island it had now vanished from sight. We were even less happy when we had to spend three whole hours getting the anchor back up by using the mast winch. By then we had a very heavy swell and were way off course so sadly gave up the idea of our visit to Paya, and headed back to the Langkawi Islands. After heavy seas and strong winds we hit a dead calm as we made the entrance to the islands, so dropped anchor off Bumbon Kechil. The day was spent cleaning up the cabin until the wind came back in the afternoon and we were able to sail over and anchor again near *'Dari Laut'* and return the gear we had borrowed and not used.

A fishing boat hailed us and came near asking for a cigarette. I had just been wondering what to give Bob-tail to eat so we passed a packet of *cigs* over in the small bailer and asked for a few fish in return. They must have thought we wanted to feed a tiger rather than a small cat. The bailer came back piled high. Bobby set to work to sort the fish out. And found not only a load of fish but also a lot of squids. Strangely, we had been talking about squibs only a few days before as apparently the crew of the *'Dari Laut'* liked eating them after first removing the ink. One man said he liked them cooked in the ink. Hopefully Bobby showed the bailer full of fish to Bob-tail, thinking he might like to eat them raw. Bob-tail gave them a sniff and walked away. Bobby prodded the squibs around and concluded he had no idea what the ink would look like or how to remove it. He doubted Bob-tail would eat them anyway, whatever he did with them. He dumped them all in the pot reserved for such things and boiled them. The result was a mass of rubbery stuff in black water.

"Well, I can't see anyone wanting to eat that," he said and set it aside to cook the fish. To our amazement our fussy little cat thought squib was the tastiest thing he had ever had and ate with gusto, demanding more to be put on his plate. When the fish was also done it was left in the pan and put on the cabin top, alongside the remaining squib. He then started on some of the fish. Even so there was so much of both he had little chance of finishing it before it went bad.

Pixie got up early the next morning and took herself on deck to see what she could find to play with before we put in an appearance. It was plain she had done something wrong when we came on deck as she put on her guilty look and ran screaming to me. We soon discovered that she had done. The pot of fish and pot of squib had been turned upside down on the cabin top. The squib ink ran all over the top and down the nice white sides in purple coloured riverlets.

The *'Dari Laut'* speedboat gave Bobby a lift to the market where he was able to buy all the vegetables he could find and even found some eggs. We moved back to Bumbon Kechil which gave us more privacy on the beach with Pixie. While Pixie and I were on the rocks we heard the now familiar squeaking in the water. Six otter heads popped up to look at us. Too shy to come very near they must like to be noticed as they always called to attract attention. Perhaps they are like us and when they see a strange animal, they like to attract the others' attention to the sight. Next morning, while still on board, we heard them, and watched as they went ashore to play. They trooped off a little way in the bush and then rolled around in the sand, playing like puppies. Later they were out of sight but we heard them squeaking from the caves. For the first time Pixie picked up a sea cucumber, it made her hands sticky and she did not like it and held her hand out to be cleaned.

The time had come for us to leave Malaysia for Phuket, Thailand, where we planned to stock up on lots of nice fresh fruits, cashew nuts and rice. Before leaving for good we wanted to spend just a few more days back on Pulau Dayang Bunting. Our little beach, the rocks, caves and the lake which we felt was our own special spot. After the first day the weather changed for the worse and we had both our anchors out, wishing we had not lost the bigger one. We managed to get ashore again on the second day but it was very windy and a hard row. Pixie was not so lively and then did not want to go in for her swim in the lake. Instead she put her head on the ground with her bottom up in the air as if she wanted it washed. It was not dirty but I noticed a small deep hole in her bottom that look suspiciously like one she had in Singapore in which we had found maggots. A fly must have laid its eggs in a tiny scratch. We returned to *'Sandpiper'* where I still had the powder we had before to put in the hole to kill the maggots. The following day the wind howled and Pixie stayed mostly in bed where I repeatedly washed her bottom in Dettol and put powder in the hole until all the maggots dropped out dead.

By the fourth day we were still getting heavy seas and strong gusts of wind. Our anchorage off our favourite island was no longer enjoyable. We decided to leave.

Bobby had just finished getting the sails ready when a police boat came alongside and requested us to leave as soon as possible. Two Thai pirate boats were in the area and they hoped to trap them just off our island.

Being ready to sail and not wishing to get mixed up in a shooting affair we set sail at once.

We made our first long sea voyage
Really quite a feat
It might have been more fun though
if we'd had more to eat

CHAPTER ELEVEN
A THOUSAND MILES

Sailing away from the Langkawi Islands, rain descended obscuring the island from view. The rain did not last long but the wind died a little for the next hour, before picking up to push us along nicely at about five knots. During the night the wind freshened to moderate gale force and we had to reef the mainsail. A jolly bit of exercise in the dark. The Bunting Islands were a known stronghold of the pirates, rather an exciting place I thought. The captain makes the decisions I was reminded, and that we did not need that sort of excitement, we would not want to meet up with them in the dark. We gave the islands a wide berth and saw no boats of any kind.

Perhaps the wind thought it a waste of time to blow just for us, by the following afternoon it died away to nothing. We had estimated we would arrive in Phuket early the next morning, now we did little more than drift off course. Bobby's sights next day put us thirty miles off course and still we had very little wind and at times dead calm; the currents in that area were strong and erratic. Thankfully the wind returned after dark and we were able to set the steering vane.

Pixie was still not herself and eating very little, then started vomiting. Bob-tail was being very sweet to her and let her lie down using him for a pillow.

The third day found us just off Phuket with the wind all over the place, how nice it would be to have the benefit of an engine. Slowly we tacked back and forth and made the big buoy Ao Pa Tong. There we picked up a kindly wind that drove us straight into the bay before it petered out. We dropped anchor in fifteen feet. We were far from the shore in this very large bay with a heavy swell and no other yachts. We hoisted our Thai courtesy flag and the yellow quarantine flag and hoped the emigration would come out to us.

Onshore we could make out a hotel and beach huts with a lot of people. Not our sort of place really, but we were still eager to get ashore and stock up on all the fruits and nuts we had heard so much about. Pixie picked up once we were anchored and got the Vim out and spread it all over the floor of the cabin and then started eating it. It did her good, must have cleaned her out as by next day she was completely well.

It was Bob-tail now that was in trouble, he had dug out my little curry leaf tree I had in a pot, got earth all over the place and chewed off the root. My small attempts at gardening on the boat were always doomed to failure. All told it was not a happy day, the wind was stronger than ever and we dragged anchor. Nobody came near us and we could not row ashore in our inflatable dinghy in such a strong wind. Our fresh food was down to a few small onions and a squash. By the third day we had given up all hope of getting ashore, instead we tried to get the anchor up and move on. That too proved impossible, the wind was far too strong.

Seeing a fishing boat pass within hailing distance with a cargo of what looked like tourists. We jumped up and down on deck, yelling until we drew their attention. Waving money we asked in sign language to be taken ashore. It worked, we thought. The person in charge indicated that he had to take his passengers round to the next bay and would then return for us. We must have read his signs wrong, we waited and waited, the boat never returned.

The following day was the same, the anchor refused to come up and not a single boat came near us. I made bread and realised our flour too was soon going to run out. Having not yet given up all hope I started making the Sri Lanka flag. It was the most attractive flag I had made and took a lot of work with the lion in the middle brandishing his carving knife, so it helped take my mind off the fact that as things stood it looked as if we might never leave the bay and might sit there starving to death. Our Thai flag was already frayed at the ends due to the strong wind and had wrapped itself round the stay as if it intended to remain there for ever.

Waking on the fifth morning something felt strange, all was silent. The wind had left us. Bobby bounded up on deck and started pulling up the anchor. This time up it came, just before the wind returned, allowing us to sail out of the bay. We were happy, happy that is except that we had been unable to get ashore for the food we so badly needed. We would not actually starve, we still had a lot of dried pulses on board, plus the dreaded canned food. We always had a plastic dustbin of rice but thinking we would get better and cheaper rice in Thailand we also had let that run low. "Don't worry," said Bobby, "sailors in the past never saw fresh food on long voyages."

"I know that, but they all got scurvy and I just hate to think of all my teeth dropping out and what about Pixie?" I replied.

In truth I felt we could go for a long time on what we had on board but did worry for Pixie. We had always made sure she had some fresh food every day. We did have mung beans and could sprout them but Pixie had always refused them, perhaps because she had other things she preferred, as after a few days she willing ate some each day.

We took a look at the next bay, wondering if we could anchor there and get ashore but that looked no better with the wind blowing strongly down from the mountains and there was not a building, road, or any kind of life to be seen. We felt it wiser to carry on to Sri Lanka without delay. It was now the ninth of December and we hoped we would arrive before Christmas or we would end up drinking everyone's health in water or coffee. The frayed Thai flag still flew defiantly from the stay. The string had snapped so we had no way of getting it down. We set the steering vane and sailed on for a while until the clamps holding the blocks for the leading lines snapped in half. I steered while Bobby drilled another hole, reset the blocks and fixed it all up again.

I felt excited as I took my sewing up on deck, this was our first long sea voyage. We would no longer have the land close by. I sat staring out to sea wondering why it did not look more dangerous. A noise made me glance at Pixie, just in time; I had placed my box of sewing things in a bucket which in turn was on a coiled rope. Pixie had managed to pull the end of the rope overturning the bucket and now all the sewing thing were spread all around. I made a grab for them. There were so many things that Pixie was not sure which to make off with, finally settling for a tube of glue to toss in the sea. I even got that back as it caught in her safety net. She was not too upset as she had managed to keep a small pin. My watch that night was midnight to four. I saw nothing and the vane did all the steering; it was a good feeling being alone on deck as we sailed steadily along. I alone was awake while all the world slumbered. By three I was hardly awake and started looking forward to the end of my watch. The clock chimes every half an hour, the length between chimes seemed very long. *Surely*, I thought, *I must have not heard the seven bells for three thirty, or perhaps the clock has stopped.* I was just about to stick my head down and take a look when the wind changed, we jibed, the boom crashing over, the clock chimed seven and Bobby rushed up on deck.

We got her back on course and reefed the main. I felt mad at myself for not noticing the wind had changed and mad at the wind for picking the time when I felt sleepy. I punished myself by not calling Bobby back until four thirty. Feeling very cold and tired by then, I wrapped up in all the blankets with Pixie and Bob-tail and fell into a sound sleep.

After the first night, being well out of the shipping lanes, we felt it not necessary to keep watches and left the steering to our Aries vane. If a squall hit during the night, we would get up. Squalls were the most bother and dangerous during that trip.

Heavy swells made the boat roll badly. Any movement on my part was a bit of a liability. I was never sure if I was coming or going. Washing the dishes might be dull work on land but at sea it took several times longer on deck and quite a bit of skill as the bowl of water slithered from one side to the next and then splashed up into my face. It was either fun or frustrating, depending on the mood at the moment as pans and plates along with the odd fork that had been washed got mixed up with the ones yet to be washed. When all was done and I would toss the water back in the sea, as often as not there would be a glint of metal, another fork donated to Neptune.

The third afternoon I spotted what I first took to be dolphins with very round heads. The dolphins we had seen before had long beaks. I loved all animals and on land would know most, but those that dwelt in the sea were all new to me. I so regretted not having obtained a book on sea life.

The wind and swell increased, most of the time now we had Bob-tail's sand tray in the cabin and it was not the most pleasant thing to have around. When we thought he was not needing to use it we put it in the cockpit. While I was doing the dishes one evening Bob-tail decided to join me. He then spotted his tray and decided to make use of it. I always hated him being on deck in bad weather, sure-footed though he was. I feared the netting we had put around the rail was not a real safeguard. A particularly heavy wave caught us, I grabbed hold of his tray to prevent it slithering along the deck. Not a very clever act. Bob-tail rolled right out and into the scuppers. Dashing to the rescue, I picked him up but managed to get his little tail which has a hook at the end, caught in the netting. Trying to keep my balance and unhook his tail while he struggled wildly was not easy, and it's a wonder we did not both go overboard before I freed his tail and tossed him down in the cabin.

On the 13th December we rounded Pygmalion Point of Great Nicobar with its deserted sandy beaches. There was not a soul in sight, nor so much as a hut, we even missed seeing the lighthouse. With Nicobar behind us, there was nothing between us and Sri Lanka. We had the pleasure of dolphins accompanying us and then quite suddenly the sea was alive with fish jumping up out of the water, and birds who appeared from nowhere, diving for the fish. Just as suddenly the fish stopped jumping and the birds vanished. The dolphins too were gone. We were alone again.

By the 14th December we still had 720 miles to cover before arriving at Galle Harbour in Sri Lanka. This indicated that at our present rate of progress we would not arrive for Christmas after all. I put our little remaining rice away to keep for Christmas. *By then*, I thought, *we might consider rice a luxury*.

On my watch the following evening, just after dark, I saw the lights of a ship in the distance. The first vessel of any kind we had seen since leaving Phuket. Later a flying fish came on board, Bobby suggested keeping it for Bob-tail but it was still alive so we returned it to the sea. The next night Bob-tail got his own fish. We had not heard it coming on board but Bob-tail appeared in the companionway with a fish in his mouth and was just about to jump in the cabin with it. Bobby jumped up and Bob-tail jumped down and under the cockpit taking, we thought, the fish with him. In his flight, unseen by us, he must have dropped the fish, as now Pixie had it and tossed it forward where Bobby took possession of it. Now the fish was quite dead so Bobby cooked it for Bob-tail.

After that, flying fish were found on the deck regularly and Bob-tail took to eating them with noodles, of which we still had a good stock. What a shame nature could not arrange things so that fruit and vegetables appeared on deck for Pixie.

The swell was still heavy at times but generally speaking the weather improved and with it our spirits rose. We were going to make Galle for Christmas after all. Just as well, as though we still had food and water, the kerosene was low and only a few boxes of matches remained. Hardly enough to keep Bobby's pipe going for a few days not to mention my cigarettes and the stove.

Towards the end of the trip I felt it a good time to learn to use the sextant and take sights. I was a dismal failure. I fancied I could use it as I did my camera, so put it to my left eye, plugging my right with my thumb. Hopeless; the sextant being much larger than my camera I needed both hands to hold it, I had evidently done a stupid thing.

"If you want to use a sextant you must put it to your right eye." Bobby sounded quite annoyed as if it was something any reasonable person would know. I now put it to my right eye, quite a good idea as I see far better out of that eye. However, I could not judge where the sun was. I was told in no uncertain terms that it was because I had both eyes open. I knew that, but holding the sextant it was too far for me to close the other eye with my thumb. "Just close your left eye," Bobby said. I did, the snag was that my right eye closed at the same time. Bobby gave up and said that I must be the only person in the world who could not wink. A defect that had never worried me before. That was my first and last sextant lesson. Just for the record, I found out later that I am not the only one in the world without separate hinges to my eyelids. I have a brother and a sister made the same way.

We started taking night watches again on the 20th as we were now closing in on the shipping lanes approaching Sri Lanka. At 2300hrs that night I excitedly noted that I could see the loom from the lighthouse. By midnight it had disappeared and was seen no more that night.

Once more on watch at seven the next morning I scanned the horizon with the binoculars; I could just see something. Was it another boat? As we drew nearer the smug on the horizon turned into the lighthouse, the sun came out and land was just visible. As we moved closer to the land a small fishing boat came up and showed us a pink fish they had caught. They wanted us to give them a drink, we would have liked to but all we had was water. Quite suddenly we stopped rolling, we were in calm water. It felt good to be able to walk normally again instead of staggering around like a drunk. I set to and started to tidy the place up. With no warning the wind changed and we jibed. The mat that I had hung over the port side flew off and covered Bobby who was steering. The bucket of water on deck shot over to me, drenching me with its contents. Our bit of calm was over and we were rolling around again.

That evening we sailed with staysail only, as we were nearing Dundee Head Light and did not want to try and enter Galle in the dark. It started to rain hard, washing the salt of our voyage away.

Our thousand miles from Phuket was over.

Christmas Day was such a treat
with lots of drink and food to eat
For Don flung wide an open door
till bellies full and heads were sore

CHAPTER TWELVE

CHRISTMAS IN GALLE

Daylight on the 22nd December found us outside Galle. A fishing boat full of Europeans came along, hailing us as they passed, telling us to keep close to the buoys. The entrance appeared very narrow with a heavy surf pounding the rocks either side, with a deafening roar.

Praying that the wind would not drop and wishing that our engine was working, we headed in. It was much wider and easier than it had at first looked once we were opposite the entrance. We sailed in without mishap. We had completed our first real sea voyage.

There were a number of other yachts all tied to buoys. There were other buoys with no boats attached but we thought they might be privately owned. We dropped anchor at a safe distance from them. Putting away the sails and feeling rather pleased with ourselves we saw a dinghy coming over from a very grand yacht, *'Capyla'*; we then made acquaintance with Bob and Carrie. We learned, a little later, that the authorities did not like boats anchoring in the harbour and that we should tie up to a buoy. The anchor came up without difficulty and we were towed over to one of the buoys. After running up the yellow flag all that remained to be done was to get the now finished Sri Lankan flag up in place of the Thai one that still flew from our cross trees. While hauling Bobby up the mast to get the offending flag down, Dick Turpin and his daughter Mary Ann came over in their dinghy to tell us they were going into town and would we like them to buy us any fruit and vegetables. Would we indeed! Anything they could get we told them would be more than welcome. Soon after they left Bob and Carrie returned to say it would be OK if Bobby went ashore to inform the authorities. Off Bobby went leaving me to tidy up again. Bobby returned with a launch full of port officials, doctor, police and emigration. All of which managed to squeeze on board. They were all extremely nice and friendly which made us feel rather bad that we had nothing to offer them. They left taking Bobby with them as he still had customs to go to first and then to find Don Windsor, the man who everyone mentioned who had been to Galle, that we certainly would meet and find him so helpful. He was the unofficial yacht club where the crew of any boat stopping in Galle landed eventually to seek advice, eat his dinners or just relax on his patio, drink beer and chat.

It turned out he was expecting us. He told us we had the largest pile of mail he had ever seen at the post office. He had also heard about us from Wilfried and Astrid on *'Kathena Faa'* who had left a week before our arrival, for the Maldives. We found a note from them at the post office. Mary Ann returned with lots of nice-looking fresh produce and Bobby later with a beer. We had a salad that we were craving for and it tasted even better than we remembered. Well satisfied Bobby went back ashore to the wonderful post office which kept open twenty-four hours daily. He was able to send a cable for just three American dollars to my parents in England to wish them a Merry Christmas and let them know we had arrived. He also mailed a large pile of Christmas cards we had intended to mail in Thailand. Don commented that he had never seen so many letters for a private yacht from so many different countries. In a safe harbour with so many friendly people around we fell asleep that night happy and contented.

Pixie was as pleased as we were to have arrived. She got up at six, dragging us with her. She soon attracted may admirers, a flock of crows kept flying round the boat calling at her and leaving their visiting cards in unwanted numbers, while frightening poor Bob-tail out of his wits.

Two young boys swam out to us, which was quite far, informing us they had come to trade. After introducing themselves, one extracted something from his mouth and tossed it on deck. A tiger tooth they informed us. A little strange, why would we want a tiger tooth and where could it have come from as Sri Lanka has leopards but no tigers? It was tooth-shaped, covered in silver each end with a band in the middle and rings on the setting to hang on a chain. It looked like a piece of bone. Hardly able to say we did not want it after their swim, we asked what they wanted for it. We had as yet no money, Don having paid all our expenses the day before until Bobby could get to the bank. Their request surprised us. They asked for a can of beer. We had no beer having drunk the one Bobby had come back with. We did have a number of empty half gallon plastic jerry cans that had contained fruit juice we had bought in Singapore We proffered two of these and the boys swam off with them delighted.

At noon we set off for the shore with Pixie. The moment the dinghy touched the steps, Pixie jumped out and ran up them ignoring a lot of dogs which all started to bark in surprise. She spotted an old boat ashore, *'Albert'*, and insisted on going over and inspecting it. Not sure what she found so interesting in it but it kept her happy while the dinghy was tied up and we trooped off to the customs gate with a line of men following us. They were very interested in Pixie as she was not the same as the local monkeys and they thought she was a baboon. Once through the gate children joined the procession in a nice manner. Pixie, well aware of her following admirers, majestically plodded on to Don's house. No sooner had we turned into Don's gate then the rain fell down. We should have expected that as we had just been told it was the dry season and that it never rained near Christmas! The garden was beautiful with plenty of trees and places we thought suitable to chain Pixie to. After she had been greeted enthusiastically by Don, his wife and the rest of the family, she insisted it was her right to sit with everyone else.

Leaving Pixie with Bobby and all her new friends I joined Mary Ann and Carrie in Don's minibus for a ride into town. Don had told us there would be a party at his house on Christmas Day for all the yachties to which we were invited and, of course, the star of our family Pixie. I volunteered to make an English Christmas pudding but pointed out the size I could produce in my pan would hardly be enough for a crowd. Prema, Don's wife, came to the rescue by taking me into her kitchen where she had plenty of giant-sized bowls and suggested I could also use her kitchen. The set up was ideal, though my attention was diverted when I spotted a little old woman and a young girl about eight years old. They sat together working away at lace making, the old lady doing a circular mat and the little girl a narrow strip of lace which, though less complicated than the old lady's, still meant using a large number of different bobbins. Lace making I later found was a popular craft in Galle.

Our trip into town was spent dashing through the rain to the different shops to make purchases and back onto the bus. I found a good selection of dried fruit and everything needed for the pudding, putting off exploring the town properly with its bullock carts for another day.

Back on '*Sandpiper*' I stoned and de-stalked all the dried fruit and washed it. I had never done such a lot in one go before. I now had to keep my eye on Pixie who kept steeling a handful when I turned my back. I then put it all in to soak in sugar, rum and molasses. Next morning we trooped back to Don's house, Pixie's retinue of admirers following behind. Leaving Bobby and Pixie to chat to Don, I went in the kitchen to make the pudding. It was fun as I had company, Mary Ann joining me to help. She was a little nonplussed to see I was not weighing anything. I doubt there was weighing scales there but anyway, I would have no idea how much should be put in. It was just a matter of using up all the ingredients that we had and seeing if it looked right. When it was mixed in this huge bowl it certainly, we both agreed, looked right and had a nice Christmassy smell as, of course, here all the spices were nice and fresh. We took the bowl out to the others, a few more yachties had arrived and got everyone to have a stir and wish. Not sure some of them had a clue why they were requested to do this but complied anyway. Covering it with a large piece of sheet we lowered the bowl into an even larger pan of water and left it on the stove with instruction to top up the water when necessary.

That night on board we had a nice dinner and then listened to carols on the little radio we had bought. Before we went to bed I put a wee stocking with some goodies on the rail of *'Rimwimata'* for Mary Ann. Christmas was in the air and we were in Sri Lanka. What could be better?

Christmas Day dawned and Jason from the junk *'Heraclitus'* came over to wish us Merry Christmas. Later we went ashore to the all-day party. Don's house had been transformed. All the tables and chairs outside were decorated with flowers. On the patio a tree branch stood in the corner festooned in lights. The crews from all the yachts arrived and we all took a hand in making decorations for the tree. The pudding looked just like a Christmas pudding should. I made a few holes in it and poured in more rum, putting it back to boil to be served hot. Trays of food now covered the kitchen; Prema had been very busy and was then making *small eats*, open sandwiches and small cakes, some of these she had cleverly sculptured in the shape of little boats. The crowd from the boats had now grown, many of them we had not met before. Italian, German, American, Swedish and British. A local lad Christopher sat playing a guitar while his beautiful little wife sang. When they left, one of the Italians produced his guitar and another a tambourine and we had Italian songs. I went in the kitchen to see to the pudding, touched the pan and got an electric shock. It stood on an electric stove but no one else was affected so got help getting it out. When everyone had eaten their fill Mary Ann and I produced the pudding, sticking a sprig of bougainvillea on the top in place of holly. The pudding turned out just as pudding should and was a big success, with everyone finding room for a piece. Drink followed but no one got drunk and a good time was had by all. All that is except Pixie who was attached to her long chain a little distance from the main gathering. She showed little interest in all the food proffered and did not approve of all the noise. By evening most of the party had dispersed to the beach and we returned to *'Sandpiper'* to give Bob-tail his Christmas dinner.

Festivities over we went back to working on the boat. Bobby scraped a lot of goose barnacles off the side. We were told that some people eat them so had considered boiling some up for Bob-tail but dismissed the idea when we found they came off with a good helping of anti-fouling and gave no indication whether they were dead or alive.

Ashore again at Don's someone kindly brought back for us twelve eggs on his bicycle. We expressed our amazement that he had managed to return without breaking even one of them. Since our grand smashing of the 30 eggs we had had several other accidents with eggs though not on such a grand scale. Don's garden contained a number of different fruit trees and he suggested I gather up some local gooseberries that Pixie was eating so she could have them on the boat. I collected some and put them in the paper bag with the eggs. They were a little wet. About to leave, Bobby picked up the bag. All twelve eggs smashed as they hit the ground with the gooseberries and the wet bag.

One day we met Don's herd of cows for the first time as they walked through the garden to the field at the back. They all passed Pixie without paying any attention until the last cow. She was the largest and lowered her head at Pixie as if to toss her. Pixie in turn showed her teeth. The cow turned back, then had second thoughts and returned to try again. That was just too much for Pixie, after giving the cow a warning the first time she now rushed at the cow who turned tail and fled up a different path. More interesting than cows was a mongoose that dashed past us as we left.

I enjoyed exploring the town where half the traffic consisted of bullock carts. Not sure what the bullocks thought about it but they were certainly more picturesque than cars. I passed houses where signs proclaimed that lace could be purchased and where the women sat working away in their open doorways. I bought a terracotta bowl of curd which was delicious. Amazingly, or so I thought, the bowl was not returnable. I was happy to keep mine and gave away any glass and plastic bottles we had which were so gladly accepted. Exploring the small shops, I was fascinated by a round-shaped thing wrapped in dry leaves. As I could get no satisfactory answer to my query as to what it was, beyond that it was something to eat, I bought one. On unwrapping it I found it to be what we called in Malaysia *GULA MALLACA*. Very raw dark sticky sugar.

Pixie soon got accustomed to going to Don's and took more interest in the garden and was often kept company by Don's dog and cat who would lie under a tree with Pixie. Having spent many years in the tropics we thought we knew all the fruits. Don had a tree with hard round fruits which were quite new to us. Wood apples a very apt name. We did not find them very tasty but they were supposed to be good for you and did make good jam.

There was another party at the end of the year, to see the new year in. This was organised by Carrie and Bob and we all put in a few rupees to cover expenses. It was held at a place on the beach some miles outside Galle. Transport was needed and we took Pixie in the back of a car. Old year's night was a wet one and we wondered if it would be cancelled but a thatched covered area had been hired and here we found masses of cooked food with plenty of different kind of vegetables. Smaller huts were dotted around the place and Pixie took her can of beer – not containing very much – and food to the top of one of these; 1979 was seen in on the beach round a bonfire.

A galley now, where once a bunk
with extra apace for all our junk.

CHAPTER THIRTEEN
WORKING HARD

The first day of the new year and we were up early; party time over it was now necessary to work in earnest. We had made arrangements to go alongside the Fisheries wharf, where the engine could be taken out and landed ashore for repair at the workshop. We also decided that it was a good place to do some remodelling to the cabin interior. We wanted to move the galley farther forward between the main part of the cabin and our new bunk, putting lockers and another long seat in its place. When building the bunk in Malaysia we had learned enough to realise that fitting lockers and shelves on the sloping side of the boat was not as easy as it appeared. When Don informed us that he could get us two carpenters to work on our boat for the daily wage equivalent of two US dollars a day we jumped at the idea.

At eight that morning a boat came and towed us to the wharf. No sooner tied up then the engineers came on board and looked at the engine; lifting it was going to be a problem. Four men were called, they were willing but small and thin; having unbolted the engine from its bed they tied a rope around it and heaved. Nothing happened. They heaved and sweated, the engine did not budge an inch. Lesser men would have given up as it was obvious they were not strong enough to move it, but they kept trying. When they were completely exhausted they went off to lunch saying they would return stronger. They returned looking refreshed but were soon exhausted again with no results for their labours. Rather late in the day it was agreed that manpower alone would not move the engine, modern technology was required. A block and tackle was produced and to the delight of us all the engine was raised up and moved under the companionway hatch, from where it was lifted out by a crane, where it was taken off to the workshop. The engineers soon found the problem, the rings in the gearbox were loose and they did not anticipate any problem in replacing them. Cheering news.

Pixie thoroughly enjoyed being alongside and was torn between trying to see what was going on in the cabin with our engine, and showing off to the admirers on the wharf. Though the local people were poor they were also extremely kind and generous and liked to give her food. Pixie, sensing she was on to a good thing here, would sit on the wharf, still chained to our rails and look expectant, accepting anything offered in a nice gentle manner. Bob-tail hated all the noise and strange people and went into hiding in the quarter berth.

We thought perhaps we might need more than just a good engine to get us through the Red Sea and planned to get the whole boat in good shape. We set to and made a long list of things to check. It was just as well we did as when Bobby went up the mast to examine the spreaders he found one was completely rotten. Why it had not disintegrated before was just our good luck. After dismantling the spreader he took it along to the carpenters' workshop to have another made. Two days later he collected the new one, rather dismayed at the weight of it being twice as heavy as the original. They assured him that it would dry out and be lighter. Seeing him carrying it back I could not understand why they had painted it yellow. On closer inspection we found it was not painted but just the natural colour of the wood. It was a new wood to us. It was jak wood from the tree that bore the huge jak fruits. It became my favourite wood. Rather like mahogany with a beautiful grain, a hardwood which darkens with age.

Before the carpenters descended on us, I removed things from the galley. "Where," I asked Bobby, "are we going to cook?" After looking round the cabin he came to the obvious conclusion that it would have to be on deck. Rather than find space on deck for the burners and large kerosene tank, I thought it better to go and buy a small kerosene stove to have on deck and it would come in handy should our two burners blow up or refuse to work for some reason. In town I soon found a cheap one made out of large cans that once held milk powder, and did not need to be preheated with meths. On the way back with my new stove a cute little boy grabbed my arm and started unwrapping wooden elephants. Black elephants of various sizes, none very well carved. One thing we did not need on board was a herd of elephants. Two were pressed into my hands. "Twenty rupee, very nice, very cheap." I tried to give them back, telling him I did not want them. Still talking non-stop he added more. I now had six. I still said no feeling six was worse than two even if costing the same amount. Undaunted he took four back, leaving me with two which were now only ten rupees, he then added a baby elephant. His English sales talk was perfect and by this time a large interested crowd had gathered to see who would win. Needless to say I came away minus ten rupees and with three black elephants. The crowd applauded.

Naively we were excited at the prospect of having carpenters do our remodelling for us. Don sent them round with Christopher as an interpreter, unfortunately neither one of them spoke any English. No problem we were told. Christopher would come each day to explain what was needed. We were not overly-impressed with their looks, one was a very old boy and the other only slightly younger, and sullen looking. They looked even more unhappy when they were told what was required. At the end of all the interpreting we were told they could do it and it would take one week to complete. Marvellous! Obviously we should not go by first impressions.

Seven thirty next day, they arrived and stood looking a bit lost as if they did not like to start. We showed them in sign language what to strip out and they set to work. They had brought their own tools: saw, screwdriver and a hammer. By the end of the day with encouragements from us they had the sink and stove out and all the surrounding bits and pieces, along with half the bulkhead to the tool locker. We wanted the galley made first so the next step was to make a new frame for the sink. Again they looked a bit lost and sawed at a bit of wood. When Christopher came we went over it all again and the way the pipes should be fitted. We needed new pipes and Christopher said he could get them for us but it would be better if Bobby fitted them.

After they had gone, we looked at each other and voiced the hope that they would be better at making things rather than dismantling. We cleared away all the bits of wood which they had left, it apparently not being part of the deal to clear up, and then went over to a tap in a little hut we had found that the workmen took their showers in. Here, keeping a watch on the doorway which had no door, in case anyone came along unexpectedly, we and Pixie had a good shower each evening. Bob-tail by then had become very bold and would come walking with us. He decided not to take a shower but would jump up on the wall surrounding it and peer down at us.

The next day was no less frustrating. More wood was needed to make the frame for the sink. The logical thing was for one of the carpenters to go and get what was needed. He refused to take the money and go alone so Bobby had to go with him. The pipes were delivered and were the wrong size. While the one carpenter was away with Bobby the remaining one started on the little locker that would go between the new galley and the seat. It was to be the same as we had had in the old galley and so the old frame and door could be used. I particularly wanted them to fit, having made the door in Singapore with a copper tooled picture. He set to work carefully measuring with a bit of string. On seeing this I offered him a measuring tape but he did not like the look of it. The base of the locker went in with no trouble, now the frame should fit between base and deckhead. There was a two-inch gap. He did not look upset and reassured me in sign language that it would be taken care of later. The wood arrived and they set to work making the sink frame; now they were looking happier and more competent, working in a professional manner, fitting the wood to the curve of the hull. I was impressed and made a mental note of how this was done.

Dick Turpin now arrived on a bike looking very discouraged. He and his daughter Mary Ann were circumnavigating and had not wished to stay so long in Galle, but he was waiting for money to be sent out from England and it still had not arrived. Pixie tried cheering him up by giving his very luxuriant ginger hair a groom.

We were delighted when the carpenters finished the frame for the sink. We put the sink in its place and it was a perfect fit. Our elation was soon dampened when we realised the bottom of the sink was now only level with the outlet pipe. Once the pipes were fitted we would get sea water coming in rather than dish water going out. We had failed to take into account that the old galley was in the higher level of the cabin. It was now our turn to look shame-faced. The sink could not be made higher or we would have to stand on a stool to reach it, and then bang our heads on the deckhead. It was the old carpenter who then pointed out we had another outlet in the head and pipes could be taken to that, we agreed that was the best idea and our opinion of our carpenters went up. We were the dumb ones. Another day over and still not much achieved but we felt more confident of our carpenters now and they more at ease with us.

Clearing up the cabin while Bobby went off to get fish for Bob-tail and beer for us, I heard a man talking to Pixie in English. Going on deck I found two engineers off one of the Sri Lanka navy ships that had just come in. Pixie was inspecting the hand of one of them as I stood talking to them Suddenly the man I was talking to, said in a very calm voice that Pixie had his wallet and that it contained all his money and papers. He was very sensible and did not move or make a grab for it. With my heart in my mouth in case she dropped the wallet in the sea I hold him to just keep talking to me and I would get it, praying that I would be able to before she dumped it in the sea. Luckily Pixie then jumped back on board with her prize and I got it from her with no trouble. When I handed it back to the owner she was very cross and jumped back on the wharf and grabbed his trouser leg and made to bite him. Like most of the people we had met in Sri Lanka he had an inborn instinct how to react to her and just stood still, Pixie seeing she could not frighten him went back to being friends. I was then shown an uncut ruby that had been in his wallet; I was not very impressed, in the dark it looked like a dented black pea but when held up to the light on the dock it glowed red. It was now dark and Pixie's friends asked me if I had eaten. I told them I was waiting for Bobby to return. It was not very late but the fact that I had not eaten appeared to give them a lot of concern and they asked me what I would like to eat and they would get it from their ship. This was rather surprising and I wondered if I was looking hungry or starved but at this point Bobby returned so was able to tell them we would now eat. They were still determined to feed us and asked for a container in which to bring back some food; I gave them one section of our food carrier. They soon returned with a bottle of mango juice, a loaf of bread, packet of margarine and in the container two fried eggs and curried potato chips, which we accepted gratefully but it felt strange to be on the receiving end. Later when we ate, adding the beans I had cooked earlier, Pixie got both eggs, grabbing them off the plates as I put them down. She knew her rights, after all they were her friends who had brought them.

We always took Pixie for a walk before bed, when we were alongside. Until that day we had never gone very far from the boat and Bob-tail had come with us. That night without hesitation she took off right round the dock to the other side where the navy ships were tied up. No doubt deciding to repay the visit to her friends. Having reached their part of the dock she was not quite sure just which ship they were on and turned her attention to an old ship the other side of the wharf, where she sat for a while thinking. Suddenly she called like she does for one of us, going over to one of the navy ships just as her friends were getting off. She must have recognised them. Now she clung onto his leg claiming him for her own, several more sailors gathered round offering her toast and lettuce, all of which she refused.

In the end I had to drag her away from her boyfriend. The old song *All the nice girls love a sailor* running through my head.

The following day the navy ships were open to the public. The dock gates were opened and men, women and parties of schoolchildren swarmed in in their hundreds. Once in they decided to make a day of it and toured the whole dock, inspecting any boat that was tied alongside. Understandably, with Pixie, we became exhibit number one. Eager to see everything that could be seen, even Pixie with all her charms was not enough for them, and light from our port windows was blocked out with dozens of eager faces watching our every move. It is rather unnerving to have your every move watched, you feel that you should be doing something very profound. Instead I was painting wood preserver on the frames the carpenters had done, every stroke was watched. A drip of preserver splashed on my leg, I wiped it off with a bit of paper. Wood preserver is not intended for human skin. It made me itch. I started scratching, aware that a dozen eyes were taking in every move. I wished I had drawn the curtains and could scratch in private. Bobby was working with the carpenter in the galley and now called me to come and look. The sink fitted nicely where we wanted it and it also fitted in the space behind which we had intended to cover and use as a draining board.

"I was thinking," said Bobby, "how about fitting the old sink behind in which you could put the dishes to drain without them sliding around and buy a new and shallower sink to wash up in?" This sounded a grand idea and I readily agreed. Bobby then left to look for a sink and change the pipes for the correct size. Thinking it would be nice to get away from all the faces I offered to go as I had finished my painting job and needed cigarettes. No, he wanted to make sure he got the pipes the correct size so I was left with the carpenters and all the faces. The carpenters were working but only on one side; if the sink frames where the sink was to be attached was done, perhaps they too didn't like to watched. I finally drew the curtains but faces then appeared looking down the hatch, that was too much. I went up and asked them how they would like it if I stood looking in their doors and windows. I then felt ashamed when a man apologised for the crowd. They all left but in no time more took their place.

Bobby returned; he had all the pipes but could not find a sink of any kind or the Arberite he wanted, and had a hard time tracking down the last forty cigarettes in town. The Bristol cigarette factory was on strike.

The next day would be Sunday. The carpenters would have the day off. The navy ships would leave, so no more faces, and we planned to do as much as possible. I wanted to put in a small shelf in the now nearly completed little locker. Bobby planned to fix his pipes to the sink. That night, taking Pixie for her walk, we were surprised to see what we thought was Bob-tail sitting on the deck of a fishing boat alongside. The cat then moved and we saw it had a long tail but otherwise bore a remarkable likeness to our Bob-tail.

Our day without the carpenters could not really be called a success. At four thirty in the morning I was dragged out of bed by Pixie. Bob-tail was ashore and had obviously met Long-tail. They were having a very noisy conversation. As Pixie and I went up to investigate the argument had come to a head and now sounded as if they were resorting to blows. Just as we got on deck Bob-tail came flying down and we were just in time to see Long-tail make a speedy retreat. We examined Bob-tail who seemed none the worse for the encounter and I left them on the seat, Pixie busy grooming Bob-tail and I went back to sleep.

Later that day Bobby and I got down enthusiastically to work. Bobby's pipe fitting was going well and I found exactly the right length of wood I needed for my shelf. I made nice supports for it to sit on. Had I left it at that, all would have been well, but then I decided to add a bit of old Arberite on the shelf. The glue must have been old and it would not stick, so I had to leave it under a pile of wood hoping it would stick under pressure but was disappointed not to have finished the job. Bobby soon had all the pipes in place and connected to the sink. Time to christen it by tipping a bucket of sea water in the sink to watch it drain away. For a moment we were gratified to see how fast it disappeared but then noticed our feet were wet and that the water was coming out of the bottom of the sink. Too late we put a pan below, by then most of the water had covered the carpet and run down the wood frames. When the sink was removed he took the rubber tube off the metal part of the pipe that was part of the sink leading from the drain hole, he found at it was bent and fractured. Another job for the workshop and a day's work wasted.

Slowly as the days progressed the new galley started taking shape. The old sink was taken to be fixed at the workshop but before we got it back we found a beautiful new Japanese stainless steel sink complete with draining board. Being much shallower than our original one it could be fitted to the original outlet and we could put the old sink behind as we had wanted. By cutting off all but a few inches of the draining board the sink was a perfect fit. We were also able to get Arberite after learning that in Sri Lanka it was called Formica. We wanted white but that was unavailable. We settled for a piece with a wood grain affect. I am not a fan of pretend wood but it was either that or red. The gimbald stove was fitted next to the sink, leaving us space for a foot-wide locker between the stove and bulkhead. The locker top would serve as a bit of counter space and the carpenters did a very nice job of covering it with the Arberite/Formica. Our new galley was complete. We were standing back admiring the effect when the carpenter picked up a plane to trim a fraction off the edge of the Arberite top. One stroke and a big chip flew off the top. I could have cried.

Dilemma

A fridge we had aboard our boat.
Some day to sell it was our hope
Prospective buyers live ashore
but smuggling was against the law.

CHAPTER FOURTEEN
SMUGGLING

"'Sandpiper', good morning, how are you 'Sandpiper'?"

Our visitor was not on the wharf but the other side, having come up in one of the crazy but fascinating local catamarans. These locally made craft are used for fishing but unlike our modern-day fibreglass catamarans with two hulls, these consist of a very narrow dug-out canoe with outriggers attached. They were far too narrow for even the very slim Sri Lankans to sit in; the crew sit astride to paddle. Any fish caught were put in the dug-out. We came on deck unenthusiastically, recognising the man we called Charts. Charts had been one of our first visitors when we were on the buoy. At first we had welcomed him when he asked in a business-like manner if we wanted to buy any charts. We were in need of some and were given the impression that he could get them for us and anything else we needed. His conversation flowed with names of other boats and ships he had done business with. It sounded as if he had a thriving marine supply business. He became a little more evasive, however, when we asked where he had his shop. Evidently, he supplied all his customers personally, bringing anything ordered to their boats. Being told what general charts we needed he promised to bring them round the following day. After several more unproductive visits he finally arrived with a roll of very old, water-stained charts. Taking a look we discovered they were all of China, Japan and Borneo. It did not surprise us when he said he had got them off the sunken ship in the harbour that had gone down after being on fire. We now wondered what other find he had dug out of the wreck, hoping to sell to us. This time, however, he had changed his role, asking if we had anything to sell. Thinking he was trying to expand his chart trade we said we might have a few old charts. Charts, he had found, did not sell well and so was no longer interested in them.

"You got any T-shirts?" he asked. It so happened that was the one thing we did have. While in Malaysia we had been told that everyone in Sri Lanka asked for T-shirts, even the customs, and it was worthwhile taking along as many as possible. I had bought a couple of dozen when in Penang, then forgotten all about them as not a soul had asked for one. Digging out our pile of T-shirts, I thought how unfortunate it was that Charts and his friend were bigger than the average Sri Lankan, so the ones we had would probably not fit them. Fearing we might be landed with them ourselves, we had purchased mostly small sizes. The size apparently did not matter, they sorted over them eagerly, not even taking them out of their plastic wrappers. They decided they would buy twelve, at fifty rupees each. That little business transaction having been attended to they now wanted to know what else we had. We confessed we had been stupid enough to come from Singapore without even a watch or any other item to sell. They just could not believe it. "What about electrical goods?"

"No," we insisted, "we have nothing." They obviously could not believe we were that crazy and went on, "No radios, tape recorders, refrigerators?" At the word refrigerator, we remembered we did have a refrigerator on board that we would love to sell. It was a small Japanese one that could be run off the batteries and had been on board when we bought *'Sandpiper'*. We had tried it once but found that to get it to freezing point we had almost drained our batteries. We put it away thinking that someday we might find a power boat who might like to buy it from us. It could also be run off the mains but being a very small portable fridge, we had never considered that anyone living ashore would want it. We showed them the fridge, most of it was the motor leaving a very small space for keeping something cold. They still liked it and went off with the instruction book to show an electrician to make sure it could be used with the current they had. First they cautioned us not to tell anyone else we had it to sell. Word must have gone around that we had T-shirts as I was even stopped in the street by strangers and asked about them. I was soon wishing I had a few dozen more to sell and make everyone, and us, happy.

At first we were delighted at the prospect of selling our small refrigerator, then Dick warned us about having anyone on board. He had just had his radio stolen from his boat while he was ashore. Don also said to be careful and that we would be in trouble if caught by the customs. Apparently, to sell our refrigerator to a local person was considered smuggling even though it was not new. Somewhat to our relief neither Charts nor his friend turned up that evening at the arranged time. Much as we wanted to get rid of the thing, which was just taking up space, and getting a little extra cash in its place, it was hardly worth running foul of the law over.

Eleven thirty that night, Pixie, Bob-tail and I already in bed with Bobby just about to join us, Charts and his friend arrived, shouting and calling out to us. Sleepily we got up and extracted the refrigerator from under a pile of junk, put it on deck and connected it to the battery, to let them see that it was in working order. Charts said he would take it for US $30. Just then we observed the policeman that patrolled the dock at night heading our way. "No," said Bobby, "I do not think I want to sell it and anyway I want $50." This still did not deter them and Charts said he would have to ask his father. To our relief they left just as the policeman and his senior arrived to ask what was going on.

Next day in broad daylight Charts came along again with a different friend who also wanted to see the fridge. I told them we were not really interested in selling it and it was too heavy for me to get out,

Bobby being ashore at the time. They left, saying they would be round again at eight that night. That evening, sitting on deck with Pixie, two well-dressed young men walked by, then stopped and talked nicely to Pixie. After asking all about her they mentioned they worked for customs. We kept our cool and went on chatting. Conversation led to life on board and one asked offhandedly if we had a fridge. As we never used it I would normally have said NO without giving it a second thought. Now I wondered, was this just a chance conversation or had they been leading up to that one question. Without saying yes or no I prattled on about having an ice box for which we got ice from the fisheries. A little more innocent conversation and they left.

To our dismay Charts and friend turned up exactly at eight. This time they made even more noise than before, shouting and yelling. The security police started moving our way. "No problem," roared Charts, "we have all the money." Digging in his pocket and waving around a bunch of bank notes. They went on talking loudly in their own language, for all we knew proclaiming for all to hear that they were buying our fridge. Bobby in the end got rid of them saying he would meet them outside the dock area the next morning. Security police again came and wanted to know what was going on.

It was clear we had got ourselves in a bit of a pickle. If we continued to refuse to sell the fridge to Charts we would probably have to put up with his nightly visits bringing down certain suspicion on us from the security guards. He might even report us for trying to sell it to them. If on the other hand we did sell it to him, with all the noise he always made, he would more than likely get caught with it and there could be no denying we had sold it to him.

Early next morning a strange man came on the wharf, asking for the fridge. He had heard from the shops that we had one. *Goodness*, we thought, *now what is Charts up to, advertising the fact all round town?* This man was very persistent but we finally made him understand that though we had a fridge it was not for sale at any price. No sooner had he left, and earlier than Bobby's agreed appointment with Charts ashore, there was wild shouting and Charts and his catamaran, together with his friend, came alongside. They wanted to take the fridge there and then in broad daylight. To have done so they would have had to balance it on top of the dugout and then presumably, once ashore, carry it through the streets. What a dumb lot of crooks we had to deal with. Bobby was now really angry and told them to shut up and go away, he did not wish to do any business with them as they could not keep to the agreement and discuss things ashore. “No problem,” they kept shouting.

This was their favourite phrase. Perhaps for them it was no problem but it was fast becoming one for us. To try and finish the matter we said we now wanted to use the fridge ourselves while in Galle and perhaps we would let them have it before we left.

We did work hard, but that's not all
for don't forget we were in Galle
So every time we went ashore
We had adventures by the score.

CHAPTER FIFTEEN

NEVER A DULL MOMENT

During the first twelve days alongside we had been working hard. The work I enjoyed but the frustration of watching the carpenters at the same time I feared might be giving me ulcers. Apart from quick dashes to the shops for necessary items I had not done much exploring. By the eleventh day the carpenters had almost completed the galley. The next step would be to strip out the set of drawers that we still had in the old galley part then rebuild lockers and seating opposite matching the set up. I needed a break ashore and this was a good time to take it before the coming ordeal.

The fort at the end of town was another world far from the bustle of shops and traffic. Stepping through the gate of the fort you could imagine you were in Europe. On the whole the Asian atmosphere of Galle town was far more intriguing to explore, but now the tranquillity of the fort was what I needed. The post office, a place in itself rather wonderful, was situated there, where we collected our mail and that was about all I had seen. The streets held few people and even less traffic. Now and then a palm squirrel would scamper up a tree, cows were contentedly grazing on the grass verges which looked particularly green against the backdrop of sea and sky.

As I strolled around this old fort, long ago built by the Dutch, a little boy with good English joined me and we chatted as we walked along; he like me appearing to be content to wander without any destination. For a little while we stopped and watched soldiers being drilled in the grounds of the old army quarters that were still being used as such. Continuing our walk we found ourselves amongst the houses. I was too absorbed in my surroundings to notice that my little friend was now leading the way. Suddenly he said, "This is where I live, please come in." I could hardly refuse such a polite request, but wondered what his parents would have to say. Most of the houses were much the same, all I guessed a couple of hundred years old. Some were falling apart, others better but rather shoddy looking, whereas the ones owned by the more affluent were done up nicely. My little friend's house fitted the second category. Of his mother and father there was no sign but his three sisters were there to welcome me. Any qualms I had that this family would not welcome my unexpected appearance was quickly forgotten. His older sister Fatimah, aged seventeen, was still at school and spoke perfect English. The younger sisters giggled shyly behind their hands. I learned they were neither Buddhists nor Hindus but Moslem, a minority in Sri Lanka. Fatimah wanted to hear all I could tell her about the Moslems in Malaysia, Singapore and other countries. A lovely young family, I was given coffee and they asked if I would send a postcard from a Moslem country. I eventually did so from Egypt.

I was finding everyone exceptionally friendly. I wanted to buy some cheese but was unable to find the shop I had been told about. A man approached me with elephants to sell. I was very firm this time having no desire to start an elephant collection. Changing the subject I asked him where I could buy cheese. Putting his elephants away he offered to show me. He took me to Walkers which I had already passed and discovered it was still closed. He now suggested we try another place for local cheese. This place was open but being a bakery I was not too surprised to learn they did not sell cheese. I thought I might as well buy some bread. This I was told they did sell but as I could see, all the shelves were empty. Bread was finished. Made me wonder why they were still open. Elephant man now took me around until we did find some bread and then bade me farewell. As I came out of the fort the noise hit me after the silence that had existed behind the walls.

Back on board, much refreshed from my walk, I found Bobby had got fed up watching the carpenters dithering around about the facing of the sink and having long conversations with each other, which may or may not have been about how to go about the job. He now had them stripping out the drawers. After taking the drawers out they were disappointed to find they could not then remove the whole framework and just set it in its new place. To us the best idea appeared to take it apart bit by bit and rebuild it in the new place. Unable to explain to them, they did it their way, knocking it all apart, leaving it as a wood pile in the cabin.

Previously I had seen a black bead necklace in Don's shop that intrigued me when I learned it was made of black coral from the Maldives. I had never seen black coral before and wanted to see it in its natural state but was told that it is found only in very deep water round the Maldives. That evening one of the security guards came along and asked me if I would like to have some coral he had got from a fishing boat. "What kind of coral?" I asked. I had a large collection of dead coral of different kinds which I had picked on beaches in Malaysia and Singapore. We had shipped this collection back to England. I would only collect more if it was of a different type. "It's coral," he said. "Yes, but is it black or white?"

"Black," came the reply. I happily said I'd love to have it and accompanied him back to his security hut. Here several rather smelly pieces of coral lay. They were black, only because they needed a good washing.

On the 14th January we waved goodbye, rather sadly, to Dick Turpin and his lovely daughter Mary Ann. They had left Fowey in England about eighteen months before and were now returning via the Red Sea to complete their circumnavigation. We knew Dick was keen to be on his way so were happy for him that his money had finally arrived and was free to leave, but we were going to miss them.

Soon after watching *'Rimwimata'* sail out of sight Mardi came to see us. Mardi was a young girl about Mary Ann's age and had left the boat she had sailed from Australia and was now footloose in Sri Lanka. Wrapped in a sarong with a hibiscus in her hair, she told us quite cheerfully that she had been arrested that morning for not renewing her visa and was given twenty-four hours to get one. She thought she would go to Colombo the following day and apply for an extension of her visa. However, it was a holiday so she rather doubted she would be successful. The prospect did not appear to worry her unduly and evidently something was arranged as she did stay for some time after that, but then one day came on board to bid us farewell, having decided to travel overland across India.

The carpenters now set to work with a will. Bassamy, as we called the older of the two, set to work making a nice frame for the set of drawers and his mate, who never seemed to be called anything but acknowledged us if we called him Chipmunk, went ahead with the facing in front of the sink. Bassamy was pleased with his frame and proudly showed it to us. All fitted in where we wanted it, we agreed it was nice but were puzzled by the fact that he had done this first with no framework for the drawers behind; still he was the carpenter and no doubt knew what he was doing. Perhaps he did, perhaps he just felt in the mood for doing the frame first. A little later he took it all down and got on with making the framework for the drawers behind. To our delight that went well and looked almost professional. I then noticed another snag. Although we had what looked like three drawers, only the top two were true drawers, the other a flap door behind which was a lot of piping to the water tank, and where we intended to keep large tools that would sit on the top of the tank. The tank also extended along under the sink, but there was no bulkhead dividing that locker from the rest of the tank top, so anything put there would slide across and perhaps down the back and be lost forever. I pointed this out, expecting that now all the framework would have to be removed to do this last part that should have been done first. Bassamy showed me that he had in fact already thought of this and had the plywood cut to fit. I knew this but what I wondered was how he was now going to get it in? For the next five minutes he tried turning the wood first one way and then the other hoping no doubt it would suddenly shrink in size and go in. No luck. Taking a saw he cut the piece in half. With a satisfied look he had got it in.

The seat now remained to be done. As this was to be the same as the original one opposite they did have a good guide as to what we wanted. They were much better at doing framework than a good finishing job. I was very impressed how they measure with their bit of string and made the perfect curve to fit against the hull. I believe they never fully understood that we did not just want lockers etc. to be practical, but also wanted them to look nice. I think too they could have worked much better had we been able to explain what we wanted in their language, as we could not, I don't think they were ever quite sure what we wanted.

We admired the way all the local seats and backs of chairs were done with split cane, woven into a pattern. It not only looked nice but was also cool to sit on. I had studied the chairs done in this way at Don's house and saw it would not be difficult to do. Therefore, we decided to have the seats and the backs covering lockers behind done in this way and also the existing seats which had only plywood seats and back. We could still have our chewed cushions on it but it would look very much nicer and allow a flow of air to the lockers below and at the back. We explained to Christopher that we wanted them to make fourteen frames in all for the seats and back. We were confident they would know just how to go about this as just about every seat they had seen must have been done in this manner. As for the weaving of it I intended to do this myself, a nice change from scraping old paint, repainting and varnishing.

Don being our fountain of knowledge as to where anything could be found, I went along to ask him where I could buy the required cane. As soon as I told him what I planned to do he said he could let us have men to do it. I insisted I wished to do it myself. "In that case you had better go to the back of the garden, I have men doing some of my chairs and you can see how it is done," he said. I now noticed two men at work on a chair, each some distance away. It was surprising how very white the cane looked; *perhaps it darkens with age*, I thought. I was horrified when I got near enough to see that these nice old chairs were now being re-done using white plastic laces instead of cane. Plastic had only just that year been imported into Sri Lanka. Even so plastic bottles and bags were still quite highly valued. Plastic has it uses, as we had found on the boat, but it was a shame to see it replacing pottery and other more natural artistic and attractive items. As I looked at the work in progress I concluded that the plastic laces must often break. The old cane work on the other chairs was beautifully done. The plastic they were using now in just the same style had been knotted in several places. Perhaps they were being thrifty and did not wish to waste any of this precious material, regardless of the appearance. I thought they might not be very comfy if you were unlucky enough to sit on a knot. Don was surprised I did not like the plastic, it was modern and cane was difficult to obtain. *Difficult or not*, I thought, *I was darned if I was going to have plastic on my seats*. My favourite hardware store said they thought the cane available about ten miles away and would try and get it for me. Feeling happy I then collected a pile of mail from the post office, my heart did beat a little fast with fear when they also gave me a cable. Cables usually bring bad news and I carried it back unopened to *'Sandpiper'* and gave it to Bobby. I breathed again. It came from Bobby's old friend of the China Seas trade of years ago, Captain Peter Foxely, congratulating us on our arrival and asking about our voyage. We noted it was a week old and had only come from Malaysia. It was fortunate it was not something urgent.

Some days later I went to the shop to see if they had got my cane. They had been unable to get it but told me to take a bus to Dodanduwa where, so they said, were several places I would be able to obtain it. I chose to go on the day our engine was to be put back, feeling it would be best to be out of the way. After enjoying the ride I set off on foot on my search. I had walked a good three miles during which time saw a couple of shops with chairs made using the cane, but no cane for sale. It was a lovely place, everyone I passed said, "Hello, where are you going?" but for the most part that was the extent of their English so they could not help when I tried to tell them where I hoped I was going. Having kept an eye out for cane while on the bus and seeing no likely place to purchase it I felt sure I must be going in the right direction. Right through Dodanduwa I went, and to the next village, still no cane. Having now almost got to the end of that village I found a young man who had a little English and was very willing to help. With pen and paper I drew a chair and the cane seat and spaghetti-like things I hoped he understood to be the cane that I wanted. "Yes, yes," he said, "I understand." *Well*, I thought, *if you do you're brilliant because no one else had when I actually pointed at the cane in real chairs*. I did wonder when he said we must go back the way I had come.

I was offered a ride on the carrier of his bike. I was tempted at first to refuse but realised we might have to cover the distance I had already walked. Ladylike I sat side saddle on his carrier feeling a bit mean as he now had all the work while I rested my legs, but we made faster progress. We stopped at a furniture shop I had already tried and he had no better luck than I had. He must have been given the information we sought, as back on the bike we went, on and on, way past where I had got off the bus. We stopped at a house, large barn would perhaps be a better description. No sign of cane, then a man appeared carrying a bundle of the precious stuff. Now the question arose as to how much of it did I want. To make things more difficult it was sold by the weight. I did not have a clue. Using my hands I measured the size of one frame and said I wanted enough to fill fourteen such spaces. The man did some sums and told me I would need three pounds. I had to take his word for it. Later I found he must have been a real expert as it was just what I needed with very little over.

At the time it did not sound much, but at least I was not going to have to hire a donkey to cart it all back. It worked out to cost a little less than four US dollars per pound which sounded reasonable. I then turned my attention to the cane he had carried. It was cane, not plastic, but sadly disappointing being very hairy and thick, not a bit like the finished work I had admired. I asked if I had to sandpaper it all as it was obvious it was not much good in its present state. I was told he would prepare it. He then showed me into his barn-like place, it was large enough to hold a dance in, but understood it was his home. He certainly did not believe in cluttering up the place with unnecessary furniture. A small charpoy in one corner and a wardrobe on the other side of the large room, together with a single chair. There was a photo of a wedding on one wall placed very high and a really big tree trunk which turned out to be his work bench. I then noticed a woman and a child stood shyly in the shadows. The man with the cane then demonstrated to me how he would prepare three pounds of cane. Taking two pieces of sharpened iron he hammered them in to the top of his tree trunk. Taking a knife he hammered that too in position, together with a piece of tin. Taking a length of cane he ran it between the knife and tin. This shaved it clean one side. Turning it round he did it again so both sides were shaved. It had now lost its hairy look but was still too thick and so was passed between the two pieces of iron. Presto! A reasonable bit of cane. Very neat but quite a business considering the amount he had to do. By then it was ten in the morning and he said he would have it all finished by four in the afternoon. My young man said he'd show me around to kill time but six hours I thought would be a little excessive, plus the fact I had told Bobby I would be back by noon. After thanking my young man and paying a deposit on the cane I took the bus back to Galle.

Back on board I found that the engine had been put safely back in its place, waiting to be bedded and tried out. Before getting the engine in Bobby had to move the boat up the wharf a little and Pixie amused everyone when she did her share of pulling in the ropes. At two thirty I took off again and caught the bus without having to wait. Thinking I was a little early I decided to get off the bus before my destination and walk along the nice stretch of road.

Unfortunately I misjudged how far away I was and ended up walking for one hour and ten minutes. I enjoyed my walk. I was able to watch a very large water monitor swimming in the stream running down to the sea. The beach had lovely clean sand and a very large surf. As I walked I got a thousand *Hello, where are you going?* Someone had been in these parts and taught them all that single phrase.

I enjoyed seeing the little houses and could see there was a lot of cottage industry. For the most part it was making string from coconut fibre. Very clever. With two wheels and a woman pulling the strands of the fibre from the wheels and twisting the pieces into lengths of string.

On arriving at the cane man's house I found my cane all ready in a neat ring and piles of the cut off stuff on the floor. They told me there was no need to soak it first, when I asked. It still looked a bit hairy and later I was told by others that I had got a poor quality cane, still it was certainly, I felt, superior to plastic. It had been an enjoyable day in which I think I had walked a good sixteen miles all told.

One day when walking Pixie along the wharf I was surprised to see a little yellow yacht moored the other side of the wharf. I had never noticed it before and it did not look like a local boat; I thought it was far too small to have come very far. Later we learned it was '*Super Shrimp*' and small as it was the owner Shane Acton had sailed her west from England many years before and was now planning on going through the Red Sea and back to England to complete his circumnavigation. We still felt we were very daring by planning to go via the Red Sea but '*Sandpiper*' at 35ft was huge compared with little 18ft '*Super Shrimp*' that looked more like a dinghy.[1]

The cigarette strike at the Bristol factory continued. I had not been too unhappy about it at first, thinking this was a good way to stop smoking, but there were still some to be had via the black market

1 '*Super Shrimp*' did complete her circumnavigation, the smallest boat to have done so.

sellers and I lacked the willpower to stop. Every time we went into town boys would be standing on the street corners asking if you wanted to buy cigarettes. You could even buy them singly at one rupee each. There was far more pressure to buy than before the strike.

One evening having run out of cigs and longing for a smoke after dinner I walked into town. I had never had the occasion to go into town at night before. The streets were deserted and all the shops closed, even the cigarette boys were not to be seen. The only thing that remained open was one or two little tea shops. In desperation I entered one of these. “No,” they said, “no cigarettes.” It was so dark inside my eyes took a while to adjust. I then saw on the counter bundles of the little rolled-up leaf things called bedi that the poorer of the population smoke. Leaf tobacco just tied up with thread. I picked up a bundle, *better than nothing* I thought. I looked at the man behind the counter, he looked back and laughed. Before he would allow me to purchase them he gave me one as a sample which I lit from the small oil lamp, a wick floating in oil, the only illumination in the place. Not bad, strong and small and tended to go out after a couple of puffs. I bought a bundle of twenty plus a wee cigar that was looking rather lonely next to the bedis.

Returning with my purchases a little girl suddenly shot out of a street and ran after me, wiping the big grin off her face when she saw I was looking, replacing it with a pathetic look. “Give me one rupee,” she said holding out her hand. “What are you doing out at this time of night, you should be in bed” I asked, ignoring her request. She giggled but I don’t think she understood a word. We continued up the road together.

She knew her numbers in English up to ten. Each time she again asked for a rupee and I would just say no. She then increased the amount she had originally asked for. By what reasoning she deducted that having refused her one rupee I might be willing to part with ten I don’t know. Perhaps she was encouraged by the fact I was now laughing. Finally, I put my hand in my pocket and gave her a few coins. She grabbed them and without a word darted off down a side street as swiftly as she had come. I had only gone a few steps farther when again I heard her running feet, catching me up she thrust the coins I had given her back in my hand. "No good," she said. I took a proper look at what I had given her, making sure it was local money; it was and perfectly good if small in value. However, this little girl was a big timer and had no use for anything less than a rupee. We continued on as before, her chanting her rupee theme.

One Sunday we declared it a cleaning day. With the carpenters out of the way we set too both in the cabin and on deck. It was impossible to keep the place even remotely clean and tidy while all the work was going on and it had now become unbearable. We were unable to find so many things that had been buried under tools, wood and other things. I found one large bin of dried pulses were almost walking away. Judging from the state of what remained of the different plastic bags they had been in, the weevils must have come with some white beans and having had their fill of them moved on to other types. Tossing away a large proportion of them and washing the remainder I placed them on paper, spread on the wharf to dry. It rather looked as if I was starting a dry produce stall. Fortunately, no one tried to buy them, perhaps because the smell was not very nice. As they dried they smelt just like a mouse cage that was in need of being cleaned out. We also noticed we had a large cockroach population which scurried furtively away when we uncovered a hiding place.

"There is only one thing to do," said Bobby. "We will have to spray them before they take the boat over." I hated the thought of doing that and so in desperation I sang to them:

Little cockroach go ashore.
I don't want you anymore.
Take your brothers, father, mother,
sisters, cousins,
all relations,
Just take the lot.
If you don't, here's what will happen:
With a spray gun you'll be SHOT!

Being rather tone deaf and having a far less than melodious singing voice, it was not such a bad idea. It made Bob-tail howl and rush on deck and Pixie started banging the deck. What was more to the point, the cockroaches disappeared, well almost. Perhaps as Bobby said they just found better hiding places.

We wanted to have something in our cabin that was not only practical but a little different and nice looking. Coming down the companionway the thing that would now take the eye first would be the drawers dividing the galley from the new seating area. So far it was complete, all but the top, as I had set my heart on having a nice top made of Jak wood. I toured all the lumber places but could not find a plank that was wide enough. We also needed to have two supports from that top to the deckhead. We had tried to find someone who could carve us something original. It appeared that there was not a soul in Galle who did any kind of carving.

I now explored the antique shops just past the railway station to see if something suitable could be found. Starting at one end of the shops I worked my way down. Most traded in second-hand jewellery. At the back of one of these shops I found just what I was looking for. Old broken furniture all piled up, some undercover, some in the open with the grass growing around them. I could find no carvings that would do but spied an old couch, the legs looked perfect. Having come armed with a tape measure I then found they were the exact size I needed and would do well. The couch was old so I gave the legs a little wiggle in the hope they might fall off. That having failed I sought out the owner and asked if I could buy just the legs. Legs were apparently rather common and eventually a pair was found that fitted my measurements and minus a couch. During my leg hunt I spotted, lying in the grass, a large square of wood. Undressed and not quite square, the top I wanted could easily be cut from it. It was very weathered and I hardly dared hope it was jak wood. Tentatively I scraped away at some of the covering mud and mildew. It was! True it was no longer flat, being very warped in fact, but felt that could be taken care of. To these finds I added a small bit of fretwork I liked the look of. The wood weighed a lot but cost little. I happily called a taxi to take me back. I had all I needed.

Our usual time for getting up in the morning was six. On the day Bobby had to get the train to Colombo and collect his money he had to leave at six to catch the train. That morning he woke, looked at the clock and thought it was five thirty. He woke me and we rushed around, he dressing while I made coffee. "No time for toast or cereal," he told me. He was about to go when our ship's clock ran its bells. One, two, silence. We looked at it. Bobby had another hour, it was only five.

Later than expected our two carpenters turned up. They were due to start making the seat frames. I was looking forward to doing the caning. Bassamy showed me a small bit of sticking plaster on his skinny leg and demonstrated how apparently he had cut it with a chisel some days before. Quite why he relayed this interesting fact to me I was not sure at first, but after he discussed with Chipmunk what to do and how to make the frames, he took off. I then gathered he was telling me he was injured and unable to work. Rather odd as only the day before Chipmunk, while working, had just about cut his little toe off which was a nasty thing to do. I had fled and Bobby had bound it up and stuck it all in place with a bit of tape and no more was said about it.

To my surprise Chipmunk, on his own, worked faster and better. Before it was time to leave he had made three frames. As he finished each one I sanded them then he just had to drill the holes. The holes were important, they had to be spaced equally apart with the holes on each side of the frames corresponding with each other. If they did not, however much care you took to weave them, the result would be uneven and a bit of a mess. When he handed me the completed one, I at once noticed the top hole started one inch down on one side but half an inch on the other. Using a tape I pointed this out to him. The impression I gained was that I was now really being petty to quibble over a mere half inch. Apart from that I did not feel it was correct and so counted the holes, one side had one extra hole. He and I counted them over several times before he agreed, shrugged and drilled an extra hole in one of the larger spaces. We could afford neither the time nor wood to have them remade so did the best I could with them. Before he did the final one I think he had grasped why I liked the holes to be evenly spaced.

Bobby returned safely from Colombo, having been amazed at the amount of traffic now on the roads. A few years back we had revisited Colombo for a few days and were delighted to find we were still in no danger of being run down on the roads. The shops also were full whereas before they had been rather empty. He had bought me two silver charms and Pixie a plastic monkey. Bassamy we were not to see again. After a few days we heard he was in hospital for something other than the cut he said he had received. We got quite fond of Chipmunk who now seemed happier and worked as well as he was able, doing on his own the same amount of work that before had taken the two to do.

Our new spreader now had time to dry out and needed painting. Bobby went up the mast and painted it all. I sat at the bottom out of the way of any drips, working on my wooden legs that I was sanding, then lowering Bobby when required. By the time Bobby had finished painting the mast he was completely covered in white paint. He washed first with a cloth dipped in petrol. He then smelt highly inflammable, and then had an even white film of paint all over his body which was a bit eerie.

While Bobby was thus engrossed I went on working on my legs. We both looked up startled when someone ashore yelled "Pixie." She had found the empty paint bucket, bosun's chair and the brush that was still full of paint. Brushes hold a fascination for Pixie, she was now sitting with it in her hands which were coated with white paint, as too was her face and even her tongue. The moment we looked at her she quickly tried to hide the evidence and tossed the brush in the sea where it promptly sank. One expensive brush gone. Bobby set to work cleaning her the same way he had cleaned himself and made no better job of it.

While we were alongside we very rarely went to Don's house and when we did it was not together, as the walk along the road was too far for Pixie. Also, with all the work we were doing we were very tired at the end of the day.

We missed meeting with the owners and crew of other boats that came in, but were anxious to get all the work done. The later we left to go through the Red Sea the worse we could expect the weather to be. Don came round one day and told us we were working too hard. He was giving a party that night for his son and daughter, twins who were celebrating their fifteenth birthday. The guests were for the most part all the 'Yachties'. We said it was now a bit far for Pixie to walk. Don had not overlooked that and was sending a car for her in which we could also ride. Therefore we drove up in style and were the first to arrive. There had been more boats coming in and we hadn't had the chance to meet the crews. We were surprised, therefore, to see Basil, an extremely amusing Australian and the owner of *'Edna Maria'* which we had last seen in Penang. The party was a great success and Pixie managed to get more than her fair share of the goodies and attention.

At the end of January we arranged to go on the slip. When the day came, a fishing boat that was used for tourists and had had her bottom badly ripped on a reef, was still on the slip. Being told we now would not go until noon I went off to get some sandpaper and thought, as there was plenty of time, I'd go first to the post office to collect the mail. We were still awaiting some books that had been sent long ago from the US, and one from my sister in England. We lived in hope that one day they would arrive. We made regular inquiries at the wonderful post office where everyone was always very helpful but could not produce them for us. The letters that were sent addressed Poste Restante were all kept in a drawer of a desk. All you had to do was go in, say excuse me if someone happened to be sitting at that desk, and open it up and have a search for your mail. That day I was pleased to find not only a letter but also a form which informed us there was a parcel somewhere in the building. Parcels I knew from previous searches were put in a large wardrobe in another room and the wardrobe was always kept locked. It never had much in it and the things that it did have remained the same every time I looked. I think they were always hopeful I would claim one of them myself. That day the man with the key was missing. I was given a seat and now several very concerned men rushed around looking for the man or the key. His desk was searched but no key could be found. After some time the man appeared complete with key and was shown my card. He agreed that without doubt it was a sign that the books I had regularly badgered him about had now arrived and that this time when he unlocked the wardrobe they would be waiting for me. As he was the only one with a key how, unless he had placed them there, they could have arrived, none of us thought to question. As soon as the door was flung open I knew there was nothing for me. Just the same old things that had been around for ages. Nevertheless, each item was again inspected to make sure my name was not on one of them.

Everyone had expected the wardrobe to produce something for me so now they all studied the card. It was all printed, the only addition being my name and number two written in the corner. Someone suggested it meant that I had two letters. We now all trooped back to the drawer. I told them that was where I got one letter and the card. Having no luck they ran around again and then someone who presumably had higher authority was shown my card. He made a minute study of all the letters in the draw, even poking around at the back. Yet another trip to the wardrobe, with naturally the same result. Now, the latest man announced, there remained just one more place and no doubt that is where we would find whatever my card referred to; the registered letter department. Here I and some of the staff had to stand the other side of the mesh grill, and an impressive looking safe was opened. It contained very little if anything. Next to it stood an old wooden chest. That too was opened up and delved into but produced nothing of interest.

Now someone remembered they had a book in which they enter mail for which cards are issued. The book was dated with each day's mail but my card had no date. Working from the time before we had arrived in Galle they went down the long list of names. Finally, there was mine dated only a couple of days before. We all looked happy, here was proof, then it was discovered it was two letters from the same friend in the States and that I had previously signed for them. Over one hour hunting for two letters I had received two days before. No one appeared to mind having spent so much time for nothing, just pleased the whole thing had been cleared up. I doubt if any post office in the world would have gone to so much trouble. I had remembered signing for some unknown reason for two letters, they were not registered but had a lot of interesting stamps on a fancy envelope, which I suppose merited special treatment.

I now feared I would not get back in time with the sandpaper before *'Sandpiper'* was on the slip. I dashed into the shop to find it packed and said it was urgent and could they just let me have the sandpaper. Looking round I noticed one of the crowd was off the boat that was on the slip at the moment. He was buying anti-fouling, no hurry, they were not yet off the slip and as he had a bike I also bought anti-fouling and had him take it back for me.

It was the following afternoon before we did go on the slip. Pixie was chained to a pole in the grass to be out of the way and a couple of men came on board to handle the ropes. We left the carpenter on the wharf so he could continue working. Unfortunately, his tools remained on board so all he could do was sit and watch. Halfway up, the block slipped out but with lots of shouting was refitted. They were then afraid to take us right up so we were not in a very good position. By the time a ladder was found so we could get off, it was getting dark so no work was done that day.

The first thing Pixie did the next morning when she got up and went on deck was to untie the ladder and push it down making us prisoners on board until Sunil, a funny crazy little man who often proved helpful when we employed him, came along at seven thirty. After that we chained Pixie to an old boat that she could climb on top and get under which she loved. She now could do what she wanted and we, without her help, might get things done a little faster. The slipway men came and put up some bamboo scaffolding. They made a nice job of it and moved away. "Hi," Bobby called, "how am I going to work on that, you think I can swing around like a monkey?" They had forgotten to put any planks. Matters were not helped when we found there was no water, the only time during our whole stay. The water pipe had broken and it was not fixed until we came off the slip the following day.

Chipmunk, now reunited with his tools, went on working at frames on the wharf. The next day, just before we were about to go back in the water, he came up the ladder complete with tools and promptly turned round and threw down the ladder! Was he mimicking Pixie? It was time for him to go and we asked in sign language how he intended now to get off. In reply he indicated he wanted to come and help so let him be.

In spite of having an extra hand on board, disaster was only narrowly averted. Sunil started pushing off one side so hard we were fast going into the next. Chipmunk was helping all he could and was more helpful than Sunil which was no recommendation. I now told them what to do, Sunil at least understanding English. Bobby was at the wheel. We had left the awning up so he could not see where he was going. Getting a rope ready I told Sunil he must jump ashore to attach it to a bollard as soon as we were near enough. Suddenly we were headed right head on to the wharf. "Stop, jump," I yelled, intending the first for Bobby, the second for Sunil. Poor Sunil, fearing we would crash right into the wharf, got frantic and tried to push us off with the pole he had but it threw him on his back. Rather funny really but no time to laugh. I yelled again to Bobby and Sunil took up the cry. "Bobby, Bobby," as if he was shouting a last desperate prayer.

Fortunately, Jim from *'Maori Lass'*, a New Zealand boat, had now come on the wharf so he ran to our assistance. Bobby had backed off in time and we made another attempt. All went well and we had Jim and Jan on board intending to give them a beer that Sunil, we thought, had bought that morning. He assured us he had paid for it but had left it in the shop; for Sunil it sounded reasonable and we had to be content that the next day he would complete the transaction and bring us the beer.

Bobby went ashore next day and Sunil, having cleared everything off our deck, gave it a much needed scrub. Pixie was tied farther down on the wharf to a bollard so she was out of the way, she and Sunil not being on the best of terms. There was no one around, and she had a nice long chain and still in sight of us. My attention was drawn to a lot of loud shouting and commotion that end. I looked up to see a local powerboat had come alongside to tie up on Pixie's bollard. Before they were properly alongside Pixie took a leap and landed on their deck scattering the crew, the boat now drifted farther away from the wharf. Pixie hung on to the boat and the clip on her chain pulled off. The crew of the boat had now all fled below leaving only Pixie on deck, with no one at the controls. I rushed along the wharf as soon as I had heard the commotion, but by then it was too far for me to jump on board. I was left standing helplessly on the wharf yelling, "Bring my monkey back," at the top of my voice. Heads appeared on board and they managed to get the boat alongside while Pixie, now very upset, screamed at them. I jumped on board and grabbed her up and jumped back on land. I don't know who was the most upset. After all that, the boat decided not to come alongside and took off out of sight. Pixie I took down in the cabin for a long session of cuddling until she stopped whimpering.

Independence Day on the 4th February. Thinking there might be some celebrations I went ashore with my camera. On the green outside the fort, schoolgirls were giving a gymnastic display. It was not quite what I was expecting but on my arrival at the back of a small crowd that was watching I was soon pushed forward and room made for me on a concrete pipe so I had a clear view over all the heads. After the gymnastic display there was a bicycle race through town – that was it!

I had been talking to a retired police officer who then took me to his home for tea and to meet his family after which he asked me to come and look at his shop. I tried to get out of this as I had no money on me and felt once there, whatever his shop contained, I might be expected to purchase something. He insisted, so off we went. The shop turned out to be a gem factory and high class jewellery shop. Lovely to look at but hardly anything I would be buying. I talked to the charming woman who asked how I had heard of the shop. I indicated my policeman, who she had never seen before. He obviously had nothing to do with the shop, just hoped I would buy something and that then he might get a little commission. It was all a little embarrassing not to be able to comply with his wishes, the more so when I was given a free packet of uncut gems.

As I had told him about Pixie he now asked if I would like to see a white monkey. Always willing to see a monkey, white or otherwise, I agreed. We then set out on a long climb up a hill to a little village with small hut-like houses nestled among the trees. A very attractive place. He made several inquiries of passing people but no monkey of any kind did we see. We then entered one of the small, poorer looking houses. Here I expected to see the monkey. No white monkey could have amazed me as much as what I now saw in this poor little hut. A wooden table was strewn with cut and polished gems. A young boy was placing dozens of garnets in jewellery settings. In the corner was a furnace and tongs where I was told they worked the silver. A small girl was now sent to bring a box to me. When that was opened to my astonishment it was full of finished jewellery. Wooden elephants covered in silver and studded with gems – one was covered in gold which surprised me, gold I thought being rare in Sri Lanka. To find such a mass of valuable gems in such a place was like a fairy tale, I could hardly believe my eyes. The value of their little hut complete with the few bits of furniture I am sure would be less than the average western garage, minus the car. The jewellery and gems on the other hand I could only guess at, but would surely purchase a grand furnished house. As it was not even hinted at that I might be interested in buying a gem or two, I suspect they were contracted to work and did not own any of the treasure the house contained. The little boy and girl turned out to be the policeman's grandchildren, I had guessed this by their reaction to him on our arrival. He now asked if I would take their photo. I was only too happy to oblige. I should have asked if I could photo the place to start with but was too overwhelmed by what I saw. I suggested taking a photo of them working at the table strewn with gems. My suggestion was turned down. A photo outside they said would be better. The area outside was attractive but commonplace and I wanted a photo of the inside. I told them for my camera the light was much too strong and that it would be better inside. I won my point but the children had disappeared the very moment I had agreed to take a photo of them. To my dismay they reappeared all dressed up. The little girl who had looked so cute and natural in her tatty little dress, now had on a long dress to the ground covered in sequins. Of course they did not wish to sit at the table where all their finery would be lost to view but stood in front of it. Grandfather then stood between them. They were all set for a typical formal family portrait with the table and everything else completely blocked from view. My film was a slide film so it was not until we got to Europe and I had a pictured taken off that I was able to send them a copy as requested.

Chipmunk was getting on nicely with the long seat and lockers, doing as well as could be with his limited tools. His main fault was he was just too thrifty, not something I thought I would ever discourage. However, we wanted screws to be used rather than nails. This had been made clear from the start when we had both carpenters. To the end it was a running battle. Brass screws were obtainable and inexpensive in Galle and I had purchased a lot, they knew they only had to ask if they wanted more. We hid any nails we had, still we would catch them banging in huge nails. In dismantling the old galley and locker the supports were found to be nailed together. Most of the nails were bent and looked useless, they kept them and would hammer them back into shape to reuse. The amount of wood that would be needed was also difficult to estimate. We left it to them to say how much was needed but stipulated what kind of wood we wanted and where. We had fallen in love with the jak wood and wanted that in most of the places that showed. The seat frames were made of it except the last three which were made while we were on the slip from another kind of wood. We let that go as they would be covered by cushions anyway. The sides were also of jak wood and looked very nice. Sadly, the front of the seat, just a strip along the top and the arm rest on one side, could only have been made from something picked up on the wharf. Still time was getting short and we were getting less fussy. A few remaining jobs were put in the hands of the slipway carpenters. Pixie was now to have her own platform, sticking out from the port side of the cockpit. Here she could be chained near us at sea, have a nice view and be out of the way of the sails. We, unnecessarily as it turned out, made a rather elaborate design with stanchions round it so an awning could be attached, the platform could be hinged, so in bad weather it could be pulled up and made fast to the rails. Parts for the stanchions proved difficult to obtain or fix for some reason. It finally took a couple of weeks to complete. We were pleased with the result and so was Pixie, after she got used to it. Later she spent many happy hours at sea working out how to remove the screws etc. My wooden legs were also attached to our little divider, a far harder job than we had realised. At one point when they were screwing the base in they asked for a saw. Why they wanted a saw I could not understand but handed one over and watched in case they were thinking of sawing my legs in half or something. I was rather taken aback when I saw they sawed the handle of their own over-large screwdriver in half. They had found it too hard to work in the space below. Had they asked, we had a whole set of screwdrivers they could have borrowed instead of the saw.

Not everything was left to the carpenters. A spoke of our wheel had broken off. Bobby found a suitable bit of wood and whittled away at it and turned out a very nice new spoke which he set in place.

By then a year had passed since we left Singapore and Pixie and Bob-tail were due for another rabies shot to keep their health cards up to date. At the vet's office I explained what I required and asked him if he could come to the boat and give the injections. He was willing but he had no vaccine and told me I would have to go to Colombo to get some. Rabies vaccine was not something that I had ever had occasion to buy before and would have thought it highly unlikely anyone would be so foolhardy to sell it to me. I asked where and how I would get it. He would write out a prescription as there were several places that might have it, he would find out. Leafing through the telephone directory he made a number of calls to Colombo. After several calls one was found, he then outlined the procedure for buying it. First the important thing was to keep it cold and so I would have to take a flask with ice in and then put it in a refrigerator. It all sounded very dodgy, so when he said he would go on the Monday and get it if I paid his fare, I readily agreed. It would cost no more than if I paid my own fare with the added risk I might never find the place, or having found it and bought a flask, dropping it.

I left, arranging to call for him on the Tuesday and bring him to *'Sandpiper'*. Arriving at his office at the appointed time I found he was not there, but waiting for me in his house on Dickinson Road. This was a lovely walk through a jungle of coconut palms and banana plants, with houses peeping through the foliage. Some of the house were not quite hidden and they were lovely old ones. The vet lived at the back of one of the grander houses. The waiting room was typical, bare of anything but chairs to sit on. Then I saw against one wall a marvellous couch, all carve, not varnished and in perfect condition. The seat and back done in the typical cane work. Oh, but how could he, the owner of such a beautiful piece of furniture have done such a thing. It was not done with cane but plastic! My eyes popped a second time when the vet showed me to his car. So far all the cars I had seen in Galle were real old bangers, by comparison this one was magnificent. He had, he explained, been to Australia and bought the car in Singapore on his return.

We arrived to find Pixie happily sitting on Jim's lap grooming his hair. Bob-tail was done first in the cabin and then Pixie was brought down. The vet was competent at this job and aroused no fear in either of them but when Pixie saw the needle she clung to me and whimpered. She was cross with the vet when it was over so we put her back on the wharf with her latest boyfriend, Jim.

Shaun now arrived, a single-handed Canadian off *'TaganitaII'*. We had previously exchanged books and flags with him and he now came at an opportune moment bringing a gift for Pixie, some chocolate, so like a child after their injection she got her reward.

Before we left the wharf the navy ship returned for a day and that night Pixie's boyfriend from his previous trip came to pay her a visit. We had just finished dinner and looked up to see someone was standing in our companionway. Pixie recognised him before we did and looked very happy. He and his friend came in and Pixie claimed him at once, grooming him from head to toe. His friend she ignored, except to examine his trousers which were nice corduroy ones. Contentedly she fell asleep between her two admirers and we all had coffee. Waking just as we had finished she wanted her share so we all drained our cups and glasses into hers. Satisfied she drank it and started grooming her boyfriend again.

Finally, all the work we needed to be alongside to do was finished, with the engine now working nicely we were able to motor out back to our buoy. Once more we could row ashore and join the other yacht owners at Don's house. Many of the boats we had known had by then left with new ones taking their place. That evening Don told us the crew of *'Telstar'* had gone to him earlier full of excitement saying a new yacht had just arrived, with a great big baboon at the wheel. "How many people?" Don asked. "We only saw one man with a beard."

"Was the boat called *'Sandpiper'*?"

"Yes, that was the name."

"Well," said Don, "it was not a baboon you saw but Pixie, the current attraction for the last one-and-a-half months."

Don now suggested that after all our hard work we should spend a few days relaxing. This he assured us would be good for us before our big sail ahead. He suggested we go to Coconut Cabana, where the new year party had been held. We could have one of the little huts at a very low rental and eat at the owner's restaurant. It sounded delightful and we agreed. Don loaned Bobby a bike. I had never seen Bobby on a bike before but he said he remembered riding one in the dim past and off he went and booked a hut for us.

The following day after taking the batteries to the fisheries to be charged in our absence, we went around to Don to see if he could arrange transport. One bike for the two of us with Pixie and Bob-tail was not really adequate. Happily, Don had a minibus waiting and put the bike in the back in case we wanted to use that also. Time to go and Bob-tail, sensing something was in the air, had disappeared and refused to even answer our calls. Knowing he just had to be aboard some place we opened up all the lockers. No Bob-tail. We then started moving the floorboards over the bilge. Bob-tail moved forward as we did, until he was cornered in the shallow part by our bunk. Into the basket he went. With Bob-tail protesting loudly we got his basket and Pixie, along with ourselves, into the dinghy. Fortunately, Pixie did not try and let him out but sat on top of the basket peeping through the small opening at him. The ride was a short one, Pixie had been in the bus before but hated the way it rattled and sat on the floor ignoring the awful noise Bob-tail was making.

Coconut Cabana was even more attractive in the daylight. There were only four little cabins and we chose one in the most attractive setting, farther back so no one would pass. Our little home was surrounded by palm we could chain Pixie on, and we took Bob-tail in the hut. This hut was perhaps copied from a fairy tale book, *'Snow White and the Seven Dwarfs'*. Being slightly raised from the ground, logs graduating in height had been placed as steps, the interior was high and so cool but tiny and all rough wood. Two single beds together to make a large one, a table and chair. No varnish or paint. We just loved it. If Bob-tail decided to sharpen his claws on some part or Pixie chew on a beam no one would be any the wiser. Bob-tail looked a bit sullen at first and refused to leave his basket. When he did and had explored the place we opened the door so he could sit in the entrance and take stock of his surroundings. With the sea in front and the trees surrounding us it was just the most perfect spot. That was until a dog barked making Bob-tail jump, instead of moving into the hut he dashed out of the doorway. Three dogs now appeared, thinking this was a good game they dashed after poor Bob-tail with us close on their heels. Pixie still chained to the palm, started screaming her head off. We had in about five minutes of our arrival turned a beautiful, peaceful place into bedlam.

The dogs turned out to be quite friendly and when Bob-tail reached a fence and went under it they gave up and went off. The fences were attractive, made by sticking large cuttings of several different types of tree reasonably close together, then letting them be woven together with vines. Such a fence Bob-tail had managed to worm his way under. He was now in the private garden of the house next door. I was encouraging him to come back the way he had gone in when a child started to yell, sending Bob-tail off again. Bobby saw him and called that it was OK, he could exit the garden near the beach. Bob-tail too had seen this opening and made a spring over to what looked like green weeds growing. He promptly sank, having landed in what turned out to be a stream. Dripping wet we returned him to the hut where he went under the bed and remained until nightfall. Pixie made friends with Richard the manager who wanted to feed her with some bread but plain bread was not to her liking and she ignored it. One of the dogs decided if she did not want it he would have it and stole it, upon which Pixie gave him a good smack. For a moment we thought there was going to be a fight but the dog having his mouth full could not snap back and disappeared with the bread.

The bay was beautiful, taking Pixie we wandered along the beach. A little farther out in the sea but still in shallow water, tall upright stakes had been planted, on top of which was a small platform. They looked as if they might be useful for some kind of seabird to perch on, perhaps even to build a nest. Instead of any kind of bird, fishermen would be perched cross legged on the tiny platform, fishing. They stayed put for hours and in fact we never did see one getting on or off his little platform. For that matter, though we spent many hours on the beach, we never noticed them catch a fish either.

Bath time in our home in Singapore.

Author steps aboard.

Bobby and Pixie now safely back on board.

Sewing the Malaysian flag.

Before entering Port Kelang we see the survey boat Bobby designed.

'Sandpiper' gets a change of colour from blue to white.

In the cockpit.

Getting the aries steering vane on board.

Lumut club house.

The Hinxman Family in their dinghy.

Family breakfast.

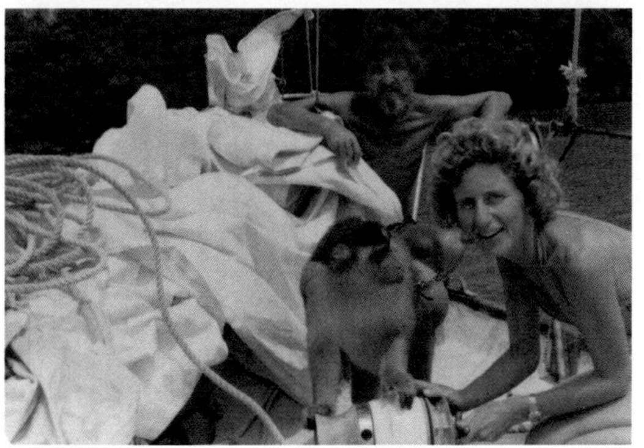

What are you doing?

Keeping cool.

Will eat up here to keep an eye on things.

Pixie and Bobby explore the islands.

Back on the single bunk with Bob-tail.

'Sandpiper' off Penang, taken by a friend.

Bobby fixes the baggy wrinkles to the rigging.

The Langkawi Islands, like sleeping monsters.

The most perfect anchorage, Langkawi.

Going ashore, 'Sandpiper' in the distance.

Climbing the rocks to the lake.

Shampoo in the lake.

Bob-tail guards the boat when we go ashore.

Heading for Sri Lanka.

Don Windsor, who gave all yachties a warm welcome and help.

Galle fishing boats.

No plastic in those days: note pots of curd hanging up.

Our delightful home for a few days. 40 years later we know it was Unawatuna. So changed.

Pixie and Bob-tail enjoy the double bunk.

New layout of the cabin.

In Suez, we tied up to an old wreck of a tug boat.

Shifting a plinth outside the church of the Holy Sepulchre.

The streets could not have changed much in 2000 years.

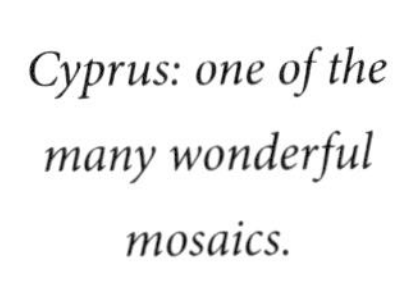

Cyprus: one of the many wonderful mosaics.

'Snowflake' we rub noses with the glass between us.

Sitges: Michael on board 'Sandpiper'.

Not quite as big as Michael but accepted as a substitute after Michael left.

It is useful to have a crew member who can take a compass bearing.

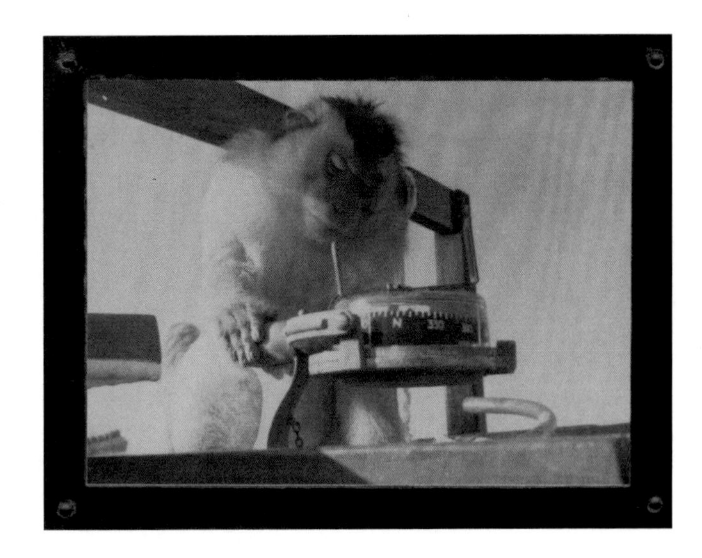

Alongside in Sitges.

Bobby takes a sight with his left eye.

Virginia and John bid us a safe journey as we leave Sitges.

The sun rises for a new dawn.

Pixie soon became the centre of attention when some little children spotted her. The children were very sweet and Pixie loved them and kept looking round to make sure they were following as she made her way to some boulders to climb up and get a better view. Spotting a banana skin she picked it up and looked at it. Normally she would not have bothered, she knew if a skin was empty or not. The children got the message, and found a banana for her. That gone another was produced, then fruit started appearing fast. Most of it came from a European sitting on the beach who had brought a lot with him, probably with the idea of having a picnic. The children begged a good portion of it and then gave it to Pixie. A young boy climbed a palm and picked a coconut, came down, chopped the top off and gave it to her to drink. Heavy though a coconut is, she downed all the water and then waited for him to cut it in half so she could get at the jelly. She had put on a lot of weight and we were hoping that if she had a few days of hard exercise she would lose some of it but with all the food she was getting that looked unlikely.

The shower and WC facilities were in a separate building near our little hut. We were enjoying a shower and nicely covered in shampoo when the water eased to a trickle and we had to rinse off as best we could. Later we saw a man working hard at a pump handle and saw that he had to pump up the water to fill the tanks for the showers. We could have done it ourselves had we known. He pumped for hours and we decided to be a little more careful with the shower water in future. The large open-sided cabana where we had celebrated the new year was going to be for food and drinks but was not yet in operation. We were to take our breakfast and dinner at the owner's restaurant a little farther along the beach. After dark the man who had been working the pump came to direct us to the restaurant. There was no electric; our hut had two kerosene lamps and we had brought a flashlight with us. We were led along a track leading from the back of the huts. We thought Pixie would object strongly to this walk in the dark in unknown territory but she realised at once she must follow the man and so he led, with Pixie walking nicely behind him while Bobby and I brought up the rear.

The owner's restaurant turned out to be his private dwelling place and we the only customers. We had been shown the menu earlier in the day. A set meal, two actually, each listed a wide range of vegetables, the difference in the two being that one also had an omelette and the other fish. We asked for the omelette. Inside we met the owner's wife and children and were shown to seats at the table. Pixie was given the best chair with wooden arm rests. Pixie, they told us, was the first monkey they had had to dine in their place. We thought we were to be joined by more people as the table was large and a number of clean but well-worn paper plates were set around, they, however, were used as mats, and dishes of food placed on them. Pixie having been placed in the chair of honour, we tied her chain round the leg of the chair to be on the safe side and sat either side of her. The owner thought it nicer if we sat the other side of the table so we complied as Pixie was on her best behaviour.

The table was soon piled with all the dishes of every kind of vegetable. We put a little of each on Pixie's plate and we all set to. It was all very good but surprisingly not very spicy, I doubt if a chilli had come within waving distance of it, perhaps they thought we would not like the food highly spiced. Pixie found the table from her chair a bit high so balanced her plate on the arm of the chair. When she finished I gave her a second helping which was a mistake. She ate only a little more and then deliberately tuned it upside down spilling the food onto the floor. We apologised on her behalf for such bad manners but they were very nice about it and said they were enjoying having her. Having eaten our fill, the wife went to clear the dishes. That was another thing we should have stopped. Pixie might not want any more but she objected to having anything removed and so made a leap at the poor woman pulling the chair she was tied to with her. The woman moved almost as fast and only got a slight scratch on her foot but was a bit shocked, not being used to her customers leaping at her for no reason. Having righted her chair and passed the dishes off the table ourselves, we arranged it so Pixie could not pull it over again and she then sat back contented, she had made it clear that she was the prime guest and things had to be done her way. We now all tucked into the pineapple that was served. Over coffee we talked with the owner. He was looking forward to having electricity, saying it would be less expensive than the kerosene lamps he used. He had a very nice Tilly lamp but the mantles were expensive as both lamp and mantles had to come from England. After a very enjoyable evening we were shown out the opposite way we had come in and found ourselves on the beach only a short distance from our little hut.

Pixie, quite worn out after her exciting day, claimed half the bed for herself and was soon asleep. We left the door open for Bob-tail so he could now go out and explore. For the most part he preferred to walk around on the rafters above us, showing off perhaps, or keeping out of danger as another cat came and sat outside and sang to him.

We went to breakfast wondering what 'string hoppers' were as quoted on the menu, making various crazy suggestions. We decided our best guess was fried grasshopper which we naturally planned to turn down, but thought Pixie would appreciate them.

In daylight we could now see the outside of the house and garden. On the beach side were trees and a wooden table right opposite the window along the dining table side. We left Pixie there. She eats little breakfast so thought she would be better off outside, and we could bring out any likely titbit like string hoppers. String hoppers turned out to be cold noodles knitted into little round mats. We also had grated coconut, fried eggs, tomato, cucumber, onion and very thick slices of bread and jam.

We spent two more days in that delightful place and if time had permitted could have happily stayed for months. We explored the beach and found a nice freshwater stream. There were more children who were kept busy finding things for Pixie to eat or just play with. Pixie and I would get up just before the sun and stand watching it rise, bathing us in beautiful colours. The view across the bay was a picture. The sea was crystal clear with the dark reefs showing clearly. We would climb the boulders and from the other side look over to Galle. Usually in our walks Pixie holds us up wishing to stop and meditate every so often. Now, when I wanted to stand and just look, she dragged me along in a hurry. We flew along leaving Bobby behind until she found a bush with clusters of red berries which she found very tasty. Later Pixie and I got to a point overlooking the temple. Looking down we saw Bobby looking for us. We called and waited for him to catch us up but he had little time to enjoy the sights if he wished to stay with us. Pixie was off down again in a mad rush. It did not matter just where we were, everything was beautiful and unspoiled, the world was as it should be and we fairly danced about the place.

Our second dinner went off with no bad behaviour by Pixie. After a day's exercise she was more tired than hungry. We sat either side of her and after eating she fell asleep in her chair while we talked and learned some interesting facts.

During my shopping expeditions round Galle I had found in the small shops near the market, woven leaf baskets with no opening. They obviously contained something. The question was what? When I asked, no one could think of the word for it in English. They did some elaborate miming, which only added to my confusion, and then took a bottle and poured a little out on my hand for me to taste. "Honey," I declared. I was fascinated by the original way they sold it. Each one was weighed before being sold and it worked out extremely cheap. I bought several and thought they looked nice, hanging down from our grab rail in the cabin. Soon they started to leak and I had to bottle the contents. I learned later from Don that the woven baskets were made from the fronds of the areca-nut palm, the nut of which is grated and chewed with the beetle leaf. The woven basket is only intended to hold the contents until a bottle can be found. That night at Don's we were given the *honey* with curd. "Is this wild bee honey?" I asked. I then learned that it was not even honey but nectar, that floored me for a little but my informant went on to tell us how it is collected. A man will climb a coconut or a kitul palm when they are in flower. They bind the flower and tap it each day to collect the natural nectar.

They then heat the nectar to make it less runny. However, if it is not heated by the next day it will have fermented and become toddy. Kept even longer it is then arrack – a fermented alcoholic drink. On the other had if you added some spice to it on the first day it would turn into good coconut vinegar. That was not all. The balls wrapped in leaves which I had taken to be *gula malacca* (raw sugar) turned out to be this same nectar that had been boiled a long time until solidified and called jaggery. I have always found palms interesting ever since discovering how very many different types there are. Now I felt they were even more amazing.

At the end of our last beautiful day Bobby got on the bike and went off to get transport for our return to Galle. Pixie and I spent half an hour eyeing a large lizard that was in return eyeing us, and accepting raw pumpkin that Pixie's little friends were eating and sharing with us. We returned by taxi which Pixie preferred to the minibus. The moment we drew level with Don's house Pixie wanted to make sure we did not go past and climbed on and over the driver's shoulder and out through the window. We had decided to have dinner at Don's that night, so I stayed with Pixie while Bobby went back to the boat with Bob-tail.

Our decision to eat at Don's had been made by us to round off our little holiday. We were expected anyway as another of Don's sons was having a birthday and so a good time to celebrate.

So far in Galle we had failed to see any wild monkeys. Don declared they were in his garden all the time. Other people saw them but it so happened they were never around when we, who so wanted to see them, visited. That day, Bobby had only just left with Bob-tail when I heard a noise in the trees. There on the other side of the driveway from where I had Pixie, a beautiful little black face looked down at me from a guava tree. I got little more than a glance from him but he was very interested in Pixie who looked back at him with less interest. I then noticed a number of them in the palms. Purple-faced leaf monkeys with long tails, very different from our Pixie. They left but returned again when Bobby arrived so we all got to see them. It was another very enjoyable evening spent with a crowd from the remaining boats. A perfect ending to our days of relaxation.

Perhaps the arrack that Don was very generous with that night had a hand in things the next day. We wanted now to stock up the boat with as much provisions as possible, everything being very cheap, and so we'd need transport to carry it all back. Every boat did this before leaving and Don provided transport in the form of either his minibus or car. Now something was wrong with both, and he went on to say if things continued this way he would put a cover over a bullock cart and use that for transport. "A bullock cart!" I exclaimed. "Have you got one?"

"Sure," replied Don. "Well why can't you let me have a bullock cart to go shopping with tomorrow?" I asked. For some reason this was considered very funny and everyone had a good laugh. "I am serious," I protested. "I don't like cars or buses but have never driven a bullock cart but would just love to. Do you have to practise driving a bullock cart?" I added as an afterthought. With a big smile on his face Don sat back and said, "If you really want to, I will have the bullock cart and driver ready for you tomorrow; he is going into town for me anyway and you can go too if you like." I said I would most certainly like to and would be there next morning and I was.

Arriving at Don's next morning loaded with empty baskets I found the bullock cart awaiting me. I climbed in and sat at the back of the empty cart, anticipating a leisurely ride into town. Speed from a bullock was the last thing I expected as I would often overtake this mode of transport when I was walking.

No sooner were we on the road to town that we took off at such a turn of speed I was nearly thrown out of the back and had to cling on for dear life. I was bouncing about two feet in the air like a sack of feathers. *Surely*, I thought, *the bullock had suddenly gone mad and there was no knowing where we might land up*. We passed another normal bullock cart and having done so the driver of that one started thrashing his bullock with a stick so that was also galvanized into the same frenzy, staying close on our heels. A race was in progress.

I had been concentrating on hanging on and was facing the way we had come. Now seeing we were part of a race I realised if our poor bullock had indeed gone mad it was because he was being given the same treatment as the one in hot pursuit. With an effort I managed to swivel round. Sure enough the driver was giving the bullock hard punishment. I yelled at him to stop beating the poor animal. He failed to hear, which was not surprising considering the noise of the rattling carts and the yells of the driver behind; at the same time a third had now joined in the race whose bullock had bells. I made an attempt to get farther inside the cart within reaching distance of the driver so I could start prodding him, the jolting was too much, I gave up, wedging myself as firmly as possible against the side. The inhabitants of Galle don't have much excitement in their lives and three bullock carts having a race into town, one with a crazy, as I now felt myself to be, white woman clinging for dear life was the event of the week. All traffic had to stop and give way to us and the pedestrians stood along the road and cheered and waved. I felt I should pretend this was a sponsored event and that I was in full control. I made a big effort to smile and wave in a queenly manner at the crowds and not to grimace too much every time I was shot into the air. Thankfully it was not far at the rate we were going before we reached the town, just before my driver's stick snapped in half leaving him with a useless few inches. The race was over.

Bags of rice, dahl, potato, onions, a stalk of green bananas and heaps of other green fruit and vegetables that would keep were piled into the cart. Our bullock looked none the worse for his race but I felt he must have enjoyed the slow plod back fully laden than the rush in an empty cart. It is hard to tell with bullocks, they don't change their expression much.

Bobby went ashore and got back the batteries that the fisheries had put on charge for him. For some reason they insisted on being paid in foreign currency which was maddening as the smallest denomination of foreign currency we had was £10 and the change was given back in rupees. A lot of money for us to spend, as now we had most things we needed and were ready to leave. While Bobby was ashore Charts turned up again. We had, mercifully, not been worried by him any more after the last time we had refused to sell him the fridge. Now he knew we were leaving and said he had come for the fridge and had his elder brother with him who also wanted to see it. When they were told that Bobby was not here, they said they would return at six that evening. We were rather pleased when the time came and it was pouring with rain and no one came. We were just preparing for bed at ten thirty when again Charts turned up. They were quieter that night deciding I suppose to give us no cause for complaint or reason not to let the buy the fridge. We gave in and accepted 700 rupees. Apart from the fact that on leaving one of them fell backwards down the cockpit well, all went well.

We could have left on Friday but Bobby decided Friday was not a good day to start a voyage and so decided to wait until Saturday and spend Friday letter writing, collecting a last pile of letters from the post office and buying a few bits of old silver jewellery by weight with the money from the T-shirts. I also could not resist buying an old ola leaf book containing, I was told, medicine recipes. It was minus its wooden cover but still I felt a beautiful and interesting item. That night we had dinner at Don's house and said goodbye. Our sadness at leaving was tempered by the excitement of getting underway again.

Up at six the following day. Three other boats besides us remained, all of us heading for the Red Sea and planning to leave that day. *'Sunshine'* and *'Maori Lass'* had both got their clearance the day before; *'Hawaiki'*, like us, still had them to get. Bobby collected all the papers and went on deck to row ashore. "Where is the dinghy," he called down to me. "What do you mean where is it?" I called back. "Well it is not where I tied it last night."

"So look the other side," I called back. "It's gone," he said. "The painter is still here but no dinghy at the end of it."

Stupidly we now both stood on deck looking all around us. Not a sign of the dinghy. *'Hawaiki'*, a New Zealand boat with John, Nora and their two sons, was on the next buoy. We called over to them.

One of the sons came over and rowed Bobby around to look for the dinghy but with little hope as the painter had obviously been cut. Bobby reported the loss to the police station. Then the police launch ran him around and they looked on all the local boats but there was no sign of it. Not surprising as anyone taking it would have let the air out and could have hidden it anywhere.

Meanwhile, *'Sunshine'* left and I continued getting everything put away in lockers, wondering if now we would be able to leave.

A few days earlier a Trimaran had arrived with Dick, Neil and a young girl on board. We had met them the night before and learned that they knew *'Sandpiper'* well having sailed on her with Charlie Green. They came on board and liked our new arrangement and said it looked a lot cosier than before. They told us how *'Sandpiper'* was the last boat out of Cambodia and how Charlie had liked to keep the boat unobtrusive looking. He had been very upset one day when one of them had decided to polish up the brass on deck. Charlie was afraid the local pirates might think it was gold. Later they came around with a big bag of paperback books. I handed over some of ours that we had read to take to Don for others to read.

Bobby was still ashore with the police when *'Maori Lass'* came up to say goodbye. Lucky them, we should have been leaving then too.

John and Bobby returned in John's dinghy looking glum. One customs officer was on leave, the other had disappeared, so there was no one to issue clearance which meant John, like us, could not leave. The police were looking for our dinghy and already had pulled in all the criminal types. Bobby said he would give a reward for the recovery of the dinghy. We desperately needed our dinghy, our only means to get ashore in places, but we also wanted to leave as soon as possible as already we were later in the year than we had planned.

Did selling our refrigerator have any bearing on the matter? We did not think so. If we had refused to sell it, perhaps, but why would they wait until after they had it to steal the dinghy? We had told them we were leaving Saturday but then that was common knowledge. It turned out it was no secret we had sold the fridge to Charts. Don had heard about it, a watchman on a boat had seen the whole thing. Charts, they now told us, was a known criminal. Just how criminal it was for us to sell, or for Charts to buy, a second-hand fridge we were never sure. It now was certainly common knowledge but we were never questioned about it.

John and Bobby went ashore again that evening to try and get clearance but still the custom man had not turned up. Later John's son came to tell us the man had arrived so once again they went off, both this time returning with their clearance. Bobby in the hope the dinghy would be found and we could leave as planned.

Don had his spies out in force seeing if they could hear anything about our dinghy. One returned to ask if we had a platform for an engine on the dinghy. We did not and the man was very secretive and said no more, but it gave us a little hope that he may be on to something.

We then heard the very sad news that *'Del Mondo'*, the Italian boat whose crew had spent Christmas celebrations with us at Don's, had been sunk on the reefs in the Maldives. Fortunately no lives had been lost. It was a beautiful well-found boat. Bobby had helped put the mast up when she was alongside and had been very impressed. We really felt for them. Our dinghy loss by comparison was nothing.

Next morning John and family on *'Hawaiki'* slowly sailed off, hardly a breath of wind but they were moving and we, now the last boat heading for the Red Sea, were still stationary. Dick on the trimaran had kindly said to give him a shout any time we needed to go ashore. In the afternoon Bobby again went ashore to see if there were any further developments. The police showed Bobby two pieces of plywood fixed either side of a frame. Bobby was easily able to identify it as having once been a shelf we had discarded from *'Sandpiper'* and which Bobby had used to put in the bottom of the dinghy to stand the batteries on and had left there. The police looked happy and felt now they were on the right track. They certainly were doing all that could be done.

The thieves must have also felt that the police were soon to catch up with them. A spy reported in that the dinghy would come to Don's house in a taxi on payment of 400 rupees. Naturally Don did not really wish to get so involved nor did we wish it. On the other hand if we did not do it their way they were likely to dispose of it which would end any chance of us getting it back. We were now all having to act like criminals just to get back our own property. More messages were relayed back and forth but they refused to deliver any place but Don's. By eight that evening Bobby and Don decided they only thing to do was to go along with them and pay the ransom. To tell the police of the latest development now would only result in certain destruction of the dinghy and untold delay by the police if they learned we had got the dinghy back, and it was important for us to be on our way. We felt bad about this part of it as the police had been good and most helpful but saw no way round this problem. The plan they worked out was that once the taxi with the dinghy arrived at Don's house Bobby would get in and they would go to the fisheries wharf and get it on board and then we were to sail at once. The last bit we did not wish to do as it would be dark but agreed to sail at dawn the following morning.

Accordingly, that afternoon we moved away from our buoy and went alongside the fisheries wharf again. Bobby went ashore as we now had to be careful and not arouse the suspicions of the security guards. We tied up right at the end, one guard appeared and stayed ages as soon as we arrived. Often, in the past, we had chatted to the security guards in the evening, now we had to try and discourage any friendly visits. I stayed below with Pixie and only a small kerosene lamp burning, with the curtains drawn over the windows. I kept peeping out and saw a guard coming our way again so took Pixie for a walk to draw them off; returning with Pixie I saw two more guards farther down the wharf but in sight, talking to each other. There was silence, I peeped out, the coast was clear and it was now eight, Bobby could come back any minute. Then the silence was broken, more talking sounding very near. Bob-tail who had gone ashore suddenly flew down into the cabin. Pixie was asleep. Turning the remaining lamp off I peeped out again, two guards and a woman, most unusual, perhaps they wished to show her Pixie. They must have decided either no one was aboard or we were asleep. All was silent once again.

Exactly on nine Bobby arrived in the taxi and the wharf was deserted. Hurriedly they got the deflated dinghy out of the trunk and on the boat and down into the cabin. The driver was dreadfully drunk and nearly ruined the whole thing when he tried to back off down the wharf and almost went over the edge into the sea. Then his engine stalled and Bobby had to direct him to make sure he got clear of us and out of the dock area before he had a disastrous accident.

Things had not gone quite to plan as in the end the kidnappers got scared and refused to even go as far as Don's. Also Galle was deserted of taxis except for the one with the drunken driver. An agreement was finally reached. We had our dinghy back which was the main thing. Now we were ready to leave.

Full sails,
warm nights,
no swell,
Moonlight.
Pure contentment,
sheer delight.

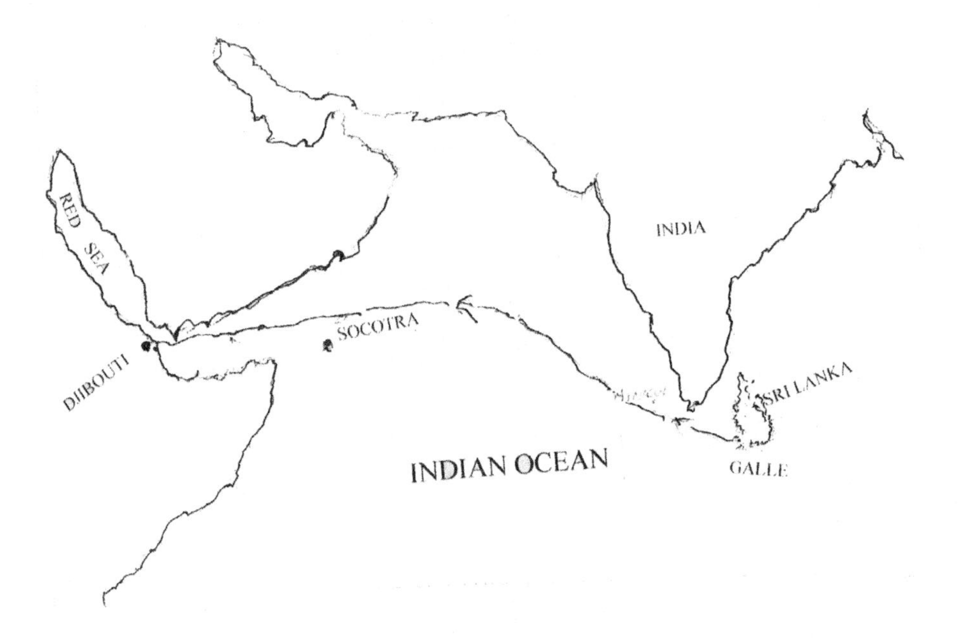

The Indian Ocean

CHAPTER SIXTEEN
THE INDIAN OCEAN

"Oh no," I exclaimed, waking Bobby. "What is it?" he said blinking. "Six o'clock," I replied, and we both dashed out of bed. We had promised to be away by five.

Bobby had the engine started and pushed off from the wharf without any help from me and before I knew what had happened, being busy trying to put Pixie on her new platform. She seemed afraid of it and was pulling back screaming. Our sudden rush out of bed must have upset her. I gave up and went to put her back down in the cabin, noticing on the way a dead sandpiper on the deck. Bob-tail must have killed it in the night and left it there like a bad omen; most upsetting.

We were off, no one to see and we still had our awning up. As I took the awning down I noticed Bob-tail's pan of fish Bobby had bought back and cooked for him the night before. A dreadful thought now hit me. Where was Bob-tail? In our rush to get away I could not remember seeing him and so often when we were alongside he would wander off on the wharf, first thing in the morning. Had we left him behind? By then we were just leaving the entrance and I was scared to look in case I could not find him. My fear was not prolonged as I spotted him lying on top of the locker looking guilty. I was so pleased he was with us, that I did not scold him for the dead bird.

We felt a little sad about the way we were having to leave what was our favourite country and wished we had left a day earlier and so avoided the unfortunate kidnapping of our dinghy.

We kept the engine going for another hour and that together with the sails was giving us almost five knots. Soon after shutting off the engine the wind dropped to nothing and we barely moved. Pixie was very naughty and though chained in the cockpit she could reach round into the cabin and grab at the curtains. They were now a year old and with sun and sea started to rot, so she could rip them very easily; this was very satisfying to her but made the place look a bit seedy. Later she condescended to go on her platform; we made a canvas covering for it to protect her from the sun. By two that afternoon we found we had done only two miles in four hours. At that rate it would take us a year to get to Djibouti, which was a bit sad as already our bananas were getting ripe. Not only the ones I had bought but another stalk which Sunil had got for us, they had been very green and were supposed to take two or three weeks to ripen. Pixie was no help, deciding that bananas now were the last thing she fancied. I started to hum, '*Here we sit like birds in the wilderness*'. That was a big mistake as from then on I could not get the wretched tune out of my head. There we did sit, hardly moving, and the hot sun addling our brains. Two fishing boats came alongside and were about to board us. They looked friendly but as we did not know their intentions Bobby shouted at them and waved them off. They went without protest.

Things livened up a little during the night and the next day we had a very heavy swell which made us feel awful. By noon on the third day we had done 148 miles by log. Our bunk was a sodden mess. The deck had been awash all the preceding night and what water had not come through a leak round the hatch had come in torrents down the chain hole. Sea water had also come up the outlet pipe of our galley sink and then splashed in the big sink behind. Our new seats had their first baptism as we had left the hatch above open and waves had come over the cabin top. The heavy rolling had caused the new seat cushions to fall forward, and the caned locker doors I had made with the idea that air could get into the lockers, of course made it easy for the water to enter and soak everything.

During the night we were hit by a gale and Bobby had to put on the safety harness to reef the mainsail. Such weather did not affect all the crew. Bob-tail was quite happy, he loved the new locker under the port seats and was quite content to be shut in and lie on top of the awnings etc.; there he stayed, safe and dry, and only had to call to be let out. Pixie was very content. Not wishing her to be out in such weather we let her stay in the cabin where she was able to take the cushions and chew a few more lumps out of them. By the afternoon the wind was not as strong. The main was un-reefed and Pixie went back on her platform though it still had water washing over it. By noon on the fourth day we had logged 237 miles. We had probably done more as when we were still moving along nicely, the vane doing the steering, Pixie took it into her head to investigate the end of the log line and pulled it in. By the time we had discovered what she had done, she had got it in such a tangle of knots that it took ages to sort it all out and soon after that we were completely becalmed, the heavy swell still with us. That evening a small breeze came and played with us, very half-heartedly. By one the next morning we dropped all sails and went to bed.

I found it interesting that when we were becalmed we had a lot of tiny flies in the cockpit. I counted six different kinds, tiny black ones, green ones, round black ones, bigger things with thin legs and some small daddy long legs. Perhaps they too had been relying on the wind to aid their travels and were also sitting out the calm, as they disappeared with the first breeze.

By nine thirty the following morning we started the engine and so by midday had done the grand total of 23 miles in the preceding 24 hours. That was the general pattern of things until the eighth day: heavy swells, light breezes and now and then dead calm. Pixie investigated the log line again and then we started using a bit of common sense and moved it to the other side of the cockpit out of her reach. There was little we could do about the lines controlling the steering vane. Pixie felt no doubt that if we changed course a little we might get more wind, as she often chose to do this. For the most part this did not prove to be very helpful.

I found maggots in the flour I had bought in Sri Lanka. I sat in the cockpit with Pixie and sifted it all but in doing so sifted out all the nice brown bits which was a waste. The maggots on the other hand Pixie regarded as a delicacy. I went on to clean several days' supply of rice and sort the weevils out of the dahl. While I was eliminating unwanted debris from the food Pixie was getting rid of larger objects, tossing the bucket we caught sea water in complete with its rope overboard. Sadly, the large plastic bowl we would fill with water for her to sit in cracked down the side, the last bit of pleasure she got from that was to dump it. Our biggest loss Pixie had no hand in. When we left Singapore, Mala had given us a very nice vacuum flask that looked like a coffee pot. This was useful as we could make coffee when the weather was calm and keep it hot for use later. Bobby had just poured himself a cup of coffee and placed it on the table for a minute while he took a look outside, we took a heavy roll and the flask rolled off leaving the inside full of broken glass.

On the seventh night out, Bob-tail got his first flying fish of the trip and we saw the light on Minicoy very clearly. We had done just over 400 miles. By eight next morning our log showed we had done one mile since four the preceding afternoon. Minicoy was very clear about five miles off, sometimes to starboard sometimes to port as we just drifted around in a circle. We were just considering starting the engine when a nice breeze blew up and we were soon clipping along. Bobby was reading below and I absorbed in my daily task of sorting the stones from the rice. For no particular reason I glanced at the compass and looked again. Here we were going along nicely but in the opposite direction. Pixie had turned the boat right round without us knowing. Guess she wanted to go back to Sri Lanka. Later, after she had chewed out a nice bit of primitive carving on the hatch cover, Bobby shortened her chain putting her out of reach of most temptations. The bananas were going ripe far faster than we could eat them. They were put out on the cabin top to dry. We all, except Bob-tail, loved dried bananas but on shore could never make them. At sea with a good wind we had better luck. This time they did nicely, though a little squashed where we had stepped on them.

Now we had days of good strong northerly winds and on the ninth day out we found ourselves in the shipping lane. Now we had to keep a good watch with ships about. We were moving well with reefed main and staysail. The tenth of March was coming up, Bobby's birthday, and I had nothing for him. I solved this by cutting up an old towel and made him a pair of shorts. With the speed we were now going we expected to log 1000 miles by his birthday. Meanwhile, annoying things were happening as usual. Finding what at first looked like a pool of water in the galley we discovered it was kerosene and that the pipe to the stove was leaking. Bobby set to work to repair it but the spares he had turned out to be the wrong size. Shampoo was leaking from the little locker in the head. I dared not open it as then everything would come tumbling out. Pixie demolished a whole cushion and chewed the top of the fire extinguisher. Bobby made a lovely patch for the leaking stove but sadly when we lit it the pressure blew it away. We gave up and lashed the burner I had bought in Sri Lanka on top of the gimbaled stove. This worked well except it was very high and by the time the pot was on top it became very top heavy. We took it in turns to stand watch over it holding the handle of the pan which was then higher than our heads.

On Bobby's birthday I gave him the shorts I had made in secret. He looked very pleased and made all the right noises. He then tried to put them on. They went as far as his hips and stuck! I still had some towel over to make them a bit larger. I made a birthday cake, rather a dirty job as cakes like to be on a low heat and when I turned down the roaring fire our spare cooker gave, I got lots of black smoke; I put up with it as it was all in a good cause. The pan fell off three times, but the lid stayed on. Halfway through the cooking the kerosene ran out so it had to be taken off while we filled the stove again. Despite all, it was quite a tasty cake though its shape left much to be desired, looking as if it had been sat on. We logged 1000 miles of that trip just before midnight.

Next morning the wind died away and when it freshened about nine it was back to northerly. I spent the day trying to clean little smuggy black spots that had covered everything, a result of my low fire on the stove. The wind was not as strong and the following day it decreased further and we began to feel cold. Our best day's sail had been on March 6th, our ninth day at sea, when we had logged 116 miles. After that, and for the following week, we averaged 100 miles a day. It was not to last. By the 14th we were hardly moving and between noon and the next did only 20 miles. We resigned ourselves to the reduced speed, read and I finished sewing new covers for all the cushions. Two days later we found we were moving a bit better. After being becalmed at noon, we caught a nice breeze which later became strong towards midnight. It was beautiful on deck that night, the moon was behind us shining on the sea making a silver trail.

When I took over my watch on the twenty-first night Bobby went below saying his usual piece about calling him if anything happened that I was not sure about. I grunted in reply, so far I had never had to call him and never expected to. It was an interesting night, pitch black, not a sign of any ships' lights. Suddenly! Right behind us a flaming red thing appeared. It was huge and far larger than any ship's light could ever be. Not only that it was an odd, almost triangular shape and getting bigger. I had not got a clue what it was but it was close on our heels and catching up fast, there was no escaping it. I dashed down to wake Bobby not that I felt he would be able to do anything, but felt he ought to see whatever it was that was after us, before the end. Bobby stood in the companionway and looked, then calmly said, "Where? I can't see anything." That he could not see a huge red flame right on our tail was impossible. Perhaps I was going mad or had a vision only visible to me. I joined him. There was still a big red thing behind us, in fact it was even bigger now that some of the clouds surrounding it had moved away and the shape was more familiar. "Oh," I said lamely, "it's the moon."

The day after being frightened by the moon was my birthday. Bobby had for days before been tending his dried bananas and then they disappeared from the cabin top. I thought I knew exactly what I was getting for my birthday. At breakfast that morning I found a card and three little packages on my plate. The card was a double postcard size print of my favourite Sri Lanka painting, no card could have pleased me more. The smallest package made me gasp. A beautiful smoky topaz set in silver. The next was even more of a surprise if that was possible. The black coral bead necklace from Don's shop. The only one I had ever seen and been so fascinated with, but never dreamed it would be mine. I was speechless, having no idea that Bobby had thought of my birthday coming up before we had left Sri Lanka, and had only anticipated the third packet of nicely dried bananas that tasted perfect. Here I should mention what we call dried bananas. Not the dry white slices of banana or the flakes but the whole banana minus the skin shrunk in size, dark brown and moist, resembling a banana in the same way a raisin resembles a grape. After years of living in the tropics and even growing our own bananas we had never been able to dry them. When we tried all that happened was the banana would go over-ripe and runny and attract flies. We thought the Ecuadorians, which was the only country we knew that dried them this way, must be the holder of some secret. Now we found the warm winds when sailing did the trick.

We had been hearing a lot of planes, mostly just the drone of the engines, until one day jets screamed their way over us. I hated them but Bobby looked through the binoculars and said they had no markings and were, so he thought, Russian. A lot more passed over us another day and one was clearly marked, showing it to be American Air Force. Perhaps they were competing with each other at making the most noise. On neither occasion was there any sign of an aircraft carrier. The wind now picked up a bit and was better at night than during the day. Bobby got a rude awakening at midnight when Bob-tail caught a flying fish while I was busy with the log. Down in the cabin went Bob-tail with his catch. Pixie saw him and pulled him away from it.

She strongly disapproved of his fish-eating habits. This was all too much for Bob-tail and they had a little fight for the first and last time in their lives. Pixie was hanging on to Bob-tail who was screaming his head off which made her get even more cross with him, and started nipping him while I was trying to part them. Bobby woke up and Pixie jumped back into bed while Bob-tail rushed under the cockpit. Bobby was left with the dead fish on the floor which he put back on deck. The fish was still there the next morning. As Bob-tail had bitten the head off before his tussle with Pixie we thought he might eat it raw. He had obviously not bothered to go and look for it again so we put him on deck. He pretended not to see it. Bobby cooked it up with a little rice and Bob-tail gobbled it down in a minute.

Sailing had become really enjoyable on our longest sea passage to date. The first week had been a bit hectic with rough seas and everything so wet, but after we had cleared up and dried out, the sailing was the best we had experienced and we did not mind the days when we had little wind and only made a few miles as there was always plenty to do and time to do it. We had books to read and I was happy sewing and wishing I had brought my hand-sewing machine along, instead of shipping it to England.

As we were nearing Djibouti, which would be our first port of call, I felt in no hurry to arrive. Our port water tank holding 30 gallons had lasted us until the twenty-third day. We were not short of water – our starboard tank with about 35 gallons and we still had a lot more in several full jerry cans on deck.

As we approached the Gulf of Aden we were seeing a lot more shipping. A German ship passed us very close, going in the opposite direction. They waved to us from the bridge and we waved back, it felt nice to have that slight contact with other seafarers. The nights were getting colder. I would sit out my watch in the cockpit wrapped in a blanket and made a note to dig out some warmer clothes before starting on the Red Sea.

On waking at five thirty the following morning I saw Bobby dousing the jib. The wind was now so strong that the vane could not handle it. There was just a quarter moon, very bright, hanging below, was a bright planet.

'*Sandpiper*' was now just bowling along as if pleased with herself for having finally arrived. We were not so overjoyed as estimated we would be arriving at Djibouti at night, not a good time owing to the reefs. We took the jib down and still flying along we doused the main, continuing with just the staysail so we would arrive at first light. When lowering the mainsail Bobby twisted his back and it really hurt him. After dark we could see the Djibouti light very clearly straight ahead. Bob-tail and I stayed on watch until midnight, our last night watch of the trip.

"Are you awake?"

"No," I answered sleepily. "Come on," Bobby said, it's four o'clock. It seemed more like four minutes than four hours that I'd slept but I got up readily when I remembered we were almost on top of Djibouti and I wanted to see land. It was still dark, the light was still there but we were now heading away from it, Bobby having just tacked, finding us too close. He was very tired and his back was hurting him and he needed to rest but insisted I call him in an hour as he wanted to take a bearing. He had fallen asleep almost at once and it was still a bit dark at five so I waited an extra quarter of an hour. I had been steering and had to keep the wheel hard over so now, as my calling failed to wake Bobby, I lashed it in place and went and woke him. Now he was less than enthusiastic about taking a bearing and asked if it was light. "Just about," I replied. I then stopped to sort out a sweater for him as it was cold and went back on deck. Everything was the same and I still could not make out land. Fifteen minutes later I again woke Bobby and he got up so I went below and lit the stove for coffee while he dressed. Within a minute or so Bobby was on deck and startled me by calling, "Quickly, start the engine, we are almost on land." I could not believe we were even near the land, just before I had been unable to see anything. From the tone of his voice I knew it was no joke and quickly started the engine and then looked out. Amazing! What looked like a long wall was almost within jumping distance. It had got a lot lighter in the last few minutes which was fortunate as certainly I had not been able to see it in the dark. I took the wheel and Bobby hoisted more sail. Danger averted. I could not help thinking that if we could do this sort of thing as soon as we got near land what were we going to do in the Red Sea?

As the light increased, the wall turned out not to be a wall, just sand. Farther along I could see a few dark shapes which I took to be trees, then, in the distance mountains materialised. I kept staring, waiting for a camel to complete the picture, someone had forgotten to paint it in.

While all this was going on we had left Pixie and Bob-tail in bed. Pixie had decided on a bit of reading and had chosen a magazine and parted it from its cover. She then absorbed herself in the West Coast of India pilot book, proof that she has no sense of direction and does not know where we are. Bob-tail as usual when we are having panic stations cried and wanted to go on deck. It was not rough but we were rolling and feared he might fall overboard so pushed him down below and put his sand tray in the cabin. After he used it he started demanding his breakfast. I collected Pixie from her reading in bed and put her chain on to fix her to the table where she still managed to carry on being naughty and Bob-tail still cried. Pixie then opened the locker door under the seat for him and he got in happily. He was not left alone as Pixie then proceeded to make more room for him and pulled everything in the locker out. In less than no time she had a wonderful shambles of stuff around her, along with the carpet in a bundle on the floor, charts, towels, cushions and plates. Still they were both silent and contented.

As we moved in towards the port of Djibouti we could see more of the country of Ethiopia. It looked a very barren landscape, hills and plains but all sand with a thin powdering of trees. At that distance there was no way of telling what kind they were, just a dusty looking green colour, very indistinct. We passed a village, all low white buildings and wondered what the people lived on. Warships passed on the horizon, Russian or French? We were left guessing. We continued on slowly with the engine and thought of all the good wind we had the day before when we did not want it. The mountains of Ethiopia were beautiful but the rest looked hostile and barren.

Passing the entrance buoy we took down the sails which were not helping much. The entrance was easy and we felt we probably could have come in in the dark. I looked round the harbour apprehensively, it was big and busy. I felt a little sad that our ocean voyage was over. We had logged 2175 miles since leaving Galle. After 29 days at sea we had now arrived at Djibouti.

Djibouti has a clubhouse,
but oh dear, dear,
the price they charge for
one mug of beer.

CHAPTER SEVENTEEN

PIXIE BANNED FROM THE CLUB

Very slowly we motored into the large harbour of Djibouti, taking it in turns to look through the binoculars to see if there were any old friends among the boats at anchor. One boat caught our eye, it looked like *'Maori Lass'* but we were too far off to tell for sure. Pixie then looked in that direction and started her call. She needed no binoculars to pick out her favourite boyfriend Jim.

As soon as we were anchored Jim came over for a chat and groom. They had been in Djibouti for nine days, having made much better time than we had, but were leaving that night. Djibouti, he informed us, was terribly expensive and the other two boats had only stayed two days. Jim was full of news having a ham radio on board. One boat, he told us, had gone too close to Socotra and got shot at. We had all heard how dangerous that island was and we had kept well clear of it. Our good friend Doug on *'Whistler'* had made the biggest radio headlines. He kept radio listeners all over the world on tenterhooks for several days. In Lumut he had eventually repaired his engine and left Lumut with two men and a girl on board, none of whom had sailed before. Somewhere off the coast of Penang, Jim told us, Doug started radioing for help. His sails had apparently all been blown out and he had bent his crank shaft so could not use his engine. His crew it seemed were all frightened to death and the girl so sick that she could not even keep down liquids and was becoming dehydrated and needed medical help. Hams were sitting up all night and passing on messages, planes and boats went out to rescue and a helicopter to take off the girl. For three days the area Doug had said he was in was searched with no sign of *'Whistler'* though he could still be contacted on his radio. They then asked him to take a sight again. This time they would work out his position which was about 100 miles from the position Doug had given them. Then it was an easy matter for them to find him. The last report was that the girl felt better and did not want to be taken off by helicopter and Doug did not want a tow. From then on radio silence, so everyone was left wondering if he would remain drifting about for ever. A long time later we learned from his girlfriend Machteld that he did make it back to Lumut.

We decided not to go ashore that day as Bobby's back was still hurting him. It was not really his day. Pixie took his best pipe, the only one that was not broken, and tossed it overboard. Bobby then sat on his sun shades breaking them in the process. As Djibouti is a French military port there were a number of warships and a few other boats and small dinghies. We liked the birds best. They sat in the water in friendly little groups.

We both felt better next day after a good night's sleep. Bobby's back still bothered him a bit but he felt that a bit of exercise would not hurt and pumped up the dinghy while I gathered up a pile of clothes that I wanted to wash the salt from. I rowed and Pixie jumped about in the dinghy very excited. Bobby smacked her in the end, but she did not care. The yacht club was situated at the end of the causeway with no ground around it let alone a tree, so Pixie came with us straight into the club and up the stairs. A splendid position was found for her in a corner where she had a grand view of the harbour and the causeway, and where her chain could be fixed to the open brickwork.

She was unusually excited at first but soon settled down and accepted gifts of food. Bobby went off to the bank and Pixie and I made a few friends. Most people were French but there were a few Ethiopians, the latter had good English and were very interesting to talk to. When Bobby returned just before noon he had a nice long French loaf with him but the only other thing he had got from the list were a few eggs and potatoes as he was weighted down with a 10lb bag of American long grain rice. I could not believe it. We had decided to only get essentials, rice was not on the list for the simple reason we still had what probably amounted to about 50lbs we had bought in Sri Lanka in a big plastic dustbin. It was beautiful looking rice that did not even need washing but might spoil us for the more regular rice we had. He also regretted it. Dashing in the supermarket the rice took his eye. He noticed it marked 1700 francs and had taken it to be only 17 francs. I had to agree if it had only been 17 francs it would have been a bargain. That it was actually one thousand seven hundred surely made it the most expensive rice in the world. The shops now being closed until four I had to wait my turn to go shopping.

After a beer we found the washroom downstairs. Not a very wonderful washroom, the French ones never are. This consisted of two showers with doors and a WC also with a door and a man's urinal, with no door, and a basin. At one time there had been two basins but all that remained of one was the tap hanging down from the wall. It was a communal place for men, women, staff and members. The water was a bit brackish but better than nothing. I did my wash and then all three of us shut ourselves in one of the showers and had a good long scrub, Pixie trying to lick the shampoo. Feeling very much better and cleaner we returned to *'Sandpiper'* to enjoy some of the bread Bobby had bought.

Later in the afternoon I went off shopping, leaving Bobby and Pixie at the club. The post office was a little disappointing as only two cards were there for us. My shopping was not very successful either. The market only had a few people selling things which all looked a bit rotten and I was only able to buy tomatoes, cabbage, half a water melon and some bananas. The souvenir market was much better stocked, they even had ostrich eggs, they were not on our list. I was unable to find the supermarket but got flour, oats and coffee in a little shop, with some difficulty as of course it was all in French.

Returning with my purchases I looked up and saw Pixie and Bobby looking down at me, I called and waved. Pixie then made a dive at a French couple who had come up behind her when Bobby's back was turned, looking at me. Fortunately, Bobby pulled her back on her chain and she had only grabbed at the woman's pants. The man appeared to be scared stiff and made a kick at Pixie. Bobby pulled her back and stopped the kick landing with his own foot. Most people would have realised it was a silly thing to do to go up behind an animal and as he was so afraid I don't know why he came near. No Sri Lankan had behaved is such a stupid manner. However, no harm done and we sat and had a beer with some new friends. I had not seen the man who had been scared by Pixie, so although Bobby told me about the incident I was amazed when someone came up to Bobby and started talking nineteen to the dozen in French. The man went on and on. Bobby just sat as if listening though I knew, like me, he did not understand a word. Finally, the man stopped. Bobby looked up mildly and said, "Sorry, I don't understand." Poor man, all his lovely speech wasted. He stood there for a minute looking as if he might explode any moment and then with a flushed face went off. A little later one of the club committee members came over and said he was sorry, they all liked having Pixie, but now one of the members had complained that dangerous wild animals were being permitted membership, so now he had to ask us not to bring Pixie anymore. Pixie had been banned from the club and Bobby had already paid 3000 francs for our membership for three days.

Next day we met John Wilburn and his young but able crew, Chris Tuck. John had sailed from New Zealand in '*Natica*', a ferro-cement boat he had built himself, single-handed until the Seychelles where he stopped a while and Chris joined him. They were both very matter-of-fact about their voyages and down to earth boys, we took to them both immediately. They had been unable to find flour or oats so I accompanied them on a shopping outing with the idea I would find the shop at which I had purchased mine. Naturally, once in the area, I had not got a clue where the street I had found the shop was and took them round in a circle a few times before, more by good lucky than good judgement, we found the shop and got our essentials. Essentials only it had to be, the prices were the highest we had ever seen, and for us coming from Sri Lanka they were unbelievable. In Sri Lanka we had been able to feed ourselves, Pixie and Bob-tail very well for one dollar a day – unless we had a beer.

Bobby settled up the bill for the beer we had at the club. A small mug of beer cost 350 francs. We now felt it was lucky that we had not gone again, Pixie being banned, or we might have run up a large bill.

Before leaving I went again to the post office knowing we should have more mail awaiting us. I stood forlornly at the counter where I had collected two cards before and which had in big letters Poste Restante above. No one was serving so after ten minutes I decided to get the stamps first for the mail I was sending and joined that queue. No sooner was it my turn than the man serving moved over to the Poste Restante counter and served the two men who had been behind me with forms. He then came back and I got my stamps but was none too happy when instead of giving me my change in money, I had to take it in stamps I had no use for. I asked him for my mail and was told to go back to the place I had been waiting at. He did not move over but another man served me. Perhaps this man was new, he did not seem to understand, and kept asking me for a number, until I realised it was a box number he wanted. A customer came to my aid and translated for me and explained that I was collecting mail from the Poste Restante. Was I hearing things? They said Djibouti had no Poste Restante. I pointed to the sign above my head where it was in large letters. I also told him I had collected mail from there only two days ago and leaning over pointed out a place below where it had come from. He found a pile of letters and then glancing at the paper on which I had printed our names, went through them, holding them in such a manner I had no chance of seeing the address side. One I was convinced was for us from my friend Hazel Kiesel in the States, a larger than usual kind of envelope with stickers of flowers over the flap, just the kind she usually sent. He passed it by and refused to take another look, saying there was nothing for me. My pleading to check again was to no avail. Could I then have a change of address form I asked? No, he had none. Giving up on that man I went to the next counter with the kind customer who was translating for me. They were now closing but it appeared that they never forwarded mail, yet kept saying I would get a letter later; how if they would not forward it I could not imagine. I made it clear that I was never returning to Djibouti. They still insisted I'd get my mail in fifteen days, even wrote it on a piece of paper. I gave up. I could only think they meant they returned mail to the sender after fifteen days.

Now all the shops were closed except one with some fruit which I was able to buy with my remaining francs. That left me with 140 francs and there was nothing I could buy with so little but they kindly let me take a small packet of biscuits which were really 160 francs. I did not really want them as had never bought biscuits before but thought Pixie might like them and they were of more use than the Djibouti money.

Bobby was stitching the mainsail along the seams when I returned and we decided rather than leave that evening to wait until next morning. We got out the genoa, a big sail we had been unable to use before feeling it was not safe when Pixie had been on the foredeck. Now she had her platform we could use it without any danger to her. We also dug out our zip jackets and sweaters for the coming cold nights.

We were now ready for the challenge of the Red Sea.

Only the stars to keep me company,
The moon has turned her back.
The sun has yet to shine again
and everything is black.

-

The wind has gone for good it seems.
The sails hang slack and limp.
The sea is like a mill pond.
I sit on deck and think

-

I think about the universe
and all it means to me.
The many different lands I've roamed
Both inland and by sea.

-

I never cease to marvel.
How all this came about.
Praise be to all of Nature
With joy I stand and shout.

Map of the Red Sea

CHAPTER EIGHTEEN
THE EASY HALF

"Well we are off," said Bobby. "Yes," I grinned back.

It had been afternoon before we got away. After starting the engine to assist us getting the anchor up we discovered it was not getting cooling water, so Bobby had worked on that for a while. Next we discovered we had three engine leaks: oil, fuel and water. Still it worked which was the main thing and finding the wind we were soon able to turn it off and were going along nicely.

That night I made a particularly fancy dinner of different dishes using lots of fresh vegetables we had and nuts. By the time it was ready, the wind had left us and we had to start the engine. As this meant manual steering we had dinner in the cockpit and thoroughly enjoyed it. We agreed to start by taking two-hour watches. I took the wheel at eight and Bobby lay on the seats. I did not enjoy my watch, I felt very tired and was getting stomach cramps. At ten I looked at Bobby and he was sleeping so thought perhaps I could manage another hour and then I would be able to have three hours sleep. Within three quarters of an hour I was feeling very ill and had to go to the bathroom. Dashing down I made it just in time and then woke Bobby. I had gone back to the wheel expecting him to take over. To my horror he just said, "As you did not call me at ten you might as well keep going until twelve and we do four-hour watches." I felt so ill by then I doubted I would last out that long and tried to protest but he never heard me as he was now saying he would take Pixie to bed and off they went to the bunk. I felt too ill to yell after him. My steering got worse, I kept vomiting and getting pains, I tried lying down to steer which was rather less than efficient. Ten minutes to midnight I could stand it no more and started calling and flashing the light down to the bunk. Bobby came up looking green and said he did not feel well. I barely heard, just flung myself down on the bunk, fully dressed and lay there, one moment freezing and the next boiling hot. I continually had to dash to the head, having dreadful diarrhoea and vomiting. Bobby on watch was the same. It was four in the morning before I took over, I don't think I had slept; Bobby was steering the way I had tried, lying down, it was only then we realised that we were just as ill as each other. It was fortunate we had not encountered any bad weather, though steering with the engine on was no joy. We had had the engine on all night and had logged only 28 miles. In all it hardly seemed worth it.

We were over the worst of the attack by late morning but did not feel well all the next day. What we had we never knew. At first I thought it was something we had eaten but Pixie had the same for dinner and she was fine. Also everything was fresh. We then remembered that on Wednesday Pixie had also had a very bad case of diarrhoea and vomiting. With her it only lasted one morning but we think we might have felt better sooner had we been able to have a good sleep. Our illness was put down as having caught some bug.

We passed through the Straits of Bab-el-Mandeb and Perim Island in the dark the second night. We were then in the Red Sea without a breath of wind. It was not until after midday on the third day that we got a very slight breeze. Our first hundred miles were logged that night at seven twenty when we could see the lights of Yemen. We tacked away, we had been told that they were not very friendly and shoot at you if you get too near.

During my early morning watch on the fourth day I had company when a lone porpoise came and blew his nose at me. As it grew light I found we had a bird on board. Not a sea bird, I could not decide what he was but to me he looked a bit like a small sparrowhawk. He kept flying around and landing on the boat and then taking off again, a very jittery passenger. When Pixie woke on her own and came up without disturbing Bobby I put her on her platform. Immediately the bird flew almost on top of her head and she gave it a light smack. I put some of Bob-tail's food out for it as he was the meat-eating kind of bird but he was not interested. While I was getting breakfast Feathers, as I then called him, came flying in and made to perch on Bob-tail's head while he lay sleeping on the seats. Bob-tail was so surprised, he jumped up. I grabbed hold of him in case he gave chase, which allowed Feathers to fly out unharmed. He then sat on the jerry can on deck. I tried without much success to take his photo, he was too fidgety, not sitting nicely in one place for long. He was friendly though and came and sat next to me and then took off returning to sit on my head. He was very fond of heads.

That afternoon we passed the Hanish Islands on our port side. A very fickle wind kept changing every few minutes. Once we thought we had lost Feathers when we tacked and he got knocked off the rail. He turned up later sitting on the jib-boom. He enjoyed diving down in the cabin and taking us by surprise and once gave Bob-tail such a start he was chased on deck where Feathers just sat on the boom rest and gave Bob-tail a defiant stare. Bob-tail looked back and came back in the cabin. We enjoyed watching a lot more porpoises. One had a very deformed dorsal fin. They must get in fights, perhaps with other sea-living creatures as several had fins that were not perfect. This made watching them more fun as we could tell one from another. They were much larger than the ones we had seen before and more of a brown colour with no white on them. Feathers became less restless and settled down on the cabin top for quite long periods. Bob-tail was very good and did not go near him. I was a bit afraid that in the dark he might change his mind and decide Feathers might make a better meal than a friend. After dark that night Bob-tail suddenly rushed out on deck, I followed in case he had Feathers in mind but saw he was just sitting on deck staring out to sea; after a bit he returned to the cabin. We heard and saw nothing. When I went round with the light I failed to find Feathers and believed he must have just flown off. Rather strange to leave at night but then he was a strange bird.

I took over the watch at midnight on the start of our fifth day and still had no more than the lightest of breezes and often becalmed. We started the engine on nearing the light on Abu Al Island. It was still ahead when I went below at four. Waking again at six thirty I was greeted by the nice sight of the Zubair Islands and Abu-Al-Chan and other small islands. They all looked very barren. I wondered if that was where Feathers went to. Two young white sharks were now playing around the boat. The weather remained calm and hot. Every now and then I would sit in my birthday suit and pour sea water over my body to cool it down, I had to keep covering up as I feared getting too sunburnt. At midnight after the fifth day we had still only logged 187 miles and then suddenly as if someone had prodded the sleeping wind awake we started really moving and before daylight we had really strong winds and heavy swell. The genoa was quickly lowered and the main reefed. We now had gale force winds from the north. Pixie, who had been very good in the calm weather, got more lively and took the coffee pot to bed with her. Unfortunately, it still contained some coffee and the middle of the bed had a pool of coffee and coffee grounds on it.

Things started flying around the cabin. The tool drawer flew out and into the head. Had one of us been in there it would surely have killed us, a most undignified end. When it got light we had the Sunbair Islands on our starboard side. By eleven Bobby could see the volcano island of Jabal-al-Tair ahead. Maddeningly, I could see nothing. The wind stayed with us for three days though on the second day we had un-reefed the main. We now expected to arrive in Port Sudan in the afternoon of our ninth day at sea That morning found us becalmed. We were still left with the heavy swell and it was very hot. We hung over the rails watching the porpoises trying to find the one with the deformed fin or others that we felt we would recognise. We decided it must be another group. A black and white bird with a very long black beak sat on the rail over the life-ring, soon it was joined by three more. They had scissor tails, their backs were all black except round the neck where there was a white ring and white underneath. They were so tame we could touch them. The day dragged on and we barely moved. After dark we had a little wind but it was just teasing us and soon departed. We moved a little during the afternoon. We were a little excited when we could just make out a boat ahead of us but it was too far off to see it clearly. We wondered if it was *'Natica'* who had left the day before us? We watched the boat going inland, perhaps looking for a beacon and hoped it would not get too near the coral reefs with which the Red Sea abounds.

Bobby had been worrying over his position which put us farther ahead than he thought possible. Then we saw the lights and entrance to Port Sudan which showed we were exactly where he had calculated. We must have had some help from a current. It looked as if we would arrive at midnight. Just as we said that the wind dropped again and we hardly moved. Then we could see the masthead light of a boat behind us, perhaps it was the boat we had seen earlier. A light wind came and slowly we headed for where the beacon light on the reefs should be, but they were not lit so we turned and came back. The other boat passed us and also came back. We both messed around until daybreak before venturing near the reef. We could then see the buoys and headed over, as we drew near we saw *'Maori Lass'*. At first we thought they were leaving but to our surprise we saw that she would be going in ahead of us and wondered where she had been as she was a fast little boat and they had left Djibouti the evening we had arrived. I could smell the land now. It at once reminded me of the hot clay smell when opening a kiln of fired pottery. Coming in behind *'Maori Lass'* we lowered our sails and started the engine. We were passing a big ship moored alongside the wharf when the engine stopped. Bobby got the genoa up fast and we just managed to clear. We started the engine again with the same result, something was wrong and so we kept up the genoa until we had anchored near *'Maori Lass'*. As we were coming in we had looked back at the boat that had been waiting for daylight like ourselves. She was now coming in behind us. It was *'Natica'*. We were all together again, arriving at the same time. Pixie was excited by it all and bounced up and down on her platform. I had a flag, red white and black stripes, and now looking around we saw if we added a green triangle it would do for Sudan. I was still sewing on the triangle when the quarantine boat arrived with the doctor. They came to us first, an extremely nice doctor who soon cleared us once we told him we were not sick.

John and Chris appeared and were soon followed by Jim and Jan. We sat around discussing the trip. After leaving Djibouti Jim and Jan had spent a week in North Yemen in Hodeida which they had enjoyed. It was nice to be all together again and with half – the easy half of the Red Sea – behind us. Later in the afternoon a customs boat came over but they only wanted Bobby to write the name of the boat and destination. We did not go ashore that day. There was not much to see from our anchorage, just a large port and a dusty road. Everything looked sand coloured.

Next day Simon from a catamaran anchored near us came over and told us he had been told we must all go to the Port Master with our papers. He was on his way in his dinghy with an engine so I went with him. I was able to get our paperwork done but for Simon it was a waste of time as he had not been cleared by the doctor. He could still land, but he could not have his papers for entering done. Simon dropped me ashore so I could go into town and he went back to wait for the doctor. I had hardly stepped ashore when I was offered a lift by a very pleasant man with excellent English. Before dropping me at the post office he invited Bobby and I to go for drinks at his house that night. A little surprising in a Moslem country. Sadly, I refused as we could not leave Pixie and was not sure he would want her.

Collecting mail was a lot of fun. When asked they just pushed a huge pile of mail forward, not in a nice pile, just a heap that you could rummage around for as long as you liked to try and find your mail. It took a lot of time as there were hundreds of letters, some very old. I could find nothing for us but at least had been able to look for myself. I now set off to explore the place. A heavy dust haze hung in the air making it hard to see or breath. I wandered about aimlessly just getting the feel of the place. The people were both friendly and fascinating: tall, handsome men with their long white night shirts and turbans and the womenfolk rather shy. When I found two camels and goats with long shaggy coats, I felt the picture was complete. This was a real place compared with Djibouti. Everything was closed as it was almost noon when I came out of the post office. I purchased a few postcards and one mango. I was soon very lost and had no idea which way it was to the sea. Wherever I looked the view ended in a sand haze and it appeared and smelt as through all roads led to the desert. When I did eventually get on the right road a car stopped and gave me a lift back.

Next morning Pixie got up at five so I put her on her platform and went back to bed for an hour. Big mistake. We heard bang, bang on the deck above us. "What is that?" asked Bobby drowsily. "I don't know," I replied, but got up and went to see. Pixie was running around the deck looking like a frustrated barber with no customers. A pair of scissors in one had which banged on the deck as she ran and a comb in her mouth. She dropped the scissors on deck when I chased her and then gave me the runaround. I only got her by stroking Bob-tail. That was too much for her and she came to me. Later we found the binoculars on the foredeck and the compass twisted upside down with its electric light wire chewed off.

Bobby found out what was wrong with the engine when he discovered a burlap sack had twisted itself round the propeller. As John had kindly offered to help him fix the engine he now went over to *'Natica'* to tell John he thought he had found the fault. Chris came back with him and then we were told by a Port Authority Officer that we had to move to leave room for a ship coming in. We started the engine and Bobby got the anchor up easily with Chris helping. Over coffee Chris delighted us with stories of baboons and other animals he had known as a young boy in Kenya.

Later Bobby accompanied the boys into town to do the shopping having not been overly impressed with my morning purchases of mango and postcards. He also hoped to get water and told me to use all the water in the tank for washing. The water we had got in Djibouti was so awful to taste we had stopped drinking it. I had a wonderful time with so much water to use. The washing all done I washed down all the paint work. When I had finished only one jerry can on deck remained full so thought I would wash the sarong I was wearing. Placing the sarong in a bowl I tipped the jerry can over it. This one even smelt bad I thought, and then the penny dropped. It was kerosene. For a long time after, and repeated washings, my sarong still had a strong smell.

Next day I went to the tourist office to get a permit to take photos. This is necessary but all that is required is filling in the form and getting it signed, no charge. I was now permitted to take photos of everything except military zones, bridges, water, gas and electric works, slum areas, beggars or any defaming subjects. These restrictions did not worry me as they did not sound very picturesque subjects anyway. Most of my photos I took in the market which was fascinating; the people no less than the goods they displayed. Standing in the market with my camera, I stood out like a sore thumb and despaired of getting any natural shots. Most of the women did not want their photo taken and either waved me away or hid their faces. Not wanting to start a riot I complied with their wishes and tried for pictures excluding them. The men and children were just the opposite and wanted their photo taken and I had to pretend to take many more than I actually did. None were what I wanted, they all insisted on posing. That though was better than nothing and we all had a lot of fun. Only one young man annoyed me. He was dressed in western-style suit and no doubt thought himself very dashing and a cut above his fellow countrymen. He wanted me to take his photo and not bother with the rest of them.

I bought some flat bread and some peanut butter paste. The guavas smelt so nice I thought I would get a few and handed five cents to a man selling them. I was handed one guava. "Only one?" I said in a disappointed way. "Only one," chirped a wee boy, we all laughed and I was given another. What I really wanted and could not find was some local goats' cheese and so when a friendly old man with good English stopped to chat with me I inquired where I could get such cheese, and he took me along to a shop. This was very typical, like Sri Lanka, the people were very helpful and would go out of their way to help.

I now needed a camel to photo and wandered around in search of one. I spotted one being led down a street and took off in pursuit. It was still a little far when I took my photo. Then I saw its owner had joined a line of some sort so I moved to get a close up of it. I was just adjusting the camera when the little old man who had been leading it started jumping around and waving his arms and shouting as if he had suddenly gone mad. People now closed in around me, looking a bit less friendly. One man tried to help and explained to me that the man did not want his photo taken. "That's all right," I said, "I don't want his photo, just his camel's." This was explained to the driver of the camel. In return I was told that he wanted a lot of money if I took a photo of his camel. "No," I said. "It's not a very beautiful camel and not worth a lot of money. I will give him a cigarette." My offer was turned down and I made my getaway, feeling rather pleased with myself for having got a shot unnoticed.

The public gardens looked like a nice place to walk in but I never did. I felt the method of entrance left much to be desired. All the gates to it being closed the only way to get in was to climb over the wall and bars at a place where the barbed wire had been removed. Certainly, the local inhabitants were not put out by this unusual way to enter. They were both going in and out that way and the gardens were full of people. I can only suppose the attendant one night locked all the gates and then either died or lost the keys. Things like that are taken in their stride in the east and if you can't get through the gate you obviously go over the wall.

I went for a drink in a place opposite the gardens. The moment I sat down the waiter gave me a delicious guava drink and refused my money. "You are a visitor, I have paid for it, be happy," he said. I was, it was such a lovely thought.

That night Bobby, Pixie and I were invited aboard *'Natica'* for dinner. Their foredeck, unlike ours, was nice and clear and tidy, and Pixie was chained to the rails with no fear she would find something to dismantle, while Chris cooked in the galley. Pixie could peep through the windows at him. We had a very enjoyable evening with dinner in the cockpit. Not only was the dinner and company perfect so was the setting, a beautiful night with a full moon.

Talking about the forthcoming trip, we decided to sail from Port Sudan together feeling it would be nice to have company and if either one of us got into trouble in any way the other would give assistance. All being well we arranged to leave in two days' time. Easter Sunday.

All was not well. John went down with a bad attack of diarrhoea which sounded similar to the attack we had experienced on leaving Djibouti. Jim and Jan were ready to leave on Sunday but the wind was so strong they too cancelled their sailing. No boats left that day. I made a cake and invited the boys over but John was still very unwell so Chris came alone. Pixie had liked both John and Chris but something went wrong that night. While sitting on Chris's lap she started biting him so I took her off. Unfortunately, soon after that, I tripped over Bob-tail on my way down to the galley and Chris stood up at the same time. Pixie might have thought he pushed me; certain that he had some hand in it she bit his finger and a real bite this time. After that she was chained up on deck in disgrace and Bobby patched up Chris's finger.

The following day the wind was still blowing strongly from the north. John was feeling much better but we all thought it better to stay put. Next morning we waved farewell to Jim and Jan who left at daybreak.

Chris got up early and went in search of kerosene, taking our jerry can along to buy for us as well. Kerosene was in short supply and difficult to obtain but somehow he had found out where he could get it if he went early. He returned with the kerosene but nearly got arrested for trying to buy more than half a gallon from a donkey cart. None of us knew you had to have a permit to buy larger amounts.

Fuel was completely unobtainable and John had only twenty gallons on board. We had considerably more so gave him a jerry can full. We were not sure what the weather would be like and expected to have to use the engine a fair bit. Bobby and John went off to get clearance and were told they had to pay nine pounds each for port dues. Bobby had only brought seven with him. John said he had more and could let him have two pounds. He put his hand in his pocket only to find it completely empty. They felt sure he could not have been pickpocketed so retraced their steps in the hope of finding it. No such luck so they both went off to change more money. Arriving back at the office to get clearance they found it closed until the next day.

At times the water in the harbour of Port Sudan was beautifully clear. Looking down you could see the bottom and all the fish. Other days oil would cover the water and leave a nasty black scum around our water line. The dinghy had a black deposit on its bottom. Bobby took it ashore and spent the afternoon giving it a good scrub.

Next morning John and Bobby had better luck and returned with their clearance. Meanwhile, another slick had appeared and the dinghy was as bad as ever. Now almost ready to leave we ran the engine to charge the batteries. It made a very funny noise and then stopped, refusing to start again. While we stood looking hopelessly at it a German, Romeo, who owned the big motor cruiser came over in his dinghy as did John and Chris, all having heard the strange noise our engine was making. Our German friend Romeo, we never learned if this was his real name or a nickname, said he knew the noise, it was telling us that the exhaust was blocked; the boys agreed. This was all new to us. They suggested to keep tapping it with a hammer to clear it but this did not help very much and in the end Bobby took the exhaust apart. He then spent hours on deck banging and poking the soot out but could not clear the U-bend. By that time it was dark and John and Chris had gone ashore to spend the money they had kept for fuel on food. On their return John came over to see how things were progressing. Between them they managed to unscrew the join and get it all clear. Bobby now looked as if he had spent the day down a coal mine.

Next morning I viewed with dismay the state of the deck, all covered in soot and black blobs. There was no way to clean it as the water was thick with oil and strangely enough masses of small purple jellyfish, a mixture I thought would not be much help in cleaning the deck. We all wanted to leave that day so the boys came over to see how we were getting on and John stayed and helped Bobby clean the remaining bit of pipe to the engine and then reassemble it all. I deflated the dinghy and got that, the last thing, packed away. We tried the engine, it not only worked but sounded in good health. We were now ready to tackle the difficult half of the Red Sea.

Roar wind roar,
do your best,
I'll do mine.
We have travelled far you and I,
companions, ever moving
moving.
When tired you leave me
leave me
I sit and wait.
Like a lover for the returning of his mate.

-

Now in anger you return.
To vent all force on I.
In this great expanse,
who will hear my cries of help?
Not you O wind.
For I shall fight,
fight and use my skill.
We may go back from whence we came
but I'll be master still.

CHAPTER NINETEEN

BATTLING THE RED SEA

At 1300hrs *'Natica'* had her anchor up and was away, we followed ten minutes later. As we rounded the bend we saw *'Natica'* was way ahead. Pixie recognised her and gave a call. There was only a light wind, we hoisted the genoa and cut off the engine, a little later the wind dropped. *'Natica'* was getting far ahead and we started the engine but were still only making two knots. After dark we lost sight of *'Natica'* though when we had last been able to see them they were only slightly ahead. We expected to be able to see their mast light, then decided like us they were reserving their lights until they should see a ship.

My watch started at midnight, by then we were going along nicely when I saw a ship ahead. I tried to put our running lights on but the switch was stuck. Bobby came to help but we could not move it. The ship did not give way and we had to change course and lost the wind in doing so. It was a beautiful moonlit night and not very cold, with just a gentle wind. I felt very contented alone on deck. It was hard to believe we were in the Red Sea. It was hard to believe all we had been told of the potential dangers. My watch ended at four and it had been uneventful. I woke just before eight, Bobby was starting the engine. He had taken the genoa down as a seam need stitching. *'Natica'* was then behind us but quickly caught up, staying far to starboard. Porpoises were around us trying to encourage us to go faster and have fun with them. Bobby having finished his repair job got the genoa up and at the same time the engine went funny and nearly stopped; we accelerated and it picked up. *Where,* we wondered, *was the wind?* At 1750hrs *'Natica'* caught up with us and I was able to finish my black and white film and start a colour one to take photos of them. We went on but *'Natica'* was not following. We turned back but found they were OK, and we all decided to motor until the wind returned. *'Natica'* was ahead of us now, then they must have slowed down as we passed. They kept close behind and we could see their light. When we lost sight of it we thought perhaps they had turned it off. Daylight came and they were gone. We did not see them again that trip.

In the early hours of the morning we got some wind but thought it too good to last and left the genoa up. The wind continued and by 0400hrs we were flying along with an ENE wind which we had never expected. Freak weather but just the kind we could do with. Very little swell, in fact perfect sailing weather. I hung out two sheets I had washed. A very old torn thing I wrapped Pixie in and our nice blue sheet. Next time I looked the old torn thing was still nicely pegged to the rails but the blue sheet had flown away. With such perfect sailing weather I felt I could not get upset over the loss of the sheet. By noon we had logged 105 miles, a fifth of our trip was behind us already. We were still flying along at eight that evening when Pixie and I went to bed.

The weather now changed and we were experiencing a heavy swell, the wind would die completely and then come back from a different direction. Bobby lowered the genoa. I got up at midnight to take over but Bobby wanted to get on course first and was having a hard time doing so. An hour later I found the log line had caught under the hull and do what we could, we could not release it. We were afraid it might be round the propeller and would cause trouble if we had to start the engine. It was impossible to steer a straight course, the boom was swinging from side to side, either because of no wind or short violent gusts.

Bobby got up to make breakfast then fell backwards just as he was putting the coffee in the pot. He was thrown against the water tank the other side. Water and coffee went all over the floor where my clothes lay. Everything was a mess again and so dirty. As the day went on we got a steady wind and again were sailing nicely. There was still a heavy swell but we were enjoying it all again.

At 1700hrs we suddenly went off course, the wind was very strong. I struggled to unscrew the vane as the nut was on hard; Bobby came up and managed to get it free but too late. The boom crashed over and we were flying along. Bobby got into his harness to get the genoa down. I was having a lot of difficulty steering and then I let her gybe. The washing-up I had been doing in the cockpit flew into the well, a can of kerosene in the cockpit turned upside down, wedging my foot. I could smell the kerosene leaking out from a small hole Pixie had chewed in the top. Pixie was hanging on for dear life as her platform was under water. An eternity passed before the genoa was down and replaced by the staysail. From then on it was rough, we sailed under reefed main and staysail only. Gale force headwinds continued all night. It was impossible to make any headway and we tacked from one side to the other. Our spirits dropped when Bobby's noon sight put us ten miles west and one mile south of the day before. Our last bottle of liquid detergent spilled out and a jar of coriander seeds opened up. The seeds could be found from one end of the boat to the other. The carpet in the galley was sodden as the water dashed up the drain hole in the sink and shot out. That night Bobby took star sights which put us much farther north which was more encouraging, but which sights were correct? It was hard to tell owing to the poor visibility and high refraction.

There was no let up the next day. Pixie and Bob-tail were beginning to get tired of it all and only wanted to sleep cuddled up to me. Even so Pixie found time to be naughty. On waking one morning the first thing I saw was half of Bobby's last pipe held in her foot and the other well chewed, stem in her hand. Bobby was mad, now he had tobacco but no pipe.

While Bobby was making porridge I mixed up some milk, then left it on the divider while I put a damp cloth on the table. Down went the milk, all over the varnish, paintwork, floor curtains and inside the head. A little landed in Bob-tail's bowl but the rest was a mess.

Still the gale went on. We were not making bad mileage but unfortunately we were not heading north, having the wind dead ahead. Now we were far to the east and in danger of the coral reefs off Saudi Arabia, so had to tack and were heading south westerly back where we came from. We were shipping water like mad, hatches leaking, the bunk full of water and then all the books managed to escape out of their shelves with a bar that was supposed to keep them in and leap around the wet bunk, to be joined by the contents of a locker the other side. The seating on the port side was drenched. Things were a bit wet.

Our beating continued yet another day. Our noon position put us back near the coast of Egypt and a little farther north than two days before. We tried to tack but she would not come round, we had to chance the log line being wrapped around the propeller and started the engine. The line snapped, the engine worked. We got her round onto the other tack. The engine now was not getting cooling water but once we tacked it was OK. Perhaps we had been heeled over too much and the intake had been above the water line.

With everything so wet the bit of carpet between the seats was the only remotely dry space to lie down. Not for long, first my coffee went over and was soon followed by Bobby's. Pixie had appeared to be fine but after eating her porridge threw up in the same place.

For the continual trips on deck Bobby was making, he found it best to wear nothing but his safety harness, as he was under water most of the time. It looked very funny, he said it was just very cold. He had returned for the umpteenth time, dried himself, and put his clothes on. He was sitting, in as much as one can sit at such an angle on the port seats. We gave an extra lurch and he shot up and did a complete somersault over the table landing up with me and Pixie on the seats the other side, hitting his head on the locker, but splintered neither.

To cook a dinner of packet soup and instant mee was quite a feat. To boil the water I had to stand on guard, it was always a lot less by the time I had finished, the water would keep leaping out of the pan before it boiled. Getting that elaborate meal on the table required us both. That night Pixie jumped on the table and to our horror wetted, so that had to be mopped up first. That done, Pixie now sitting on the seat turned over the ashtray just as we placed the bowls on the table. Grabbing her bowl, she jumped when she found how hot it was, spilling some on the table which mingled with the ash and ran down in a black mess on my knee. As I was jammed between her and Bobtail, and hanging on to my soup bowl, there was nothing I could do about it.

I went to sleep that night with my head on the floor near the steps. I'd just dozed off when it felt as if a pack of books had fallen on my head and my hair was being pulled tight. It turned out to be Bobby. He had been to get the log book and was sitting on the steps when he fell trying to stop the book falling on me. He nearly broke his neck and mine, and hurt his behind. He looked a bit green and said his ear hurt and lay down, going to sleep almost at once. I took over his watch but an hour later he woke and said he was fine.

Keeping watch was a harrowing experience owing to the bad visibility coupled with the fact I never can seem to see anything until it is almost on top of me. That night a ship suddenly loomed up within spitting distance. We were having to run without lights as the hurricane lamp would not stay lit in such weather. We would put it in the cabin where it would show a bit of light through the windows. We had a flashlight to use if we saw a ship and would then also put on the electric running lights if necessary. This ship was so near I certainly needed to do something fast so shone my light and tried to signal U – the switch for flashing stuck. I leaned down and put the running light switch on but nothing happened, then realised that neither of us had remembered to turn on the battery switch which was located in the head. Dashing down, as well as one can dash in a rolling boat, to the head, switching the batteries on and then back to the switch under the chart desk. By this time the ship was right on top of us and I could see all its super structure. I would never manage to get the vane off in time to tack and it was too late for the ship to get out of our way. I called Bobby thinking he might like to be awake at the end. He came up and by then the ship was just crossing ahead of us, missing us by what looked to be only a few feet.

Just when we thought we might spend the rest of our life battling the elements and getting nowhere the wind died down a bit. The storm was over and we were just left with the heavy swell.

The sun came out and life became more normal. We could now move about and assess the damage. The first thing Bobby did was to get the genoa that he had left lashed to the pulpit rails when the storm had first hit us. The damage was worse than we thought. "Just come and look at this," he called. I went up and could hardly believe my eyes. The stainless steel pulpit rails were bent right out level with the deck on the starboard side. The near new genoa was now ripped in several places and would have to have large pieces cut out and replaced. Bobby sat on deck sewing it using a palm, a leather quarter glove used to push the needle through. I dragged things from the cabin out to dry.

That night we were sailing along beautifully again, tacking at midnight and finding we could go a little more north as well as west, instead of south as we had had to do on that tack previously. We were also out of the shipping lane and so had no ships getting in our way which is so irritating and worrying. By daylight we were almost becalmed, the sun was out and it was hot. A perfect time to get everything possible on deck to dry. We could hardly move half the mattress it was so heavy with water. I made bread and cleaned the galley and cleaned out the sink. As the water went back down to the sea where it belonged, I felt my feet getting wet and looking under the sink saw that the pipe was leaking at the top, further investigation showed that the sink had just rusted away all around the hole. That wonderful new Japanese stainless steel sink we had bought at great expense in Sri Lanka, which we were so delighted with, was now ready for the scrapyard. It had started rusting almost from the day I first used it and I had to continually scour it, this last trip being under water so long had really finished it. The cabin soon started to look nice and cheerful and more liveable again. Looking at the engine Bobby had another surprise. The water pipe had bent in a most odd shape. He managed to get it out and replaced it with another, but that was a bit leaky too so he covered it with some messy stuff and waited for that to set, then back to sewing the genoa.

We allowed Pixie to play on the foredeck but later in the afternoon we had such a heavy mist that the water was just dripping from the sails. I found that night very eerie, the boat motionless and shrouded in the heavy wet mist. All was silent. There was no sound of other shipping apart from one that sounded too far away to worry about. My four hours on watch passed and we had not moved. I took a look at the stuff on the engine pipe that Bobby had been worried might never set. It was hard. I woke him up with the good news but on seeing how thick the fog had now become he felt it better to bob around where we were out of the shipping lane until we could see where we were going. During Bobby's morning watch he heard a ship sounding its whistle and did not think it was far away but could see nothing. Next morning by nine the sun had managed to fight its way through, the fog lifted and the deck started to dry. Bob-tail had not used his tray on deck since I cleaned it at midnight. It had an inch and half of water in it, just from the heavy dew. We now started the engine and cheered when it worked and the pipe held. Pixie went on the foredeck again for a change and was hanging over the side watching one small black fish swimming along with us. Later, while making bread in the galley, I looked up to see her little face upside down peeping in at me through the porthole. It disappeared and then a rope suddenly appeared coming down the hatch over the bunk and was wiggled about to attract my attention; she had found that worked well with Bob-tail the day before.

The netting we had festooned the rails with to keep Bob-tail safe we dismantled. It had become very dangerous as we kept getting our toes caught in it. It did very little good as it had to be tied up where the sheet blocks were and Bob-tail had proved to be very sure footed and in the main preferred to be on the cabin top in bad weather. Once the net was removed we looked a lot neater. In the afternoon we had a beautiful little yellow bird visit us. I was on deck at the time picking stones out of the rice and looked up to see him sitting just two feet away. He flew off but came back and sat near Pixie but she has never been very friendly with birds, they seem to bug her. She slapped the deck and the little bird removed himself. The next day we failed to see him but his wife paid us a visit.

Two more days of dead calm, we kept the engine going all the time. It was a far bigger strain than the storm had been. The monotonous noise of the engine and having to steer ourselves in the boiling hot sun during the day made us tired and cross, and the nights were little better as then it was cold and damp and we were only averaging 60 miles a day.

After four days of dead calm we felt a little breeze and shut the engine off. Oh, the peace of it was wonderful. Bobby had done a good job on the genoa and it was accordingly hoisted.

We had a lovely little bird in the cockpit with a white body, rusty red throat, deep blue head and blue-black wings, he was just as tame as the others had been. Bob-tail sensed they were passengers and never made any attempt to catch them. It was the first of May and that night we could see the light on the Brothers. By the following morning we were barely moving again. I thought of a new way to do the washing. I would tie it on the end of a rope and trail it in the sea. That way I lost a couple of items. We almost lost a jerry can with some diesel oil in when Bobby was filling the tank and knocked it overboard, he moved fast and caught it with the boat hook. By evening we were back using the engine. The next day we had a heavy swell which in the afternoon eased down a bit when we ran through heavy oil pollution for over an hour. At 1630hrs we were hit by a squall but had seen it coming and

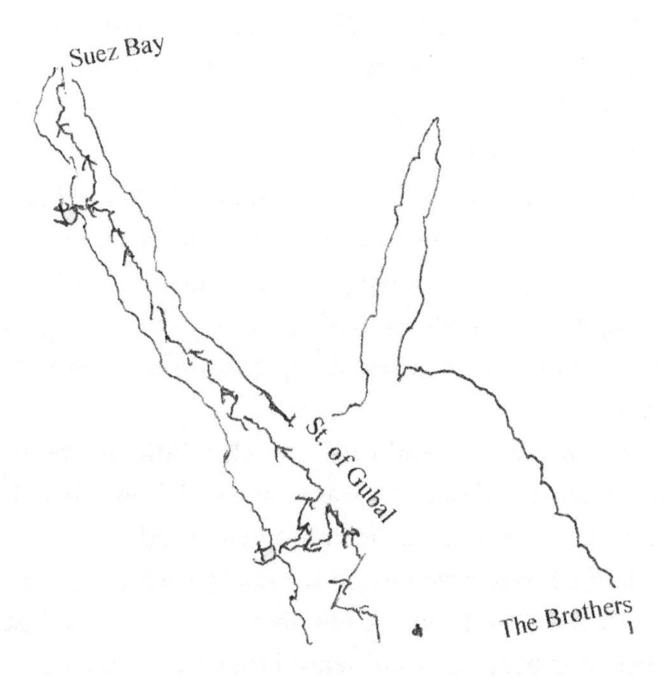

Gulf of Suez and Strait of Gubal

got the main reefed in time and the genoa off and down the hatch. We were glad of the rain to wash the salt off the deck but it was not for long and left a very confused sea. We continued sailing when possible, using the engine when the wind left us. May the fifth brought strong winds again and a heavy sea, we were tacking up to Shadwan Island. Now the wind was back in force just when we did not want it as we could not be tacking all over the place in the narrow Gulf of Suez. The decision was made to look for an anchorage when it was daylight. We headed for a small bay on the west side of Shadwan Island. Suddenly there was a reef just ahead, Bobby tacked fast. Everything flew from one side to the other and when we had tacked and I found Pixie had the waterproof flashlight into which Bobby had just put new batteries. It was waterproof and break-proof but sadly not monkey-proof. She had stripped off the rubber covering and got it all apart. Bobby was able to put it all back together again but she had done something that rendered it useless. This left us with just one flashlight that only worked when it felt like it. Shadwan Island was lovely looking, in a very dry, barren way. It appeared to have nothing on it except the lighthouse. We were within one mile of where we intended to shelter when we were met by a boat full of armed men who came as close to us as the rough sea permitted. One man stood up waving his arms indicating to us to get away from the island and shouting something, not sure what but he had made it very obvious we were not being welcomed or allowed to anchor. This was the height of bad manners in such a position as we were in. The only thing now for us to do was to go back south and shelter behind the Gifatin Islands. The wind and swell were very strong and we hated to go back. Then the sheet of the staysail jammed, we lowered it before realising we had not got the main up, we were getting tired and forgetful. We started the engine fast. Pixie, seeing we were occupied, grabbed the parallel rule and a can of glue. The parallel rules were no longer parallel but a little bent. At first the engine was not getting water but that righted itself, while we got the staysail un-muddled and back up. Pixie took out a large can from one of the lockers in which I kept spices in plastic bags.

For months after we were finding mustard seeds in every crack. All the time when she knew we could see her she acted like a little angel, sitting on the seats below with her feet up on the table and hands over them or busy grooming Bob-tail. It was only when we were busy that she would take a quick stock of things to see what devilment she could get up to.

We were now flying along but kept having to tack. A strong smell of fumes assailed my nostrils when I went below. Pixie had nothing, so assumed it was some broken bottle in a locker, until I noticed a flood of kerosene in the galley. The pipe to the stove had broken again.

The sun came out and large birds were flying around. I was filled with a surge of excitement as if we were in a race to get to the islands before they disappeared. In spite of now being in sheltered waters by the islands, we still had a strong wind and heavy sea and swell. Pixie was also excited, still bent on sabotaging the trip. How could she know this whole journey was because of her and the rules on quarantine?

I went to turn on the echo sounder to help us find our way over the reefs. Pixie had thought of it first and I found she had pulled the wire up where it led down into the bilge and was starting to chew on it. She could not have had it long as she had not yet bitten right through and the sounder still worked. The sails were lowered and the engine started; slowly, we worked our way in. For no reason the engine stopped and refused to start. Nothing left but to hoist the foresail and go in a little farther, anchoring in five fathoms in Gifatin Channel. Even there in relative shelter we still had strong north westerly winds and heavy swell with water washing over our deck. Coming in we had seen another large motor boat and wondered if we were going to be told to move on again, but it turned out to be a fishing boat hugging the shore and not interested in us.

We could just make out a town on the mainland but it was a fair distance off. We had a strong dry wind, the accompaning dry smell reminded us of Sudan.

We put Pixie in the cockpit which she objected to, not liking the wind, but she needed some fresh air and it gave me the chance to tidy up the cabin while Bobby did the same on deck. We were extremely tired, having had only about two hours' sleep the night before. We also had not eaten but did not feel it was worth getting smoky joe out to cook on, the pipe to the stove would have to be repaired again before we could use that. We made do with a can of beans and one of beetroot which we thought we would add to some rice left over from the day before. Bob-tail had his rice with sardines. He must have been extra hungry as the rice tasted of kerosene and we could not eat it. Bobby fell asleep after dinner sitting at the table. I cleared away and curled up on the floor, Pixie and Bob-tail on the other seats. It was rough but nice to know we were at anchor and there was no need to keep watch.

Strangely neither of us had a very good night's sleep. It was cold and we kept waking, perhaps because we were not used to having any more than four hours' sleep at a stretch. After stripping off and having a good salt water bath on deck, Pixie included, we felt a lot better and set to work with a will, trying to ignore the strong winds. Clearing out the lockers I found we had far more empty containers now than full ones, but came across a full bottle of coconut oil which was worth celebrating over as I had felt sure we had finished the last one. Bobby got the mattress and all the bedding out on deck to dry and then looked at the engine. After cleaning out a very dirty filter the engine was back in working order.

During the bad weather we had seen a metal rod fall down in the bilge and thought it was the anchor winch handle. We were going to need that to get our anchor up as we had put down a very heavy anchor Bobby had had made in Sri Lanka, a copy from someone's Danforth but in heavy steel. This was the first time we had used it and now we feared it might be caught in the coral. Bobby went fishing with the boat hook in the bilge, finally managing to get the rod. It was not the winch handle after all. What it was we were not quite sure, but too small to serve our purpose. We then had a hunt for the real thing and in doing so cleared out a lot more places. It turned up in the very last place left to look, under the seats.

During the afternoon the wind dropped and the sea was calm. The water was a beautiful green to green-blue and so clear we could see right down to the bottom, five fathoms below. There was a black thing in the water some distance off, it would disappear and then emerge again. Sometimes it looked as if it had wings, Bobby thought it was a ray. A little later the wind blew up again. That night we were able to sleep in our bunk for the first time since Port Sudan. The mattress having dried hard during the day.

We had hoped to leave in the morning as the night before the wind had come from the west. Now it had changed and was blowing from the north causing a heavy swell. Knowing it would be rough outside we waited another day. I did a lot of washing and the strong wind blew most of the salt out. Bobby fixed the stove; with that working again we felt everything was in good shape. Before dark it was dead calm again and Bobby pulled some of the anchor rope in, noticing the anchor was lying on a patch of coral which was bad luck as all around it was sand.

The next morning we were up early and before six I had managed to lose our last bucket overboard when it came off the rope and floated down to the sea bed. Pixie took breakfast with us but did not eat all her cereal and let it fall, making a nasty mess on the floor for which I smacked her. That made her mad and she thumped on the table sending my coffee flying to add to the mess.

"Well it seems a nice day, let's see if we can get the anchor up," said Bobby. The engine started first time and within half an hour our big anchor of 45lbs was up. The fluke had caught in the coral as we had feared and it was bent.

We were away by 0715hrs with genoa and staysail up, but what little wind we had kept dying on us. We made the entrance to the Gulf of Suez, the Strait of Gubal, in the early hours of the morning. Ships were visible in every direction and we were not too sorry for the lack of wind. Using the engine it made manoeuvring around the ships much easier. There was a bow of a red and white ship sticking up out of the water, wrecked on the rocks off Sha ao Ummush, a sad sight. The paintwork looked bright. The chart showed it had a light there but it was crossed out now, we wondered if that was the reason for the wreck.

My midnight to four watch was a very well lit one; a full moon and going through the oil fields the oil rigs were all lit up like Christmas trees with flashing red lights on top and tall flames of burning gas, a nice sight at night but felt it must be very polluting. I enjoyed that watch and did not feel tired and so continued on steering until seven thirty when there was enough breeze to put the steering vane on.

Our flour was almost finished and we were now eating typing paper with our bread. Having run out of foil to line the pan I used typing paper, covered in oil. This prevented the bread sticking to the bottom of the pan but the paper stuck firmly to the bread. It was very difficult to cut through and we could not afford to waste the crust so ate it, paper and all, quite nourishing.

That evening we had strong winds and had to take down the genoa but not for long. By three in the morning we were becalmed again and started the engine. It was now the twelfth of May and we were almost there and hoped to make Suez the following day. By noon we had gale force northerly winds and were being blown sideways. The channel was so narrow we could see both sides. Our bunk was saturated again and sea water poured up into the sink and on to the galley floor that soon had inches of water over it.

"We can't manage this narrow stretch in this weather," called Bobby. "We will have to try and anchor." We edged in towards Ras Za'farana lighthouse where we saw a wreck, keeping the jib up and the engine going and with the echo sounder on. The sea was horribly rough and howling for our blood, which it very nearly got. Then bump! We were aground! The nearest we had been to disaster. The wind still rolled us about but there we were stuck just off Marsa Thelement. The spit extended much farther than shown on the chart. Fortunately we were on sand, not coral, but even so, if we could not get off, '*Sandpiper*' would be finished. With sail and engine Bobby tried reversing off. An eternity went by, probably in reality five minutes, and then slowly we came off and back in deep water. We breathed again.

We continued on, ten fathoms, ten fathoms, the echo sounder never showed less. It was deeper than we would have liked but decided to anchor. Dropping our 45lb anchor and eight fathoms of chain with 20 fathoms of rope I glanced again at the echo sounder and now it showed the depth to be dropping rapidly, we ran out of fathoms and I switched over to feet, it was still dropping and we were dragging anchor and drifting on the shoal. Moving fast we put out the smaller Danforth and plough anchors which held her and we stayed in nine feet with a sandbank too near for comfort. The wind continued to howl but the anchors now held. In our haste we had not tied the mainsail properly and it was catching the wind. I went to tie it, the wind was so strong I had to straddle the boom and hang on for dear life or I would have been blown away.

Meanwhile, Pixie had concentrated on ripping up everything she could lay her hands on. She had chewed a float we had picked up, that had fallen on the floor and it was now in a million little pieces. An awful mess but fortunately nothing of value was destroyed.

We still had waves coming over the deck forward and sand was blowing about. We were tired and disappointed, given another twenty-four hours of only light winds we could have made it to Suez. We cheered up when we found the lower half of our mattress was relatively dry and that it would fit on the floor of the cabin allowing us all to curl up on it in comfort.

Clang! Bang! We woke at five the next morning to this strange noise and a roaring wind. Bobby went up top to find that our large new anchor had gone, taking with it all the chain and two thirds of the rope. Only our small plough anchor was now holding us. The rope on the Danforth was also slack. When it was pulled up we found the stock was badly bent. We dropped it back, it was no use, but perhaps its weight would help hold us. Bobby was not a happy man. He had lost his knife and got soaking wet and cold. He came back to lie down. We all stayed in our nest on the floor until ten.

The weather was so bad we let Pixie and Bob-tail stay in all day. We were close enough to see the shore and it looked much the same as the rest of the landscape we had been seeing recently: dry, barren and all sand or sandstone hills and mountains. A little village lay halfway up a hill. Gebel Thelemet we thought. Lower down some traffic could be seen.

We had some non-fat milk powder, bought by mistake in Djibouti, useless stuff. I decided to have a go at making cheese with it using some sea water. That afternoon the wind was so strong we were nervous, feeling that our little anchor may not hold. Bobby said he would start the engine and move farther up to the anchor.

Removing the boards over the engine we both stared down in amazement. There, like a gift from heaven, was a can of Danish Camembert cheese, just perched on top of the engine. At first all we could do was to stare at it in amazement. We both could see it so it could not be a figment of our imagination. Suddenly we knew we were going to really enjoy a real treat tonight. Typewriter paper bread with Camembert cheese, what luxury. Bobby bent down and picked it up, being extra careful not to knock it down the bilge or drop it. He felt or saw something move. A maggot! The can looked still sealed with a ring pull, which he pulled at the same time noticing it had been open just a crack. Visions of a grand feast were rudely shattered when we then looked more closely and saw, not just one but a number of very fat bloated maggots on the outside of the can. Inside all it contained was the foil and some dark grey looking stuff in a small pile that had no resemblance in any way to cheese. Our disappointment was acute. It was just such a cruel trick to have been played on us. When we gave it a little more thought we guessed what had happened. We had bought several such cans in Malaysia and put them in a small section of the bilge to keep cool, as we did with other things. This one must have slipped down, out of sight. Perhaps all the water that went down the bilge from the sink the day before had somehow washed it up on the engine. Why the maggots had not been drowned was another mystery. Perhaps they had only come out when they knew their house was high and dry. The inside of the can was also dry. Odd.

There was no let-up in the wind the following day and we woke feeling very cold. Pixie was shivering and did not stop until I wrapped her in four layers of blanket. As soon as I made coffee the kerosene started leaking again. We did little that day but keep a wary eye on our one holding anchor.

By the fourth morning the wind had dropped considerably and the sea was calmer, our spirits rose. We could leave now but waited for the sea to go down a bit more so we could retrieve our anchor, it being our last we could not afford to leave it behind. Bobby blew up the dinghy and then as the sea was still not calm enough to see down he changed the oil in the engine and let it run to charge the batteries. We felt a jolt, looked at each other and then rushed on deck. We had just touched ground but had not really grounded ourselves. The engine was still running so we were able to put it in gear and move off. I pulled up the anchor rope, with no effort, as expected it came up easily with nothing on the end of it. Sadly, with only our useless bent anchor on board and our two good ones down there on the sea bed, we moved out. Whatever the weather there would be no more stops until Suez.

As we moved farther out the wind increased and we changed the genoa for the staysail. The night was spent tacking and making little headway north. By eight the following morning the wind had dropped a lot. The sun was well up but it was freezing. We were continually crossing the shipping lane which was packed with ships. Bobby had fixed the stove and tried heating the bent anchor over the flames to straighten it, this proved impossible.

With the last of our flour I made a small loaf of bread. The cheese I had made from the skimmed milk was at least edible but a far cry from the Camembert we almost had.

By late afternoon the wind had increased and it was hot. We expected to arrive about midnight but were knocked back by a heavy swell. Around midnight the wind died down and the swell decreased also but I was so cold on watch I put both the zip jackets on and two pairs of jeans.

We were coming up to Suez and I was dressed for the Arctic.

When on a camel I did sit
I really felt a stupid nit,
for on my head a veil I had
With modern jeans it looked quite mad

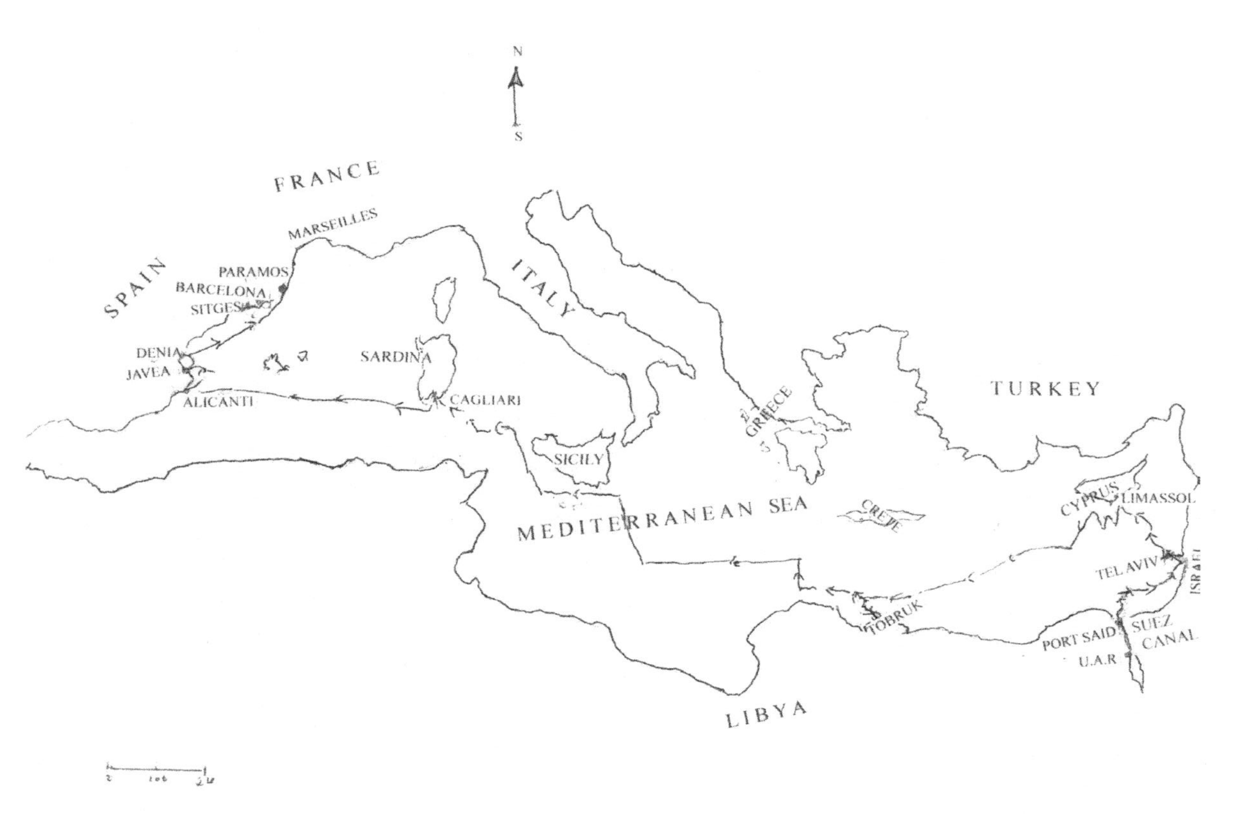

Mediterranean Sea

CHAPTER TWENTY

CAMELS AND KISSES

"Hello, hello, we are your agents, we will help you."

We were now motoring in dead calm into the Newport Channel of Suez. It was the seventeenth of May, twenty-eight days since we left Port Sudan just five hundred miles away, but we had logged one thousand one hundred miles. We felt tired and strangely deflated and wanted nothing to do with the little boat that was now bothering us. We knew that it was best to have an agent to arrange the passage through the Suez Canal but wanted to pick our own. So, we ungratefully waved the boat away. They stopped calling us but followed behind. When we started to turn where we thought the yacht club was, they came alongside and said we must go to another place. We never did understand whether the yacht club was still operating and if it accepted visiting yachts. We were told they recently had some bad experiences and had closed their doors to visitors. One other story was that the Canal Company had forbidden visiting yachts to reach the club which was partly in the Canal. In fact, we had been given so many different stories that the truth could have been anything. Now the men on the boat had finally claimed our attention they handed up a card, proclaiming them to be 'Prince of the Red Sea' agents. They told us we had friends waiting for us and a letter. In that case we thought they were probably legitimate and we would be needing their help so we stopped being unfriendly and followed their advice. They took us near the big German cruising boat we had known in Port Sudan. They told us to anchor.

"We can't, we don't have an anchor," we told them, as if it was something one might have, but we chose not to. We actually felt rather foolish to be sailing around without an anchor and think they were a bit surprised too but they probably meet all sorts, and took us alongside to tie up to an old laid up, probably bombed, tugboat. What a place, they certainly were not trying to impress us. Everything around us had been shelled and bombed, a big crane had been sunk right next to us. What buildings still stood were in ruins. A most depressing place.

No friends were waiting for us, they had all gone through the Canal but we cheered up when they handed us a letter from John on '*Natica*'. John and Chris had made the passage in twenty-two days and had now left. This was good news as we had not set eyes on them since the second day out of Port Sudan. We had thought and talked of them often, always in the hope we might catch up with them. Always wondering how they were getting on. John wrote that he had used 'Prince of the Red Sea'. We now agreed to do the same. They did not waste any time, they were fast, friendly and efficient, and had we wanted we could have gone through the Canal the following day but first we wanted to get a new anchor made, among other things, so delayed our departure.

All our paperwork was taken care of in no time and I was taken ashore to shop in a grand car. The ride to town, however, was depressing. Devastation, I had never seen such a place before and it brought home the fact how awful war is. Bombed buildings and road and rebuilding going on surrounded by rubble. I was taken from shop to shop, there appeared to be no supermarkets, just small shops which had most things except disinfectant. That was the only thing that no one had ever heard of. Strange as that was something the whole town looked badly in need of. I had, of course, not yet got any money but that was no problem. My tubby little guide had a pocket full of notes he shelled out like playing cards, saying he could be repaid later. I hoped he was keeping a check on things as I soon lost count. Most things appeared to be expensive but there was a lot of very nice fresh fruit and vegetables. I did not feel too comfortable with my agent as he insisted on guiding me around the shops by taking my arm or holding my hand, though he seemed harmless. Later when it was Bobby's turn to go ashore he also had his hand held. Men kept stopping us and would just say "Welcome," to me which was rather nice but would keep staring at my hair and even tried stroking it. I started to wonder if I had remembered to comb it before starting out. My shopping trip ended at the agents' office where I was given a few puffs on a water pipe and a cup of Turkish coffee. Before getting back to *'Sandpiper'* I was shown where we could get water and wash. A most strange place, it appeared to be a courtyard of a mosque. The buildings all around had been bombed but the water pipes had miraculously remained intact.

Another boat arrived and was tied up alongside us. *'Timkin'*, British, having sailed from Saudi Arabia where the owner and crew had been working. Bobby joined them going into town. We were very surprised to see Bob-tail had gone ashore, before dark. He must have had to do some high jumps as it was no easy matter to get ashore over the big derelict tug we were tied to.

"Would you like to go to Cairo?" Bobby asked me on his return from town. Would I indeed, that was just exactly what I wanted to do, having never seen the pyramids. The two boys off *'Timkin'* were hoping to fly out from Cairo to England and Bobby had arranged that I share the car with them and stay on to see the sights. I was thrilled to bits.

Pixie, thoughtfully, woke me at five the next morning, giving me time to get ready for my trip to Cairo and leave at six. I and *'Timkin's'* crew crossed the harbour by boat. Here their luggage was checked and they handed out the customary packets of cigarettes. We then proceeded to the office with the agent by car. After sipping Turkish coffee for some time, Mohamed arrived to drive us all to Cairo, about 75 kilometres away. The view consisted of nothing but desert, a few scrubby bushes and now and then, some army tents or a few tanks and a road check every so often. Quite suddenly Cairo was there. Unlike most other cities where it's hard to tell where it starts, Cairo was quite different. Nothing, then the city starts with an army school surrounded by a high wall behind which tower numerous trees. It was as if someone had gathered up all the trees and put them behind the wall. The city was also full of flowers, yet outside nothing grew. Our first stop was the airport where the boys came up against innumerable problems in trying to book and confirm flights. One of them had a wife who should, by then, have produced him a second baby and so was understandably keen to fly out as soon as possible. Had they been able to confirm a late flight they would have come with me on the tour of Cairo but nothing could be confirmed and they hoped to get an early plane so wishing them luck we parted at the airport.

I was disappointed that the boys were not joining me on my sightseeing trip as this now left me with Mohamed. Tall, young and good looking, and probably half my age, it should not have presented a problem. Unfortunately he, like all the Egyptian males I had met, mooned around me like a lovesick schoolboy. I got the feeling that any female under the age of 100 would have received the same unwanted attention. I found it very irritating when I wanted to just be left alone to ponder on the sights. Telling them my age did not help, they simply did not believe me. For a while I thought the trip up the Red Sea had in some miraculous way transformed my face back to a youthful appearance. I had not seen myself for some time so looked in the looking glass at the airport ladies, it reflected the same old weather-beaten face looking decidedly the worse for wear. If it had changed, it was not for the better. Later I learned that what one's face looked like had little relation to age. All the local women over the age of about twenty start growing outwards in an alarming fashion. That I still resembled a bean pole to them indicated I had not yet reached full womanhood. Before we left the airport, Mohamed presented me with a lovely bunch of roses but nothing in which I could put them in water, so sadly they wilted and died in a very short space of time in the car.

Our first stop was the Mohamed Ali Mosque, the largest so I was told, of the 300 or so mosques in Cairo. I found it to be less impressive than I had expected but bought a postcard to send to my young Moslem acquaintance in Sri Lanka. Our drive then took us past huge cemeteries full of very small domes. I wondered if all the bodies slumbering there had died a natural death or were victims of the war. The tops of the pyramids came into view, then round a bend the city stopped as abruptly as it had started. There, surrounded by desert, were the pyramids and the Sphinx. So very familiar from pictures but now there in real life. Breathtaking! I would have liked to have stood alone for a while and just try and take it all in. It was not to be. Mohamed was a tourist guide and I a tourist. I was driven round to a friend of his who owned a camel and a shop. Here I was introduced to a well-dressed camel with lots of tassels and things, who obediently folded his legs under his body allowing me to clamber on his back feeling like a real dumb tourist. I am fond of camels and had the camel been allowed to canter off into the desert and around the pyramids I would have been quite happy, but this was not the plan. A very young boy was in charge of the camel and his business was to make the tourists look complete idiots. Deftly he now stuck a headdress on my head which even the most hippy of hippies would have thought a bit incongruous, worn with a pair of black jeans. However, according to the young boy, I had now turned into Cleopatra. He now relieved me of my camera with which he said he would take my photo. I protested saying that my camera was too complicated for him to use. He declared he knew all about cameras, which it transpired he did, and I had to allow not one but two of my precious pictures to be wasted, with me on the camel. I only got to ride a little way just so we would have the pyramids as a back drop to this charade. The shop then had to be inspected, full of beautiful things I had no use for or money to buy. When I gathered we would get no further that day unless I did buy something I purchased a few postcards and the smallest, cheapest brass ashtray I could find. At last I was free to see what I had come for.

The pyramids were within walking distance of the shop so I thought now we would be done with the car and walk. No. I would apparently die of the heat, so back in the car I must go. Stopping a short distance from the first pyramid, Mohamed gave me a ticket, telling me everything had been paid for so I would not need money, so I left my purse in the car. I entered the pyramid, happy to be able to do so alone. At first I was excited but then found it rather depressing inside, with narrow tunnels going up and down, which necessitated bending down to get through, leading to the centre. There was little to see, everything having been taken out and put in the museum. I had entered behind four American tourists, who I soon caught up with. They had a guide but I derived little benefit from him. His English was so accentuated and he spoke at such a rate I gave up trying to understand. Back in the open air again I was about to move off when the guide grabbed my arm and told me to give him something. I told him I had nothing to give him, not having my money with me and that anyway I had my ticket and had not asked him to be my guide. At this he nearly had a fit and as he was rather on the ancient side I was afraid he might collapse at my feet. However, he remained standing and his tongue wagged nineteen to the dozen. *Was he to eat stones, was that what I wanted?* he demanded of me. That was the last thing I wanted the poor old boy to do, he would probably have considered it a neat trick and demand more money for having done it. He wanted to know who the evil person was that told me I did not have to pay him. In true British spirit I refused to divulge the source of my information. When he loosened his grip on my arm to wave his own in the air in frustration I made my escape and raced back to the car.

"Quick," I said to Mohamed, "move away, the guide is after me." Too late, the ancient one was as nimble on his old pins as was his tongue in his head. He now clung onto the side of the car nearly burning up poor Mohamed with a torrent of Arabic curses. I expected any moment he would produce a dagger from the folds of his robe and I would be without a driver. Mohamed, who had remained silent, now managed, a bit late I felt, to get the car moving. I looked back to see the self-appointed guide jumping around behind us in what appeared to be a war dance of a sort, waving his arms and no doubt calling down the wrath of Allah upon our heads.

I went into the second pyramid on my own and found it much like the first so declined Mohamed's suggestion of a visit to the third. What I really enjoyed was seeing them from the outside and being able to wander round the Sphinx watching horses and camels being ridden in the distance. While wandering around thus, I bumped into two more old guides but made it quite plain to them that I had no money and did not require their services. They said they could see I was a student and it did not matter if I had no money as long as I was happy. That was rather nice, and I wished they had told my first old boy that. They showed me around, pointing out carvings over doorways and other points of interest that I might have missed. As we parted they told me that one day I would come again and then I would be rich and could pay them. Meanwhile, they asked to be allowed to each give me a kiss on the cheek.

Returning to the car Mohamed took my hand and slipped a ring on my finger, white modern metal with turquoise and a red bead. The stones and beads were supposed to have come from a tomb. Judging by the amount of cheap jewellery that was being sold, all with this type of tomb stones, every tomb that had ever been opened would have had to have been packed tight with them. We now went to lunch and later I received a bangle to match the ring. I wondered if I was supposed to estimate the value of these gifts, double it and present a tip. The lunch had been enjoyable but I wished we had gone instead straight to the museum, which was fantastic but closed half day, so I was only able to spend an hour before being told I had to leave, by which time I had seen less than half the exhibits on the ground floor.

During that hour Mohamed had gone to the airport and found the boys had managed to get on the afternoon flight to London.

We now went back to the pyramids and farther out into the desert to look back and take photos. Looking at the pyramids from outside I found far more satisfying than going inside. I was let loose in the centre of Cairo to wander around the shops while Mohamed washed the car and changed a tyre. A very modern city with shops that overflowed with expensive goods of every description. It was another world but one that I had little interest in.

Back at the dock the gate was closed and the guard refused to allow the car in. It was pitch dark and I would have to walk but it was indicated that the guard would escort me. His idea of escorting me was to put his arm around me and I had to fight him off and shout at him which brought another guard who must have been his superior and wanted to protect me by doing exactly what the first had done, who also remained with us. We proceeded to where *'Sandpiper'* was moored, which seemed twice as far as it had been in daylight with me running and pushing away hands and faces in the dark. At last the old tug boat that we were tied to was there and I pulled away and clambered on board. From that I would have to climb down to our deck but suddenly I was lifted off my feet by one of my escorts who carrying me jumped down on the deck and started across to *'Timkin'* with me in his arms. I yelled for him to put me down and Bobby appeared with a flashlight. I was dumped on deck and the guard vanished.

"I'm back," I said inanely, rather expecting Bobby to ask why I required to be carried aboard. Bobby had had his own troubles. He had been sitting in the dark in the cockpit with a flashlight, in the beam I saw Pixie silhouetted on the end of the remains of a wrecked pier. Bobby had been watching her since four that afternoon when she broke her chain and went on to *'Timkin'*, from there she had worked her way along their mooring line to the wrecked pier. Bobby had tried to get her back but she refused to go to him and he was afraid she would make her way ashore and get lost and probably shot. We both have different roles in Pixie's life. One of her rules being that when she is loose, it must be I who bring her back. We now pulled our way over in the dinghy holding the mooring lines. The dinghy had deflated a bit due to the low temperature but still floated. I then had to climb up the weed-covered and slippery rotten wood struts that remained of the pier, in my best jeans and white blouse. Pixie just looked. So I had to crawl along to where Pixie sat waiting for me. Taking what remained of her chain in my hand we scrambled back to where we could get back down to the dinghy. I was a little afraid she would hurry and pull me off the rotten wood structure we had to walk along. She was good and understood I was not as nimble on my feet as she was and took her time, stopping and looking back and waiting for me to make my way along.

It had been an unusual day and we were all very tired that night.

We now had a new anchor. The first day ashore Bobby had gone to a blacksmith and drawn a picture of the anchor he wanted and the very next morning it had been made and delivered. We were impressed.

The morning after my Cairo adventure we were woken just before six when the agent jumped aboard. He had come to tell us that *'Timkin'* and ourselves, by Port Authority instructions, had to go out to anchor. They had already moved *'Timkin'* and now towed us out to anchor. We were then told that a surveyor would come and inspect our engine to see that we were capable of going through the Canal. This we dreaded. While in Sri Lanka we had talked with other boats that were doing this same trip. For all of us it was the first time but somehow the idea was put about that you had to be capable of six knots. None of us smaller boats had that kind of engine power. We had then thought that we could be towed by the bigger boats that could do that and more, and they were quite agreeable to do so. On arrival in Suez we were surprised to learn that all our friends who had passed through had done the trip under their own power. Dick Turpin had had a little trouble when he discovered his engine would not turn his propeller. A large American yacht had offered to tow him but towing by anything other than the canal tow boats was not allowed and they were very expensive. Dick's troubles came to an end when it was found the fault lay in the fact that a length of rope had wrapped itself around the propeller shaft. When that was removed he was OK. Bobby started to do a little work on our engine but had hardly begun before the so-called inspectors came on board. They sat down and the agent went to where I had my cigarettes and took two packets, handing them to the inspectors. We did not have much in the way of drinks to offer, only Pixie's lemonade. Bobby started the engine. It ran for about two minutes and the inspectors, who evidently thought it sounded OK, nodded their heads and went off. We had not even had to move. Now all the paperwork was completed and we paid our bill. It took every penny we had, and even then fell a little short of the total but no one minded.

We were now set to go through the Canal the following morning.

Up the Canal we did go,
though progress was a wee bit slow.
Our pilot would not hold his tongue,
All told the trip was not much fun.

CHAPTER TWENTY-ONE
UP THE CANAL

Engaging a pilot is compulsory for the Canal. Ali, our pilot for the first half of the trip, jumped onboard while Bobby was still trying to stop a leak in the engine. *'Timkin'*, with her remaining crew, had left ahead of us. Keeping our fingers crossed, hoping our engine would not let us down, we got up our new anchor. Pixie and Ali ignored each other. Ali spoke English, as he informed us, very well. He certainly spoke it very fast, also continually. He never stopped, half the time we could not understand what he was saying and when we could, found him very boring. Perhaps being the smallest, we were last in the convoy and from the start *'Timkin'* was out of sight. Soon we started meeting ships coming the other way. They looked huge, their crews all waved to us as they passed. Ali took the wheel and was getting very concerned about our poor turn of speed. We thought we were doing marvellously with the engine going flat out and black smoke billowing out behind. This had never happened before, we took it as a sign the strain the engine was going through. We thought we must be doing almost three knots. The log had not been streamed as this would have given away our slow speed. After a while Ali's talk changed its tone a little, he was talking of papers he had not been given him and about how we had to give him something. As Bobby was not responding in the way he hoped, Ali told me to take the wheel and took Bobby down in the cabin for a real heart to heart talk that went on and on. Ali explained in great length, and several times mentioned that we should not have used 'Prince of the Red Sea' as they were not good. They should have given him a piece of very important paper he needed but had failed to do so and now he would be in trouble. Bobby pointed out that he should have settled with the agent before coming on board. Ali also claimed he had not been paid and that he was a poor man and that it was the custom for Bobby to give him money. Bobby told him the truth that we had no money, he told him several times and Ali looked sadder and sadder. Bobby relieved me at the wheel. I then had to put up with Ali teaching me Arabic. I learned a few words but was not clear what the English equivalent was. Ali soon became very sorry for himself, not only had he not been able to get any money out of us, but it was clear we were never going to reach the bitter lakes before dark, this was where his stint ended. We were not allowed to travel through in the dark and resignedly he said we would have to stop at Genifa and moor alongside the jetty there. It had been a wearing trip and we were pleased to stop.

We spoke to the official who told us that there was no problem and that Ali could sleep ashore that night. Ali had other ideas and said he wanted to sleep on board. He then said that our bunk was big enough to let him sleep with us. We quickly dampened that idea and told him if he did not wish to sleep ashore he would have to sleep on the seats. He was a small man and it would have been no problem. "What about Pixie?" he protested. "Pixie and Bob-tail sleep with us in the bunk," we told him. He agreed to sleep on the seats.

At dinner in the cabin that night we had to rearrange things as Pixie obviously was not too keen on Ali, she tolerated him as we did but if he got too near she glared at him and showed her teeth; a thing I rather fancied doing myself. Knowing she would object to him eating at the table, we pulled down the folding seat at the end for Pixie and put her chain on, attaching it to the seat so that she could only move a little. Ali we placed at the other end of the table. Ali told us about all his English friends and how he did not mind eating their food and would even eat roast beef. He showed no disappointment when we gave him rice and red beans which was our meal that night. He talked his way through it all so it was doubtful that he even noticed what he ate. Pixie objected to his manner and every now and then Ali would raise his voice, then Pixie would stand on her seat glare at him and slap the table hard. This had the desired effect and Ali moderated his voice until he forgot again and the same thing happened. We felt Pixie had him under much better control than we had.

It was arranged we start out early at four the next morning. We felt if Ali had his way we would be up all night listening to his stories, only half of which we ever took in. At eight, feeling truly weary, we told a whopping big lie and said we liked to go to bed early, especially as we had to get up at the crack of dawn. We took Pixie and crawled into our bunk, leaving Ali playing with our radio.

In spite of our early retirement we did not wake until four thirty when someone ashore started calling Ali. We jumped up and started out just before five. Poor Bob-tail hated having company on board and would not even come out of hiding to eat. Before we left, Ali obtained a cup of sugar from ashore. We knew all the Arabs liked tea and coffee very sweet but had forgotten to get any sugar. We had specially bought some tea bags and had coffee of which Ali drunk endless cups, but we had to let him use honey to sweeten it. I transferred his sugar to a jar with no lid, so he could return the cup. Stupidly, when lighting the burner, I knocked the jar over. It had not been very clean looking sugar to begin with so I swept it up extracting all the larger bits of dirt I could see.

Cigarettes were the tipping currency in Egypt and everyone who so much as poked their nose on board the boat for any reason at all expected a pack. Ali smoked my cigarettes non-stop, I noticed doctoring about every third with drugs. Ali now started asking for chocolate, how he thought we could have kept chocolate on board without it melting I don't know. Then it was hair oil, which we also had to confess being without. Finally, he thought he needed some cream for his face. I did have an open pot of Nivea but felt my skin was more in need of it than his. I offered him a dab of it but he wanted a new unused jar so he was just out of luck.

Thankfully, we arrived in Ismalia before dark that afternoon and as soon as we anchored a boat came out and took Ali off. Happily, we waved goodbye to him. We sat back, Bobby was not feeling well. We both agreed it had been the most boring two days we could remember.

We woke at four thirty the following morning when our new pilot arrived. We immediately nicknamed him Hippo. Hippo was HUGE. At first he was as silent as Ali had been talkative. Still he did his job and took over the steering and stayed in the cockpit. I did wonder if it was because he could not get down the companionway, owing to his size. I quickly made him some tea wondering how much food he would need to fill him. I passed the remains of the sugar up to him and he emptied it all into the tea. Hippo had no jacket of any kind, just a cotton shirt stretched across his chest and it was very cold. He shivered and indicated he was freezing to death. It was the height of foolishness for a man of that size to expect to be able to borrow clothes. I handed him a zip jacket which he put over his shoulders where it became little more than a collar, but it was the largest item of clothing we had. He still shivered so I gave him a blanket. Even that looked ridiculously small on him.

Bobby by this time was feeling really ill; he had a bad cold and after getting up lay on the seats and went to sleep all morning. I took over the steering for a short time but Hippo seemed to be happy at the wheel. To my surprise he did manage to get down into the cabin for breakfast for which I made an extra quantity of toast for him. He left his lemon juice but ate all the toast and cheese and finished off with cereal. He accepted honey in his tea and coffee without comment and was very much more pleasant than Ali had been. I cooked a large lunch to keep him going. Rice and beans left over from the night before, mee with fried chilli, onions and tomato on top. I cut lots of bread and also made a salad which I planned for us. I set it on the table and invited him down and let him eat first and alone, feeling he would be happier that way and anyway he needed all the space. To my amazement he ate a lot of bread and butter and all the salad except the olives which he picked out. The cooked food he never touched and we were left to try and plough our way through that. Later I thought he was probably a strict Moslem and feared the cooked food might have contained some meat that was not Halal, and wished I had explained that it was all stuff he could have eaten.

After lunch Hippo slept for a while and it was after he woke that he noticed we were making less speed than he hoped. The tide and wind were then against us. He was steering when a large fishing boat was passing. Hippo then leapt from the wheel and started shouting at them and picked up a coil of rope. He obviously wanted a tow though this is contrary to the Canal rules and we said nothing. The fishing boat ignored him and passed on ahead of us. Hippo stood in the bow and just bellowed after the departing fishing boat. After that he sulked and did not want tea or coffee and even refused a cigarette. We now had a great big baby on our hands. Another fishing boat came along and the same scene was repeated. We passed the last station and were hailed by a loudspeaker. Evidently they wanted us to stay the night as it was getting late and we were so slow. We left it up to Hippo. He needed no loud hailer, he just bellowed back and we continued on, the loud hailer still shouting after us. Now for the first time he asked us for money and we had the business again of trying to explain we had none. We did in fact have a few Thai notes we had been given in Malaysia but not used, being unable to get ashore. We offered him these but they were refused. We then came up to a small jetty on which stood a man and a bus parked on the road. Hippo now made a last try to get us to give him something and kept saying Luba. I felt sure I knew that word, then rightly or wrongly, remembered it was milk. I grabbed a can of milk powder we had open and gave it to him and he appeared satisfied and steered for the jetty. Only then did we understand what he was doing when he shouted at Bobby to take the wheel, and flung himself off *'Sandpiper'* and onto the jetty. I waited with bated breath for the splintering of the boards but they held. He must have told the man on the jetty how mean we were as that man shouted out after us that we were supposed to pay the pilot's taxi fare.

Alone at last, just where we were not quite sure, but Port Said was just ahead and we continued on, intending to find a quiet place to anchor for the night if possible as Bobby was still not feeling well. Two men on the last jetty waved us in, they took our passports and we explained that our pilot had jumped ship. They suggested we go to the international club, a new yacht club that was being built there. We explained the embarrassment of having no money. They assured us that everything was free. We gave in and went as directed to the yacht club

It was a happy decision. Four other yachts were there. We immediately recognised '*Natica*' and John and Chris standing waving us in. It's a lovely place they tell us and if we hurry we will just be in time for a hot shower before the gas is turned off.

Our ordeal was over.

Lucky us to have a friend,
with money he was glad to lend.

CHAPTER TWENTY-TWO

THE PROMISED LAND

We stayed three days in the delightful little Port Said Yacht Club. Part of the attraction was its manager, Ali, same name as our pilot but oh so very different. This Ali was both friendly and very helpful. On being asked to sign the visitors' book we found many others had enjoyed this little stopping place. Among names we knew we found *'Kathena Faa'* with a drawing by little Kym, they had stayed there over a month before. We made friends with two grand Australians, Tom and Mimi, on *'Amatuana'*, a beautiful boat Tom had built himself. They also had a cat they had named D27: big, white and fluffy. We exchanged experiences about our trip discovering that John and Chris had been around Shadwan Island at the same time as ourselves but they had been more fortunate and had actually managed to get in and anchor but did have shots fired at them.

Apparently, everyone who had gone through the Red Sea had come under small arms fire at some point or other. That was one adventure we had missed out on; we had sometimes heard gunfire but always at a distance and believed it to be natives playing their usual games with each other.

We were all a little concerned over Jim and Jan who were also old friends of Tom and Mimi. They had left Sudan two-and-a-half days before we had but so far no one had seen or heard from them and they were presumed to still be in the Red Sea. Knowing they were good sailors and with a well-found boat, it was the general opinion that they must be anchoring and exploring places. Privately, I think we were all a little more concerned than we liked to voice. About a year later we learned that they had gone to Jeddah and Jim had found himself a job there.

Rather to our dismay, we found we were required to pay harbour dues and clearance of five pounds and also one pound stamp duty. This meant we would have to stay and get money transferred from our bank in England. We had wanted to delay doing this until Israel which we thought would be more efficient. John came to the rescue kindly loaning us fourteen pounds which enabled us get our clearance and buy some fresh food.

'Natica' and *'Amatuana'* left and we waited another day as Bobby was still feeling unwell. We were surprised the following day when Bobby went to get clearance to find it was a public holiday, May 25th, our wedding anniversary, the holiday though was for rather wider interests. The border between Egypt and Israel was being opened. Our departure was put off until the next day.

Pixie and I were up early the next morning and took a little walk around the club grounds. Pixie made friends with a little dog and I picked a few wild flowers for the breakfast table. Bobby was still not himself but said he felt fit enough to leave. We bade Ali farewell and were away by ten with just a light breeze. In navigating out of the harbour we passed many wrecks, a ship broken in three parts and others upside down. All presumably war causalities, but it was hard to say. There was very little wind on our way out but we were contented, and that evening opened a bottle of Omar Khayyam wine Bobby had bought in Suez. The next three days we had poor sailing weather, very little wind and becalmed a number of times. The weather was a reminder that we were now approaching Europe, it was cold even during the day. Bobby still felt unwell and I was not feeling too grand. Pixie had a bad case of runny tummy and vomiting and Bob-tail was off his food. In all not a very lively crew, it was lucky that the weather was not rough. We sighted the coast of Israel, all heavily patrolled, on the morning of the twenty-ninth. At first we did not like all the patrol boats but then found they were all very friendly. They came slowly near us and asked where were from and where we were going. They were all smiles and did not mind we had come from Egypt. We were looking for the marina where we had arranged to join up again with *'Natica'* and *'Amatuana'*. It was not marked on the chart but had been described to us. Seeing some chimneys farther south we thought we had overshot it in the dark and turned back. Another patrol boat came alongside and asked out destination. We had boobed, the place we were then heading for was Jaffa, where we had first planned to go before being told about the new marina at Tel Aviv. After we turned onto the other tack the wind increased and we hit very heavy seas. Once more our bunk got swamped.

In the early hours of the next day we were becalmed again. I was sitting in the dark, trying to steer with no wind when a searchlight suddenly shone on me, yet another patrol boat wanted our destination. When I replied they asked if I knew the way to the marina, I expect I looked a bit lost. "No," I called back, feeling a bit of a fool. They kindly told me to steer 055 instead of 030 as I had been trying to do and with that the wind returned which was even more helpful. Until then the word marina was just a word, I had never seen one and did not know what to expect. We came up to the marina just before six that morning. I was stunned. "Bobby, just look at all those boats, there are hundreds, we will never get in, I don't like it," I wailed. It was completely beyond me to understand how all the boats could be packed so close together. It was crowded but the majority of boats were small fibreglass ones, belonging to the local residents. We were directed into what looked to me the only remaining space near *'Amatuana'*. Once in I started to breathe again. We had not hit a single thing and were now nicely tied up. *'Natica'* was just a little farther along from us. A number of different officials and security officials came on board and searched among our things, putting back anything they disturbed in the exact place they found it. I think they were searching for bombs. If for some reason we had had a bomb aboard Pixie would have either dismantled it or blown us up months ago.

Assuring them, when asked, that we did not have a gun of any sort and the most lethal weapon we had was a knife, they left. The searches were routine and we did not mind as they were all friendly and polite.

"'*Sandpiper*'," a shrill familiar voice was calling us, one we had not heard since Singapore. We popped our heads up and sure enough there on the wharf was little Carl clad in a bikini in spite of what we considered to be cold weather. She looked well and happy and had been there about a year and was now on '*Noelani*' with Graham, another clever person that had built his own boat. Tom and Graham had already found they had a lot in common. Tom and Mimi had been on their way to England to start building boats to sell. Now they had decided to stay in Israel and go into the boat building business with Graham. Chris decided to stay and join their business as he was hoping to build his own boat some day in the future. We found we were not the only cruising boats when Norma came round, she and John had their boat '*Wawaiki*' the other side of the marina. We were together with a nice little circle of old friends again.

Carla took me shopping for some fresh food, showing me the best shop nearby and paying for my purchases. It also proved to be an education in how to get served. The shop was crowded with a crowd of very rotund ladies who though not tall, were a lot taller than little Carla who cannot have been much over four feet. It appeared they were all going to stand around talking forever and while I was prepared to resign myself to having to wait at the back, Carla elbowed herself to the front, her sharp little elbows digging in fleshy ribs. The fruits and vegetables were beautiful and inexpensive. I stared at some huge red things, surely they were radishes: right shape, colour and leaf but they were as big as grapefruits. Carla confirmed they were radishes. I regretted later never having bought one but I was not sure what to do with such a giant.

Carla also had a cat who considered the marina was his territory having spent all his young life there. He marched on board and inspected our deck, leaving his calling card in Bob-tail's sand tray just to show him who was boss around there.

Our first priority was to telex for money to be sent out to us from England. We had not done this in Egypt as we were labouring under the misapprehension that Egypt would be inefficient and Israel would be ultra-efficient. Just how efficient Egypt would have been we don't know, but certainly we were impressed with the manner in which everything was dealt with in Suez, even to having our bent anchor straightened and a new one made overnight.

When we had money sent to Sri Lanka it had taken three days. Bobby went to the bank on the Thursday to send the telex, with hopes of receiving the money at least by the Monday. At the bank he was told they would send the telex but that owing to some holidays the bank would not be open again until the following Tuesday, when he could come and collect his money. John was in no hurry to leave so there was still time to pay him. The bank was unable to exchange what remained of the Egyptian money John had given him, or the Thailand notes we still had. John then kindly came to our assistance again and insisted on loaning us more money to tide us through until Tuesday.

Tuesday was Pixie's sixth birthday. We called it her birthday as it was the day we first had her but she must have been at least a year old then. Bobby went to the bank after telling her he would return with lots of nice fruit for her. He returned empty-handed, the money had not come. That evening I joined Carla on Mimi's boat and confessed to still not being able to repay her for the fruit she had paid for the first day. "Oh that's nothing," declared Carla. "Do you want money?" asked Mimi offhandedly. She had just been made treasurer of the new business venture they were forming and had a pile of Israeli notes. "Here take this," and she handed me a 500 pound note. This generosity and helping out among cruising friends, which after all we had not known very long, was something we would not forget. Pixie after all was able to enjoy her birthday that evening as she gorged herself on peaches which were the most delicious we have ever tasted, and also the cheapest.

The next day there was still no money and when the same thing happened the following day Bobby became very angry and saw another girl in the bank who immediately went off to see just when the telex had been sent. The telex, it transpired, had not been sent at all. Bobby now demanded to see the manager. The woman Bobby had been dealing with before, and who had assured him each time that it had been sent, was now called into the manager's office. Here she now confessed that she had not sent it as a telex but by airmail, which from Tel Aviv was extremely slow…so this time the telex was actually sent off and Bobby continued his daily visits to the bank. Two weeks from his first visit we had borrowed again from Mimi. The bank still said they did not have our money but by that time they were getting tired of seeing Bobby each day so tried to be more helpful and telephoned other branches of their bank. At the end of it all they located a branch that had received the money and had been wondering what to do with it. By that time the bank was closing, it being half-day, he was told to return the following morning. Full of hope now Bobby set out for the bank, only to be told they still had not got his money. This was now getting beyond a joke. John was soon to leave and though he did not appear to be concerned we wanted to return his money before he left. The bank that had claimed to have the money was again contacted, they had sent it off to yet another wrong branch. When that branch was contacted they said they had not received it. This was all too crazy to be true. Bobby now insisted they give him the money which after all they knew to be somewhere in the country in one of their branches and if they kept losing it, it was hardly his fault. They compromised and he came away with one hundred pounds, the rest to be collected the following day when it finally found its way to the correct bank. It was nice to be able to make the rounds and return all the money we had borrowed and we were now able to purchase other things that we needed to get *'Sandpiper'* in a seaworthy condition again.

Partly due to the hold up of our money our stay in Tel Aviv was prolonged to twenty-nine days, most of the time being spent working on the boat. Mimi had bought some nice new bed sheets in Egypt and kindly gave me her old ones to replace ours which had all blown away at sea. We were all working on our boats, turning out lockers. We gave away a lot of jerry cans in which we had kept water on deck and now had no use for. John gave us a little saucepan with a lid. Gradually all the boats were beginning to look smarter.

Bob-tail had a series of adventures. He was lost the first twenty-four hours after we arrived and finally turned up on another boat where he was unable to get off until we pulled the boat in and put a gangplank down for him. He had not spent all his time there, as before that Mimi had found him when she had opened a locker and Bob-tail jumped out. She had fed him turkey before he left and he remained her friend forever after. Bob-tail did not mind D27, Mimi's cat, but Carla's young cat bossed them both. One night Bob-tail came in completely waterlogged and it was obvious he had fallen in the water, how he got out again we had no idea. Another morning I woke at four to a banging sound which sounded like the anchor chain. As we were in the marina and had no anchor out I thought I would investigate. As I stuck my head out of the hatch I saw Carla's cat just getting off our boat and stalking off. No sign of Bob-tail who usually howled every time that cat paid a visit. The banging continued. Grabbing a sarong to go on deck and investigate further the noise stopped and I heard Bob-tail on deck. Again, he was soaking wet. We never did find out how he got back on board but it was now clear that he had been pushed overboard. In the end a truce was called among the cats and was exercised by them going on each other's boats and eating the food which worked out quite well as far as we humans were concerned. We were able to get dry cat food which is good for their teeth, but none of the cats cared for it, that is from their own bowls, but they would eat anything if they thought it belonged to the others. So, we all kept bowls of the stuff in our cockpits. Mimi's boat was the most popular around dinner time, when she would start cooking fish or meat, the smell would attract all three cats. One would sit on the cabin top with its head hanging down the companionway and heads would appear either side of her galley. Every now and then she would post titbits in the waiting mouths.

Bob-tail, though the oldest of the cats was by far the smallest, now grew a bit bolder and one day decided to give D27 a push. They were both sitting on *'Amatuana's'* cabin top, D27 with his back to Bob-tail who suddenly shot a paw out and hit poor D27, who taken by surprise was knocked straight down his own companionway into his cabin. He did not reappear and Bob-tail just sat there looking innocent but well satisfied with himself.

The market was a wonderful place to shop with piles of beautiful fresh produce, flat bread and local cheese. The only problem was limiting oneself to what one could carry back. One day returning from the market I wanted to get some butter in the supermarket but arrived just as they were closing and was refused admittance, even though I pleaded with the doorman to let me in for a moment to buy butter. Giving up I went my way when someone started calling, but in Hebrew; though not understanding I turned and saw two young girls calling and trying to catch up with me. Laden as I was I thought I must have dropped something. It turned out they had heard me ask for butter and seen I had been refused entrance when they themselves were just coming out. They understood what I had wanted and handed me a packet of butter, which I was very pleased to accept but when I dug in my purse to pay for it they ran off refusing payment.

'Natica' now left. John had decided to go to Cyprus. Chris was to remain in Tel Aviv working with Tom and Graham. John would not be sailing alone, he had signed on three charming young girls who were all very keen but had never sailed before. We could not decide if he was very brave or very lucky.

The best day for visiting Jerusalem I was told was Saturday, when the tourist buses don't run, making it less crowded. Accordingly, I set off one morning but arriving at the bus station I discovered that the ordinary buses did not run either but share taxis (Sherut-taxi) did. When I stood waiting for one to come along a private car stopped. *Good*, I thought, *I am getting a lift*, and moved forward. A man leaned out of his car but instead of asking where I was headed for asked if I was hungry, offering to give me food and about to hand me a large bag, presumably containing food. He gave me a lift instead when I told him I had had my breakfast. The lift did not help much as he was not going my way so only took me a little farther on before dropping me off. I hope he found a hungry person to give his food to.

The ride to Jerusalem, when a share taxi did come along, took three quarters of an hour and the landscape was amazing. I had expected something like my trip to Cairo with nothing but desert between the two cities. What I saw was more like England. Everywhere was cultivated and in the newly planted fields the soil looked rich. Sprinklers were going and all the slopes were terraced. No desert remained but parts contained a lot of rocks which had been dug up and positioned to make walls for the terraces.

My transport stopped in Jaffa Street and from there it was a short walk to old Jerusalem. Entering by the gate known as 'Bab el Khalil' (Gate of the Friend) a thrill of excitement went through me to think that for the first time I was actually entering Jerusalem, the city so steeped in religion and history. It was sad I had only one day, as there is far too much to see in such a short time. All I could hope to do was to wander around and drink in some of the atmosphere. I wanted to visit St. James Cathedral in the Armenian quarter, having previously seen a picture of it, but having got there found that it was only open during services. There being no service at the time it was closed. I was not too sad, it was after all a place of worship not a tourist attraction and by closing its doors when no service was taking place was perhaps the one place that retained its purpose. I thought this after visiting the Church of the Holy Sepulchre. The last Stations of the Cross are here and the tomb where it is held, Christ was placed. I believed this to be the most important church in Christendom. I don't recall any religious place that left me so cold. I was dreadfully disappointed. The church as a whole I did not find attractive and it was in a shocking state of disrepair, with ladders and buckets all over the place. The atmosphere of most places of worship is such that everyone automatically lowers their voices and walks slowly. Here people were hurrying about and raised voices of tourists and guides could be heard, workmen trundled in wheelbarrows shouting between themselves. A woman entering just behind me was stopped. She had a sleeveless dress on and with much giggling between her and her companions they dug out a long dress probably just bought in the bazaar to drape over her shoulders. I nearly left then but did continue. The holy sepulchre itself, a domed building over the tomb inside the church was, I considered, ugly and very out of place; crowded in and around it were a group of young boys all wearing YMCA T-shirts, punching each other and laughing and giggling and talking loudly. Feeling completely depressed and wondering what I was doing there, I hurriedly made my way out passing on my way the 'Stone of Anointing'. Three women knelt with rosaries praying, bending over and kissing the stone, rubbing their rosaries beads on the stone. Evidently some people were finding solace but for my part I felt all religious significance had been long ago erased and hidden under a pile of masonry. Perhaps not being a churchgoing person myself I was too critical. I spoke to many churchgoing people who had made the pilgrimage to Jerusalem since, all of whom went in church parties on guided tours and none said they were disappointed. Perhaps they relied on the strong belief that I did not have.

The almost frightening depression that had assailed me in the church lifted once I was back in the open air. Outside the church a drama was taking place to the wide-eyed wonder and amazement of a large number of onlookers. A new marble object that looked as though it might be a base for a large column was being moved. They had by some means got it on to a wooden platform with very, very small wheels, that had seen better days. From this platform stretched two ropes. What appeared to be the front rope was tied to a tractor and the back one held by a man who certainly was no Hercules. They were attempting to pull it nearer or perhaps even trying to get it inside the church. The problem was that the courtyard of the church was on a slope leading down to the church. The tractor was not being used to stop the natural force of gravity which would have allowed the trolley to go down of its own accord and crush into the church, but it was placed at the front. As soon as the tractor moved, taking up the slack, the man on the end of the rope behind was forced to let go and the trolley, with its heavy burden, moved of its own volition after the tractor crashed into it. On impact the tractor swung round and the driver jumped clear, after which the tractor and trolley ended up against a pile of rubble and came to a standstill. I did not stay to see what would be the next move, thinking it might not take place that day. The workmen were having a very heated argument around the collision and an American tourist with a movie camera stood shaking his head in utter bewilderment and saying over and over again, "I just don't believe it."

Quite the most impressive structure I saw was on Mount Morian. The temple compound was peaceful and the quiet, rising in the centre was the 'Dome of the Rock'. At first I had not considered going in, but sat in the courtyard looking at the view all round. Apart from the mosque itself, there were many other structures of interest around it. It was peaceful and there were less tourists, why I don't know, being one of the most sacred shrines with an incredibly long history dating back to Abraham. The mosque is of course Moslem but the rock has been held at different times by Jews, Christians and even Roman Jupiter worshippers as a sacred place. After a while I decided to remove my shoes and go inside hoping I would not be disappointed. A party in front of me handed the guard a bunch of tickets. However, I was not asked for anything and allowed in. It was worth it, here was the reverence that one expects in such places. The floor was covered in different carpets and even the smallest children acted respectfully. There were beautiful mosaic patterns and stained-glass windows. Surrounded by wooden railing is the sacred rock itself.

I walked down to the Wailing Wall and then wandered through small streets until I came out on Dolorosa, this being the street where the rest of the Stations of the Cross are. I went through and looked back on several of the gates which are all quite different in style. Going through one I found myself out in the open, no buildings, just mountains in the distance. I started to walk a little way but a man came running after me and made it clear that it was not allowed, for some reason which I was not able to understand, to be there. He then led me to a graveyard just outside the wall, the significance of which I also did not understand unless you only went through that gate if you were going to be buried.

The bazaars were lively and colourful selling an assortment of souvenirs, gifts and religious articles. A man was playing a haunting melody on a small wooden flute, this took my fancy and I bought four, thinking they would make nice gifts for my nieces and friends' children. Back on board neither I nor Bobby could get a single sound out of them. About a year later having asked many people to try without success, my brother Michael discovered by accident when he stuck the first two inches in his mouth that it worked, it also made you gag.

When in Suez, not then having been told about the marina at Tel Aviv, we had considered anchoring off Jaffa and had accordingly given the Jaffa Post Office address for our mail to be sent to. Although we had now come to Tel Aviv we thought, not unreasonably, that our mail would have gone to the place it was addressed to. I took a bus to Jaffa. The visit was enjoyable, wandering around the reconstructed artists' quarter, collecting fallen figs for Pixie in the gardens and haggling in the flea market for things I had no intention of buying at the time. The only disappointment to this visit was there was no mail for us at the post office. We did in fact track down our mail before leaving, at the Tel Aviv Post Office!

After our money arrived we thought a few bargain carpets from the flea market would do wonders for our cabin. Our old brown bits of carpet we had inherited with the boat were falling apart and ready to be thrown out. The black rubber backing remained in lumps on the floor each time they were taken up and Pixie had discovered if she picked at a thread she could unravel large areas in one satisfying go.

I returned to Jaffa to spend several hours in the carpet area of the flea market. Here hundreds of carpets were spread out for my perusal and I crawled over them with my tape measure, then haggled away like an old Arab. The asking price in the end dropped to half the amount stated at first and sometimes dropped even lower when I turned away. There were very few customers so all the carpets I had inspected were left out after I had left in the hope I might return, and eyes watched me start my measuring and haggling at the next stall. I had found the perfect one for the main part of the cabin at the first shop but had left it to be sure there was no better bargain at another stall. I settled in the end for two strips of bright handmade carpet with a thick pile for the galley area which could be cut to fit perfectly. When they were rolled up the size and weight was a bit staggering and I joined in the laughter as I tottered off under my burden. I then passed a shop I had been to on my first visit, just testing the waters, so to speak. Then I had haggled over the price for two bed covers which I liked but at the time had no intention of buying. The two had started at 1000 and finally ended at 220 – the man remembered me and had them out as I passed, he had a better memory for faces than prices as they were now 300. "Rubbish," I said. "You told me 200," thinking I might as well play the same game and knock off the twenty. Placing my carpets on the ground I got out 200 and passed it to him, gathering up the bed spreads. He helped me, still begging for another 10, it was all in good humour and he joined in the general laughter as I carried off my prize. I then reached the place with the carpet I had first wanted and which I still did. I could still afford the 500 they had brought it down to, however, there did remain the little problem of how to carry it, but decided that could be figured out later. They now wanted 750, no doubt realising that I had been to every other stall so must really want it.

"No, 500 or nothing, anyway I don't think I can carry it," and with that I bent down to pick up my bundle. Before I could hoist it off the ground they accepted my 500. On seeing it was quite impossible for me to carry all I had, they tied the bedspreads up with the carpet in one bundle and tried to make the smaller on of the other carpets. I now had two large bundles, both of which I could manage separately but not together. The bus stop was not far and I made my way along by setting one bundle down, going a few paces with the other, setting that down, and dashing back for the other, a little scared I might lose a bundle to some nimble thief. I was lucky, perhaps because too many interested eyes were watching my comical progress. I still had two buses to get on and off but always found willing hands to help me out. With the new carpets on the floor and the two bedspreads covering the seats our cabin now looked bright and cosy. The bunch of flowers Mimi had sweetly given me the day before set it all off to perfection.

The Tel Aviv Zoo was a sad place and I could not really enjoy it. Plenty of animals but far too may for the space they had. Most of the animals were kept in small old-fashioned cages. To my surprise they had two female pig-tail macaque monkeys which they said they had had for six years. A keeper showed me around and got the hippo to open his big mouth and had his teeth scraped, an act I could see the hippo really enjoyed. For such a big mouth he had surprisingly few teeth, six up and six down. I was also able to stroke a black jaguar when he kept rubbing himself against the bars. I felt sorry for him and all the others and wished I could set them free.

There was a motor boat moored not far from us that had on board a little hairy dog called Daisy. A prim little lady who wore a ribbon in her hair, she would look over at our boat and Pixie and Bob-tail would stare back. It was not until the day before we left that Pixie and Daisy actually met. That evening I was walking Pixie around before dinner and we had spent some time with a man who really admired her. He wanted to give her his keys to play with. I warned him not to give her anything he wanted back as she never returns gifts. He wished to give her a gift of some sort so then presented her with a coin. Pixie accepted it and put it in her mouth, by this means she ascertained that it was of inferior value and took it out and gave it back to him placing it nicely on his shoe. Continuing on our walk I stopped to chat with a friend while Pixie was busy picking up some sweets that had been dropped. Suddenly a boxer dog ran up, he did not bark and seemed friendly enough but had taken us by surprise. Pixie, who until then I had never seen turn away from a dog, gave a shriek and sprang into my arms, nearly toppling me over in the process. The dog was called off but Pixie made me carry her back to the boat.

That night Bobby produced a bottle of wine to have with our dinner and Pixie insisted on her share, after which, feeling sprightly, she wanted another walk. I thought perhaps she now felt brave enough to face the boxer dog. At the far end of the marine a party was in progress on and around a large boat. We had not been invited so I felt it was not very polite to join in. Pixie had no such inhibitions and insisted on gate-crashing. We were made very welcome and had a delicious piece of cake each. Pixie had her photo taken. We had remained on the jetty and not noticed that Daisy the dog was part of the party on board. Daisy now tripped down the jetty to play with Pixie. Pixie took one look at this wee dog, crammed the remains of her cake in her mouth and fled, dragging me behind her. I don't think I have ever moved so fast and swear I flew, my feet barely touching the ground. Why this sudden fear of dogs I could not understand unless it was because neither dog looked like the kind she was used to.

The next day we were all ready to leave by nine. Bobby went to get clearance which they had told him the day before would be given as soon as we were ready to leave with no delay. This time there was just one girl on duty who appeared not to know what to do and said it would be two hours before we could have our clearance. Sure enough, by eleven we had our clearance, said goodbye to all our friends. Bobby started the engine and Chris was standing by to let go our ropes and was just about to do so when Bob-tail came flying along the deck and jumped over to *'Amatunana'* and dived under the upturned dinghy. A shore-based traveller we had made friends with, Annette, was on board, and she and I dragged him out by his hind legs. I pushed him in the basket we had and closed the lid until we were quite clear, we could not have our youngest crew member jumping ship. Slowly we motored out past all the little windsurfers and waving goodbye to Mimi, standing on the end wharf.

We were now on our way to Cyprus.

Along a little grass-grown road,
an old man on a donkey rode.
I stopped and waved my hand at him.
He waved right back and gave a grin

CHAPTER TWENTY-THREE

TOMBS AND MOSAICS

With only very light winds that left us becalmed a number of times, it took us four days to get to Limassol. However, on the third afternoon when we were wondering if the wind ever blew in that part of the world, it returned with such force that we had a struggle getting the genoa down.

The second night out Bobby sighted whales on his morning watch and leader of them was white. "Some people have all the luck," I said, wishing it had been me that had seen them. "It did not bring me much luck, look what Pixie has done," he mumbled. She had got his much-mended pipe, which he had painstakingly fibreglassed together in Tel Aviv, and had broken it in half yet again. We had another little problem that night when the stove refused to light. Bobby did not feel up to tackling whatever was wrong with the burner so we ate the vegetables I had prepared raw, which probably was better for us and Pixie who, seeing we were also doing without cooked food, ate hers without any fuss.

The Israeli patrol boats were the only shipping I had to contend with on my midnight to four watches. The first night, one was heading in the opposite direction, as it came near we eyed each other through the binoculars and waved. They then circled us and having concluded we looked harmless went back the way they had come.

The following night I was almost run down by what I presume was another patrol boat. It was three in the morning and I was wide awake and alert. Our kerosene lamp had run out of kerosene but as there were no ships around I felt it did not matter. Should any ship turn up I expected to see their lights and I was armed with a flashlight that worked to warn them. Suddenly I heard the loud noise of an engine. Standing up I took a good look all round with the binoculars but could still see nothing. I even looked in the sky wondering if it could be a plane I was hearing. There was no moon but the sky was full of stars so it was not really pitch dark. Try as I might there was nothing I could see. I gave up and had just sat down and thought for good measure I would wave my light about when we were floodlit in a blue light. Now I could make out a huge dark shape passing by within touching distance. That really shook me! Not a word was said, the spotlight was shut off and I could just make out the outline of the ship as it went around to our stern and then vanished from sight, not a light showing.

We had originally been heading for Paphos but when the wind finally came back with such force on our last day we changed our minds and made for Limassol, feeling it would be more sheltered. It was on the whole an uneventful trip and we only lost one cockpit cushion and a towel overboard, which was not too bad considering our usual losses.

We literally flew into Limassol. '*Natica*' was anchored there which cheered us up at the prospect of seeing John again. John was ashore but had seen us coming in and had rowed out to us as we came to anchor. He had apparently had an enjoyable trip with his three girls, who all turned out to be willing sailors but now they were gone and he was happy to see us. John was a little lonely on his own and was waiting for his mother to fly out from New Zealand and join him for a holiday.

The water was beautiful, clean and clear. We could see right to the bottom with its long wavy grass-like weed with fish swimming in and out. Pixie enjoyed watching the traffic on the road and made contented noises. Bob-tail did not bother to go on deck at first and when he did he seemed surprised. Perhaps he expected to have returned to Tel Aviv and was disappointed he could not jump on any other boat and see what was cooking. John joined us for dinner that night and we had a very pleasant evening chatting about past sailings and friends.

A couple of days later I found myself bowling along at a terrific speed in a service taxi to Paphos. Part of me wanted to shut my eyes tight while hanging on for dear life. On the other hand I wanted to see the countryside which was interesting, looking as if God had taken a lump of dry clay and tossed it down so it broke into smaller lumps.

After a visit to the post office to collect mail I did a little exploring after spotting some ancient monuments on a lower level to the street. Going down the crumbling relics I found seven domed affairs were in a small area, but the door was locked and there was no one around. I contented myself with peeping in through the window and some other odd intentional holes in the smaller of the domes. The inside was nicely whitewashed and had items on display so took it to be a museum. It was a peaceful place and I sat under a pomegranate tree which had fruit bursting open invitingly. I ate one and took another for Pixie. I next found a donkey path that led towards the sea. Taking this path I thought I might see where we would have anchored had we come to Paphos. I soon found out I was on the wrong track for that as I found myself on the other side of the lighthouse. It had been a nice walk even though a bit hot, and I was able to add some wild figs to my collection of things to take back for Pixie. I passed the odd house now and then, but did not really expect my track to lead anywhere so I was somewhat taken aback when I came to a barrier where I was asked if I wanted a ticket. "For what?" I asked. The other side of the barrier looked no different from where I had come. "This is the Tombs of the Kings," Demetros the ticket man told me. "Oh!" I said lamely. I had never heard of them and could see nothing the other side that resembled a tomb or anything that was worth buying a ticket for. "You must have walked a long way," said Demetros. It had not seemed very long really but he probably thought I was a little potty to have made the walk for no reason. I told him I had thought I would be able to look over the port.

I was invited into his office to sit and rest and have the use of the bathroom where I could swill my face in water and take a drink. I then sat chatting with Demetros and smoking his cigarettes. Cyprus was the reverse of Egypt, where you were expected to hand out packets of cigarettes to all and sundry. In Cyprus they insisted you smoke theirs. The tombs were closed for lunch and Demetros now suggested I take a look at them but refused my money for a ticket. I learned that they had only recently been discovered and were thought to date back to 200BC. They were more interesting than they had looked from afar, being below ground level and all hewn out of the natural rock. I was able to take several photos and was very glad I had not missed them. Returning to the office there was a cup of coffee waiting for me. Demetros then kindly drove me in his car to the port.

Paphos is a lovely little port and would have been ideal for us had we gone there. There stood the castle and the wall ran out to sea one side to make the bay. Most of the boats were small fishing boats but there were a few foreign yachts. All along the front were open-air cafés to which we could have taken Pixie, and little shops. I found it was only a short walk to the mosaics which I loved and thought well worth a visit. I treated myself to a vegetable salad at one of the cafés on the front. On top of my salad were some very interesting leaves, of what I could not find out. They did not look like edible leaves but felt they could hardly be poisonous and they tasted OK so I ate the lot and then wished I had kept one to try and identify it. It was a jolly ride back to Limassol. I plied the driver and his four female passengers with questions and though their English was limited they did their best to answer, while plying me with cigarettes. I do not like smoking in cars but they insisted. I wondered how non-smokers got on.

An incident took place that afternoon back on board that was a little unpleasant, as everyone so far had been so very friendly. Bobby was ashore and I in the cabin when I heard a lot of noise and looked out in time to see a youth jump off John's boat. I was worried as I knew John was ashore at the time. They then swam over to *'Sandpiper'* with the idea I think of getting aboard. One surfaced under Pixie's platform and got a shock when she flew at him. I shouted at them for good measure but they still hung around pushing at the steering vane and looking to see what they could do at the same time keeping out of Pixie's reach. I went to arm myself with the boat hook to prod them off. However, they swam off fast when John arrived having seen them from the shore on his boat. When Bobby returned we both went over to John's boat to drink some local wine, strong stuff, and then transferred to *'Sandpiper'* for a spaghetti dinner. We sat talking and time flew. It was two in the morning before we broke up. John hardly needed his dinghy as *'Natica'* had swung round and was nosing our stern. Well trained boat it had come to get him.

The following day Bobby enjoyed himself when he found a good ship's chandler who would even accept a personal cheque. He returned loaded with a number of little things we had needed and had been unable to get in Tel Aviv including a new fire extinguisher which I was pleased to see was blue instead of red, as the old one had been. Pixie had done in the old one for good when she bit a hole in it and all the stuff inside came out.

We had wanted to visit some of the Greek islands but the wind was in the wrong direction. A local man said it was unusual for that time of year but thought that now it had come it would probably not change for a month or two. Time was getting short so sadly we felt we could not afford to see any more places and would sail non-stop for Spain. John presented us with a lovely brass methylated spirit container that he had purchased in Egypt and which we could use for our stove. We said goodbye and arranged to all meet again in England where John thought he might go and work for a while and we thought we would visit, taking turns if we still could not bring in Pixie.

At 0030hrs on the Saturday we were off.

First they tried to shoot us,
really rather shocking.
Next day they then repented,
and paid for all our shopping.

CHAPTER TWENTY-FOUR
FRIEND OR FOE?

The sea was dashing up the sink outlet pipe and soaking everything, before finding its way down into the bilge. We had a strong westerly wind and a very heavy swell. True we were free of the dangers of reefs, shipping and the likelihood of being shot at, as in the Red Sea, but our progress was about the same. We were going south but being blown sideways and so unwillingly were heading in the general direction of Tel Aviv.

We had started out with a light breeze and by noon had only logged seventeen miles when we hit the heavy swells. The following day the weather was better, though we were still making very little headway west. By the third day it was calm enough to have a proper strip-down and an all over shampoo on deck but the water was surprisingly cold and in future we would wait until noon for our ablutions. The nights were not as cold as in the Red Sea and the days not so hot. We felt better without these extremes in temperature and would have felt better still if we could make more headway in a westerly direction.

The heavy swell returned on the sixth day and the only thing I saw while on watch that night was an empty oil drum float past. Then at breakfast a fleet of six ships on our starboard side was the event of the day. We were shipping water again. Bobby had an idea and drilled holes in the boards over the bilge by the galley to let the water escape faster, it did not help appreciably. Two days later Bobby had a much better idea. He squeezed himself under our port seats and turned the valve off. Our days of water sloshing up the sink were over. A few hours later we were becalmed and so he had the fun of wiggling back under and turning the valve on so we could use the sink.

We had now done 500 miles but were very far south and were afraid of getting too near Libya, so tacked and started going due north.

A tremendous crash, Pixie shrieked! We dashed on deck fearing we had hit something, only to find Pixie's platform had fallen down because she had undone both holding ropes.

Coming below from my watch one night I was hit by fumes the moment I got my head in the cabin and my eyes were watering. Bobby thought he could detect something but it was not bothering him as it was me. We tracked down the source of the trouble. In Limassol Bobby had managed to get some blue liquid for our wretched loo; for a long time we had to use ordinary disinfectant which did not work at all satisfactory. The blue stuff worked well. Now we found the bottle had fallen over and though the cap was still on as well as it would go, a considerable amount of the liquid had leaked out and all the fumes with it. Why such stuff could not be packed in better containers that were leakproof was a source of amazement to us.

Tap, tap. We looked at each other. My suggestion that we might have a woodpecker on board was, not taken seriously. Bobby discovered a rigging screw holding the chain on the bowsprit had unscrewed itself and jumped ship, leaving the chain loose and banging against the hull. This was fixed with another smaller rigging screw leaving Bobby to lament the loss of his nice stainless steel one.

We now had a very short sea. The jib was taken down and soon after that we found we had gone off course. The rope of the steering vane had broken. That was unexpected but it was fortunate that the thin rope that Bobby had bought, with the idea of cutting it up to tie up the sails, happened to be the correct size for the vane. By the time the vane was rigged anew the wind had left us.

I had the engine going all the time for my early morning watch following the fixing of the vane. It was certainly preferable to trying to keep the boat on course with no wind and had the added advantage that the noise of the engine drowned out any noise I cared to make. I was able to sit there singing and not frighten anyone.

We were heading north away from the coast of Libya which we had not seen and did not wish to. Our supplies were getting low so we planned to put in at Sicily to stock up, giving Malta a wide berth, having heard alarming stories of their paranoid attitude towards animals on boats.

Our twelfth day since leaving Limassol. Pixie was tired that morning having come on deck and shared the last part of my watch with me. We let her stay in the cabin and sleep on the seats. We now had a light wind, a rough sea and heavy swell but had cut the engine off and were going about two knots.

11:30 am: Bobby was on deck and spotted a navy boat, it flew no flag but was heading directly for us. Drawing closer the crew started shouting, the noise of their engine preventing us from hearing what they said. Presuming they wished to know where we were going we yelled "SPAIN." They still kept shouting.

"Quickly, go and get our flag out, they must want to know our nationality," Bobby called. I rummaged in the locker for our red ensign. Bobby took the flag and holding it up, waved it at them. The result was startling to say the least, like a matador flapping his cloak at some poor bull. A sailor on deck handed the big man in white a firearm, and while we stood there hypnotised with amazement he took aim and fired. All I could think of was thank goodness Pixie and Bob-tail were not on deck. Pixie had sat up at this startling turn of events and I quickly attached her lead to her belt and the leg of the table to make sure she did not take part in this one-sided little war. It did not look as if the shot had hit us, either it was a bad shot or they were just trying to frighten us, if the latter they were succeeding.

The big man in white was now waving his arms around and shouting about going into port. What port we did not know, or for that matter what country, as they flew no flag, though we had a good guess. Why they could not have motored up to us to put their questions like the Israeli patrol boats did, was strange. "What course shall I steer?" Bobby bellowed. "120," came back the reply. We obediently pointed our nose in that direction, heading right into the wind so the two forward sails hung limp or flapped in different directions. We were making no headway of course but obeying orders which was being prudent as they had now swivelled the big cannon-like gun on deck, round so that it pointed in our direction. One bang from that and they could hardly fail to miss and blow us all to little bits.

Their boat hung around us until they finally decided we were never going to get any place. We were hailed again, from a safe distance, did they think we could return their fire? They shouted to steer south to Tobruk.

We found Tobruk on the chart. We were not just losing time but had to go south and so losing our hard-gained ground. "Now we will have an even harder time getting west," I moaned. "That is the least of our problems, they probably won't let us go anywhere," Bobby replied.

Very jolly, here we were being captured in the middle of that civilised sea, the Mediterranean, out of sight of land, having come through the Red Sea with not so much as one shot fired at us. I confess I did feel it was all rather exciting, or would have been if we did not have Pixie and Bob-tail with us. If they decided to arrest us for some unknown reason would they allow the pets to share our cell? I was not sure.

It was more comfortable sailing in the direction of Tobruk. We kept Pixie in the cabin and I finished making some bread that I had started before all the excitement, wondering if it would be the last time I would be able to make bread. Not being sure if Libyans allowed washing facilities to their captives, I filled a bowl with fresh water in the cabin and took a luxury wash down, shampooed my hair and changed into clean clothes. This made me feel so good I soon forgot about being under arrest and wondered if we would be able to get some fresh fruit.

As we neared the harbour of Tobruk, our gun-happy escort sped ahead and disappeared. This left us wondering what to do. We could hardly stay and tack about the harbour in case, as we turned, they thought we were making a break for it. We lowered the sails and started the engine.

Three men in a Zodiac dinghy with a Johnson outboard came along. We were pleased to see they were unarmed. After circling around us they led us to tie up alongside in the naval yard. No need to put our fenders out, the whole wall was lined with very good ones, like a padded cell.

By 16:20 we were all tied up waiting for the next move. We had expected to be boarded and searched for whatever it was they thought we had, but now they showed a singular lack of interest in us, apart from the fact we had a guard walking back and forth keeping his eye on us.

Bobby changed from his old salt-impregnated jeans to a clean pair of decent shorts. He had just pulled them on when they came and asked him to go ashore. Sticking his head up he told them he was just getting his papers. In fact he was struggling with the zip on his fly. It refused to close. I now suggested that Libya being a strict Moslem country, they might not care to see him in shorts anyway, and certainly not ones that could not be done up decently. He gave up pulled the old jeans back on and stuck a hat on his head as had not had time to find a comb and comb his hair. The result was far from impressive but a car was waiting and it would have to do.

No one tried to board us or ask me any questions. Bob-tail went on deck and our armed guard saw him and made friendly noises which sent Bob-tail rushing back in the cabin but it showed they had no animosity to animals. I then took Pixie out and put her on her platform. To make sure all was going to be OK I sat with her for a bit. Nobody said a word to us. Guess they were not keen on females.

Trusting to luck that Bobby would be returned to us in due course, I now busied myself getting the mattress, pillows and sheets up on deck to dry and set about preparing dinner.

Bobby returned at 18:30 none the worse for his interrogation. Most of the time he said had been spent answering daft questions. They wanted to know why we were in Libyan waters. Bobby told the truth that he did not know he was in their waters as the land was out of sight. They insisted he was. He asked them how far their waters extended. If they knew the answer to that, they were not letting on. Why, they asked, was he not flying a flag? That was easy. He considered himself in the middle of international waters and pointed out that we had shown our flag after they hailed us and was then fired on. He also mentioned that they themselves flew no flag so he did not know who they were. Why when hailed had we not stopped? How they thought you could just stop with sails up we wondered and, as we were only going at a snail's pace, they could so very easily have come up to us. They also asked why he had made them fire on us? Apparently that too was our fault. As it was clear they had hauled us in for no specific reason, he asked if he was now free to sail tonight. They would not let us sail that night but as we were in a naval area, we must move to a different berth and they would think about letting us leave the following day.

Although he had been driven the short distance from the boat by car with two escorts and the driver, he returned walking with just one very sympathetic man who had good English. This man said he was sorry about it all and that we should never have been made to come in in the first place. So we did have one friend.

We now had to move to the commercial shipping wharf. We had been told just where to go and could see a man on shore beckoning us into a berth between two ships. However, a tug boat came alongside and insisted we go the other way. What to do? We had no way of telling who of the two were the most important and so obey. The man on shore was going frantic and the tug boat moved away so thought we should go as bidden to the berth. We started to head that way but then realised our mistake as one of the ships was just leaving and we were in danger then of being run down. A quick about turn and we just managed to get out of the way in time.

Once the ship had gone we went in nicely to tie alongside. The man who had been waving us in turned out to be customs and was waiting for us with Bobby's sympathetic friend. Still they did not come on board, just asked how many cigarettes we had and what drinks. Permission was given for us to walk Pixie around the dock. As they left another customs man came and he apologetically came on board to have a look at the three half-used bottles of booze we had, telling us we must on no account give any of it away. This we promised not to do and agreed we had better not take a drink ourselves either, in case the drop in the level of the bottle was noticed. If that happened we could be accused of spoiling the morals of someone on shore. We were also told not to take any photos and to make sure, he would take our camera to keep until we left. I handed my camera over and then he and I exchanged cigarettes. I getting the best deal.

We were left with our own personal armed guard. Whether he was protecting us, or the rest of the dock from us, was hard to say. In all the treatment was very good, and less trouble than in some other places, except of course we did not want to be there in the first place. After dinner I took Pixie for a walk and our armed guard dutifully trailed behind, only stopping us once when we must have been heading for a prohibited area.

We had just finished breakfast next morning when two navy commanders stepped aboard, both in beautiful spotless white uniforms. Sadly, Pixie grabbed the leg of the pants on one just before he stepped down in the cabin. Her hands were dirty. His uniform was no longer quite so spotless but nicely decorated with monkey handprints. It was all taken in good part and the two Farags – they both had the same first name, could not have been more friendly. They were apologetic for all the inconvenience we had been put to and said it had all been a mistake and kept asking if there was anything we needed. I told them I would like to go ashore and do some shopping and they left saying they would send a car for me. As they departed the customs man came dashing over. He also was apologising and asking why we had not told him we were special guests of the commanders. He now returned our camera and presented me with a packet of cigarettes. From having been treated with such suspicion the day before we were now VIPs.

Moored next to us was a container ship *'Gisela'* flying the Monrovian flag. She had English officers and Hong Kong Chinese crew. They now paid us a visit with masses of bananas for Pixie, several small bottles of pear juice and a large bottle of syrup.

The big car duly arrived for me but before we could set off the trunk was opened and cartons were unloaded and handed down to us on deck. Two cartons of biscuits, 'Julia Creams', a carton of evaporated milk in small cans, cans of beans, chickpeas and four large cans of olive oil. Olives, gherkins, two huge cans of tuna fish and two very large bags of loose tea. I was wondering not only where we would put it all but if I did need now to go shopping. I had twenty English pounds to do my shopping and wanted to change it but Farag Zaky, one of the commanders who accompanied me in the car, refused to let me change it, saying they were paying for all we needed.

We had a driver but he was a driver by name only as Farag drove. We first stopped at his house so he could change his monkey printed uniform for civilian clothes. None of the buildings on the outside were very impressive and his house was no exception. The cement was of very poor quality, mostly sand, and all buildings had holes and crumbling walls.

I had a list of our needs, mainly I wanted to stock up on fresh fruit and vegetables, so the market was our first stop. Eggs were the first thing and I had my container that held twelve. That was filled but was not considered enough and twenty more were put in a bag. The market was surprisingly filled with lovely fresh produce. I was surprised as the countryside appeared dry and barren and looked incapable of growing anything. Boxes were produced and soon filled with aubergine, garlic, onions, cabbage, carrots, tomato etc. I now knew why we had a driver who did not drive. He was kept busy carrying the filled boxes to the car. Every time I said I wanted something I got several times the amount I had asked for. This was a little worrying as I had no idea what it all cost and at that point was not certain we would not be paying for it in the end. I was sure my £20 would be inadequate to cover it.

I think we had something of all the fruits and vegetables they had in the market. We then started going to all the little shops. Each shop we visited in search of ghee which was all I needed. It must have gone under another name as it was proving difficult to find. We did get a very large can of something which later I discovered was the ghee I was looking for. Meanwhile, we did not disappoint the owners of any of the shops as in each one Farag insisted on buying more things that were a luxury for us. Honey, canned peas, cheese, butter, orange and lemon drinks and even Baygon for cockroaches, poor things. Never had I shopped for so much in one go. Two things remained on my list: tobacco for Bobby, which did not appear to be sold anywhere, and methylated spirits to heat the stove. That was banned being alcohol.

Shopping over I was then taken on a sightseeing tour. There was in fact little to see, the main attraction being the war cemetery, which was very well kept up and contained Christian and Jewish graves with of course Moslem. Also, huge geranium plants. It turned out I could have taken my camera, and wished I had, but as it had been taken from me in the first place I thought they did not allow photos, but of course now I was a VIP and told I could have taken photos. Unlike Egypt no one tried to hold my hand, or touch me in any way, except for my hair. I kept feeling something touch my hair lightly and would turn to see a man trying to stroke it.

We now returned to Farag's house for coffee and also for tobacco for Bobby as Farag had several cans of Erinmore he said he did not want. As the outside was not very imposing I was not prepared for what I saw when we entered. It was staggering. Large rooms and floors covered with beautiful Polish carpets. The furniture was all Italian, dining table and chairs. Modern smoky glass display shelves, and a huge settee. Everything was in perfect order and looked like a showroom. It even had Italian prints on the walls. Farag confirmed he shopped in Italy. The driver, Farag and I now sat in this western living room and were served coffee by his beautiful young wife, she looked very shy and their three little boys peeped round the doorway at us. I was then shown their *Libyan* room. Carpets covered the floor and low cushions round the walls. This room I was told was just for entertaining men. His wife had her own quarters, which I was not invited to see.

Back alongside *'Sandpiper'*, Bobby stared with amazement as box after box was unloaded from the car. He thought I had gone mad to buy so much and wondered how we were going to pay for it all. Laughing I handed him back the £20 note. Bobby had a lot to show me also. The steward of *'Gisela'* had been round again and we had another box on board with butter, sauce and loads of canned beans and also some *Time* magazines. We were certainly not going to starve for the rest of the trip. Later the commander delivered us diesel, kerosene and methylated spirits, plus a large bag of meat. I had declined to go in the meat section of the market saying I did not need meat and did not like to see it. Perhaps he thought it was a certain type I did not want. Bobby made himself a large beef curry and Bob-tail thought it was his birthday with all the meat he had, both raw and cooked.

Our only problem now was where to put all our goodies. Most of our lockers had been empty when we arrived but we had never had so much to put in them before. First, I cleaned out all the lockers and sprayed with Baygon. Hundreds of poor little cockroaches came tumbling out and lay dead on their backs. After they had been buried at sea I set about filling the lockers. Farag Almarian now came over to see if we had everything we needed and seemed disappointed that we could not think of a single thing more we could possibly want.

We were now free to go anytime we wished but thought we would wait until the following day to give me time to get everything put away and do a big wash as we also were given as much water as we wanted and the opportunity was too good to miss.

Both the Farags signed our visitors' book and we really meant it when we said that we hoped they would visit us sometime in England. They handed us a typed weather report – our first and last – it was issued to each ship in port. At the bottom were the names of the ships it was going to, ending with '*Sandpiper*'.

The Libyan flag is just a plain green, quick and easy to make. I made one that night and we ran it up as a gesture of courtesy.

Next morning a man fishing on the dock insisted we accept a fish he had caught. He told us he had many English friends and regretted they had now all left the country. Farag Zaky came to see us to say goodbye. It was Friday, the day of rest, the port was very quiet that morning. Just after eleven we let go the ropes and moved off with the engine. The dock now was completely deserted but I waved to the land which we had not wanted to go to and yet had received so much kindness from.

The stores on board, we thought would last,
to Spain without a doubt.
But Pixie got the kerosene,
then tipped half of it out.

CHAPTER TWENTY-FIVE

MEDITERRANEAN BLUES

It was nice to have full food lockers and we set out confident that we would be able to head straight for Spain. There was no let-up in the weather which remained typically Mediterranean, never letting us head the way we wished. First we went north east just to get away from the coast. By noon the second day our position was only a little north west of where we had been the day before, when we went into Tobruk. Huge sea kept hitting us and breaking right over the cabin top. We had a swell nearly all the time and the only consistent thing about the wind was that it was never in the direction we wished it. When the wind got tired of battering us about, it left us alone completely to bob around becalmed or to start the engine.

On the fourth day out, the pipe on our cooker broke again and we had kerosene all over the place. We had been nicely off for kerosene after getting a full container at Tobruk but on the second day out Pixie unscrewed the top of the container and spilt half of it down the cockpit. Until the pipe could be fixed, we would have to use our spare stove which, being a wick kind, burned a lot of fuel. To save time

Bobby fixed the stove by using plastic tube instead of copper pipe. A neat idea, except as soon as we lit the burner our plastic pipe melted away and we were back were we started.

It was the vane that gave us trouble the next day. The rope we had fixed about a week before was cut almost through. We thought the rope must have chafed on the plastic tube it went through, but on examining the tube found that was also cut. How, we never discovered.

The sixth day was nice and sunny so I pegged a blanket out to air along with Bobby's swim trunks, that was the last we ever saw of them. Our remaining cockpit cushion also came to grief that day when Pixie ripped off the cover, opened the undercover and had fun chewing at the bits of foam inside and tossing them in the sea. These small inconveniences were compensated for when later in the day we were fairly galloping along for a change in the right direction, just north of west. With a strong wind we wondered if we should take in the jib but could not bear to do so, as we were doing so nicely. Every now and then we would hit a really heavy sea and one cracked the glass in the porthole above the sink. It was only cracked and let in no water, but it was a bit worrying as on that tack it was under water, and if it went completely we would be more than a little wet. By noon that day we found ourselves at long last off the chart we had been on ever since Port Said. The new chart was a small photostat copy. The change in the chart coincided with the change in the weather, we kept our fingers crossed and hoped the good weather would continue.

The next morning I woke for my watch at eight to find Bobby had dozed off and Pixie was very busy raiding the tool box. We were now setting a bit more to the north, still with a strong wind and heavy swell so it was not possible to have Pixie on deck. We lowered the jib, finding it did not slow us and that made it possible for Pixie to have a turn on deck.

Until then I had not had to make bread as we had been given a lot in Tobruk. A lot of bread still remained but was very mouldy. We cut it up, toasting all the good parts. In preparation of making our own bread again I looked at the flour. It all had to be shifted, having hatched a good supply of worms.

Taking the log at noon we saw we had come 79 miles in the last twenty-four hours, the best day's run since Cyprus. It was not to last, the wind dropped considerably later in the day, the swell also went down. One compensation for the lost wind was that we could sit reasonably at the table to enjoy our dinner. It was a good time to open a bottle of wine to have with it. Pixie was very insistent on having her share. Being smaller than us we gave her a smaller glass but she swigged it back fast and then demanded we give her some of ours. We both complied with her wishes, several times, so in the end she got more than we did. At eight twenty we sighted a ship. The first we had seen since leaving Tobruk.

Strangely, the nearer we got to the UK the harder it was to get the BBC on our transistor radio. We gave up listening, the reception being so poor and we could not even get a time signal.

For most of our trip I would take the midnight to four watch, Bobby finding he could sleep better during those hours. I, on the other hand, except in bad weather, enjoyed the nights alone under the stars. On the night of the 28th July I lay down at eight to get my four hours sleep but found I was still wide awake at ten, so got up. As Bobby then felt tired we changed our watches so I took mine to end at two in the morning. It was a nice night and not so cold. As I stepped on deck a very pretty sight greeted me. A falling star, unlike any I had seen before, it appeared to be slightly green with a splash of red. I wondered if it was a star or a rocket and stared in the same direction with the binoculars for about an hour but no sign of anything and no more falling stars.

The following night I took my watch as usual at midnight. Half an hour later a strange thing happened. I could see the lights of two ships, one on our port side the other to starboard. Both were quite a distance and I watched them for some time. While looking at the one to starboard, which was going in the same direction as we were, I saw a very bright red light, some distance from the ship but much higher. I could not think where it had come from. With the binoculars it looked like two red lights close to each other but nothing else, and they were flashing. As it had appeared so suddenly and moved fast I turned our lights on and continued to watch it. I saw now that it seemed near enough to the ship to be a tow, a moment later realised it could not be when it caught up with the ship and passed it, now being ahead. That is how it looked but rather think it must have been much nearer to us than to the ship as the light was so bright. It then went back the way it had come and around to our stern so fast I wondered if it could be a low-flying plane. That did not seem likely as my hearing is good and I heard no engine. Just as suddenly as it had appeared the light vanished, I had not taken my eyes off it. I turned our light off so I could see better but no sign of it or anything, it never reappeared. When Bobby relieved me I told him of these strange goings on. He thought the light may have been a helicopter. If he was correct how come I heard nothing? It made we wonder though, just what had been going on. From its movements it could have been searching for something. I wondered again if my falling star from the night before was perhaps not a star but a distress flare. I just hope it had not been anyone in need of help, or if so that they had been found.

During a calm Bobby worked on the cooker and put in new copper pipes and got both burners working. It was a two-burner stove and it was very rare that I ever had both burners working at the same time. It was luxury to have two pots bubbling away together.

For my part the most unpleasant experience I had was when an aircraft carrier passed us one day. I hated the thing with its endless planes that kept taking off and landing and the noise as they went over us was enough to drive you crazy, or me at any rate. Bobby considered them interesting to watch, saying not many people get the opportunity. All I could say was lucky them, I would prefer to be shot at.

We were now getting very little wind and were often becalmed. I spent hours trailing washing in the sea and washing it in sea water and egg shampoo, the detergent having run out. I then shampooed Pixie and myself from head to toe. We kept nice and clean if a bit salty.

The nights were getting colder and very damp. During the night the sails would drip moisture so that by the end of my watch my hair would be as wet as if it had been raining.

Our position was always more disappointing after being becalmed as there was a strong easterly current that pushed us back. We were now into August and beginning to despair of ever getting to Spain that summer. There was little excitement to keep Pixie happy and she kept inventing her own forms of entertainment. One night I heard her banging around while Bobby was on watch. I investigated and found she had lifted up the small floorboard at the bottom of the steps and dropped it in the bilge below. Had I not noticed, Bobby would have stepped down and gone the same way as the board. As it was it took Bobby ages to retrieve it and he made Pixie feel decidedly unpopular.

Sixteen day since leaving Tobruk and the sun came out, I could smell the land. Bob-tail could too, he was up on deck lifting his head and sniffing. Later with the binoculars I could make out hills and mountains to starboard: Sicily. We had been using the engine for twenty-four hours so shut it off to give it a rest, thinking we had a little breeze. It was quite hopeless, we were again being pushed back by the current so gave up and restarted the engine to make our way along the south coast of Sicily. My night watch started with a little breeze and I had the genoa up but the wind kept dying completely, just coming back now and then to taunt me, in little gusts. The genoa was more of a hindrance than a help and kept blowing on the spreaders where I feared it would tear the sail. Feeling I would be better off without it, I went to take it down. The moment I left the wheel we went off course, I started to lower the sail but it was hard on the spreader so called Bobby to help. Half-asleep he came up and, not realising why, I said, "Wait until I change course and blow the sail free." He hauled it down. As expected it got ripped after all and there was another sewing job for him.

The day continued with little or no wind. Our log turned slowly. Twice it stopped, though we were moving. Once it had tar paper stuck on it and the next time a plastic bag. Bobby's reading glasses disappeared and we figured Pixie must have stolen them and dumped them overboard. We were now having to use the engine far more than we had expected which meant we would have to put in to Sardinia for more fuel or we might end up drifting around in dead calms for ever.

Wind returned on the 22nd day and we now had a storm. Bobby got the genoa down and tried to get it in its bag but the wind took charge and blew it back out. He got soaking wet for nothing as in the end he just lashed it to the rail and reefed the main. It was times like that we wished we had more than one safety harness between us so I could have helped. Without one we feared I would have been blown overboard, had I tried to join Bobby on the foredeck.

The storm continued into the next day and ripped a batten out of the mainsail. The seams looked as if they were going on the staysail too. By 0800hrs the wind was not so had but we still had a heavy swell. Sardinia was just showing in the distance. Gale force winds returned, we were getting frustrated. Bobby had long ago run out of tobacco and started tarring up my cigarettes for his pipe. Now the cigarettes had all gone.

That afternoon the wind suddenly turned itself off and we started the engine. This for some reason took some doing and when we finally did succeed to start it the wind came back. As it was Sunday the following day we thought we would anchor in Pula Bay for the night and go into Cagliari the following morning. By midnight we were still a long way from where we wanted to anchor and found we had lost the log rotator, our second and last one. Our last reading on the log had been 1940 miles since Cyprus.

Twenty-four days since leaving Tobruk. In the early hours of the morning, we anchored in Pula Bay. Tired and cold but thankful to be able to stop, I made hot cocoa for the three of us and milk for Bob-tail. We then all fell exhausted into the bunk.

Next morning we could see where we were. A delightful little bay. Two small islands with old towers on and what looked like a holiday village. Houses all white or cream with windows, doors etc. that were arched or half-moon shaped: very attractive. The soil was rather barren with a backdrop of more craggy mountains. After breakfast Bobby got busy sewing the sails while I investigated wet lockers and got things out to dry. We had several small sail and motor boats come out to look at Pixie and she enjoyed showing off. Nice as our bay was, we felt it would offer little protection if it blew hard and so that afternoon we got the anchor up. Just a gentle breeze that made for very pleasant sailing. We passed an oil refinery which was not very attractive and before dark we anchored in the Bay of Cagliari. Here we could look ahead to green trees and a stretch of yellow, probably something growing rather than sand we thought. The other side was ugly oil refineries and chimneys. The town looked large with a mass of buildings. We planned to go into the harbour early, the engine had other ideas and refused to start. Bobby gave it some oil but it was not getting to the engine and he felt that the filters were blocked. We had spare new filters but the old ones had been put on so tightly in Sri Lanka he was unable to move them. We managed to get the anchor up without the engine but there was no wind to move us for hours. A slight breeze finally favoured us and we hoisted the genoa and sailed into the harbour to anchor. We were the only boat at anchor. Others all appeared to be Italian or French and were tied to the pontoons. It was either a club or marina, we were not sure which.

The place was large and we had passed several big ships coming in but no work was going on and the whole place had the air of a ghost town about it. Bobby blew up the dinghy and rowed ashore to see where we could go and if he could find a mechanic to look at our engine or at least get the filter off.

Bobby returned to say he had found only one person who had a little English but had been able to make it clear that anyone could tie up where they wished. We wanted to go alongside and tie up but felt it was going to be difficult getting in with no engine, even if we could get the anchor up again. We experimented with the engine and found it would work if I played nurse and stood feeding it drops of oil every minute. By this means we managed to motor into a space and with a bit of help from others, tied up. People having kindly helped us tie up were now trying to tell us something which we gathered was that that particular space belonged to another boat who would be returning the next day. We thought we would cross that bridge when we came to it. More cheering news, the banks were closed so we could not change money. When we asked about a mechanic a man shrugged his shoulders and said "August," by which we took to mean that mechanics did not exist in that month.

Bobby went ashore while I washed the salt off all our things. Surprisingly he returned with another man who could even talk understandable English and better still was a mechanic! He had brought along a special little chain thing to remove the filter and had it off in a minute. When the new filter was attached the engine worked. He was a charming man and said it was true that all mechanics had left town, this week in particular was a holiday, but he was working on a contract and so had stayed in town. He gave Bobby the chain thing he had used to remove the filter and refused to take any payment for it, or his time. He could not, he said, charge for working on a holiday week.

Before finding this kind man Bobby had changed some money at the hotel but had been unable to buy anything as all shops were shut tight. We had picked the worst week in the whole year to arrive. Our kind mechanic now took Bobby off to show him where a few places would be open. Bobby returned smiling with four bulging bags. Things were expensive but one shop was open and had a good assortment of fresh food plus cigarettes, tobacco and a new pipe. He displayed all the goods for Pixie and I to admire except the pipe which he intended, when not in use, to keep hidden from Pixie.

We had a nice meal that night without cooking, feeling the need for fresh raw food. Pixie delighted in the lettuce the most, rather than the cucumber which she usually went for. Perhaps I should have peeled it as it was not the kind we were used to and the skin was a bit bitter.

To round off the evening we had a bit of excitement. We heard shouting and saw a light flashing so went out to see what was going on. A very angry Italian was shouting his head off and was very drunk. We understood that he did not like us being there, or the French boats, and wanted us to all get out. Bobby shrugged his shoulders, smiled nicely, and said he did not understand, whereupon the drunk gave up on him and went to start on the French boats where they spoke Italian. We watched as they all marched off to a shed still shouting. Later one of the crew of the French boats, who could speak English, came over to explain to Bobby that the drunk was in fact the security guard. He was well known for his drunken outbursts and was called Buffalo Bill as he carried a gun which apparently he quite often fired when drunk. All was well now, we were told, as they had told him they were going to write to the authorities and the newspapers saying what a bad reception he gave foreign boats. That shut Buffalo Bill up and we were now safe, at least until the morrow.

To make sure we got all our water on board before we were made to move we started filling our tank, finishing at midnight. Next morning as no one told us to move we stayed put and Bobby took another walk ashore. It was amazing that we had run out of things since Libya considering all we had been given. We certainly would not have starved as we had masses of canned goods but had run out of all fresh things. We would have been in a very bad state had we not stopped in Libya. Perhaps there is a reason for everything. We now felt very grateful to the gunboat that had forced us in, resulting in all the provisions we had so kindly been given.

The most important requirements now were diesel and kerosene, neither of which we could locate. The other boats told us both were not easy to locate at the best of times but diesel, when it could be had, was sold at the gas stations. Bobby managed to get two jerry cans of diesel. The problem was carrying them back. He had to keep setting them down. Cars past but no one offered him a lift. I went for a walk taking the small kerosene container with me in case I could find some as we now had very little left. The first shop I asked sent me back the way I had come to a gas station but they had none. Next stop a man took me around in his car to three more gas stations but no one knew where to get it. I thanked my lift and continued my walk. I found fascinating places with small narrow streets I would have liked to photo, but film for my camera had run out. I was not able to find kerosene nor yeast, which I also needed, but did find a much-needed bucket as the one we had got in Cyprus had gone the way of the rest, overboard. I also picked up a small paintbrush and some cat food so felt my walk was justified, and picked some wild flowers in a vacant plot which sadly all drooped before I returned. Even they did not go to waste. Bob-tail started eating them as soon as I put them down.

The next day we planned to leave in the afternoon. Bobby wanted to go on one more hunt for kerosene. While he was gone a South African boat came in: a middle-aged man with two young lads and a girl. I told them what I knew about the place and that little remained open owing to the holiday and how we could not get kerosene. Amazing! They had kerosene having recently changed their kerosene stove for a gas one. They wanted gas. While we were unable to help them to get gas they kindly said they would give us kerosene if Bobby could not get any.

Bobby could not find any kerosene that he had walked for miles in search of, even to the top of a hill. That day was Wednesday the 15th August and the most important day of the whole holiday. When he did find one tiny place open he used up all his money buying all they had: a few cigarettes, tobacco and toothpaste.

We left that afternoon with our kerosene container half full. Regardless of the fact we now had no money to pay for it the South African boat had given us their kerosene, for which we were most grateful.

Oh Doctor, Doctor, do come quick,
There's a fish hook in my monkey's lip.

CHAPTER TWENTY-SIX
ALICANTE ANTICS

Leaving Cagliari that afternoon with a fresh breeze we were moving fast. It looked as if the wind would get stronger so we bagged the genoa. A few hours later we had to get it out again as the wind had dropped considerably and by eight that evening we were becalmed and had to use the engine. Three hours later with still no wind and finding ourselves back in Pula Bay, we dropped anchor in the same place we had been the previous Sunday.

It was just after five the next morning when we woke, there was still a heavy swell but a nice breeze. Getting the anchor up was not easy, even with the use of the engine. We had the big Danforth down and when we finally hauled it aboard, found the shaft was bent and it would have to be straightened before we could use it again. We were rough on anchors, having by that time lost three and bent two since leaving Singapore.

While getting the anchor up we had left Pixie and Bob-tail cuddled together asleep. I checked them once, shining the flashlight down on the bunk from the deck, just in time to see Pixie had got the small plastic folder with the health certificates in. When I went down to take them from her she was lying as before with the stolen certificates under her body. I pulled them from under her while she pretended to still be asleep.

We missed not having the log but appeared to be doing reasonably well until the afternoon, when we were becalmed for an hour, after which the wind freshened and we had a howling gale which stayed with us all night and the following day, getting worse with seas over the cabin top. We had left the jib lashed on deck and could see strips of it had torn and were flying in the wind. There was little we could do about it until the second day when Bobby got on deck wearing his safety harness, handicapped by the fact he had strained his arm and cut his hand when getting the anchor up in Pula Bay. The wind dropped during the night and disappeared completely by daylight, leaving us with just a very heavy swell. Pixie and Bob-tail were able to go on deck again. Bobby put his wet sweater out to dry and that was the last we saw of that. By noon gale force winds were back and we reefed the main again. The wind kept changing directions and the sun disappeared. "Looks more like England in December," commented Bobby.

Next we had rain, real rain, but not for long and it all went to waste, being impossible to catch any in such a heavy swell. Two hours later the wind left us. That night being becalmed we started the engine, it was hard to start and we were less than happy when our one and only flashlight fell down into the bilge.

At midnight we had light intermittent winds, not enough for the vane so I steered for one-and-a-half hours after which a rain squall blew up. Now the wind blew with such force I could hardly hold the wheel and had to call for Bobby to come and help. He quickly got the mainsail down and just then the rain teemed down. Earlier in the trip we had wanted rain, now we could have done very well without it. It was not the tropical rain we were used to but freezing cold stuff like ice. We both got soaked in the half hour it took to get on course and set the vane.

I then noticed our one remaining jerry can that had been on deck was no longer to be seen. Bobby remembered he had anchored his sweater down with it, both must have blown away. I did not know which I felt worse about, polluting the sea with our belongings or the loss of them. I finished my watch, mainly staying below, just checking our position now and then. We only had the staysail up but daylight showed us that it had ripped. Becalmed next day, Bobby sat sawing the sail, he had time, there was very little wind for two days.

The unpredictable weather was even getting on Pixie's nerves. One morning she was sitting next to me on the seats, half asleep. Bobby came out of the head. She looked up at him as if she had never seen him in her life before and screamed, then bit me on the leg. She did not bite too hard and I had jeans on but it was a bit of a shock. After nipping me she cuddled up, groomed my hair and was as sweet as ever.

The engine was giving us trouble again. It started leaking oil and then the pressure was almost zero so we had to turn it off. Bobby could not see what was wrong, we sat becalmed and just drifted. I put some dahl on to cook and in minutes smelt burning. My pot had yet another hole in it. Bobby had repaired it so many times there was little of the original pot left. I just managed to finish the cooking that night before the kerosene in the tank came to an end. Had the kind South Africans not given us kerosene, that would have been the last cooked meal of the trip.

Bob-tail now had black, instead of white feet, having investigated the oil leak in the engine. I washed them but they remained black so sprinkled Pixie's baby powder on them. We now had little white paw marks on everything but they were easier to clean off than the black ones had been. The days passed, we sailed when we had wind and drifted when becalmed. One day we had just enough wind to keep the sails full but the current was in the opposite direction so we stayed completely stationary. The world had gone deadly silent, not a movement from the sails, not a ripple in the water. An odd sensation.

We now discussed where in Spain we should head for providing we got the wind to allow us to head for anywhere. As the engine was out of action we thought Alicante would, being a large port, be the best place to go first. Here we would be more likely to find someone to come and fix it. Eleven days out of Sardinia we were only twenty miles off Alicante. Bobby started attacking the engine again and put more oil in. Surprisingly, the engine started and we only got a little oil flying off the fly wheel. We would not chance running it but felt we might be able to use it if needed, to get into Alicante.

The coast was now in full view. The town looked huge with lots of multi-story buildings. We asked some passing fishermen where the port was located. Just our luck it was, they said, the other side of the bay so we would have no chance of getting in that night.

Bang! Bang! Bang! I rushed on deck to see who was shooting at us. A shower of coloured fireworks lit the sky.

We were only five miles from the land next morning but no wind. As the sun came up the light ashore went out and the land was no longer visible through the haze. A slight breeze touched us and we tried to tack, she would not come round. We started the engine just to help us turn. More oil came out and later Bob-tail appeared with not only his feet black but his tummy too. After cleaning him up nicely with baby oil and powder, I shampooed Pixie and myself from head to toe and cleaned up generally, expecting we should soon arrive. We could now see a breakwater but it all looked wrong and we wondered if the fishermen had understood and directed us correctly. By the afternoon there were a lot of boats about but none came within hailing distance until a speedboat came up having seen Pixie. Bobby asked in his best Spanish where the port was. They did not understand and motored round us and then asked in English if we wanted the harbour. Horrors, it turned out we were not even in the correct bay and had to go round the point into the next bay for Alicante.

Bobby was kicking himself for mistaking the bays but the bay we had been in looked to have such a large town we took it for granted it was Alicante, and for once never took a sight to make sure. It was a long day with very little wind. A couple of times we used the engine but it was not keen to help and after a bit would stop of its own accord. We rounded the point after dark, then it was clear this was the place we were looking for. Alicante was decked out in lights with a castle on a hill that was floodlit. It looked beautiful, far nicer than the other bay, and we felt we were being welcomed in as more fireworks were set off. We anchored the other side of the breakwater so we could go in in daylight.

We had strong winds next day which made it quite impossible to get the anchor up without the help of the engine. We talked to the engine nicely and were rewarded when it roared to life. The anchor came up. We thought it best to keep the engine running and the staysail up, with our fingers crossed we entered the harbour. It was chock-a-block with boats all moored Mediterranean fashion, stern to wall, we were almost to the end before we found a space. It was going to be a tight squeeze so we put Pixie in the cabin and pulled her platform up. It took a lot of manoeuvring to get alongside a big tripper boat. We prayed the engine would keep going. It did its part but we still made rather a hash of getting in. We did not like the idea of mooring stern to the wall where all the people passing by would be able to look down into the cabin. We also wanted to keep Pixie farther away from the people on shore. We now nosed into this small space. Already we had an audience, leaning over the wall rails watching every move but offering no help with the ropes. We breathed a sigh of relief when we were finally nicely tied up having managed to avoid hitting anyone or anything. A few boats down we had seen *'Sunshine'*, the California boat that was in Galle the same time as ourselves. We had not expected, after leaving Cyprus, to meet up again with anyone we knew.

As it happened *'Sunshine'* was locked up, the owners having left her there and flown back to California.

We had been handed immigration forms to fill in while we were still dashing around like monkeys, tying up. Pixie in the cabin was just as busy. I made a quick dash down to see what she was getting up to. She was sitting on the table with a very large bottle of Crème de Menthe. She had unscrewed the top and was sitting there drinking from the bottle, which had been about half full. As it was a large and heavy bottle she used one foot to help her tilt it back. I grabbed it off her gave her a spanking and shouted at her. Normally she would then have whimpered and clung on to me to say sorry. She must have taken more than a sip and now she just sat, quite unconcerned that she had been caught out, and acted as if she could neither see, hear nor feel me. The moment I turned to go back on deck she was already looking around to see what next she could get into.

Meanwhile, the man on the tripper boat, who had just hung over the side and watched our antics in getting in without offering any help, now spoke. We felt we understood what he was saying but did not wish to believe it. We could not stay there he said but it seemed a bit late in the day to tell us after we finally got tied up. So we decided it was us who could not understand. An Englishman now came along and confirmed that we would have to move and that there was now a space farther down we could have.

Our engine had behaved so nicely coming in, we hated to have to put it to the test again. We had dropped a small stern anchor which now had to be pulled up. Bobby now had the job of both steering and pulling the anchor up while I rushed around madly with the boat hook pushing us off the tripper boat and the little boats the other side of us. We were going from side to side for ages as if our whole aim in life was to plough into another boat. I could not think why Bobby was taking so long to pull up the little anchor. We pulled out from between the boats but were still trying, it appeared, to bang into the others. Never had I been kept so busy with the boat hook. Our wide-eyed audience on shore hung over the rails and enjoyed every minute of it. If I had not been so busy I would have hung a hat on the end of the boat hook and passed it round. Bobby, now purple in the face, had finally managed to get our little anchor up along with a very much larger one belonging to the tripper boat. The captain of the tripper boat was watching with interest. Bobby sorted the anchors out and tossed the big one back. This galvanized the captain into action. He was shouting we had not put it back down just where he wanted it, as if we were not busy enough trying to get out without damage.

The berth we now went to was very narrow, our chances of getting in nicely looked slim. I took a quick peep down below. Pixie had a book but had chewed a bit off the echo sounder, perhaps trying to make it work, knowing we usually put it on to go into a place. She was then getting into the locker after the booze again.

Although it was a much tighter squeeze to get in our second berth we made it nicely and tied up without mishap to the disappointment of our audience.

We were now so close to a very large wooden Danish fishing boat that we had no room to put down Pixie's platform. We could just chain her to the rails but then she would be able to get on the next boat. For the time being we left her in the cabin and warmed up our cold porridge which I had started to cook hours before.

We were feeling now that we rather hated the place and wanted to get our engine fixed and get away as soon as possible. While Bobby went off to find a mechanic I kept Pixie in the cabin chained to the table. It was a noisy place but she found it interesting and stood on the table looking out of the window. Two hours later Bobby returned having been unable to find a mechanic and all the banks were closed.

A little later Pixie was getting restless so I examined the next boat which was laid up with nobody on board. There seemed nothing she could get or destroy so I put her out, chained to our cockpit rails. She had been out about five minutes by which time she had got a laughing crowd watching her and had stolen two clothes pins that were on the next boat. *Never mind*, I thought, *that is all she can get and we can easily replace them*. I then noticed she was pulling at her lip. I thought nothing of it at the time until I noticed she had a thin nylon line with wee balls on, something presumably to do with fishing. I went to get the line etc. back, gathering it up I found it ended in a small hook which was firmly attached to Pixie's bottom lip. After cutting the line I brought her back in the cabin to try and remove the hook. She will always allow us to doctor her if she is hurt in some way so I did not expect trouble. Perhaps the hook did not hurt her, for as soon as I tried to remove it she pushed me away and hid her head in the cushions as if I was trying to steal the hook. I sat with her wondering what in the world I was going to do now. I was called on deck to fill in some more forms. I was gone some time and expected to return and find Pixie had got up to some more of her tricks. Instead I saw she was now trying to pull the barb out herself.

When Bobby returned, again empty-handed, we thought that together we might be able to remove the hook. "All we need to do," Bobby said, "is to push the hook right through her lip and cut the barb off the end."

I was so pleased Bobby was so practical and knew what to do. There was a simple remedy after all. I watched as Bobby threw himself into the role of doctor. Covering the table with a dish cloth, he set his pliers and wire cutters out as if they were surgical instruments. With Pixie wrapped tightly in a towel, I hung on to her while Bobby tried to push the hook through her lip. Poor Pixie, I gripped her wrists but she pushed her feet against the table and screamed. It was all for nothing, her lip was too thick and Bobby could not budge the hook either way. The only thing to do was to call a doctor. Again Bobby went ashore, this time in search of a doctor. He found several doctors' offices but no doctor, only watchmen. Apparently people don't get sick in the afternoon and we would have to wait until the morning. He did, however, manage to change some money and get a nice selection of fruit and vegetables. Pixie perked up at the sight of the fresh food. She had become tired and listless and had continued pulling at the hook and now a blood blister had formed.

Next morning Bobby thought he would go to the British Consulate to ask where he could find an English-speaking doctor. About noon he came dashing back. He had found the British Consulate but it was closed for the day. He then investigated the doctors. One sent him to a large hospital, there a man at the desk had said to bring Pixie in at around one that afternoon. Pixie had a good wash, we put a roll of loo paper and a towel in a bag and set off.

We had never walked Pixie in a big city before but she walked nicely eager to see the sights, not a bit embarrassed by the fact she was wearing a hook in her lip. I carried her across a busy road and she preferred that as it gave her a better view. She was far too heavy for me to continue to carry her so I handed her over to Bobby. We duly arrived at the children's casualty hospital. The same man Bobby had talked to was there, he seemed nice but turned out to be species prejudiced when he saw Pixie was far too beautiful and hairy to be a human. He said the hospital was only for people and wrote out the address of a vet on a bit of paper.

We were not very keen on taking her to a vet, thinking it unlikely they would have the tools for the job. A fish hook in the lip of an animal was hardly, so we thought, a common occurrence. Also, the vet was the other side of town.

Pixie was enjoying her day out. We now took a taxi and she sat nicely on my lap with her arms round my neck. We were lucky the vet and his surgery was an excellent one, large and well-equipped and one of the doctors spoke English. Asking the taxi to wait we joined a lot of dogs in the waiting room. Pixie was still on her best behaviour and sat on my lap and let a few people stroke her.

Our turn came and the first thing was an injection to put her to sleep. The moment she saw the syringe she knew what was coming and screamed. As she is heavy and I am inclined to faint if someone else is getting an injection I sat on the floor holding her. The vet administered the shot but as he withdrew the needle Pixie grabbed the syringe out of his hand, and pushed it at Bobby as much to say 'Look what he stuck into me, jab him back'.

I sat rocking her, her head nodded, she started talking and then dropped off into a deep sleep. She was then laid out on the table with Bobby holding her hands. On a television screen we could see an X-ray of her lip, this showed just how the hook and gone in. The hook was soon extracted in three parts and her lip painted with some red stuff. We asked the vet to give her a good checking over. She had developed a pot tummy and we were not sure it was natural, and that it might be full of foam rubber she was always chewing out of the cushions. Happily the vet announced it was all quite normal with no odd things in it but gave her another injection for eczema as she had a little bald patch on her back. A long time after we realised this was due to the rubbing that area of her back got when she went under the lower safety wire on her platform. We had 1500 pesetas and had not yet paid the taxi. The vet bill came to just over that amount but they made no fuss and accepted what we had. We returned in the taxi with Pixie still fast asleep. The taxi driver did not mind being paid in sterling.

We laid Pixie on the seats. After an hour she woke and took a banana and started eating but her head nodded and she fell asleep before she had finished. This happened several times. I soon found out she was quite normal again, if a bit sleepy, when I went on deck just to get some towels in and came back to see her still sleeping but black oil all over the seats. At first I thought Bob-tail had been down to the engine again but it was not just paw marks, but lines of it over floor and table as well. I looked at Pixie's hands, they were covered in black oil. I cleaned her up while she pretended to still be asleep. We had a jar of oil in the cabin that Bobby had taken out of the engine and set aside to see if it had any water in it. Fortunately, Pixie had not overturned it, just stuck her hands in to do a little finger painting with.

Bobby took a three-mile walk to try and find a mechanic without any luck. Returning tired and fed up he then hit his head a resounding crack on the boom. Blood gushed out. I volunteered to go for a doctor. "No, we can't afford it," he said.

Next morning both Bobby and Pixie were back to normal. I spent the morning washing and painting and Bobby went off yet again in search of the Volvo Penta people. He now had the address and knew it was in the next bay, the very bay we had spent two days thinking was Alicante. This time he found them but not before he had been given a big runaround, going to four places in different directions first. The mechanics came on board that afternoon but were unable to remove the flywheel. They left saying they would come again the next day.

We had a pleasant surprise the next day when we saw *'Hawaiki'* arriving. We had last seen John and Norma and their two boys in Tel Aviv. Since then they had been round the Turkish coast which they loved. They had also visited a few Greek islands which we had so wanted to do but they had not liked them, finding them dirty and the people unfriendly. This made us feel better about having missed them.

The immigration men came round yet again with more forms to fill out. They really liked forms. I saw that they were the same as I had filled out before. When I told them they informed me that we had left since then and returned, so must fill them out again. This was news to me. I assured them we had not moved, that it was the Belgium boat next to us that had gone. They believed me but as they had put us down as having gone they now had to say we had returned. It all seemed a little haphazard to me but they were a friendly lot and it kept them happy.

We wondered how long it would be before our engine was fixed. The mechanics had turned up again and got the flywheel off but then needed to lift the engine for which they required a block and tackle and they had forgotten to bring that, so would come the next day.

Bobby left early the next day and took a bus to Denia to collect our mail and get some more money. The mechanic duly arrived with the gear he needed to complete the work on the engine. I had a hard time holding Pixie who did all she could to stop the poor man getting himself and his gear down into the cabin. He rather liked Pixie and kept talking to her but he had a loud voice and it only made her more mad at him. I stayed on deck painting the life rings. Norman, an English lad off a boat farther down, stopped by to chat. He had come through the French canals on his boat '*Windslip*' and wanted to know if we would like to exchange charts. We had intended, if we found we could, to take Pixie into England going through the Strait of Gibraltar, but we were worried as the summer was going fast, and several people had told us about the French canals which sounded nice. I was chatting to Norman when the mechanic called me. I went to find the life ring that I had half painted had blown within reach of Pixie. She had bitten a nice hole in it and ripped a strip of canvas off the same side. A bit annoying as it turned out to be the newer of the two and the side I had just painted Sandpiper on. I took it away and returned to continue my conversation with Norman. I was called again. This time Pixie had managed to just reach around into the cabin and get the foghorn, the canister of which I had painted only the day before. The paint work was still good but she had pulled out the pin, rendering it useless. I told Norman we would continue our chat another day.

The repairs to the engine were completed that day and the mechanic's boss came to inspect it. Unfortunately, he also brought the bill. On learning I could not pay it until Bobby returned with the money, he said he could not leave us with the engine in working order. I could see his point, we might have flown the coup. Sadly, I had to let him remove some vital part again which seemed a shame after all that work.

Bobby returned late that night having spent most of his day waiting for buses and things to open. However, he had his money, which turned out was little more than the bill we now owed the mechanic, never having expected it to cost so much. Best of all he had picked up a big pile of mail. We sat up late that night reading all the news from our friends and relations. Bobby's mother in Liverpool had been burgled and pushed around by thugs. Little Tristan in Lumut had been kidnapped for 36 hours before the ransom was paid and he was released; when he was able to lead the police to where he had been held they caught the kidnappers. Living ashore we thought was now rather dangerous. Letters from my family showed they were expecting us in August. It was now the last day of that month.

We had spent time in most ports writing letters to anyone we could think of concerning quarantine for Pixie and Bob-tail. We still had hope that someone would come up with an idea to let us take them to England and stay with us. I had even asked if we could take a non-paying job in quarantine to be with them. It was highly ridiculous anyway to put them in quarantine for six months and let us roam about, having lived in such close contact with them all this time. Anything they may have caught we would have also. The replies we received were all disappointing. There were still only two quarantine places Pixie could be accepted at and they could not take Bob-tail.

There were plenty of others that had places for cats. We were at a loss to know what to do. I kept wishing we had not been able to buy the Mill House and promised to return to England and be near my parents. Neither of us fancied settling down, especially in England, but we had promised and now got ourselves in a horrid situation. We had kept hoping against hope that something could come up and Pixie at least would be spared the horror of six months confinement.

Bobby wanted to spend the winter in Spain and put off the inevitable. The trouble was it was only putting it off. If it had to be, then I wanted to get on and get it over with. At the moment we were one happy family, the four of us together, if we went to England we would all be miserable and split up.

The house in Devon was not near the sea and Bobby would not be able to work. He had found out he could get a job in Holland, this we had not told my parents but we knew we did not have enough money to retire and not work. The thought of what we intended for the pets was like a big black cloud spoiling our waking hours. To not go to England as we had promised my parents that summer would be foolish, having gone through the Red Sea for just that purpose, rather than round the Cape of Good Hope as we had wanted to, arriving the following summer.

Sadly I wrote confirming arrangements and enclosing a deposit for Pixie to go into Ravensden Zoo quarantine and to St Giles asking them to take Bob-tail, feeling a traitor as I did it. I still felt that we should really not be doing this and that something just must turn up.

We had now made up our mind to go through the French canals. We had talked to a lot of people who had come that way and it sounded very nice and something different from our previous sailing. We had to hope that now our engine was fixed it would keep on going. As we discussed this I had a secret thought. Perhaps the engine would let us down and we would be forced to stay in France on the boat. After all France was almost England, or very near. We could visit and my parents could visit us. I was just daydreaming but felt that something other than the quarantine business just had to happen.

Norman and his girlfriend Ann on *'Windslip'* were very helpful and had piles of information and books on the canals. Some of the books we borrowed and read and others with charts we bought off them. Now we would be leaving Alicante turning north not south. The feeling I had in the pit of my stomach should have been excitement but it was fear. What were we doing? Why had I sent those letters? Why were we going all out to do something we dreaded?

Apart from dashing off to the shops now and then I had seen little of Alicante and wanted to visit the castle which had looked so nice lit up at night. I gave myself an afternoon off and walked along the sea front and turned off up a path getting about halfway up to the castle. As I got nearer the castle did not look so nice but the walk was beautiful. I had the whole place to myself and the ground was littered in pine cones which I collected for no more reason than that they looked so pretty. Halfway up the hill I walked in the direction of the town to find another way down. It must have been a beautiful view once but high-rise apartments, slummy ones at that, had been built between the hill and the sea cutting off the view. Spain, we were later to see, had gone crazy with building apartment blocks. Many nice views from sea and shore were being spoilt. There was, it turned out, no way down to the street the way I had come. I made my own way down a difficult patch landing up on someone's roof which I fortunately managed to get off without being spotted.

It was then easier going for a bit, but for the last half I gave up looking dignified and went down on my bottom, landing in a nice little street which I knew was near Woolworths. It was then that I noticed the proper road up to the castle and thought my walk had been more interesting. It would have been a nice walk for Pixie but too far, and she had been content for short walks along the front and to the beach.

Just before leaving we were introduced to a man called Uncle Peter. He had a boat permanently moored in Alicante. When he heard we had sailed form Singapore he asked if we knew of a boat he heard of that had a cheetah and a chimpanzee on board, also from Singapore. We certainly had never heard that story before and felt it could have been one retold many times about us, and with the telling Pixie and Bob-tail had been somewhat enlarged.

A sheet was loose
and flying free
when Bobby cried,
“I cannot see.”

CHAPTER TWENTY-SEVEN

CALAMITY

There was very little wind on leaving Alicante. On the second night we anchored inside the breakwater at Javea. The mornings were quite cold now which served to remind us that the year was coming to an end and we had little sailing time left. Javea we found very peaceful after Alicante. Behind the harbour we had a view of hills with just a few buildings dotted around plus a number of towers.

Something was still very wrong with the engine. When we started it to get the anchor up we had strange knocking noises. As the engine would be our soul means of power going through the French canals we thought it best to have it looked at once again in Denia.

Chirp! Chirp! We were sitting in the cockpit and looked with surprise at Pixie, thinking she had invented a new sound. Just then a little yellow finch landed on Bobby's foot then flew down into the cabin. Bob-tail sprang from the seat in surprise and the bird flew out of the hatch quite unconcerned.

A few hours later we anchored in Denia, just outside the club moorings. In Denia we owned an apartment. We had never lived in it. We had bought it some years before as an investment and had rented it out in the summer months. At that time we had thought that one day we would sell it and buy an old farmhouse inland.

We were still worrying continually about putting Pixie in quarantine and racking our brains for some way round it, knowing it was hopeless as we had tried every approach possible. If only, we thought, Spain had been our destination there would have been no trouble, the pets being free to go ashore. We now had one forlorn hope, that we might find another letter from my parents, who, realising that it was now late in the year for a safe passage to England, would write and suggest we stay the winter in Denia, where they could come out and visit, staying in the apartment. We were clutching at straws. Mail took some time to reach them and they probably thought we were farther along than we were. Another worry was the Mill House. They had told us as it was an old house and it needed to be lived in and have heat in the winter. Quite what would happen if left alone we were not sure. We could of course take it in turns to fly back and see what needed to be done.

"Let's stick to our plan and just hope something will happen," I said. Later, I was to regret those words. I had a strong feeling that somehow or other we would avoid going to England. A feeling or just a hope I was not sure.

The second morning we woke to very strong winds and a bumping noise and found we had dragged anchor and were bumping alongside another yacht. We managed to get away without any damage to either boat. Something odd was happening. The engine was running but we were not moving. The reason was quite simple really, we were aground!

Gathering up lengths of rope and joining them together Bobby got into the dinghy carrying out an anchor and we kegged off. After we had re-anchored a man from the club came out who was very helpful and showed us where to go and found a buoy for us to moor to, which was much safer than anchoring in the poor holding ground. In all it took two hours, good exercise before breakfast.

While all this was going on the wind must have blown the bag of garbage we had on deck within Pixie's reach. She had only extracted one bottle from it, the last thing I would have wished her to find.

An old bottle of gentian violet that had spilled out over everything in the locker and I had tossed out. Pixie now had purple hands and mouth and the deck was also nicely painted the same colour to match. When we spotted what she looked like and cried out, she got rid of the evidence by flinging the bottle in the sea.

Bobby went ashore and I was surprised when a small sailing boat came slowly under power very near us, almost touching our sides. It was a bit odd they should come so near with all the space in the harbour, so stood watching. To my surprise they had come to ask why we were tied to the buoy. I explained; I was then asked if I wanted to buy the buoy as it was not club property but belonged to them and they now wished to move it. When I told them we had no wish to buy the buoy, they gave us until the next day to get off. When Bobby returned he went and told the club what had happened. They insisted we stay on the buoy which was in club waters and they were responsible for us. The owner on the other hand claimed it was outside the club area. We appeared to have become entangled in a private dispute. It was all a little embarrassing. When the buoy owner came the next day we went off and anchored. As it turned out they had no means to remove the buoy and in the end all they took off was about twelve feet of rope which hardly seemed worth all the fuss.

We had a mechanic to come and look at the engine but he did little, then with the help of an interpreter explained that the whole engine needed de-carbonising but that if Bobby mixed a *diesel treat* with the fuel and the oil, the engine would clear and get us to England.

Before leaving Denia we wanted to get the yellow hard weather suits everyone was wearing called oil-skins. We had been made to feel by others in Alicante that we were quite mad to sail without them. We, on the other hand, were amazed to learn many boat owners did not even have a sextant on board and would not have known how to use one if they had. People merrily navigated from point to point with a radio direction finder and many never sailed at night, making sure they made harbour each evening. To do this in the Mediterranean necessitates the installation of powerful engines. As near as most ports are along the coast to each other, if there is no wind you don't get to them very fast. Weather reports too were something everyone was keen on. Certainly, a good thing to have, but we had never heard one. Bobby had asked Norman how he got them on his radio as it was an ordinary transistor, much like ours. All the twiddling on the dial never produced these reports he said he heard. After coming on board and looking at our radio he said it was impossible. There was, we learned, such a thing as a longwave as well as the medium and short we knew about. It was the longwave that gave out weather reports, a wave we had somehow missed getting on our radio.

Shopping ashore I found a pair of plastic pants and top which were not too expensive, they were very thin too but at least they looked the part. I had to buy medium size, the smallest they had in stock, which would have fitted a good-sized giant. When Bobby saw them he said we should have a pair each and was not put off by the fact the now only remaining pair were extra large. We could have both got into them and Pixie too with room to spare.

We had to stay at anchor as a dredger was at work between the jetties. It made the most awful noise like an elephant in pain and worked day and night. We were happy to be leaving but not so happy when the club presented us with a large bill, charging us the same as if we had been alongside with use of water etc. We objected strongly, as there had been no place for us alongside and we had the trouble over the buoy. In the end they cut the bill down to half, still a lot we thought for just being at anchor.

We received a little more mail before we left. A friend in Venezuela, Bernadette, wrote a very descriptive account of their troubles trying to take their birds with them back to the States. The world it seemed was only free for humans to travel around. No, even that is not true in very many places.

Leaving Denia we reluctantly headed north to France. We both felt miserable and so was the weather, with little wind, and we kept having to resort to the engine. Then the weather turned even colder and we were already wearing all the clothes we had at one time. *How,* we wondered, *were we and Pixie and Bob-tail going to survive the cold?* Now the only time we laughed was when we looked at each other on deck in our yellow skins as we called our new plastic wear. The suits would fill with wind, making us look like Michelin tyre adverts. Until then we had been happy, enjoying this life, even the hardships and mishaps that occurred. Now we were nearing the end of our voyage that had been undertaken just so we could all stay together, with Pixie and Bob-tail not having to undergo six months quarantine. We had failed, the thought of what we now intended to subject them to played on our minds. Bobby became more silent and each morning my pillow was wet with tears. We were getting rain now, a cold miserable European rain having no resemblance to the heavy tropical showers we had delighted in and taken showers in.

The 21st September had been a particularly miserable day, the weather having turned even colder as we now had plenty of wind. That night, just before dinner was ready, Bobby said he thought he would tack before eating so we would not have to do so later. "Do you want me to help?" I asked. I was having to hang on to the pot as we now had a heavy swell but felt I could leave it if necessary.

"No, I can manage," he replied.

I guessed he had lost a sheet when I heard him go for'ard. We had it seemed suddenly become more careless and twice that week had not secured the loose sheet when tacking. One night I had an awful time trying to capture a flying end; I had mentioned that we must check we had put a turn around the winch and check that Pixie had not taken it off before we tacked. I listened, as I always did, when he moved around on deck feeling reassured when I could hear him and knew he had not been swept overboard. All was well, I could now hear his steps returning. He appeared in the companionway. "Can you help me, I have just lost the sight of one eye."

How horrified can one be? The words slowly penetrated my mind, what I could do I had no idea but went to him expecting he needed some king of help for his eye. Instead he again went on deck and I followed, he wanted me to help untangle the sheets which had flown together and made a huge knot. It was this knot that had hit him in the eye. Bobby was completely calm and started trying to catch hold of this flying knot. He must have been suffering from shock. It was obviously necessary to first lower the sail and when I suggested it, he just said, "Oh yes."

We lowered the sail, only one person can work on a knot, and Bobby now insisted on unravelling it himself. It took ages in the cold and the dark. I stood there helplessly watching, not able to see his eye and wondering if he had really lost the sight in one. Finally the sheets were sorted out, the sail back up and we were on the right tack.

Back in the cabin I saw his eye for the first time. The knot had hit him full force in the eye and it was now swollen and shut. Bad as it looked the sight reassured me in thinking that the only reason that he could not see was the fact that it was swollen so much that his eye was closed. Bobby said he knew it was open a crack and he could see nothing. I prayed he was wrong and that he would see again once the swelling went down. It was his right eye, the one he called his good eye.

We now headed for the coast to anchor for the night so that next day Bobby could go ashore and see a doctor.

In spite of all the anguish.
In spite of all the pain
So many people helped us
We learned to smile again.

CHAPTER TWENTY-EIGHT

KIND HEARTS AND FRIENDLY PEOPLE

We edged towards the coast, we were still in Spanish waters, just south of Cabo de San Sebastian. At one in the morning we dropped anchor in Palamos Bay. The wind continued strong easterly and the anchor dragged so we laid out a second and the two held us in position.

Bobby's eye looked terrible and now it had started to pain a little, having not hurt at all at the time of the accident. After a drink of hot cocoa we fell into the bunk wearing our socks and T-shirts in an endeavour to keep warm.

I woke just as the clock sounded six bells. Seven I thought, and was surprised that Pixie was still sleeping. When I got up and looked at the clock I saw the seven bells had sounded for eleven o'clock, not seven. I had certainly had a good sleep and the others were still sleeping. It was sunny outside but still cold. I washed and dressed and went on deck. Looking across at the beach I could not believe my eyes, the place was full of humans stretched out on the beach wearing bikinis! Many were even swimming in the sea, which I knew from my wash was freezing cold. A number of windsurfers passed, the people regularly falling off them into the icy water. I wondered if we would ever get as acclimatised to the cold as these people were.

Bobby woke but felt, not unnaturally, generally unwell and stayed in bed for another hour after which he ate and went ashore to find an eye doctor.

Bobby found an eye doctor but the information he received was hardly encouraging. He was, as he had said, blind in the right eye. The natural lens of his eye had dislodged and had moved to behind the eye and must now be considered a foreign body. The doctor further explained that the condition was such that there was no way he would ever be able to see from that eye. The doctor went on to tell him that an operation was imperative to remove the lens, and subsequently an artificial lens could be inserted and with that he would also have to wear glasses. The doctor stressed that the operation be performed as soon as possible, in the meantime Bobby must rest and do no physical work. The operation could be done in Barcelona but it would cost about five hundred pounds. Failing that he could go to England and get it done under the National Health which might be free. When Bobby returned with this disheartening news we sat trying to work out what to do. To continue our journey on *'Sandpiper'* was now quite out of the question if Bobby could do no physical work. To fly to England would mean first we had to find a place to leave the boat, that is if we all went, that would work out more expensive than having the operation done in Spain, plus the fact we would have to rearrange all the quarantine for Pixie and Bob-tail who would have to be collected at the airport; Bob-tail had had short journeys in a basket but Pixie had never been in any kind of cage. Bobby would also have to find somewhere to live in London until admitted into hospital. We assumed that he would have it done in London. Added to that we were not sure that the operation would be free in England. We are both English but had not lived in England or paid into the National Insurance for many years, having lived mostly overseas. Even if it could be arranged in England we feared he might have to wait months to get into a hospital from all we had heard of the present state of affairs in England. Then of course we would still have to get '*Sandpiper*' to England. Strangely, until that moment, we had never considered what we would do with '*Sandpiper*' if we did settle down in England. We came to the conclusion that if he did go to England he would go alone, and I stay on the boat with Pixie and Bob-tail.

We sat debating, going round in circles, all the time with the awful realisation hanging over us that Bobby had lost the sight of his right eye. In the end we decided the first thing to do was to go to Barcelona and get a second opinion. At least there we would be better located for him to fly to England if necessary. Also, we expected we could find a berth where I and Pixie and Bob-tail could remain until his return.

That night the wind howled and it was freezing cold, the sort of weather we imagined existed in the north or south poles. Fortunately, the anchors held. In the morning the sun came out but could not compete with the cold wind that continued to blow hard. Now it was too cold for even the bathers we had seen the day before. The beach was deserted except for a lone man with his dog.

We sat in the cabin doing nothing for perhaps the first time since we had started living aboard '*Sandpiper*'. There was of course plenty of things to be done but now it hardly seemed to matter and we had no heart to do anything. Bobby fortunately was feeling very tired and slept a lot which was the best thing he could do. I felt wretched about the whole thing and wished fervently I had agreed to spend the winter in Spain. If we had gone no farther than Denia the accident would never have happened. I had also been wishing, hoping, praying, for some miracle to take place so we would not have to go to England and put Pixie and Bob-tail in prison. Now it looked as if it was turning out that way but not in the way I wanted or expected. I remember a story that said you should always be careful what you wish for, you might get it but not the way you expect.

The following day the wind had died down somewhat and that afternoon we hove up the anchors and left, this time heading back the way we had come for Barcelona. We had a nice wind to start with and by midnight had to reef the mainsail. I nearly froze on my watch and wondered if all had gone as planned we could have made it to England or frozen to death in the attempt. The wind dropped a bit but we had very heavy seas. A wave knocked me off course and the mainsail boom slammed across, the ropes getting entangled in the steering wheel. When I had sorted that all out, I tied the boom to the rails but before my watch ended she luffed again. I struggled with the rope I had tied the boom with, but it was now so tight I could not untie it. Matters were not helped by the fact I was trying to hold the flashlight in my mouth to see with, but being faulty, it kept going out. I hated to call Bobby who needed to rest but in the end had to, and together we made things ship-shape again. To make up for it I called him half an hour after my watch should have ended, I had intended to keep going longer but by that time felt so sick with tiredness and cold I could no longer cope.

By daylight the wind had dropped and we were left just floundering about and stayed virtually becalmed until noon, when we picked up a light wind.

We arrived at the long breakwater of Barcelona before ten the next morning, reaching the yacht club about three hours later, passing the statue of Christopher Columbus and interesting looking buildings. The club moorings looked full, with hundreds of yachts, mostly Spanish and not lived on, and a number of what we called gin palaces, huge motor boats. We were then waved to a space and tied up with no bother.

"Well," said Bobby, "that is our first problem solved. This is a nice safe place and you would be quite comfortable if I had to leave." I agreed, then we read the form we had been handed. The maximum allowed length of stay was fifteen days, and that only if we could show we were members of a yacht club. We had fortunately still got our membership cards from Changi Club. Fifteen days we knew would not be long enough but thought we would cross that bridge when we came to it.

The main thing now was for Bobby to get a second opinion on his eye. He was feeling a little hopeful now the swelling had gone down a little and he could see light through the eye. The club gave Bobby the address of the eye clinic. Here he found a nice doctor with perfect English who gave him some eye drops which he had to put in morning, noon and night and return to be examined again the following afternoon. Only then would they be able to say if he needed an operation or not.

We felt quite happy the next day, having made up our minds that the doctor would find he did not need an operation after all and that in time his eye would return to normal. His only pair of jeans were not only tatty but were several sizes too large for him as he had lost weight since leaving Singapore. I had two pairs of good brushed denim jeans a friend had given me but which were too large, we now found that Bobby could get into them and they looked far smarter than his own and made him feel better.

Bobby was gone hours and as the time ticked away my spirits flagged. I felt it could only mean the worst. The doctor had been very thorough and had called in another to confirm his findings but sadly they both said he would have to have the operation. He was then sent to the hospital the other side of town and examined again and told to return the next day. Here he was told he was too old (he was 58) to have a lens inserted in the eye as the doctor in Palomas had said, but after the operation it would be better to have a soft contact lens.

The next day he saw yet another doctor who was the head of the eye department. The necessity for an operation was confirmed without a doubt. The doctors were extremely nice and explained to him that it was not an emergency as the lens would stay where it was as long as he did no work. In Barcelona they would have to do it in a clinic as the hospital was for emergency cases and short of beds.He'd have to remain in the clinic for about a week and keep returning for check-ups for two months after that, before the contact lens could be fitted. All in all it would cost, as we had been told before, just over £500. They then suggested it might be cheaper for him to have it done in England. He was then advised to think about it and let them know on the Monday.

This time we did not have to think too hard before deciding that it would be far better to have it done in Barcelona. If he went to England and they decided it was not an emergency he might well just be put on a waiting list for months and told to rest. It would probably be far more expensive in the long run and he much preferred to get it all over with as quickly as possible.

A French boat had now come in and moored not far from us. A very nice couple, Oliver who was French and his English wife Louise. They had a small fluffy black-and-white cat with whom Bob-tail had already made acquaintance. I think it was the first girl cat he had met.

When Bobby returned to the hospital to tell them he had decided to have the operation there, they kept him most of the day taking tests and filling out numerous forms. The doctors were extremely kind, understanding men and told him there would, that night, be a vacant bed in the hospital. If he would like to take it he should return that night before eight and they would get him in rather than going to the private clinic. The difference meant that the operation would now cost 15,000 pesetas rather than 60,000 pesetas as the clinic would have done. A fantastic reduction and he would have the same treatment and the same doctor.

It was rather a shock to find he was leaving that night but it was good that it was going to be done so soon. For some reason they now told him he would be staying in for two weeks, rather than the one they mentioned before. Bobby had bought a lot of things on his return to keep Pixie, Bob-tail and I well fed while he was away. We were nervous that night and ate little of the dinner I cooked. Even Pixie caught our mood and was very restless, but refrained from getting into mischief. Bobby tried to start the engine to charge the batteries before he left but the engine refused to start.

Bobby left at seven that morning. I was not even going to be able to visit him as I could not leave Pixie on her own and Bobby had said he wanted us just to all stay together and not risk anything happening while he was away. That evening I took Pixie and Bob-tail for a walk around the marina, we returned to the boat in darkness and went to bed. It felt strange without Bobby and I fell asleep wondering what sort of bed he was now in.

We did not know it then, that it would be twenty-two days before Bobby would be back with us again. It was the fourth day after he left that it dawned on me that although I could not visit him, I could phone him from the club and learn how he was getting on. I remembered the doctor's name, Badell. Well I thought it was the doctor but it turned out to be the name of the clinic. After several tries and lots of help I managed to get the correct number and finally even talked to Bobby. He had still not had the operation but had undergone all manner of tests and X-rays. He was very bored as all they wanted him to do was rest. All the other patients were mostly old men with something wrong with their throats so they could not talk much and anyway knew no English. I gave him the club phone number, at least now we could keep in touch by phone.

In some respects it was good that the boat was in poor shape and there was plenty to be done. I filled all the daylight hours painting and varnishing in the cabin and getting everything washed and clean and putting up the odd picture or catches on the lockers etc. I wanted the place to look good when Bobby returned and also needed to keep busy. I would make dinner early and Pixie and I would eat before it got dark and then, with Bob-tail, we would go for a walk. I had tried to start the engine several times but without success so I could not use the electric light and the kerosene lamp leaked so after our walk we would go to bed.

To keep life interesting the foot pump for the stove refused to pump. I spent a day trying to get the club to find me someone who would fix it. Nobody wanted to even look at the thing. We had a spare pump but that also was not working. In desperation I took one apart. It did not appear to have anything wrong with it so I cleaned it and put it back together. Amazing! It worked and I fixed the spare the same way. I could cook again, that is until the tank ran out of kerosene and I could not remove the top to fill it.

Bobby and I now talked on the phone each day. He was still waiting for his operation and getting fed up. On the eighth day he was told it would be the following morning so he decided to sneak out of the hospital and come and see us. It was good to have him back even if only for a few hours. Most of that time we did not spend together as there was some shopping I needed to do and while I went off Bobby got the top off the kerosene tank and filled it for me. He also tried to start the engine but had no better luck than I had. Bobby was feeling tired in spite of all the rest, the hospital was so noisy he got little sleep. Nevertheless, he was grateful to the doctors for getting him in.

I felt very depressed the following morning thinking of Bobby now undergoing his operation, then remembering that the quarantine places in England were still expecting Pixie and Bob-tail I wrote letters explaining what had happened and cancelling their reservations. I felt so much happier doing this than when I had made the reservations. I requested the return of the deposit with little hope we would get it. I was wrong, people are kind and the deposits were refunded. My letters finished I got in the dinghy with paint and brush to paint the hull when I was called to the phone. Bobby's operation had been put off as a nurse had given him that morning what passed for breakfast. A glass of milk with a drop of coffee to colour it and some English biscuits: the operation could not take place on a full stomach.

Oliver and Louise on the French boat had only stopped a couple of days, leaving before Bobby went into hospital. I had since made friends with a charming Argentine couple off the only other occupied boat on our wharf. Christina had been a great help when I first tried to get through on the phone to Bobby; she taught me what to say once I had the number. I never knew if it was the ward I was asking for or the doctor. Hardly mattered, as that one simple word I could not pronounce. One operator, smarter than the rest, would tag on that I wanted the only non-Spanish patient and would say 'Americano'. From then on it was simple, Americano worked every time. In the ward he was just called English.

One night returning with Pixie and Bob-tail from our walk I found an English couple with a little girl looking at *'Sandpiper'*. They had just come in and were moored nearer to the club, late in the year though it was – October 9th – and they were returning to England via the French canals. I unfortunately never saw their boat as it left the following morning, but they had told me it was also ferro-cement which they had built themselves. The strange thing was the name. It was also called *'Sandpiper'*. It sounded better equipped for that part of the world than our boat, having a powerful engine and a heater. Something we would have been very glad of.

The day after Bobby actually had his operation, I phoned and was told he could not come to the phone as had both eyes bandaged. However, they were able to tell me he was OK, so I had to be contented with that and pray that the operation had been a success.

Christina and her husband were flying back to Argentina leaving their boat wrapped in huge sheets of plastic, which made it look as if it was gift wrapped for Christmas. I helped scrub their dinghy which had a prolific underwater garden on the bottom. It was sad to see them go but I was happy to accept all their fresh food they had left over.

Bobby remained in hospital suffering more pain than he thought possible to bear. After the first couple of days they removed the bandage on his undamaged eye, so he no longer had the humility of having to be walked to the loo and be spoon fed. He still had no vision in this right eye but that was to be expected and it remained covered. The pain was intense and they had to keep giving him pain-killing injections that wore off soon after, and he would be in torment before it was time for the next. He longed to get back with us on the boat fearing he would go crazy if he stayed much longer in the hospital, but sounded more cheerful one day when he phoned saying he expected to be out by the following Friday. Sadly, it was another five days after that before he was discharged. They found he had a blood clot behind the eye and had to do another operation to remove it.

Pixie was extremely well behaved all the time Bobby was away, perhaps sensing something was wrong. However, I never dared leave her and go shopping just in case she got free and into mischief.

About a week before Bobby returned an American boat come in named *'Walulu'* and moored directly opposite us. Lee and Bruce Wedlow, the owners, had just come from England where they had lived for the past five years. Lee was a very kind and helpful person and offered to mail some letters I had written. She also purchased fresh food for me when she went shopping and suggested she should monkey-sit so I could get out for a change. She said it so naturally as though we had known each other for years and she was accustomed to monkey-sitting. Praying Pixie would behave, I took the opportunity to do a bit of my own shopping. Pixie I learned, had just sat on the rails like an angel. She spoilt her reputation when Lee came on board one day for a chat, she behaved so badly. Though chained in the cockpit she was as naughty as she could be, pulling herself in and chewing at the fiddle rails in the cabin and getting very jealous when I tried to talk to Lee. In spite of that, when I learned Bobby was not coming back as expected, Lee wanted to look after Pixie again so that I could go and visit him. I wanted to and phoned Bobby to find out the visiting hours and just where the hospital was located. Bobby felt it was not worth running the risk of Pixie getting up to something while I was away as the travelling alone would take two hours.

We had more company when *'Helena Christina'*, a Dutch boat, came in early one morning. Helena and her husband were an attractive young couple with two little girls, one being only a baby. Helena was also going to be on her own for a week while her husband flew back to Holland. Things were now getting busy around us as later the same day *'Sula'* from England joined our little gathering with Christine and Barry Phillips on board. They had come to book a flight back to England where Christine had to go for an operation. We were not the only ones with troubles.

Lee's husband Bruce, on learning we had no lights at night owing to the fact I could not start the engine offered to try and start it, but

I put him off explaining that something had to be wrong and would need fixing first.

The next day I had Christine and Barry on board. Barry I soon learned was a mechanic and loved engines. It is hard for me to believe that anyone could love such noisy ugly things but in Barry's eyes they were beautiful. Once on board one of the first things Barry said was, "How's your engine?"

"Sick," I replied. "It refuses to work." This was all the encouragement Barry needed, he was down on his knees looking at it and trying to start it. He had no luck then but the following day he returned with a bag of tools and a blow lamp to heat it. Among other things our engine, like us, was used to warmer weather and did not like the cold. With Barry's intervention it suddenly roared into life. That was the start of a good day as Bobby came home that night.

It had been a busy day as *'Rolling Wave II'* joined us with Mike and Diana Harper on board. They also had come from England with Lulu their beautiful female cat, another girlfriend for Bob-tail. Lee and Bruce left that day but first Lee and I went on board *'Rolling Wave II'* and just gasped at the interior; it was beautiful, a real floating home with a lovely little stove with a chimney that burnt wood; it also had silver framed photos and ornaments. The hull was steel but once inside it looked like a wooden boat.

That afternoon, full of excitement, Pixie and I shampooed and dolled ourselves up and waited for Bobby. When we spotted him coming up the wharf we both raced to meet him. What a joyful reunion that was but it was distressing to see him with a huge white bandage over his eye and he looked so frail, appearing to have aged years in the three weeks he had been away. He was still in so much pain and could not bend his head down.

After dinner Pixie wanted to return to her custom of grooming his hair but gentle as she is it was too painful for Bobby. Later I had to watch helplessly while he was in agony waiting for the painkiller he had taken to work. He was certainly far from well.

Later that night the pill Bobby had taken took effect and the pain stopped. We lay in the bunk and he recounted his experience in hospital.

At first he had been alone in his room but could get up and visit the other patients. This was not very enlivening as the men patients were all very old and spoke little, even to each other. Unfortunately they could not speak English and Bobby had no Spanish. He felt he was walking among zombie-like people who had completely withdrawn into themselves. He was then taken to visit the women patients which he preferred, one lady having very good English, he could talk to them all and she would translate. He then took his meals with them which was preferable to eating with the men who would shuffle in, eat the unappetising food and shuffle out again. One of the female patients he felt particularly sorry for.

She was only in her twenties and was completely blind and would lie in bed crying all day which made Bobby realise how lucky he was to still have the sight of one eye. The matron was a bit of a tyrant and treated them all like naughty children. She had no English but by facial expressions and finger-wagging would make her disapproval quite plain. Pyjamas were the thing to be worn in hospital and she showed her disfavour of Bobby's sarong and gave him a pair of tatty pyjama bottoms which he wore with his shirt. Later a nurse did not approve of that get up and promptly changed it for a complete pyjama suit of top and matching bottoms. Having not worn pyjamas for years he now felt he was being turned into a permanent inmate. When the matron then wanted to shave his beard off he put his foot down, it being the only thing of his own he was wearing.

After a few days he had a roommate who had something wrong with his legs. They both tried to talk to each other, each sticking to his own language. One day Bobby managed to understand that his roommate wanted him to sneak out of the hospital and buy him some wine and gave him the money to do so. Feeling sorry for the man who had been quite sane when he arrived but had started to show the first signs of madness, he agreed. Bobby sneaked out but failed to locate any place in the area that sold wine and had to return empty-handed to the dismay of his roommate who shook his head in bewilderment that he should be landed with such a loony that could not speak Spanish and could not even find a wine shop. Bobby's disappearance had not gone unnoticed by the nurse and he got a ticking off, with much finger-wagging and frequent, "English no Bono." This did not refer to our language or our country but just to Bobby in particular who was never called anything but 'English', except by the doctor. Perhaps owing to the fact that to explain his lack of the common language we would point to himself and say, "English."

The floors of the whole place were of tile or stone and very cold, so all the nurses wore wooden clogs and were crashing around the whole time. At two-hour intervals all through the night they took every patient's temperature and blood pressure to ascertain, presumably, that everyone was still alive; to do that they had to wake the patients up if they had the good fortune to go to sleep. Opposite his room the stretchers and wheelchairs were kept in a small alcove and day and night people would be dragging the things out and tossing the stretchers to the floor to the accompaniment of loud shouting. At three thirty in the afternoon each day the visitors were let in and he could hear them coming from a distance with a roar like an avalanche.

Bobby swore the nurses had a playtime when they would shriek, giggle and chase each other up and down the corridors in their clogs. Being on the seventh floor the food always arrived cold and completely tasteless. Apparently, chillies, garlic, and even onions and salt were unheard of. One man went crazy and would take off his pyjamas and run around naked. In the end he got so bad they locked him in his room. He had Bobby's sympathy, he thought he was going mad too. Despite all this unexpected entertainment, some hilarious and some sad, he had nothing but praise for the doctors and the kindness of everyone in general. He felt assured that they had done all that was possible for his eye and would continue to do so in his status as an out-patient when he had to attend twice a week.

Bobby had expected to receive a bill for his treatment before being discharged from the hospital, but the doctor just said there was plenty of time for that and not to worry. It was nice of the doctor but it was a little worrying as he wanted to know just how much it had cost. The amount they had quoted him when he said he would have the operation there was only about £100, a fifth of the cost they had quoted for the private clinic. But he had stayed in much longer than originally expected. It was over a month before he got the bill, the doctor had to go round to the almoner with Bobby and fill in numerous forms. The doctor was extremely sympathetic having realised that Bobby had not come from abroad for treatment but had suffered the accident while sailing off the coast. He arranged that he only be charged the minimum rate as if he was a local resident and it did in the end only cost about £100.

Bobby slept and rested a lot during the first few weeks after leaving the hospital. It was a trying time for him, not liking to be idle but being unable to do anything, and when he was up he could only sit, as it was not possible for him to read, he had no glasses and straining the one eye only made the other pain more.

The weather was getting colder all the time and Bobby felt it even more than I did being immobile. I bought a camping gas cylinder and a fire which helped to warm the cabin. Pixie and Bob-tail loved to lie by it. We often had to move them when we smelt their fur burning. Later we got an electric fire, also which we could plug into the mains ashore and I bought some bright woven cloth and made thick curtains which when drawn over the windows at night made the cabin look cosy and warmer.

On relating to Diana and Mike our troubles over quarantine for Pixie and Bob-tail, Diana said that the same rule extended to Gibraltar and so they must have a quarantine place and perhaps it would be more suitable. Our spirits rose, this was one idea we had not thought of. Perhaps there they could be together and we could visit them. In this case as soon as Bobby was well enough we could go to Gibraltar, stay six months, and leave sometime in the summer and go to England, where they could be flown out to join us. I at once wrote to Gibraltar and in time received an answer. Any animal that was going to be taken ashore in Gibraltar had first to do six-month quarantine in England. Back to square one.

So far we had been lucky, we had far exceeded our maximum allowed stay at the yacht club but nobody had said anything and the club had been very sympathetic about Bobby's hospitalisation. Then came the day when the male secretary of the club, a man we had little dealings with at that point, came along to our part of the wharf and with gestures made it plain to us and the other three boats that it was time we all moved on. No more was said but within a couple of days our friends all left. We were in no position to do so yet and Bobby asked the hospital doctor to write a note to the club explaining that he was in no fit state to sail. Perhaps it also helped matters that we had found our way by then to the heart of the secretary. He was an avid stamp collector so when one day he pointed to some nice stamps on a letter that had come for us indicating that he would like them we handed them over and then collected a pile of different stamps we had on board and presented them to him. The smile on his face was enough to let us know we had a friend and no more was said about moving. After that, whenever there was mail for us, he would come out and wave it in the air shouting, "Sandy Peeper, Sandy Peeper." Most people by then would have recognised me and thought my name was Sandy.

The doctors were pleased with Bobby when he returned to the hospital for his first check-up and told him he could now take the bandage off his eye. He could not see anything from that eye but the light gave him intense pain. He had to wear sun shades even on the cloudy days we were having. I was unable to buy an eyeshade in Barcelona. When I wrote of this to my parents my mother sent a nice black eye patch, this cut out the light and made life a lot easier for him. One day a young English boy Aran came up to me. "Are you off the boat with the pirate and the monkey?"

Our decision to have the operation done in Barcelona had been a good one. We learned later from English friends that Spain, and in particular Barcelona, had the best eye surgeons in Europe. People with eye problems came from England and other places in Europe for treatment. The doctors never mentioned this fact to Bobby.

Sometime before we were to leave Bobby thought he had better ask how much it was costing us to stay so long at the marina. They showed him the rule sheet: 250 pesetas for each of the first three days, rising to 600 pesetas for every day after that. Our bill was going to be a big one we feared. We left finally on the 20th December having stayed almost three months. Our bill was less than half what we had expected. They only charged us 250 pesetas per day for the whole time. We certainly had a lot to thank the Spanish for.

From our mail we learned that both my parents, and uncle who was visiting them, had gone over to our Mill House and worked on necessary outside repairs. While there they had found a card pushed under the door. John Wilburn off *'Natica'* had left his boat in Cyprus for the winter and flown to England to work; expecting to find us he had paid a visit to the Mill House. Our first visitor had arrived before ourselves.

Before arriving in Barcelona the only thing I knew it was famous for was the fact that the zoo housed 'Snowflake' the only albino gorilla in captivity. I had read about and seen many photos of him and was thrilled to think I might now meet him in person. Strangely when other friends had gone sightseeing they would return saying they had visited the museums, cathedral, churches etc. but none had visited the zoo to see Snowflake, worse still they had never heard of him until I asked. I was a bit apprehensive that having lost touch with so much of the outside world in the last two years that something might have happened to him.

Ciutadella Park where the zoo is located is a beautiful place, and the zoo was well planned and clean, most of the animals being in moated areas rather than the old-fashioned cages I had seen and hated in Tele Aviv. I enjoyed it but saw no directions to Snowflake. I inquired of some of the other visitors, they did not understand what I was inquiring about. What I had not realised of course was that quite naturally he was known in Spain only by his Spanish name of 'Copito de Nieve'. The English language accounts I had read about him had translated his name. I eventually found the gorilla complex and there unmistakably was Snowflake. He was not much like a Snowflake having grown into a huge beautiful gorilla. He shared his section with two black gorillas. Sadly this once famous gorilla, for anyone interested in primates, was no longer the star attraction. While many others animals had plenty of room and outside accommodation, the poor gorillas had concrete cells with plate glass in front to observe them through. The cells were very small compared with their size and contained nothing to interest them. No chance to tickle them and the glass was rather smeared and not so good for taking photos.

Snowflake was occupied when I arrived trying to prise up the dividing door from his room to the next. He was well mannered and seeing me came over to the glass to grin and pose for me. Gosh he was lovely and he knew it. We rubbed noses, the glass separating us. When he considered he had given me enough of his time he went back to work on his door. I went to the next section to see what the attraction was. Here the scene was repeated. A black female gorilla also was working on the door, just as intent on getting to Snowflake as he was at getting to her. I thought at first she also was alone. She also knew her manners and seeing me, moved over holding up a tiny baby by its hands for me to see. I was nearly in tears. There was no information up in any language, but I felt sure that Snowflake was the father, how cruel to have parted them. They are big but such gentle giants. Their life could not have been much fun but if they had each other it would have been some consolation. I saw no one come near them. Poor Snowflake had been a nine-day wonder.

I am not a city lover but liked Barcelona and wished we were there under happier circumstances. A stroll down the Ramblas would always put me in a cheerful frame of mind. The day I decided to track down some spires in the distance and found myself finally confronted by La Sagrada Familia was a day to remember. That fantastic piece of architecture that no photo can do justice to, held me goggle-eyed for some hours. During our stay in Barcelona I saw most of the sights, including the naval museum with hundreds of beautiful models of ships of all kinds. I enjoyed that much more than I expected and wanted Bobby to visit it but he never felt up to it.

One of the sights I took in was more of a personal nature. Pop had written telling me of things in Barcelona he had enjoyed about fifty years before. He also mentioned having stayed in a hotel in Santa Ana Street, Hotel Novel. I found both street and hotel. The street I am sure had changed a lot, the houses having the bottom floor turned into shops with modern glass fronts, but the hotel looked as if it might not have changed in the last fifty years. I went in out of interest and enquired the cost of the rooms. They were very reasonable and the old boy at the desk looked as if he had probably been there at the time of my father's visit.

As we had few warm clothes and Barcelona had a large number of wool shops I thought I had better take up knitting. It would also give me something to do when sitting in the cabin with Bobby. There was one snag, I could not remember how to knit or how to get started. I mailed off a letter to my friend Adéla in England, a prolific knitter. She came up trumps and sent me two patterns that would not tax my limited knowledge of the art, instructions on how to get started, plus samples of the kind of wool the patterns required to be used. This was very thoughtful and would enable me to turn out something the correct size and shape. I dashed off to the wool shop as soon as I received the letter. I could easily have obtained the right thickness wool but fell in love with some really thick stuff which was probably intended for rugs. It was odd stuff, I found some of it contained string in the middle of the wool but the colours were nice, being a natural sort of off-white and grey. I purchased a load of both colours. Then I picked out the needles that the pattern directed to be used. The shop lady suggested that they would be rather useless for the type of wool I now had and gave me big fat things instead.

I set to work that evening picking the smallest size and then halving the number of stitches to compensate for the thickness of the wool. Pixie and Bob-tail took a keen interest in this novel new hobby but irrespective of their unhelpful assistance I managed to finish the back that evening. When I had arrived at the point of shaping I found it a bit dodgy. If I had cast off all they told in the pattern I would have been left with no more stitches. I just cast off a few. The result looked much like I had expected, even though on the big side. By the third day it was finished and all that remained to be done was to stitch all the bits together. No needle I had would take the thickness of the wool and in the end Bobby came to the rescue and suggested I use a sail needle and thread.

Hairy, as we called the resulting garment, was finished. It could be worn quite nicely over the top of our zip jackets making us look less skinny.

I felt rather pleased with myself when the sweater was finished. Bob-tail was also going around with a smug look on his face. That evening he jumped aboard with a dead fish in his mouth which he took in a corner and ate raw. Unusual, he usually demanded fish cooked. He was quite dry so I could not think how he had caught it. Next day I told someone about his cleverness in catching a fish without getting wet. "I should not say anything about it if I were you," was the reply. Apparently one of the other boats had caught two fish and hung them on their rails to dry and were now trying to puzzle out how one had got away.

A number of cruising boats had come in but usually only stayed a day and left. In November two yachts arrived on the same day, staying long enough for us to get to know them well and enjoy their company. *'Persistent'*, a British motor sailer with Bill Williams and his daughter Polly and her friend Heather Broomfield on board, arrived first, soon to be joined by *'Chrisma'*, she had been bought and sailed in England by two wonderful Americans, Virginia and John Mulenburg. Virginia invited us over for coffee. Bobby, still not feeling well, declined the invitation, so leaving Pixie with him I went alone and was soon joined by Bill and the girls, and two English families who had their boats tied up along the wall. We crowded into the cabin and had a very jolly afternoon. Virginia, we learned, had had an upsetting time that morning though it did not appear to have dampened her spirits. While wandering around the cathedral looking at the cloisters a man knocked against her, it seemed innocent enough and the man went his way, returned with a handkerchief and started wiping some brown sticky stuff off the back of her coat, making some explanation in Spanish. Virginia then placed her bag on the floor and naturally took off her coat the better to clean it. The man indicated he wanted to get water to wash her coat and as she removed it they had a little tug of war. The man suddenly let go his end of the coat and grabbed her bag and ran off with Virginia in hot pursuit. A Spanish man joined in the chase but they lost sight of the thief at a crossing, the man stopping to pick up a bunch of keys the thief had dropped, they were not Virginia's.

Many more interesting tales were told that afternoon. When we asked Virginia and John what they had done before taking up life at sea, they told us they had been missionaries. A little more prompting revealed they had been in Amoy China until 1950 and could speak and read Chinese. They had continued their missionary work in the Philippines and the States and were now both in their sixties and retired. They felt they wanted to meet more people outside the church and had chosen to go to England, buy a boat and learn to sail. Later we got to know them really well. They were wonderful people who never preached their religion but lived it.

During that afternoon someone said they had heard of a good place to spend the winter just twenty miles south of Barcelona. The two English couples, Val and Ian, and Steve and Lynne, decided they were going there, a few days later when *'Chrisma'* had her engine fixed she too left for Sitges. *'Persistent'*, like us, was doomed to stay much longer. They also had engine trouble but it proved more complicated to fix. We felt sorry for Bill who had come out with the girls, looking forward to cruising the Mediterranean, they were grand people to have around and with Polly and Heather to enliven things there was never a dull moment.

My first outing with them was one Sunday. I was setting off to see the local dancing, the 'Sardana' that took place outside the cathedral every Sunday. Until then every Sunday had been too cold for me but this time it was nice and sunny. I happened to meet Bill before taking off and was told they were also going and suggested I join them. On arrival in the vicinity of the cathedral we were approached by a Spaniard who was making a feature film for TV. I think he needed a nutty looking tourist to join in. As it was not the tourist season he had little choice and I was asked to take part. I was none too keen. Heather had not yet joined us but Polly thought it a good laugh, I suggested she take the part. No, no, the producer must have wanted someone more ancient looking. While it was me the producer wanted he tended to ask Bill and said he would take all of us out to lunch after my performance. That settled it. I could not deprive them of a free lunch. The producer must have been desperate and having found us was not about to let us go so we were invited into a café to have coffee with him while the professional dancers were rounded up.

Once the ring of dancers got going it looked quite simple. All I was required to do was to break in-between a girl and boy and try to copy them. I did my best, the first time I was told I was jumping up and down so much I was getting out of the camera; *rather clever*, I thought, as the boy next to me was about six feet tall. We all had to chant 'uno, dos, tres, cambia'. One, two, three, change. My Spanish was up to that, guess my footwork was nothing to shout about as we had a number of repeat performances before they were satisfied. I had earned us lunch. The producer then found he had to dash off on some other assignment, he had probably seen enough of me by then. Instead of being wined and dined, a wad of notes was pushed into Bill's hand. Perhaps they had taken him to be my agent or more likely my carer. We took ourselves off for a feed and a good time. Even after this there was still 600 pesetas left which I took back to Bobby and told him I had earned it dancing in the street.

Later that night I got awful stomach pains. I could not decide if it was the toadstool in the mushroom omelette I had for lunch or if it was because of my energetic dancing.

After that, most evenings I would accompany Bill and the girls for a beer after dinner at the nearby tavern. They were always lively company and it made a nice rounding off of the days for me. Bobby, meanwhile, was slowly getting better. He should still have been resting all the time but after the first week he started finding little things he could do. He was paying regular visits to the hospital after which he would return sometimes pleased, others times not so happy. Then they finally took the last stitches out. A few days later he found he could see shadows, just light from dark but it was an improvement. He was then told he could be tested for a lens within the next three weeks. This was wonderful as it might mean that he would have sight well before Christmas.

We celebrated too soon. On a later visit they told him there was a haemorrhage that was not healing as it should and contemplated having him back in hospital; perhaps they felt that would be just too cruel so said that if he was good and just rested more it would clear. We had hoped to leave Barcelona and join our friends in Sitges, from there he would be able to catch a train to Barcelona for his visits to the hospital. The doctor told him that he was still not well enough to be tossed about at sea for even that short distance.

The trouble I had experienced finding suitable things to send to my family for Christmas was nothing compared to what I went through trying to mail them. I had, at last, found enough paper to pack up the first four and took them along to the post office. Here I wandered around until I found the appropriate counter to join the line to get them weighed and stamped. When my turn came I handed over the largest of the parcels and saw a 600 pesetas stamp slapped on it. This was frightening as it was far more than expected. I had 2000 pesetas with me but intended to do some shopping as well. On taking the next parcel she asked me if I wanted it air mail. I decided against this, figuring it still had time to go overland to England but wondered why I had not been asked this question for the first parcel. When all four had been done I parted with 1385 pesetas and thought that was the end of it. I was, in fact, still far from getting rid of the things.

The two largest I was made to understand had to be taken to another counter, there I joined another long line where I saw two women accepting parcels and sealing the knots with red wax, thumping them with a seal and charging for it. My turn came and one parcel got the wax treatment. The next she grabbed and to my dismay took scissors to it and snipped off the nice blue nylon string I had tied it with. After a rummage in a cupboard full of a mass of string she chose a soft bit and retied the parcel giving it the wax and seal badge. I parted with 40 pesetas. All this had taken place in the basement. I was now told to go to counter 32 which was upstairs. This counter had something like 'Certificates' written above it. People were getting rid of their parcels and accepting receipts in exchange. My turn, the woman looked with dismay on finding all four were mine. She weighed the largest and asked if they were air mail. I said no. She then looked with distaste at the two smaller ones which were considerably bigger than many I had seen her accepting from other people. Looking hard at me she said very clearly, "Poco, peti, little." *So what,* I thought, or was she letting me know she could say the size in three languages. After that she considered them all for a minute and decided she did not want to have anything to do with any of them and sent me to yet another counter with 'Aero' above it. When my turn came the largest was again weighed and passed along to another counter. The woman then got to work on the remaining three. The next largest in size appeared to be to her liking and she could find no fault with it and so I received a receipt and she disposed of the parcel. Of the two smaller ones she wanted to know the contents. One had an assortment of things but included some cassette tapes. "Music," I said, trying to be helpful and then remembered that cassette was the same in Spanish. That established she wrote in on the parcel. Now we came to the last parcel and its contents. It was a small carved box. I had no idea how to say box in Spanish so mimed a box with my hands, now two customers behind me joined in the quiz, to try to understand what it was I was trying to explain. One man nearly got it when he decided it was a musical box. No musical I said, and pointing to my ring pretended to place it in an imaginary box. Everyone now caught on at the same time and a happy cry of 'Joyeries' went up. I agreed and repeated it also having belatedly remembered the word on jewel boxes in the shops. The value they did not ask for. This was not the end of getting rid of my parcels as for some reason unknown, the lady now took a dislike to the sticky paper on the ends of both parcels, they were both handed back to me and it was indicated that I pull off the brown paper tape, as if it was something contaminating. I had no objection to getting my fingers sticky but the reason I had used it was because it held the outer paper onto the inner as I had been unable to find one sheet of paper large enough. I removed some and showed her what was about to happen; she agreed that a little of it could remain. I received one receipt to cover the two parcels.

Now I was three down one still to go. I now lined up at the counter I had seen my larger parcel go to. It was weighed again and aero stamped on it, I obviously had paid for that one to go by air. I was now given a form with carbon paper and several copies that had to be filled in plus another almost the same, but made of cardboard. It looked very complicated and all of course in Spanish. I just filled in the bits I could understand. They hardly looked at the forms, tore a bit off and returned it as a receipt. I had got rid of all four parcels!

One evening I had shown Heather and Polly how to make macrame holders for hanging plants. Heather really took to it and made a lot in the hope of being able to sell them. I heartily endorsed this idea as I wanted also to make them to sell but, like Heather, did not know how to go about it. Heather spent a few days building up her courage, and looking up words in the Spanish/English dictionary and practising what she hoped was something like 'Would you like to buy these?' Feeling brave and word perfect she sallied forth to the shops. Sadly, both her work and her linguistic studies had been in vain. They told her, in excellent English, that a year ago they would have bought them but now the demand for them had fallen off. Bang went both our hopes of making some pocket money. Later she had another idea, she would go to Sitges and try and sell them there, and at the same time she would go and see Virginia and John. Another trip doomed to failure. Just after she left Polly met Virginia and John in Barcelona, they had come up for the day. They planned to attend a concert that evening. Polly, Bill and I were invited to join them. The two men were very smartly dressed with yachting jackets and ties, the first I had seen. How they managed to keep them so nicely on a boat I don't know, but felt it was just as well Bobby had not been able to join us. We females had our usual jeans and zip jackets. It was a small church, rather plain, with large marble altar and side altars. We were handed a sheet of music with words. Virginia and John knew the words in Latin and astounded us by singing beautifully while we stood but remained mute. More singing in which no one was required to take part. I think this was the concert part. Then a regular mass.

The church was packed and people came in their everyday clothes and work clothes. Men in paint-splattered dungarees. Women had the same clothes as we had and no hats. I liked this feeling; it was wrong for people who may not be able to afford good clothes having to dress up.There was a long sermon which gave me time to look around the place and decide I did not like it. The altar needed closer scrutiny, as one angel appeared to have only one arm and both angels looked as if they were armed with weapons. At intervals we stood up and sat down. Once when we were standing, the man and woman in front of me turned to each other and shook hands. Most odd, they had been sitting there together for some time. Then the man turned round to us and waggled Bill's hand and then mine. Bill caught on fast and turned round to shake the hand of the woman behind him; I did the same. Next a collection plate went the rounds, everyone to which it was offered placed on it, not coins but notes.

It was all a bit disorganised and did not come our way which was a bit of luck. The purple-robed priest blessed the bread and wine, then held them up, upon which someone hit a gong which was so surprising, I jumped. It put the priest out a bit too as he then promptly downed all the wine and got a refill. Some of the congregation went up and received the blessed bread, if they thought, as I would have done, that they would get some wine too, they were out of luck, the priest had taken care of it all. It was all done at fast speed and no one knelt at the altar. At the end the priest downed his third cup of wine, wiped his lips on a napkin, using the same napkin to polish the silver cup vigorously, folded the napkin neatly on top of the silver cup. Someone came and took it away. All a little mystifying to say the least. This was the first catholic service I had attended. Later I found it was a typical catholic church service. The hand shaking, which surprised me, I was told was was an offering of peace. Knowing that, it all made more sense. Our little group then went and had coffee. Virginia and John and young Jacey who had come with them from Sitges left to catch their train. On the way back we looked in at our tavern expecting to find Heather had come back and would be there waiting for us. It was not Heather's lucky day, she had given up and returned to their boat.

The next day was one for rejoicing. Bobby had gone to the doctor and had his eyes tested and they had found a lens with which he could see. He still had blood behind the eye so they said they would wait until the next week to see if it had stopped bleeding. On his next visit he went off with high spirits and had more tests. It was found the haemorrhage had still not stopped and it was not advisable to get a contact lens until it did. More visits and he was told the haemorrhage was showing signs of clearing, but before he could have a lens fitted a minor operation on the lid of his eye was necessary, as it could not open sufficiently for the lens to fit. This was disappointing but he was told he could now make the passage to Sitges and return to the hospital after Christmas.

'Persistent' had left on December the 8th, their engine now fixed and working. Polly and Heather had to soon return to work and so they were just going to Calpe to leave the boat for the winter and then would return to England by plane. Life was a little dull after their departure.

We were now preparing to leave on December 20th. Bobby had gone out shopping and returned with a sprig of holly, the first real holly we had seen for years. The stalls around the cathedral were full of cribs and decorations. Christmas, I was pleased to note, was far less commercialised here than in many places. Any decorations that were put up were not until two weeks before Christmas. I made a cake and pudding and got in some nuts. Two days before we were to leave, Pixie insisted she wanted to go out for a walk just before dinner. I was cooking so Bobby took her and Bob-tail. Dinner being ready I was hoping it would not be long before they returned when Bob-tail flew in crying and a bit wet. I thought that Pixie must have turned on one of the taps on the wharf, as she often liked to do. I then heard Bobby calling. Going up I was amazed to see him just standing there with water pouring off him, soaked from head to toe. "Go and get Pixie, will you," he said. "Where is she?" I asked, not being able to understand why Bobby was standing there soaked to the skin on this dark and cold, wintry night, and without Pixie on the lead. He pointed, there was Pixie just sitting farther down the wharf chattering to herself and refusing to come until I went up and took hold of her lead, wondering if they had all gone mad.

While Bobby stripped off and gave himself a rubbing down and some brandy, he explained what had happened. It seemed they were just returning when Pixie decided to sit down. Bobby turned to pull her along and stepped back, not realising he was so close to the edge of the wharf and fell off the wharf into the sea, going right under with a big splash, which accounted for Bob-tail being wet. He let go of Pixie's lead so as not to pull her after him. Instead of following Bob-tail's example and coming back she shot off in the other direction, no doubt taking a dim view of Bobby's idea of fun. Bobby was able to surface and climb out, a task not being made easier with all the clothes he was wearing including shoes. His eye patch was still in place but sodden. He had lost his one and only pipe which he had been smoking at the time. I gave him the one I had bought for him for Christmas and then set about washing off the salt water from all his clothes and hoping they would dry before we left. Generally speaking it was not a good day. I had lost my watch that morning when doing the washing on the wharf and could only think I had, after taking it off, knocked it down between the slates. Perhaps it was then lying next to Bobby's pipe but we had no way of getting them.

When Bobby paid the bill at the club and told them we were leaving the secretary seemed upset and wanted us to stay for Christmas. We thought they would be pleased to see us go, as we had stayed so long over the allotted time. The Spanish we found, once you got to know them, were very kind and friendly people.

So now we had to think again,
was it right our life to plan?
The direction of this life of ours
is surely written in the stars

CHAPTER TWENTY-NINE

WHAT NEXT?

I struggled into my layers of clothes: two T-shirts, sweater, zip jacket and hairy on top. The lower half of me clad in wool tights, socks, socklets, jeans and about to top it off with yellow skins. "Come on," called Bobby, "what are you doing?"

I was having difficulty getting my yellow skins on my legs, it was the top half of the suit I was stepping into. I now found Pixie had the electric fire upside down and was endeavouring to take the back off. We had unplugged it from the shore which left Pixie wondering what had happened to the heat.

It was cold sailing but a good wind, so there was no cause for complaint except we had to do all the steering ourselves as we could not get the rudder of the steering vane submerged.

Pixie ate the tops of a whole box of matches. Spanish matches with their pink heads were evidently of inferior digestible quality and she threw up pink vomit twice before we arrived in Sitges later that day. We moored with our nose to the wall, not far from *'Chrisma'*. Ian and Val, with their children Aran, Domane and Clyde the dog, were nearby, next to Steve and Lynne, daughter Jacey and Bumble their dog. We were back among friends.

A small Belgian boat was also nearby with a young couple on board, the wife could speak English and Coco, her husband, was trying hard to do the same. He had studied Spanish before leaving Belgium and had since found himself always in the company of English-speaking people so was having to learn fast. Rob and Chris were nearby on another small boat with their beautiful round-faced son, he was only a baby but never stopped smiling.

Young Jacey was there to greet us as soon as we tied up and said she would like to show me the town the following day. To this I gladly agreed. She turned out to be an excellent little guide and we had fun visiting the different shops and market. Another day she said she wanted to show me something very beautiful and we visited the old part of town which we both delighted in.

On Christmas Day, having opened the gifts we received and decorated the cabin with cards and holly, we invited all the children round for cake and little gifts I had hurriedly made for them. They brought along the gifts they had received to show us. They were all very sweet and well behaved and made the day for us and Pixie more like Christmas.

In the morning there had been an announcement in Spanish over the loudspeaker, Coco told us all that it said everyone could go to the office for free drinks. We were all very keen to obey this summons. We, with Pixie, started out a little late, just in time to see the others returning. The drinks were only for the brave people the other end of the marina who were apparently in some swimming competition.

That night after we had consumed a large dinner, rounding off with our Christmas pudding, we were invited to join Chris and Rob for a drink along with Coco and his wife. Bobby felt tired so stayed with Pixie and I enjoyed the company. It had been a happy day and before going to bed we toasted all our friends and relations in brandy, Pixie gulping hers and Bob-tail only giving his a sniff.

Sitges was a perfect place for walking Pixie with many places to explore. Walking along the dock looking at all the boats, or along the front past the cafés where, if anyone was sitting outside eating, we would sit down and look at them until they tagged on and passed her something. This was a nice way to make new friends. The best walks were up the steps and on to the cliffs, where Pixie found a number of things to eat and I collected wild flowers and herbs. We would climb the rocks and then go down to the beach. Our morning walks were usually accompanied by Aran with his dog Clyde. Pixie was always happier when they came along. Pixie and Clyde wanted to make friends but Aran loved his old dog and was very protective, afraid Pixie might damage him. On the beach Aran would build sandcastles for Pixie to break down

Pixie was the boss on these outings and decided where we should go, sometimes insisting we climb up and down the rocks, choosing the way that was more suitable for her little feet than mine, which often resulted in landing me in a position where I had difficulty moving either way and was in danger of hurtling to the bottom. Reaching the top after one such climb, Aran appeared. "Do you think you should be climbing the cliffs at your age?" he solemnly asked.

Pixie was even happier when all the children joined us. She knew they were at first a little timid of her and so she paid them scant attention but was aware they were there and would watch what they did and copy them. One of their pastimes was to pick up stones and throw them over the cliffs at some target. At first Pixie would just sit watching them. One day she decided to outdo them, going to the edge of the cliff and digging out a large rock, no puny little stones for her. Once she had dislodged it she pushed it over the edge and watched as it bounced down taking other stones with it. When it landed she jumped up and down with delight. This soon became a favourite pastime of hers but was dangerous when she chose a spot where there were people below on the beach.

Despite the cold we often came across nude sunbathers on the beach which was surprising. I remembered a time many years before that bikinis were not just frowned on they were banned. Perhaps they still where, as so many did not wear them. Pixie had a sense of humour, albeit not always funny. One day, seeing one such unclad couple lying in the shelter of the rocks, she sent down a rock before

I had spotted them. I watched in horror as it bounced down, feeling sure it was going to be a direct hit. Thankfully it landed by the side of the man who immediately jumped up furious, slamming his hat on his head, (I felt he might have put it elsewhere) then looked up. I was now trying to pull Pixie away from the edge but she wanted to see the end result and hung on leaning over the cliff. Fortunately, the man realised it was she not I that had tried to stone him and he roared with laughter. He also had a sense of humour.

Bobby was feeling more himself each day, though in spite of weekly visits to the doctor he had still not had the minor operation needed before a lens could be fitted. When a local man kindly offered to let Bobby buy a sheet of marine ply from him that he was using to build the interior of his boat, Bobby had something now that he could get on with and happily set about replacing the bulkhead between the chain locker and our bunk. We would no longer have wet pillows when the rain or sea came down the anchor chain pipe.

On the 6th January we had just started dinner and felt our rigging being shaken. Bobby rushed up, saw two people and asked them what they wanted. With his impaired sight and it being dark he had not recognised Christine and Barry, who had just arrived back from the UK in an old car they had bought, and on which Barry had fun fixing the engine. It was nice seeing them again. They too were going to stay a while in Sitges.

That night we turned on the radio just in time to hear the sad news that Joy Adamson had died, the author of *'Born Free'*. I think it was the first time I have cried on hearing of the death of someone I had never met.

Bobby now arranged with Barry to decarbonise our engine for us. I dreaded the thought of all the mess I expected; so far, every time anyone so much as looked at the engine the cushion covers and all the paintwork needed a complete wash. Still it had to be done and I resigned myself to it. Barry shook his head over the state our dirty engine was in. It was quite obvious we did not give it the tender care an engine should receive. Barry set to work dismantling it and taking all the parts ashore to clean. At the end of the day I could not believe it, I could not detect so much as a fingerprint. By the third day, in freezing cold weather, our engine was back together again. I would not have recognised it, it looked so shiny and clean and he had done it without so much as a mark or drop of oil in the cabin. I guess he really did love engines.

The next day was such miserable weather that it was midnight before Bobby got up courage enough to go over for his shower, which fortunately for us was directly opposite our mooring. When he returned he removed some shackles that were making a noise on deck and accidentally dropped one overboard. Back in the cabin he remembered he had left his socks in the shower and went to get them. Before getting into bed he found he was not wearing the little whistle on a cord round his neck. That too he found in the shower. By the time he did get under the covers the effect of his hot shower had completely worn off and he lay there shivering.

The Belgian boat had left soon after Christmas and on the 17th January we waved farewell to Chris and Rob and their little rosy-cheeked boy sitting in the cockpit, secured by a safety harness, still grinning from ear to ear.

That day Bobby paid one of his visits to the hospital in the hope of finally getting the operation but came back disheartened. The surgeons were going to Madrid for two weeks and he was now told he would have to wait until the first week in February.

I was invited by Barry and Christine to go to the Barcelona Boat Show with them. I had never been to a boat show before and found it interesting, seeing the interior of so many different new boats. They all turned out to be made of fibreglass which surprised me. I was particularly interested in seeing an Endurance 35, the design of '*Sandpiper*'. The interior proved much grander with a completely different layout. To my surprise they had the galley in the same place we had moved ours to. This was the first time I had seen any boat with a galley in that position. It was all very nice but would not have suited us so well with all the lost space given to extra bunks and very much less locker space. This fault we found applicable to all the boats, they also all had gas stoves with three burners and an oven. That, to my mind, was quite unnecessary.

On our return from the boat show Barry turned his car over to John, Ian and Steve; they had arranged to purchase it from him. Together with Val they took off to drive to England and stock up with food and things for their boats. Lyn had flown to Canada and Virginia was going to care for all three children.

Bang! I woke with a start and Bobby opened his eyes. “What was that?” we both asked. Pixie was no longer in bed with us. Bobby got up and found her on deck and brought her back to bed having found it was four in the morning. We got little sleep as she was so restless and kept scratching her bottom. We gave up in the end and got up. It was a beautiful day and I put Pixie on her platform where she continued to scratch. We then noticed the remains of the plastic bottle that had contained Bobby’s eye drops was chewed up. That was not all. On deck was a can of rust remover she had been banging around, we now saw it was open. The cause of her discomfort was obvious, she had tried de-rusting her bottom. We washed her thoroughly in hot soapy water but it did not help and she continued to scratch and soon had made sores which then bled. We became more worried over her as the day went on when she sat with her back to us and refused to eat anything. Next, she started to shiver though the weather was sunny and warm. We brought her back in the cabin and she just lay down. The next five days were spent doctoring her as best we could. She had obviously poisoned herself with either the eye drops or the rust remover though we could not be sure she had drunk either. She was unable to relieve herself, though kept straining to try. By the fifth day sores had broken out on her face, chest and tummy, she kept scratching. We tried to give her laxatives but little went down. Then we thought of soap, she loved eating soap and we always had to keep it out of her reach. I washed her and left the soap in her reach and turned my back. A good amount had disappeared. We got up with her twice in the night, she now had diarrhoea. This did the trick, her period started and after a few more days she was once again herself.

The 29th January did not start off very excitingly. I had the day before found a dentist, and having had toothache decided to pay him a visit. My tooth by then was fine but thinking it might have something wrong with it, I thought it best to have it checked. Christine and Barry were leaving that day so I said goodbye thinking I would not return in time to see them depart. My visit to the dentist proved a waste of time as he declared my teeth perfect and did not charge for that bit of information. That cheered me up and I arrived back in time to catch sight of '*Sula*'! moving out. Seeing Bobby on deck I called out I was going to run along and wave to them from the top of the hill. "No, they will not see you and I have a surprise for you," he called. What surprise could Bobby possibly have for me, I knew he would not go out. Getting aboard I could not believe my eyes, there in the cockpit was my brother Michael. Completely forgetting that Pixie hates us to shout, I yelled with delight as I raced up to him. Pixie did not mind. She had never met her uncle before but had taken to him at once knowing he was part of our family.

Hardly believing he was really with us I turned out the quarter berth of its accumulated junk, the berth that at one time I thought would make a good dog bed, never thinking it would be used for my six-foot tall brother.

Michael stayed with us for a month. It was his first time on a yacht and he was never going to be able to say he actually sailed. For most of the time he joined us in scraping and varnishing and all the other jobs we were working on. Perhaps it was not quite what he expected. He told us he had seen pictures of people on yachts who never did anything all day except lie on deck sipping gin and tonics. We had seen such pictures too but it never seemed to happen in real life.

On Sunday Michael and I took ourselves off with our cameras to photo the old part of town. It was a nice day weather-wise but the wrong day of the week. The usually near-deserted little streets now had cars and people getting in the way of our lens. However, the museum that before had always been closed was now open. The building was of the most interest especially the ceiling and windows. I liked best the wonderful lizard in iron and some winged dragons.

The trip we did to Tibidado was by way of a pilgrimage, Pop having taken this trip on his visit to Spain so many years ago. He had enjoyed it so much that on his return he had for a while been nicknamed Tibby. We took the train to Barcelona and then the subway. Next we rode on a beautiful little tram, that and the funicular railway we later had to change to must surely have been the same that Pop had once ridden on. The view was terrific and the church was nice, the altar as usual I found a bit too ornate, like most in Spain. What did surprise us, leaving us a little stunned, was to find the main attraction was an amusement park built round the church with loud music blaring out. There were few people, mainly just a party of old aged pensioners. We wandered around, took photos of the view and had a beer in a large but empty restaurant. We then joined the pensioners in a help yourself place for a meal. It was a beautiful day and we wanted to eat outside but there was no place to do so. We thought of walking back down to the tram but found no proper path and feared missing our connection. Coming back down we met a baby monkey on the handlebars of a tiny motorbike, we tried to make friends but it was very shy.

The only time Bobby and I ever went out together was just on short walks with Pixie. It was rather fun for us when Michael got up one morning and made breakfast before sending us off to Sitges while he got on with the daily chores. It was Thursday and market day so we shopped and wandered around enjoying ourselves. Michael enjoyed being captain in our absence and his crew had behaved well. He was a bit taken aback when Pixie growled at him as he was giving her some bread and chocolate. She had seen us coming and does not like to be caught enjoying someone else's company.

The bulkhead was completed and all it needed now was some fancy wood trim. Michael and I now explored the woodyards buying two suitable long length pieces which Michael carried over his shoulder like a lance, looking for all the world like Don Quixote. We then looked for some polystyrene to line the lockers and stop the condensation forming on the cement sides. After being told it was not obtainable in Sitges we came out of the shop to find a man loading sheets of the stuff into the back of a car. He directed us to a large warehouse where we had a good laugh at their cooking arrangements. On top of a high stove sat a blackened pot. Michael peeped in and then between fingers and thumb held up a bit of string from which dangled a few inches of shrivelled up sausage. "Would you care for a bite Madam?" he said.

We were now in possession of a very large sheet of polystyrene. It was a light as a feather but far more fragile and too large to carry even for the two of us. We begged the man to cut it in half, or to give us a knife so we could do so ourselves. The establishment did not run to any form of cutting implement. "Which only goes to prove," said Michael, "that they pick up that horrible object in the pan and just bite a bit off when hungry."

Our difficulties proved more than we expected. When we got outside the wind threatened to blow our sheet of stuff away and us with it. We tried holding it on our heads, walking sideways like a crab with this sheet of poly stuff pressed to our bodies, our arms stretched out over as much as we could cover. We each held an end so one walked forwards and the other backwards but none of these methods were very satisfactory and people kept staring at us and dodging away from the long lengths of wood Michael was armed with. Slowly we made our way, keeping close to the buildings and as much out of the wind as possible. Once out of the town and on the cliffs on our way back to the marina it proved completely impossible, the wind caught the sheet and we were whirling around in circles with it, collapsing with laughter we lay it in the long grass and anchored it with our bodies.

"Are you sure you don't have a knife?" Michael asked me for the tenth time. "No, you are a man, you should have a knife not me," I retorted. "But I don't have one and you do."

It was true I had found a wee penknife on the cliffs one day. It would have done nicely to cut our sheet in half but I did not have it with me. After turning out my pockets and convincing him I did not have it, Michael went running off to the boat with his wood over his shoulder to get a knife. I was left to anchor our purchase to the grass. I was glad nobody passed by, they might have thought I was a little odd lying face down, spreadeagled on a patch of white in the long grass.

Once safely back with our polystyrene, now cut into two manageable pieces, we collected Bobby and Pixie and took them up to one of the cafés for a beer. Pixie sat on the pavement for her drink but then realising we were legitimate customers this time, took a chair; she liked the chairs, they were plastic and good to chew on.

After seven trips to the hospital since being in Sitges it was February 12th when they had promised Bobby faithfully that the operation to cut some of his eyelid would be performed. He went off to catch the Barcelona train and Michael and I got on with varnishing the bulkhead he had put up. Going on deck for something Michael shouted down, "Hey, Bobby is back."

I did not believe it but sure enough there was Bobby walking along helping Aran with a jar of water. The trains were on strike and he had not enough money on him for a taxi and had been afraid to try and hitchhike in case he did not make the hospital in time. Collecting more money he set off again. That trip was worth it. He actually had the small operation and returned with a big padded bandage over his eye. At last that was done.

A couple of days later Bobby went again to Barcelona as the doctors wanted to check on his eye. That time he was lucky. Ian and family were going to Barcelona in the car and gave him a lift. He returned, now just wearing his eye patch. The doctors were pleased with it but when he removed the patch it looked awful and very swollen.

Meanwhile, Michael and I had a busy day. For some time the galley light and starboard light had not functioned. Michael played around with wires and got the galley light working. Bobby had told him he thought both lights must be on the same line. Michael now wanted to see if the starboard light also worked. I was busy fixing the trim on the bulkhead, so just pulled the switch for the starboard light and told him to go and see if it was working. I forgot that the boat was still as new to him as it had been to me a couple of years before. He left and went on deck, a few minutes passed before he called down that he could not find the starboard light. I went up to find him peering over the port side with his chin resting on the port light which he had not realised was a navigation light, let alone that he was on the wrong side.

That day we managed to lose both Bob-tail and a small saw we had left on deck. After a complete search of the whole boat neither could be found. We decided that the saw must have blown off the cabin top and was now at the bottom of the sea and that we would refrain from mentioning the fact to Bobby. Bob-tail we knew must be around and kept calling him and walking about the other boats in case he had gone visiting. We never found out where he had gone but he came in late that night behind Bobby who had gone out on a last search.

It sounds a bit ghoulish to visit a cemetery. Michael and I were on the way to the shop and the gate that had been before always closed now lay invitingly open. The large wall we found was made up of tombs with other bigger ones in the grounds. They were all different and most were nice but one of the wall plaques was very macabre. A skeleton holding a skull and a scythe, a tree branch the other side with bones depicted beneath it.

Michael being fond of old cars, it was fortunate that one Sunday during his stay an old crocks race was staged from Barcelona to Sitges. At first we considered all going along to see the end of it and taking Pixie. Bobby decided he would prefer to stay back and paint the anchor so Michael and I went along. Seeing the crowds of people we were glad we did not have Pixie with us. Some of the crowd were dressed in turn of the century costume. When the cars started to arrive even I was impressed: beautiful old cars in perfect condition, some with wooden wheels and lots of brass work, the drivers and passenger all in period dress. Bringing up the rear was a motorcycle with a monkey on the handlebars, not the same one I had met previously. This one was less timid and I gave him a kiss and took his photo. I hope his life was happy. I am against keeping monkeys as pets but hardly in a position to say so.

That afternoon we took Pixie up to the café and Michael bought her an ice cream. It looked far too big for her to finish but she sat in the road and ate it in one go, holding the tub with both hands which made her shiver while I spooned it into her mouth. By the time we had finished we were surrounded by a watching audience.

That was really my day. Bobby now said he would take me out to dinner and Michael would monkey-sit for us. After wandering around looking at all the menus we chose a Dutch bar for dinner. A jolly place with music and friendly people. We could not help staring a little rudely at one customer who was dressed like a Dutch doll and had three legs, male or female we were not sure. We enjoyed our dinner but at the end of it we were told the coffee machine had died. We left to find another place to take our coffee. The square was now full of people all in a festive mood. On one of the balconies overhanging the square two men dressed up as female models kept coming out and posing. Every now and then there would be a break in the crowd as groups of dressed-up people dashed through. We followed and found our way to the end of a number of decorated floats and heading down a side street following, we found ourselves back in the square, where we then had a good view of all the floats as they passed by, tossing sweets and confetti into the crowd. At the end of it all we had our coffee and brandy in another café and returned to *'Sandpiper'* clutching candies we had caught for Pixie, covered in confetti like a newly-wedded pair.

All was well when we got back to the boat. Michael had smelt burning in time to prevent Pixie setting the boat on fire when his back was turned. He was able to remove the bag she was happily setting light to from the fire.

Michael's month came to an end. His visit had done us a lot of good. We had fun and had done a lot of laughing. Walking with him for the last time past the cemetery on his way to the station to start the first lap of his journey back to England, we noticed a huge hairy orange toy donkey just tossed on a rubbish heap. "I bet Pixie would love that," Michael said.

After sadly seeing Michael off on the train, I walked back and picked up the orange donkey. It had a broken leg but was big enough for Pixie to sit on. She accepted it as compensation for not being able to groom Michael anymore. I returned having forgotten to do the shopping on the way back. Bobby went off and did it and returned with a bunch of red carnations.

Having had the stitches out of his eye Bobby went again to the hospital with high hopes of getting the promised lens. The test on the injured eye went well and a lens was found to give him a certain amount of vision. When both eyes were tested together it was found he had double vision. The doctors had not expected this and now needed time to think of a way out of this unexpected defect. Many more visits followed in which they could do nothing either because the eye was still very bloodshot or, as they said later, his eye had high tension.

While Michael had been with us a nice little Dutch boat *'Sterk Staeltsje'* had come in and berthed next to us. Her owners, Rinus and Helga van Klingeren, were a happy couple and good company. Pixie being a female always favoured the men but strangely enough she took to Helga at once, but of Rinus she reserved some doubts. We had also made friends with Tony Upton, an Englishman who was looking after a large gin palace of a boat moored at the end of the wharf. Pixie liked him and never objected to him coming aboard.

At the beginning of March we came out of the water and set to work scraping off the barnacles that had grown on *'Sandpiper's'* bottom. From the slip it was a long walk to take Pixie to the cliff and our usual beaches. but a good opportunity to explore the beach the other side of the marina. We named it the stony beach there being more stones than sand. It was not a very pleasant beach really as the tide deposited an accumulation of plastic bottles, rusty cans, old shoes and other debris. Pixie did not agree with our dislike for the beach. She thought it was grand fun and enjoyed herself looking over all the strange things humans litter this word with. On Sundays families would come in cars and picnic just above the beach. It looked as if they were setting up permanent residence. From the inside and tops of their cars would be brought tables and chairs. These would be set up and tables covered with cloths. Then a larger kitchen table would be produced on which the women would lay out all the food and piles of dishes and cooking utensils, while the men lit fires on which to cook the meal. Pixie thought she was on to a good thing here, walking over to examine it all. For a long time she sat expectantly, near a woman who was frying a huge pan of chip potatoes. Everyone was fascinated by Pixie but had a poor idea of what she liked to be given. One solitary peanut was solemnly handed to her. She thought little of that and immediately threw it down still eyeing the chips. Next a piece of bread came her way, she thought even less of that and refused to even take it.

In the end I managed to drag her away and took her to the café for an ice cream on a stick covered in nuts and chocolate. That met with here full approval.

A tiny little old lady worked in the expensive restaurant near the slip. She and Pixie got on very well together and when we passed she would dash out and produce a banana or some goodie that she had hidden under her apron. This was watched in wonder by Emanual who worked for the marina. Emanual was desperately in love with Pixie, never failing to call out to her and was always trying to buy his way to her heart with the offering of assorted gifts. All his efforts were in vain, Pixie would have nothing to do with him and would refuse to touch anything he brought for her. The only reason we could think of, as to why his courting efforts were in vain, was that he had a very loud voice and would bellow out his affections for her. Pixie had many different kinds of reactions to people depending on how she felt about them. She could be affectionate and show it by grooming them. If she felt threatened in any way she would show here teeth and then scream. Some people she just did not think worth bothering with, one way or another. With others she could be very aggressive. Emanual did not fit into any of these behaviour patterns. We think she just enjoyed teasing him. If we were walking along and he came in sight, she would do nothing until she saw he had spotted her then would turn and take off in the opposite direction. He would leave gifts on the pavement or wall or any place she was going to pass. She always knew if he was watching and ignored them, but once she felt he was really gone would take the gifts. Poor Emanual, he was never able to come within yards of her.

We spent eighteen days in all on the slip, far longer than we hoped but Bobby had found a new hobby, digging out rust spots made by the wire coming through the hull land then filling them. Tony kindly lent us an electric drill on which we could attach sandpaper discs and smooth down the surface. Pixie longed to help us and one day found an old paintbrush in the dump. It was hard and covered in paper and paint but it was hers and she treasured it. She spent days grooming it until in the end she had a respectable brush.

It was rather miserable working as the good weather soon changed and many days were cold and windy. We were a fair distance now from all our friends but they would frequently wander up and pay us a visit. Val came one day and all work was forgotten as she kept us in stitches at the stories she told. She had some people around she wanted to serve coffee to. She was accustomed to using instant coffee but had decided to use ground coffee as we did. What she had not realised was that we bought the beans and then had them ground. Val picked up a packet of what she took to be ground coffee in the supermarket and went back with her shopping. Opening the bag to make coffee she found beans. Now everyone had gathered waiting for coffee. She put some of the beans in a pan and boiled them. That did not work. She then took two beans at a time and tried to grate them on a cheese grater, all this while everyone was still sitting around expectantly waiting for their coffee. She told us this so seriously, asking how we managed. We let her in on the secret.

Their trip through the French canals was another source of amusement. Val was slim and young but perhaps a little nervous of heights. She had great difficulty in climbing and getting on and off the boat, coupled with that she was terrified of spiders. On their journey through the canals Aran, her son, who could climb like a little monkey, would go ashore at the locks and open the gates. One day Aran met a dog and being an avid dog lover went to stroke it and got a bite for his pains. He was not too badly hurt but had to be patched up for a day or so, so could no longer act as lock opener. His sister Domane, though nine was tiny and looked no more than five or six, far too small for the job. This meant Val had to take over. Though none too keen she felt she could manage to climb up the lock walls as there were steps for this purpose, but she was terrified that lurking on the wall might be a spider or two, so refused to start her assent until she had taken a broom and given the walls a good sweeping. This was usually watched by the lock-keeper and any passers-by who would look on with interest and amusement, while husband Ian would cover his eyes in embarrassment and in a pleading voice say, "Val, go on please, please don't shame me."

Glad as we were to have the sander, working with it was far from pleasant in the strong winds we were now having. We choked on the dust and our hair and clothes were covered in it. There was no hose to wash down and so had to make use of a bucket of water and a hand scrubber. This was not very comfortable as all the icy water would run up our sleeves. When Jacey and Domane came and said they wanted to help us I could think of nothing at the time they could do, and did not want to send them back covered in dust. Needing myself to get out of the cold and it being Bobby's birthday in two days' time, I suggested we go up in the cabin and they could help me make a cake for the occasion. Without really thinking I dumped some flour and margarine in a bowl and got them to mix it up which they did without a word. We then set about cleaning and stoning all the dried fruit, we added some nuts and spices, the result looked a bit odd so in went two eggs. Only then did I remember I had bought some sugar especially for the cake, on digging that out we all remembered the proper procedure was for it to have been mixed with the margarine.

"Oh well," I said. "It's too late now and I don't suppose it really matters."

Jacey then told me that only that morning she had made a cake for her father under Virginia's instructions. Virginia had a recipe and had told Jacey that it was very important to measure everything exactly, now I had gone and undone all the good Virginia had tried to do. No wonder Jacey was a bit taken back by my method of adding things until they looked about right. The girls had now got into the spirit of things and we dug around the locker to see what else we could find, a little treacle was added, then some cocoa powder, plus a bit of powdered milk to top it off. I had to draw the line at flinging in our last banana as Pixie might have objected. Jacey again looked doubtful when I tipped the resulting mass into the pressure cooker, expressing the thought that a cake tin might be better. I agreed that it probably would, had I had one and an oven to cook it in. The next morning the girls returned with icing sugar and instructions for making it. The end result was approved by the girls and we finished it off with a large B done in chocolate spread and nuts.

The cake had been hidden from Bobby and if he had guessed what we were up to he pretended not to. On the afternoon of his birthday, Jacey and Domane came round and wished him a Happy Birthday. We then got him to stop work and come into the cabin where we brought out the cake and sang the usual song. They had both made him nice cards and gifts of peanuts and a cigar, these handed over we all sat down to do justice to the cake, which had turned out edible. We were all on the second piece when Aran arrived, another cigar for Bobby in a colourful holder he had made for it. It was very sweet of them and Bobby enjoyed his little party.

"HELP! I am on fire!" Bobby must have been under the boat and not heard my cries, there I was with a flaming meythlated spirits can in my hand, trying desperately to blow it out. Stupidly I had tried to fill it over a lit burner and the whole thing caught fire. When blowing on it had no effect I tossed it into the sink and madly pumped water over it, that quenched the flames but I still felt and saw flames leaping around me and found that the front of my sweater was also on fire. I now started beating my chest in best *King Kong* tradition just as Bobby belatedly appeared.

"What are you doing?" he asked. *What an insane question*, I thought, *surely he could see I was roasting myself for his birthday dinner.*

Apart from the birthday party we saw little of Aran. He had now found himself a job. He was interested in building and all the new construction work that was going on around us of new shops and apartments gave him the idea to do something himself. He wisely decided to remake the steps from the marina to the cliffs and begged some cement from the workmen. Painstakingly he set to work in a very professional manner. He made some beautiful steps in spite of having to contend with people walking up and down them all the time he was working. Very often he would find his work had been spoilt at some point when it had been left to dry and then trodden on. On these occasions he would get very cross but five minutes later he would be busy repairing the damage.

The crane carrier came to lift us off the blocks and back into the water. As the blocks were removed I painted over the patches with anti-fouling. I left the pot on the ground while Bobby gathered up the electric cables. Finding the pot in the way he picked it up with the intention of moving it but it slipped and fell on its side. We now had paint all over the ground. I started wiping it up as best I could with paper, fearing it would get trodden all over the place. Emanual said in effect not to bother and took the paper from my hand, getting his hands covered in paint in the process. Bobby now scraped under the keel and painted the bare patches and knocked the pot over yet again. We had made more mess in the last few minutes than in the eighteen days we had been there.

We were now back home in our berth along the wall. We were alone at first. *'Chrisma'* had come out on the slip just before we left and Val and Ian were waiting their turn to go on as we got off. Helga and Rinus had gone out with Tony fishing in the big gin palace, at the end of which they returned with one small fish.

Our Spanish had not improved much in our long stay. I had trouble with pronouncing the words I did know. Needing some glue I cheated by just asking for UHU. This appeared to work. I did think it a bit odd when she went to the fridge but it was made clear when she handed me two cartons of yoghurt. I took them anyway even though they were not a lot of good for sticking.

Pixie had accepted the children from the other boats and soon they felt safe with her and could touch her. Aran was the first, having by then allowed Pixie to gently groom Clyde, his dog. He came on board one day and sat next to Pixie and had his hair groomed. A little tussle took place when he wanted to move and she hung on to his hair but all went well and the girls soon found they too could handle her.

One morning we watched an artist sitting sketching our boat. It was easy to see why we had been so honoured. With all the mess and muddle on the deck we were by far the most interesting from an artist's point of view. We liked the drawing and thought he might sell it to us when finished but it was wanted for his exhibition at *Niv D'Art*, a place that still had yet to open on Good Friday. We were all surprised at the chosen date, thinking most places closed on Good Friday. The sketch had pride of place on the easel but the price tag was beyond our means.

During the Easter holiday the beach would often be quite crowded and our walks were not the same. One day a large German shepherd bounced up barking. Pixie ignored him as he dashed round us in circles. To show her contempt of such boisterous behaviour, she sat down and started playing with the sand, now and then looking up and glaring at him. In the dog's mad dashing he was tossing sand all over other people lying nearby on the beach. They naturally started to complain. The dog's owner, a very well-endowed woman sunbathing topless, now got up to try and catch him. Things were now more interesting and the bathers stopped complaining and watched. The dog continued racing round, followed in hot pursuit by this hefty bouncing topless female, who had no chance whatsoever of catching him. More of her family or friends now took up the chase and the woman, who had by this time realised what a funny spectacle she must appear, and that the laughter of the onlookers was not just for the dog, stopped chasing and put on a shirt, bringing cries of dismay from the onlookers. The dog had no collar on so even when occasionally caught would get away again. Being in the middle of all this we had no chance of continuing with our walk, so Pixie joined in by making rushes at the dog. In the end he was caught by the tail and taken off the beach. We resumed our walk. Farther along two young girls were playing with a bat and ball in the shallows of the sea. Pixie loves a game of ball and we stopped to watch. She was rewarded when they missed the ball and Pixie neatly caught it. The girls were singularly unimpressed, seeing that she had a quick chew of the ball before I could take it from her. Making for the cliff base we passed a Coca-Cola can. Thinking it would be empty I never gave it another thought. Pixie picked it up and found it still was about half full and downed the lot just as the owner came up to claim it, the same girl whose ball Pixie had caught and taken a bite. The girl had a definite anti-Pixie look on her face. We came to the conclusion that there were too many humans about for comfort and we might be becoming slightly unpopular, so headed back to the boat.

That afternoon was the wedding anniversary of Virginia and John. They invited Helga and myself for coffee and cake. We had a very nice time and the cake Virginia had baked was just delicious. Perhaps she was right about having a recipe and measuring the ingredients.

England is renowned for its variable weather but doubt that it could outdo our weather experiences in Sitges. In December and January we experienced days which were so warm and sunny that people, far tougher than us, would lie naked on the beach. Then the next day would be so cold the beach was deserted and we only wanted to huddle in the cabin with both fires going. On April 5th we were awakened in the early hours of the morning to the sounds of thunder and heavy rain, or what we took to be rain. We got up later to a beautiful sunny day. On my way to the market I could not believe my eyes when right there in front of me I could see patches of melting snow. In town I met Paul, the owner of a nice wooden converted lifeboat. He had been celebrating his birthday the night before at a disco when in the early hours of the morning the electric failed. Two candles produced by the management did little to shed much light on what was going on. Leaving he stepped outside and found it was snowing. Though not particularly cold, snowing it certainly was. The snowstorm had done something to our beach too. It was now two beaches split in two by a deep gully in the sand, much to Pixie's bewilderment.

Bobby finally had his eyes tested for a lens and wore it in the hospital for about an hour and a half. He was a little disappointed as it gave him back nothing like his normal sight, but it could not be made any stronger or again he would experience double vision. He then made repeated visits to the hospital to learn and practise how to insert the lens himself. It was after a number of such visits that he was able to do it to his and the doctor's satisfaction. Even so he could see little from the eye. The difficulty of inserting it on the boat was made easier when my mother sent him a mirror, something we had never got around to buying This was no ordinary mirror but double sided. One side greatly magnifying. His ordeal was over and he now had to learn how to live with very impaired sight.

Helga and Rinus signed on a new crew member with jet black hair and blue eyes: a beautiful little male kitten which they promptly named Zapata after a Mexican revolutionary. Pixie liked to watch this wee thing on the deck of their boat but had more fun on the beach with a new dog friend that resembled a polar bear. He often came sniffing around her and would give her a kiss, after which Pixie would groom his long fur. He spoilt his copy book when one day he decided to play and rushed around us barking. Pixie reacted to such silly behaviour by showing her teeth and making dashes at him which drew laughter from other people on the beach. A bamboo pole about four feet long then caught her attention. She picked it up, upon which the dog, fearing she was about to beat him, raced off. Everyone laughed and clapped. Sadly, that was the end of that beautiful friendship.

The weather now changed for the worse, the wind howled and the rain fell down making working on deck literally impossible. We all kept to our cabins and battened down. The noise made by the wind was greatly exaggerated in the marina. Most of the boats had aluminium masts upon which their halyards beat out a continuous tattoo, making a mad jingling sound which Michael had likened to hundreds of people eating off tin plates with knives and forks. Pixie would still insist we take her for a walk. Walking was one thing but she would sit down and meditate, while we would have to stand there shivering. Her stops to us seemed to have no purpose until one day when we looked over the water in the direction she was staring we saw our hand brush, used for sweeping the cabin floor, merrily bobbing around in the sea. To Pixie's annoyance we had no way of retrieving it. She was fond of that brush and liked to sit grooming it. We had no doubt who had dropped it overboard in the first place.

It was strange I thought, how in a couple of years I had got so used to terms used at sea that I had to smile when the parents of the owner of a boat we said we would keep an eye on, came and asked if we would help them as they had water in the lounge. I rather liked the fact they stuck to names they knew and surprised that for a moment I was taken aback.

When the weather cleared I got working on the deck which was looking very bad with patches of non-skid paint peeling off. An elderly English couple passed by one day while I was engaged scraping off all the loose paint. The sweet lady then pointed to our dinghy and asked, "Would that really save you?" After explaining it was the dinghy, not the life raft she must have taken it to be. Her eyes were taking in *'Sandpiper'* which was obviously not making a good impression. "Did you come all the way from America in THAT?"

"No, we came from Singapore," I replied. That surprised her even more and with a note of disbelief said again, "IN THAT?" I was glad *'Sandpiper'* did not have ears.

When the deck was painted and we had got used to it being ice blue rather than light cream we thought we looked rather smart. I now polished up all the brass on deck. The best feature I considered about '*Sandpiper*' was that she had brass and bronze fittings rather than the stainless steel nearly all other boats had. We much preferred the brass fitting, feeling that they gave a warmer look to the boat and much more authentic. It was not possible to keep them polished all the time. One splash of salt water and the polish was spoilt. Jacey and Domane came and helped me and Erica from the German boat next to us gave me a tube of paste stuff which was excellent for getting off the thick coat of verdigris. When the two big handmade, brass ventilator hoods were polished along with the frames round the windows and other bits and pieces we were no longer the scruffiest boat in the harbour.

More wild flowers were coming out now on the cliffs and we always had a bunch of some kind in the cabin. The wild grasses too were so attractive I liked to use them, but Bob-tail would eat them though I gave him his own bunch on deck, and there was no reason that he could not go ashore and collect his own. When Bobby went shopping he also would stop and pick a bunch for me on his way back. One day he came back with flowers but minus his pipe. Oh, those precious pipes of his, something was always happening to them. Had we left Singapore with a locker full they would all be gone by now. Now he was very upset as it was a beautiful pipe that my parents had sent him at Christmas and so far Pixie had not damaged it in any way. Taking Pixie, who we felt sure would find it, we searched among the flowers on the cliff but no sign of it. On meeting Aran, Bobby told him he was offering a reward to the finder of his pipe, feeling sure if anyone could find it he would. No result. Next day Domane came round and we told her. "I'll find it," she said confidently. Off she shot on her little bike, returning almost immediately having found it, not on the cliff but on the path near the steps where we and so many people had passed.

A little Dutch girl appeared one day, she was ten but small for her age, with such a lively mind she never ceased asking questions. She was fluent in Dutch, English, Spanish and German. The first time she saw Pixie she went right up to her and put her arm round her with no hesitation. I think she could communicate with her also. She joined us on the beach where we met a nice Spanish family who gave Pixie a piece of chocolate. A little child of about four years had in her hand a lovely piece of chocolate cake and gave Pixie some which she took nicely. The child still had a large share in her hand and Pixie very gently took her hand in both of hers and ate the cake. The child stood there holding it for Pixie as if it was the most natural thing to happen. We were happy to find we could once again trust her with children and also her sudden fear of dogs when in Israel had long been forgotten.

We felt rather sad on May the 5th as we gathered on deck to say goodbye to our friends, Helga & Rinus, with their fast-growing kitten Zapata; Ian and Val with their children Aran and Domane and dog Clyde; and Steve and Lyn with Jacey and their Bumble. We were losing so many friends in one go. Pixie gave all the children a last hug and kiss before they left. Our winter together had come to an end. We hoped to leave later that month.

Bobby now had his contact lens and a pair of spectacles but the doctor wanted him to make a few more visits for them to check on his progress.

Pixie was restless for a few days after the children left and did not enjoy her walks so much. One morning we woke early to find she was not in bed with us and could hear her dragging something about on the deck. We found her sitting on the bowsprit watching a black cat. Nothing looked disturbed and we put her on her platform. Bobby had to go to Barcelona for another visit to the doctor so we did not mind the early start. I then noticed Bobby's new glasses were out of their case with both ends badly chewed. Not only that, one end of the glasses lay in a small pool of water in which floated his contact lens. It was very lucky I had noticed it, the lens being clear and so small it could only be seen from a certain angle. Pixie had generously left the lens un-chewed. It had been in a small bottle of distilled water which was hidden, so we thought, behind the curtain. We never found the bottle so that must have been dumped overboard. Bobby was going to feel a fool going to the doctor with his brand new spectacles all chewed at the ends.

"What is he going to think?" Bobby grumbled. "All the trouble the doctor has taken to help me get the lens and glasses and now he'll see them for the first time looking as if I have spent my time eating them."

"Well just tell him what happened," I said. He did and came home to tell Pixie he had a message for her from the doctor. "The doctor has told me to tell you that he will send the police round to arrest you for spoiling glasses." Pixie sat listening to him and then gave him a kiss. That was not the last visit to the doctor who now said that Bobby should return the following week and they would remove the little pimple thing that was growing on his other eyelid. It did not cause any discomfort but he thought he might as well get rid of it.

A family was collecting mussels off the rocks and Pixie, now in search of new friends, insisted we climb down and join them. We sat on another rock watching them for some time and when they left in a boat Pixie dragged me along to the spot they had vacated to discover what was so interesting. She worked hard dragging up handfuls of weed and mussels as they had done but gave up when she decided there was nothing there worth bothering with.

We then made the acquaintance of Mingo. Little Mingo was a bit of a mystery. I had met him once before when he had turned up and begged Aran to let him help repair the steps. Mingo could speak both English and Spanish but we never did find out just where he came from, or if indeed he was Spanish or English, or perhaps both. We did not see him again until Pixie and I met him on the cliff eating a box of sweets. He promptly sat down and told Pixie to sit next to him which she did without question, having her eye on the sweets. Mingo then carefully tipped the remaining ones out and divided them equally and the two of them sat huddled together in the wind while he popped one in his mouth and one in Pixie's until they were all gone. He told us he was going to be seven in a few days' time. The same amount of years we had had Pixie.

The only complaint we had about Sitges was the dust. There was a cement factory farther down the coast and when the wind blew from that direction a film of very sticky grey dust would cover everything inside and out.

We were now almost ready to leave and had a grand clean-up. Bobby had the little pimple cut off his eye and ten days' later the stitches removed. All that remained to do now was for Bobby to give the hull a last coat of paint. Sadly, this last painting job was not a happy one for him. To start with he had left the brush he had used the day before in Turpentine which had softened the red on the handle so when he used it in the white paint the red dripped down and he found he was painting the hull pink. Not wishing to leave the pot of paint in the dinghy where it might get overturned, he carried the pot up on deck and placed it there while he got a new brush. He only turned his back a short while but Pixie could not resist putting her hand in and then wiping it off all over the nicely painted deck and varnished wood. We managed to clean that up and Bobby went back to his painting. A little later I went on deck and looked with amazement on a most extraordinary sight. The bottom of the dinghy was full of white paint, which Bobby was trying to scoop up with the brush and get it back where it belonged in the pot. This method did not appear to be very successful and he was himself covered in paint, it was even squelching out of his shoes. It was a horrible sight and Pixie thought so too. She untied the dinghy from the stanchion and Bobby, dinghy and the whole mess would have floated away had I not noticed just in time and grabbed a line to toss him.

I then found newspaper and rags to use with the bottle of turpentine which he put on deck minus its top. I went down in the galley and noticed the turpentine was now running down the outside of the port hole when it could have been used more profitably on cleaning the dinghy. Poor Bobby, I would not have been in his paint-logged shoes for anything. He looked so glum, and who could blame him, but I could not stop myself from laughing. When the dinghy was as clear of paint as he could get it, he continued painting under Pixie's platform. She liked that and hung down and started drawing patterns in the wet paint with her fingers. That was, for Bobby, the last straw. Pixie and I were told in no uncertain term to make ourselves scarce. We went for a long walk, hoping everything would be back to normal and the paint dry on our return.

We were now ready to leave, but where? During Bobby's convalescence we had spent many an hour talking it all over. The guilt we had felt when we had first come to Spain and decided to go on to England, regardless of the fact that it would mean six months quarantine for Pixie and Bob-tail, had been too much. I knew deep down I could never let that happen and think Bobby felt much the same way. We had waited for a miracle, in a way it had happened but not how we imagined, but it had given us time to think. It was up to us now to do the right thing, which we should have done all along. We would sell the house in England and become true cruising people. Pixie was a handful on board but in her own way she had adapted well, and was happy that we were always near and she could find new things to do and make new friends.

This would not have been a hard decision for us to make had it not been for my parents, who for so long had been looking forward to the time we would return and live near them. They had gone to endless trouble for us over the house, looking after it and seeing to repairs and so on. How was I going to tell them that we now wished to sell the house and go on sailing? Our money was running out but with Bobby now having impaired vision there would be little chance of him finding work along the way. We agreed not to really plan anything, just see what the future held for us but did agree I would go overland to England some time that summer. I owed that to my parents.

May 29th, 1980: Bobby jumped back on board after getting clearance and let go the mooring rope while I started the engine. We then got John and Virginia to pull us in again so I could jump off and kiss them goodbye feeling sad as I did so.

As we let go the rope for the final time we floated out nicely, Bobby took the wheel. Nothing happened, '*Sandpiper*' was intent on kissing a larger boat alongside. "She won't steer," called Bobby. "We must have caught something."

I looked back and saw that we still had the mooring rope secured to our stern, *just like old times*, I thought, *we never remember to do everything right*. We got untied before we actually hit anything which was in a way a good start.

As we waved to that lovely couple, Virginia and John, without perhaps realising it, we had come to another crossroads in our life. There would be no more ideas of putting Pixie back in the wild or of subjecting her and Bob-tail to quarantine. We would remain together seeking whatever new adventures presented themselves.

Sitges, Spain 1980

The path we finally took led to many more adventures but as I wrote the last words in my diary on leaving Sitges the future remained unknown.

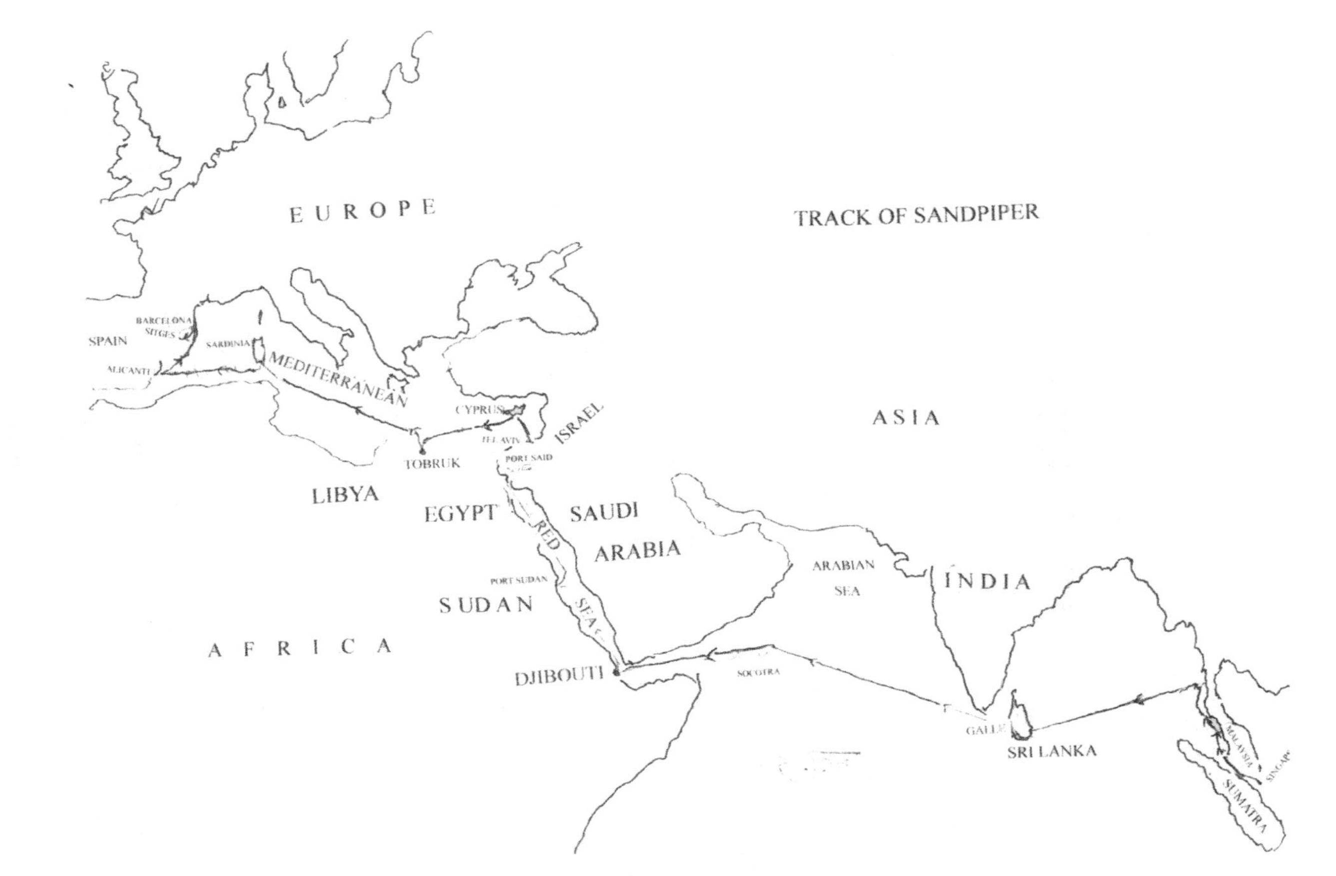

Track of Sandpiper

APPENDIX

1977

September 8th	We purchase '*Sandpiper*' in Changi, Singapore

1978

January 30th	We move aboard
February 19th	Set sail from Changi
March 1st–May 13st	Port Kelang (Malaysia)
May 16th–October 22nd	Lumut plus trips to other islands
October 24th–30th	Penang
October 31st–December 2nd	Langkawi Islands
December 5th–9th	Anchored off Phuket (Thailand)

1979

December 22nd (1978)–February 26th	Galle (Sri Lanka)
March 26th–30th	Djibouti
April 9th–18th	Port Sudan
May 17th–20th	Suez (Egypt)
May 22nd–25th	Port Said
May 30th–June 28th	Tel Aviv (Israel)
July 2nd–7th	Limassol (Cyprus)
July 18th–20th	Tubruk (Libya)

August 12th	Pula Bay (Sardina)
August 13th–15th	Cagliari
August 26th–September 7th	Alicanti (Spain)
September 9th	Javea
September 10th–15th	Denia
September 22nd–24th	Palamos
September 26th–December 20th	Barcelona
December 20th–May 29th (1980)	Sitges

ABOUT THE AUTHOR

Angela Coe was born 19th March 1937 in Surrey, England. As a small child, she was attracted to the outside; the animals and plants. With few chances of finding wild animals where she lived, it was the insects and amphibians that she liked to observe as a child.

In later years, when reading about other countries, she longed to grow up and travel. Leaving school at fifteen, she worked in London while living with her parents. London was not to her liking and she obtained a job as a holiday organiser for children in Deal, Kent. She later moved to a job as a house matron in Broadstairs.

Still searching for the way of life that she wanted, she went to Norway and learned that other young people were moving around by hitchhiking and working. At nineteen years of age, her real life started.

For four years she hitchhiked and worked while travelling, first through Europe: washing dishes, child-minding, picking grapes and office work. She then went through, Turkey, Iran and Iraq, mostly doing office work or teaching English. Then through Afghanistan, Pakistan and India. Upon running out of land in Sri Lanka (then called Ceylon), she hitched a lift on a cargo boat to China, Hong Kong and later many countries in the Indian Ocean and South China Sea. In Burma, she made the return trip to England.

Since then, the author has travelled to many parts of the world, either alone, with her husband or with her brother Michael.

The author now lives with her brother Michael and three dogs in Sri Lanka.